Communicating
Design SECOND EDITION

Developing Web Site Documentation for Design and Planning

Dan M. Brown

Communicating Design:
Developing Web Site Documentation for Design and Planning, Second Edition
Dan M. Brown

New Riders
1249 Eighth Street
Berkeley, CA 94710
510/524-2178
510/524-2221 (fax)

Find us on the Web at: www.newriders.com
To report errors, please send a note to errata@peachpit.com
New Riders is an imprint of Peachpit, a division of Pearson Education.

Copyright © 2011 by Dan M. Brown

Project Editor: Michael J. Nolan
Development Editor: Margaret Anderson/Stellarvisions
Production Editor: Tracey Croom
Copyeditor: Darren Meiss
Proofreader: Gretchen Dykstra
Compositor: Kim Scott, Bumpy Design
Indexer: Rebecca Plunkett
Cover Designers: Dan M. Brown and Charlene Charles-Will
Interior Designer: Kathleen Cunningham

ISBN 13: 978-0-321-71246-2
ISBN 10:   0-321-71246-3

9 8 7 6 5 4 3 2

Printed and bound in the United States of America

For Richard and Zora,
who raised me to be a communicator with an educator's touch.

And now for Harry,
who proves that second editions are far better than first ones.

And especially for Sarah,
who continues to inspire me to be better at everything I do.

Contents

Foreword

A few weeks ago I received a call from a client. She asked if I could send "that model document" I'd created earlier in the project in order to roll out what was a global project on an impossible timeline. I was surprised. That model document was, in fact, a concept model diagram I'd created strictly for myself—not the client, not the project team. In fact, when I tried to share it with the team early on, their eyes seem to lose focus while I explained what I believed to be a perfectly organized diagram, one that helped me fill the gap between requirements and design. But now the client was requesting its presence in a moment where the project needed focus. The project manager had seen it—poster size—behind my desk and knew at a glance it would bring needed clarity to the project.

This has been my experience in almost a decade of knowing Dan Brown's work. Over the years I have known him, where we have needed clarity, Dan Brown has provided it. What he does so well is separate the idea from the document so that a diagram is fluid and flexible, and importantly, he is agnostic about methodology. Dan's no prescriptivist.

The artist Sol LeWitt, who was known for separating the concept of a work from the execution of a work, in the 1970s explored making instructions intentionally vague so that others could interpret them. He gave his teams and the galleries who showed his work latitude to interpret his instructions, "Vertical lines, not straight, not touching, covering the wall evenly," he said to describe *Wall Drawing #86*, one in a series of visual diagrams. It was up to the galleries to interpret them. If two were the same, so be it. If they were different, that was that. While the instructions were given in the same way, it was the input of others that differentiated the pieces.

As designers, it's our role to issue instructions to those we work with. Clarity is paramount, whether we work as part of a team or a large organization with a process or a single freelancer working remotely with a team over Skype—we often use diagrams, or deliverables, to communicate our ideas. Dan's natural approach to creating clear diagrams can support a web team of any size and is a critical resource for students of user experience. As an educator, I have looked to *Communicating Design* both as a formal textbook and an informal guide. Its design systems ultimately make our ideas possible and the complex clear. Successful diagrams let us communicate.

Documentation used to be a dirty word in web design. Everyone knew its value, yet no one wanted to talk about it. I first came across Dan's diagrams in 2002 at a conference for information architects, and was immediately taken. Dan wasn't afraid of documentation. And over the course of one conference, we had decided to publish his diagrams in a magazine called *Boxes and Arrows*, making them accessible to a wider audience. Eight years later, I'm looking forward to having this second edition accessible for many to experience.

Sometimes the way you design is just as important as what you design. You will come to this book knowing the "what" already. This book shows you the way.

Liz Danzico
Chair, MFA Interaction Design
School of Visual Arts

Preface to the Second Edition

This book, in a word, is about documentation. Sounds boring, doesn't it?

Documentation—the collection of documents prepared over the course of a project—is, in many ways, the underbelly of web design. After all, documents usually appear on paper and end up sitting on a shelf where no one reads them. How cool could that be?

But anyone who has designed a web site knows that documentation can make or break the project, that it moves the process along by capturing the design concept and helps project team members communicate with each other. Web design documents—or deliverables, as they're sometimes called—also serve as milestones, marking progress in an otherwise seemingly interminable process. They're historical, allowing people who come to a project later to get up to speed on the decisions made by earlier project teams.

In short, a document captures an idea. Perhaps this is a little existential for the web design business but, getting down to brass tacks, if we can't communicate an idea effectively, how can we hope to create a web site around it?

On the surface, this book will help you improve your documentation, providing advice on how to plan your deliverables and use them effectively in meetings and on projects. In the course of doing so, it will also attempt to uncover what makes a document good, and help you recognize the difference between a bad document and a bad idea.

IS THIS BOOK RIGHT FOR YOU?

This book is written for people who make deliverables, use deliverables, and approve deliverables as part of the web design process.

- **Making deliverables:** Whether you're new to web design or have been doing it for years, if you're making deliverables, this book will help keep your efforts on track. It will either introduce you to new techniques for planning or presenting deliverables, or provide a refresher if it's been awhile since the last time you had to crank out a deck of wireframes, for example.

- **Using deliverables:** It may not be your responsibility to create the site map, but you're the one who has to consult it for the next several days or weeks or months as you migrate content from the existing site to this new structure. Or perhaps you're a developer who needs to write code for making the web site behave as documented in the wireframes. Or maybe you're the client, and you face an uphill battle in your organization in selling the idea of this redesign—those personas will sure come in handy, but you want to make sure they're airtight. This book will help you make sure you know what you're getting and prepare you for conversations with the user experience designers on your team.

- **Approving deliverables:** If the buck stops with you, you'll want to make sure all the i's are dotted and t's are crossed. As the client or main stakeholder—let's face it, the money person—you have a lot riding on these documents. They're essential for moving the project along, judging whether you're getting your money's worth, and keeping the design team honest. This book can help you make sure you know what to expect from your team's deliverables.

"But I Don't Use Deliverables"

Really? You've never written an email or drawn something up on a whiteboard? You've never thrown together a sketch to get some feedback? You've never assembled a flowchart in a diagramming application just to make sure you have all the steps covered?

It's true that some software methodologies eschew creating anything other than assets that will go into the final product. At least, that's how some people interpret those methodologies.

Every design methodology, however, entails drawing, sketching, explaining, or modeling. Every design process acknowledges the value of creating pictures or representations of the final product as a means for working through the problem. Every good designer takes a moment to envision the problem, to understand (at whatever extent is feasible) what the requirements and constraints are.

Even if you're not creating formal, multipage deliverables, you still need to describe complicated ideas, or work out a design problem, or tell a story about your approach. The diagrams and documents in this book let you do that. They're described in a way that allows for varying levels of effort: from 15 minutes in front of a whiteboard to longer periods of time to dot the i's and cross the t's.

What's in This Book?

The second edition of this book tries to build on philosophy and objectives of the first edition:

- **It doesn't cover every deliverable.** This book discusses five common diagrams created as part of the web design process, and deliverables—the ones you won't be able to avoid if you spend any time at all in this business. These are user experience deliverables, so if you're looking for advice on creating entity relationship diagrams or unified modeling language diagrams, you might want to go elsewhere. There are countless documents for user experience work that this book could have addressed, but many are not common, or they're proprietary, or they've been discussed elsewhere.

- **It doesn't care what methodology you use.** Methods come and go, but documents remain more or less consistent. One of the central assumptions of this book is that anyone should be able to use it, regardless of the methodology they use. That being said, it's difficult to write about documentation without any sense of timing or dependency, so I will make a few methodological assumptions. These assumptions provide structure for the book, but they won't render it useless if you're using a different method.

- **It's a how-to book, but not a software book.** This book will help you make better deliverables. It will help you present those deliverables better to your clients and team members. It will even help you anticipate risks in creating and sharing deliverables. But it will not tell you how to use software applications to make those deliverables. Different people prefer different tools, but the choice of tool should have little impact on the message and purpose of your documentation.

- **It's a cookbook.** Each chapter in this book is a recipe for working with a different kind of document, and you'll have your own ideas about what makes a dish work and what doesn't. Feel free to add notes in the margin. You may even find that a technique described for one kind of document works well for a different kind of document. Although the book tries to make each chapter self-contained, you may find inspiration for one kind of deliverable in other chapters.

WHY A SECOND EDITION?

Believe me, I ask myself this question every day. Here are some of the answers I came up with:

- **The web has changed.** The web can do a lot more in 2010 than it could in 2005. The role of the web in our lives has changed. Our means for accessing the web have changed. As pervasive as it is, it's hard to think of it as a "channel," and as flexible as it is, it's hard to think of it as a "medium." If nothing else, the book needed to accommodate the new perspectives, new technologies, and new role of the web.
- **Design methodologies have changed.** For a while there, the web design process seemed to stagnate. In the last couple years, however, a renewed interest in prototyping, collaborative design, and sketching has reinvigorated web design. It's becoming easier to model things, and the technologies available to designers allow them to iterate faster.
- **I've changed.** Not that you care, but my own thinking on how to prepare and talk about design documentation has changed in the last five years. Witnessing the evolution of the web and of the practice of design, and working with many designers to help them refine their own documentation practices and skills, has encouraged me to evaluate my own place relative to design. I've had the extraordinary opportunity to work closely with a business partner, Nathan Curtis, who thinks about this stuff even more deeply than I do. We've built a company of people who also value good visual storytelling, and I learn something new from them every day.

CHANGES FROM THE FIRST EDITION

So, what's different?

The Format

The first thing you'll notice is that this is a bigger book. Inspired by a textbook for making comics, *Drawing Words & Writing Pictures*, I sought a larger landscape format to accommodate larger drawings. I always wanted fat margins to give you, the reader, the opportunity to embellish the book with your own lessons learned, and the larger format affords one.

The Structure

One of the biggest problems with the first edition is that it treats every deliverable at an equal level. It positions a flow-chart as a stand-alone deliverable on par with a competitive analysis. Reality suggests otherwise: Preparing comprehensive documents poses a different set of challenges than preparing a diagram. There is an inexorable push-and-pull between diagrams and deliverables, a tension that makes documentation challenging but also feeds the creative process. Discrete diagrams and multipage documents both tell stories, but they do so in different ways.

To that end, I've restructured the book into two sections:

- **Design Diagrams** contains chapters on Personas, Concept Models, Site Maps, Flowcharts, and Wireframes. Each of these is a separate, stand-alone diagram that needs a document around it to provide context.
- **Design Deliverables** contains chapters on Design Briefs (new!), Competitive Reviews, Usability Plans, and Usability Reports. These are multipage documents that tell extended stories, incorporating diagrams from the first part of the book.

Each section starts off with a "Basics" chapter to lay some groundwork for creating diagrams and deliverables, respectively.

The Content

I've rewritten many of the chapters, especially for the design diagrams. While the first edition laid great starting points for helping readers think through the preparation of design artifacts, there were opportunities to provide more concrete guidance.

The first edition became part of the curriculum in many academic programs for web design, interaction design, and information architecture. To that end, I've included exercises at the end of several chapters to facilitate the use of the book in those settings.

What's missing

I took out a couple chapters: content inventory and screen designs.

- **Content inventories** remain valuable tools in the kit of a web designer, and I strongly believe that content must be a part of the design process. In recent years, content strategy has emerged (though like most design endeavors, it's likely been there all along) and formalized the tools and techniques used to "design content." Personally, I haven't done a content audit since the first edition, and I had nothing to new to say.
- I also didn't have anything new to say about **screen designs**, at least anything that isn't being said better and more comprehensively elsewhere. There are some beautiful books on designing web sites, and how to talk to project teams about design.

What's new

Lest you think removing a couple chapters diminishes the value of the book, let me take a moment to inventory what's been added:

- **New chapters on basics**: One of the things that bothered me about the first edition was that while most advice was specific to individual deliverables, there were some points that covered all documentation. The new structure gives me a chance to add some chapters on basics for both diagrams and deliverables.
- **New chapter on design briefs**: One of the documents I regret leaving out of the first edition is the design brief. I'm glad I could remedy that.
- **More illustrations**: From the moment the first edition came out, I was disappointed with the small number of illustrations. In a book about pictures, there was a dearth of them. I've tried to remedy that in this edition.
- **Advice from experts**: Many chapters incorporate the opinions and practices from experts in our fields. These sidebars pose a question about a more advanced topic relating to the specific diagram or deliverable.

The Tone

Perhaps it's my age or my evolving role relative to design, but I have less of an us-versus-them attitude. Being a designer in an organization whose culture evolved around something besides design (like a government agency, or a manufacturer, or a services business), it can be hard to feel a part of the designer culture. For years here in the Washington, DC area, the web design community thrived on a camaraderie that came from being a lone wolf inside organizations that usually didn't know what to make of their "webmasters." Our meet-ups were like support groups.

Much has changed.

As the web has become even more pervasive, and as everyone has begun to play a role in the design, construction, or maintenance of their organization's web site, there's a greater appreciation for the designer. The web designer has a new challenge, maybe even a greater and more important challenge than educating people about the web and user experience. That is to help everyone contribute to the design process, to establish a vision and help a multidisciplinary team realize it.

PICTURES AND WORDS, WORDS AND PICTURES

Communicating design is about combining words and pictures into a story that elaborates on a vision, describes a user experience, and remains meaningful in the context of a project. Web designers face new challenges every day (or similar challenges within dramatically different contexts), but we can think through those challenges and communicate potential solutions by combining words and pictures. So, whether you have to describe a new type of interaction, explain what kinds of content appear on the home page, summarize user research, or think through a complex navigation structure, you need to pick up a pen and start drawing and writing. This book, if it does nothing else, should help you think about the ways in which we combine these elements to tell those stories that address these and many other challenges.

Acknowledgements

Let's get some clichés out of the way: Writing a second edition was far more ambitious than I anticipated. You know what they say about clichés: they're all true. Needless to say, I blew my estimates way out of the water, and all I can say is that I hope it shows.

The following people were crucial to getting this book in your hands, providing more support and flexibility than any one author deserves. Collectively, these people established a path for me that would lead me to a successful book; diversions from that path (by design or by accident) were ultimately my choice. Should the text contain any discrepancies or errors, the responsibility is mine alone.

The team at New Riders has been a great support throughout the years. **Michael Nolan** never gave up the pressure for me to do a second edition, and I'm grateful for his persistence. **Nancy Davis** provided some much-needed advice at the beginning of this project, and I'm grateful for her wise input.

Margaret Anderson led a team of editors to help make my vision a reality. She understood immediately when I told her I wanted more structure, more practical advice, and more pictures, and I thank her for helping me keep the book aligned with those objectives. Without her patience and thoughtful prodding, I might still be churning on the Personas chapter. **Tracey Croom** and **Gretchen Dykstra** were instrumental throughout the process but especially in the final throes. **Charlene Charles-Will** led the design team, and I appreciate our conversations at the start of the project to realize the visual experience of the book. **Kathleen Cunningham** had the difficult position of designing a book for a designer. Her gentle touch and attention to detail turned my rough vision and elaborate content model into a real book.

This second edition would not have been possible without the experiences I've had over the last several years. A great deal of those experiences came from talking with people in workshops and conferences. I'm grateful to the organizers of those events for giving me the opportunity to share my experience and to learn from theirs. **Jeffrey Zeldman** and **Eric Meyer**'s An Event Apart attracts some of the brightest minds in the business, and getting to speak with the attendees there opened my eyes to some of the challenges of documentation. **Jared Spool**'s Web App Summit gave me the opportunity to turn Concept Modeling into a full-day workshop. **Donald Norman** and **Jakob Nielsen**'s Usability Week conference was instrumental in nailing down my thoughts on deliverable basics.

I've also led workshops at industry conferences like the IA Summit and Interaction. Participants in these sessions are industry leaders and they provided lots of good discussion, input, and war stories. I'm grateful to **so many of you** who had great input, shared great experiences, and actually like talking about documentation.

Reviews of the first edition appear all over the web. I've tried to read each and every one of these and consider them as I pushed this second edition into existence. Several of the kinder tweets made it to the back cover: thanks to everyone who let me put their 140-character quotes there, and especially to @yoni (**Jonathan Knoll**) who helped me dig up those tweets.

Bruce Falk provided some candid and thoughtful feedback on the first edition. It gave me a lot to think about for the second.

In 2009, my friend Jackson introduced me to technology guru and comics fan **Ben Scofield**, who in turn introduced me to the equally talented and equally comics-obsessed **Nick Plante**. Ben, Nick, and I had some great conversations about comics, and we were determined to reinvent the online comics experience. Several other start-ups beat us to it, but those brainstorming sessions were among the most memorable creative experiences I've had. Those discussions yielded the concept model example in Chapter 4, and I'm grateful to those guys for letting me participate in that (however short-lived) endeavor.

Todd Zaki Warfel and **Will Evans** constantly make great things, and turn around and give them away for free. Their sites and blogs are a treasure trove of great design ideas and methods. I'm grateful to them for letting me reprint some of their work in the Personas chapter.

Tamara Adlin, **Stephen Anderson**, **Dana Chisnell**, **Nathan Curtis**, **Chris Fahey**, **James Melzer**, **Steve Mulder**, **Donna Spencer**, and **Russ Unger** all offered their wisdom in sidebars throughout the book. I appreciate their sharing their thoughts and squeezing them into the weird format I imagined. (Thanks especially to Chris who inadvertently gave me the idea when we started up a side email conversation about flowcharts. His agreement to reprint part of that conversation is what started this whole thing.)

Liz Danzico is an information architecture powerhouse, someone who stands with one foot in the professional world and one foot in the academic world. I'm truly honored she agreed to write the foreword. (Frankly, I still can't believe it. Just double-check that her name is on the cover…) I appreciate her constant support throughout the years and her beautifully written essay that perfectly sets the tone for the second edition.

The team at EightShapes (**Jennifer**, **Chris**, **PJ**, **John**, **James**, **Dimple**, **France**, **José**, **Jason**) probably didn't notice too much of a change: I'm always a little distracted. This means only that I'm grateful day in and day out, book or not, for their perseverance, their quality work, and their commitment to EightShapes. They teach me something new every day, and I'm glad to count them as colleagues.

Nathan Curtis is the perfect business partner. I'm grateful for the (apparently never-ending) space he gave me to explore this project, and I appreciate our mutual roles as advisors, critics, champions, and friends.

An extended visit from my mother-in-law coincided with the weeks before my deadline. **Merle Holden** was the picture of serenity, providing a rock for my family and preventing utter chaos from descending upon us.

Harry and especially **Sarah**—well…I can't thank them enough.

Chapter 1

Introduction

Design is a complex process composed of many smaller activities: listening, analyzing, evaluating, brainstorming, synthesizing, experimenting, composing, describing, discussing, exploring, reacting, and countless others. Documenting is not one of these activities, but engaging in any of these activities yields artifacts—diagrams, notes, sketches, lists, inventories, annotations, and larger documents—that result from the act of performing the task. At the same time, each task requires inputs, and these artifacts that come from **doing** design are the same things that can help **feed** the design process. The success of the task directly relates to the quality of the inputs, and may be measured on the quality of its outputs.

As a web designer, I don't set out to create wireframes or flowcharts (two artifacts typical in the design process). My aim is to design a web site. These diagrams are merely useful tools in that endeavor, and I'd quickly discard them if more useful tools came along. This is an important point: *Wireframes (or any other design diagram) may be the output of a design task, but they are not the product or the objective.*

So, I like to think of design documents as both catalysts and by-products. Catalysts help facilitate a chemical reaction, and by-products are additional outputs but not the central or most important one of the reaction. Design documents contribute to the design process by facilitating creativity and communication, and they are a result of the design process itself.

Documentation contributes to the design process in many ways, but, ultimately, there are three reasons to produce it:

- **Consistency of vision**: As the design process explores deeper and more detailed aspects of the user experience, the team can easily lose the thread of the project. Design decisions at the deepest levels—obscure functionality, unlikely but possible user scenarios—may neglect the overall design vision. Yet good design depends on consistency because users count on consistent approaches to the user experience. Documents that capture that vision, those unifying themes, help remind the people working on the project of the appropriate direction. They give the project team the opportunity to evaluate new design ideas in the context of that vision.

- **Insight**: Drawing a picture of an idea gives the project team an opportunity to see that idea in a new way. Whether the idea is rendered in Adobe Illustrator or as a sketch on a whiteboard, the mere act of drawing the picture gives people something to react to, evaluate, and expand on.

- **Traceability and accountability**: Documentation is a paper trail, even if you never print out a single deliverable. By capturing the decisions as the project progresses, you have a record of the entire project and can see where crucial decisions happened and who made them. Reaching the end of a project, you may realize that you don't remember why you did certain things—was there a reason for this button's placement or that page's unusual layout? Having a collective history in its documentation allows you to uncover the rationale behind these decisions.

Is formal documentation bad?

Documentation for its own sake is bad. A document that's an item in a checklist is bad. Documentation without a purpose, without a clear role in the project plan is bad. In this case, "bad" means wasted time.

At the same time, documentation is inevitable, even if it's a sketch on a whiteboard, a list of insights from a usability study, or a wall of stickies organizing content. In short, creative endeavors can't help but produce artifacts. The choice you make as a design team is the extent to which you formalize these artifacts—that is, make them highly structured, polished, and playing an official role in the management of the project. The extent to which you formalize should be determined by need. Some reasons why you might formalize your deliverables:

- Distributed project teams need formal documentation to facilitate communications across space and time.
- Creative teams wholly separate from the business team (as in consultant-client relationships) need to prepare documents as part of a contractual relationship or to ensure they're meeting their commitment.
- Projects with long timelines benefit from formality to ensure the longevity of design decisions.

Formalization takes time (though that varies from designer to designer depending on proficiency with the tools). Deciding whether the investment of time is worthwhile is up to the project team. With limited resources (people, hours in the day, budget, and so on) the team needs to determine where to focus efforts, especially if the same group of people may be responsible for multiple design activities.

One danger of an overemphasis on formal documents: You can end up spending tons of time and energy specifically on the artifacts and diagrams without keeping in the forefront how they serve the overall goal. I believe this is the reason that the user experience community flares up against documentation, and new methodologies are proposed that discourage extensive (or any!) documentation. When this happens it is an opportunity to refine and focus our understanding of the purpose of documents. Like any tool, documents can be misused. The greatest misuse of a document is to create it for its own sake, and not to ensure its contribution and value to your project, your team, or the end product.

THE WHOLE STORY: DELIVERABLES

This book uses the term "deliverable" to refer to a complete stand-alone document. You can hand a deliverable over to someone completely unfamiliar with the project, and it tells enough of a story to bring him or her up to speed. A deliverable spells out context relative to the project, provides rationale for the ideas within, and explains how those ideas will lead to the next set of design activities. A deliverable tells a story by positioning the ideas it contains within the context of the larger project.

Deliverables are described in great detail in the second half of this book. That section leads off with a chapter called "Deliverable Basics," describing the fundamental parts of a design document. It includes chapters on four other deliverables, dealing with specific communication challenges (Table 1.1).

The chapters in the first section describe diagrams.

Chapter...	Discusses...	Which are deliverables that...
9	Design Briefs	Set the tone of the project, defining the problem, objectives, and direction.
10	Competitive Reviews	Capture other approaches to the design problem.
11	Usability Plans	Establish a structure for conducting a usability test.
12	Usability Reports	Report on the findings from a usability test.

Table 1.1: Four deliverables typical in the design process.

PARTS OF THE STORY: DIAGRAMS

Individual diagrams are expressions of ideas and insights, but they don't inherently acknowledge the larger context of the project. A diagram is like a scene or a vignette in a story: It may be entertaining and evocative on its own, but it comes with no context. A deliverable incorporates artifacts, just as a good story connects scenes in a way that evokes a particular theme.

This book describes five different diagrams, listed in Table 1.2.

Chapter...	Discusses...	Which are diagrams that...
3	Personas	Describe the target audience.
4	Concept Models	Facilitate an understanding of the domain of information for the site.
5	Site Maps	Establish a structure for the underlying concepts of the site.
6	Flowcharts	Capture a process for completing a task.
7	Wireframes	Communicate the structure, behaviors, and content of individual web pages, templates, or portions of pages.

Table 1.2: The five diagrams described in the first half of this book.

Separating artifact from deliverable is something I internalized throughout my career, but it was Nathan Curtis, my partner at EightShapes, who articulated this distinction. In documenting design, you will switch between working on the deliverable and working on the diagrams. Sometimes feedback on your work entails adjusting the elements of the deliverable that support the artifacts, and sometimes you need to change the artifacts themselves.

Content in the deliverable may be independent of the artifacts, describing the project objectives, or carrying summary information from a previous deliverable, providing

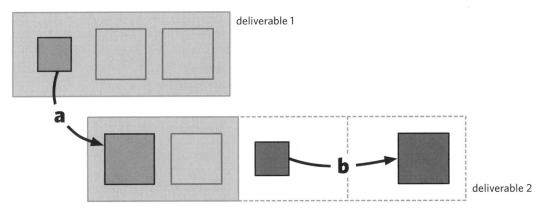
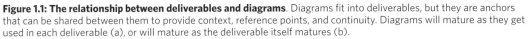

Figure 1.1: The relationship between deliverables and diagrams. Diagrams fit into deliverables, but they are anchors that can be shared between them to provide context, reference points, and continuity. Diagrams will mature as they get used in each deliverable (a), or will mature as the deliverable itself matures (b).

context for where the deliverable fits into the design process. Content may relate directly to the artifacts in the deliverable, elaborating details, providing rationale, or drawing connections to other artifacts.

TOOLS FOR CREATING DIAGRAMS AND DELIVERABLES

This book is tool-agnostic, which is just a fancy way of saying I don't care what tool you use to create the artifacts and deliverables described. Because I know you'll ask, my applications of choice these days are OmniGroup's OmniGraffle, Adobe InDesign, Apple's Keynote, and Apple's Preview (for displaying and annotating PDFs). The vast majority of my design work happens here:

Regardless of the tools you use, the book makes some assumptions about them:

- **You can separate diagrams from deliverables**. Adobe InDesign is brilliant at this, letting you embed files inside each other. Files can remain linked, so if I change a file that happens to be embedded in a document, the updates will be reflected in the document. This isn't to say you have to use Adobe InDesign. You could use Microsoft Visio for the diagrams and Microsoft Word (or Power-Point) for preparing the deliverables.

- **You can create multipage documents**. As much as we'd like our diagrams to stand on their own, creating a deliverable usually means telling a story where the artifact plays a major role. Multipage documents allow for more comprehensive storytelling.
- **You can create node-and-link diagrams with relative ease.** Node-and-link diagrams—those that boil down to shapes connected by lines—constitute three of the seven artifacts described in this book. Its format is ideal for describing the underlying structures of web sites.

One more note on tools: Do not let anyone tell you which is the "right" tool for design. (Unless that person is signing your paychecks.) As a designer, you are responsible for communicating your design ideas. Find the tool that works for you in your circumstances and learn it inside out. You

Figure 1.2: Take a notebook everywhere you go.

rely on a tool to help you do design, but you do not marry that tool. Through thick and thin is for spouses only. The moment your challenges change and the tool becomes insufficient for capturing your ideas, drop it and learn something new.

DELIVERABLES AND THE DESIGN PROCESS

Design methodologies vary in terms of theoretical basis, activities, and overall approach and process. Because documentation is so closely associated with the design process, a set of outputs often becomes a convenient way of identifying a particular methodology. In my experience, however, many methodologies rely on certain basic documents—and project teams find value in these documents—regardless of the methodology they're using.

That said, this book makes reference to three different kinds of activities. Most methodologies include some variation on these concepts, if not the specific activities themselves:

- **Understanding the domain**: Sometimes you have to design a web site around content or functions that are unfamiliar to you. Web apps that serve health professionals, for example, reflect a domain that most web designers are not intimately familiar with. (Unless you're a doctor, but then why are you reading this book?) A "domain" is a loose, but generally broad collection of information about a specific field. Besides basic information, any domain has its own jargon, labels for target audiences, unique relationships between content, functions both essential and obscure, and numerous other attributes that make it unique. As designers, our job is to get up to speed on a domain as quickly as possible, enough so that we can apply design expertise to the challenging problems inherent to the domain. My point: Deliverables can help with this.

- **Stating the problem**: Most methodologies are based on the premise that you can't create a web site unless you know what it needs to do. To capture this need, web site designers and developers define "requirements." Requirements usually appear as a collection of statements describing different things the system should do. Different methodologies do this differently: Some methods put little emphasis on requirements-gathering, while others make it the central activity. The process of documenting requirements also varies dramatically, from voluminous spreadsheets to drawings of stick figures to three-sentence "stories." Ultimately, the purpose is to define the problem you're trying to solve. Your methodology may insist that you have a complete definition of the problem before attempting to solve it, or it may recognize that you can never truly understand a problem until you try to solve it. Regardless of your approach, this book assumes you will spend at least a little time listening to the client and doing some research into the target audience to figure out what it needs.
- **Solving the problem**: Once members of the project team have an understanding of the problem at hand, they create an approach to solve it. For the purposes of this book, I assume that the solution is a web site that will meet the needs of the business and the target audience. Like requirements-gathering, this activity varies from methodology to methodology. Some call for quick bursts of design followed by testing, while others call for extended design cycles punctuated by occasional testing, and still others call for building a prototype and refining it over time. This book assumes that you use design documents (like wireframes and flowcharts) to establish a direction for how the final product will look and behave.

All of these activities constitute "doing design," and they all make use of artifacts and deliverables to a greater or lesser extent. I won't dictate that particular documents have to be prepared as part of certain activities, but it is true that some artifacts are more appropriate for certain activities.

Choosing the Right Deliverables

Should you create every deliverable in this book for every web design project?

In a word, "no."

This book describes typical design artifacts and a technique for composing them into meaningful deliverables. It identifies how you can use one to provide context for another, like site maps showing the relationships between different wireframes.

The book assumes, however, that you have planned for activities that yield these artifacts, but that you've selected those activities based on the needs of the project, not the kinds of outputs they produce (Table 1.3). This bears repeating: *Choose activities for your project based on their ability to take you closer to an objective, not because you want to make a particular kind of output.*

Good	Bad
During the design phase, we'll focus on the checkout process. We'll likely do wireframes to describe changes to those screens.	After we validate the requirements, we'll make wireframes.
This is a project to learn more about our target audience. One possible output is personas, which is a pretty good way of summarizing user research.	This is a project to create personas.
While I'm confident we can transition to screen design after hashing out a draft structure for the site, I'll want to dedicate at least three weeks to revise that structure.	We'll spend three weeks on site-mapping.

Table 1.3: Positioning deliverables in the design process. Design is about activities that lead to a web site, not activities that lead to wireframes and flowcharts.

The chapters are pretty explicit on appropriate circumstances for creating the different artifacts. They describe the activities that generally yield those documents. If your project plan doesn't call for those activities but does specify those deliverables, you might re-examine the plan.

This is the best time to determine the appropriateness of different artifacts—during project planning. You don't want to get to the "wireframing phase" (you should all be shuddering) and wonder at that point, "Why am I creating wireframes?"

DELIVERABLES AND THE PROJECT TEAM

Beyond methodology, project teams maintain an unwritten set of rules for working together. This is the project culture—an understanding of the value each team member brings to the table, how communications happen between team members, and the role of documentation in the organization. The dynamics between team members lead to potentially interesting challenges in creating documentation. And "interesting" is probably the best word for it.

The People That You Meet

The book frequently references "the project team." This group of people includes anyone directly related to the project—decision-makers, designers, project managers, developers, and so on. Your company may have a finance person, for example, but his role doesn't necessarily make him part of the "project team."

- **Designers or the design team**: The protagonists throughout this epic, the people with titles like visual designer, interaction design, information architect, content strategist. These are the people who are most likely on the hook for creating and maintaining the deliverables described in this book.

- **Project participants**: Other people on the project, maybe not designers per se, but people heavily involved in making things happen. It's a general term that can refer to everyone in this list.
- **Project manager**: The central member of the project team, the project manager runs the show. Different organizations use project managers differently, but for the most part, they have daily contact with the client and facilitate activities between the team members.
- **Discipline leads**: People who "own" particular aspects of the design or implementation. You may have five different designers on a project but one "creative lead." The book assumes that with respect to design decisions, the buck will be stopping here-ish.
- **Client**: The organization financing the web site. Clients contribute one or more stakeholders.
- **Stakeholders (such as product managers and domain experts)**: People who have a vested interest in the success of the project, perhaps because they own the project on the client side or they will be users of the web site or they have an intimate knowledge of the domain.
- **Developers, engineers, and quality assurance**: The people responsible for building and testing the stuff you design. They are, in a sense, your main customer. Even though they may not be buying design services directly, your process and outputs need to provide the right information for building the web site. One way I look at my job is how I can make their jobs easier.

Can one person play more than one role? Definitely. Can one person play all these roles? Yes, but he's very, very lonely. And busy.

Team Dynamics

This book assumes, perhaps naively, that a good project team should be built on collaboration and consensus. Most projects fare better when they operate under the assumption that everyone wants to make a worthwhile and meaningful contribution and that people should feel some ownership for their work. Such an approach comes with potential risks: Ownership can become about ego, decision-making takes longer, innovation doesn't happen in groups. A group committed to a successful project needs to take steps to mitigate those risks.

Good designers (author's opinion here, based on years of experience) learn the dynamics of the project team, observing:

- **Collaboration**: Some teams are structured to encourage collaboration. They insist that designers work together to establish big ideas, review the details, and provide almost a constant stream of criticism. Other teams bring designers together more infrequently, and perhaps in a more formal way.
- **Transparency**: Making the sausage, opening the kimono, and a host of other slightly inappropriate metaphors all refer to the same thing: How much does the team expose the dirty underbelly (another one!) of the design process? Some design teams are happy to share works in progress, quick sketches, and not-yet-fully-formed ideas with each other and with the rest of the project team. Other teams take more of a "black box" approach, hiding their efforts until they have something fully formed.
- **Disparity in hierarchy**: Watch an episode of AMC's *Mad Men* and you'll see hierarchy at the workplace. It represents the 1960s in the advertising industry as structured and divided as feudal England. Strong hierarchies may have somewhat arbitrary rules for reviews and approvals of deliverables before they "go out" (get sent to project stakeholders). The other extreme would be a place so relaxed that they don't even require second pair of eyes on a deliverable (scary thought).
- **Strength of leadership**: Being a leader on a design team implies many different things. Good leaders establish and

stick to a vision. They provide meaningful and actionable critiques. They know what it takes to get from the current state to a worthwhile conclusion. Strong leaders—those who do these things well—establish a role for documentation on their projects. They understand how deliverables support their vision and advance the project toward objectives.

- **Respect for clients**: With any design team, the elephant in the living room is their relationship with their clients. While you may know about web design, they know their business, and both are needed for the project. I've heard horror stories of design teams creating web sites disparaging clients they don't like.
- **Respect for users**: Those of us who subscribe to a user-centered design philosophy seek to understand how people will use the products and web site we design. This drive to understand them doesn't automatically entail respecting them. Design teams and clients alike, as part of the design process, may generalize about their users, a recipe for breeding disrespect, thinking of users as incompetent, ignorant, or worse.
- **Strategies for conflict**: Teams employ particular approaches for dealing with conflict. Teams ill-equipped to resolve conflict may be unprepared to work in highly collaborative environments. This changes the role of documentation.

Understanding these dynamics is crucial because they affect how you prepare, position, and present your documentation. These topics could fill a book by themselves, but for now design teams can determine an approach to their documentation based on these dynamics by looking at:

- Clarifying the role of documents
- Establishing a vision and design principles
- Agreeing on a project plan
- Defining project ground rules

Navigating Politics

Politics hamper design by quashing voices of reason and enabling arbitrary design decisions. When design is subject to politics, design decisions are made without regard to external requirements.

This isn't to say that strong personalities or leadership wielded with a heavy hand can't do good design: Designers who have internalized external requirements, who maintain a consistent vision, and who have a rationale for their design decisions can be both successful and difficult to work with.

Client Relations

The client is the person or group of people who identified the demand for the product and seek to fill the demand. They've asked you, the designer, to help them create a web site to do just that. They are the ones who bear responsibility for the product and who finance it. They're the ones who have to deal with the logistics, support, and deployment of the web site. They, at once, have a broader view (the logistical, business, and financial ecosystem in which the product lives) and a narrower view (their business and the product, and not necessarily any other relationships).

This book is about working with people with these perspectives as much as it is about working with people with the same perspective as the designer. Good documentation must communicate something abstract—the design of a web site—to this larger group of people, each of whom regards the design approach from their unique perspective. Good artifacts accommodate these alternate views of the product, at the very least recognizing that other members of the project team will be evaluating the deliverables from a different vantage.

The relationship between a design team and its client is crucial, and again has a dramatic impact on the deliverables. In addition to considering the dynamics listed earlier, project teams can assess the relationship between the designer and the clients along a scale (Table 1.4).

What about "innies"?

The content of this section is very much focused on my experience, being a consultant external to a client. My relationship with many different internal design teams has shown that they have a similar scale, one that measures their integration with the entire organization. Design teams can be carefully integrated into every aspect of a firm's operations, or could be siloed, expected to "do the web site" and nothing more.

Like outside consulting organizations, internal design teams should have an objective: What kind of relationship will let them do design most successfully? With this objective in mind, teams can shift the approach for their documentation to begin to build that kind of relationship.

DESCRIBING VS. DOING

Do documents and design artifacts reflect "real work?" How much progress are you really making on the project by tweaking line weight on a wireframe or typography on a persona? How much does the design vision depend on your formalizing a deck of screen designs or creating PowerPoint presentations about personas?

Documentation can feel detached from the design process. Diagrams are abstractions of ideas that are in and of themselves abstractions. If we need to describe something that isn't a direct reflection of a screen design (a site map, for example, or a visualization of the underlying assumptions), the documentation can feel even more detached. At least once on every project I push my chair back from my desk and wonder aloud, "What am I doing?" (Basement offices are the best places to wonder aloud. And listen to unpopular music genres.)

These moments of doubt are useful. They keep us honest relative to our process and force us to renew our commitment to great design time and again. Stepping back and giving documentation a critical eye, I give myself a chance to validate my efforts and make sure I'm contributing to the design in a meaningful way. I look out for at least three things:

- Is the level of effort on the deliverable on par with the utility derived from the deliverable? Spending hours upon hours on a document that won't see the light of day beyond a single meeting may not be worth it... unless that meeting is meant to secure funding for the rest of the project. Spending a morning on a document that will drive and inform the design process for months to come may set the stage appropriately, but likely isn't commensurate with its value.
- Am I having more fun making the document or working through the design problem? I love making diagrams. I love making diagrams that speak for themselves. I love making diagrams so much that sometimes I forget why I'm making them. The joy should be in solving the real design problem. If I've lost sight of that context, perhaps my efforts will be better served elsewhere.
- What I can I be doing that better reflects the final product? If I'm working in a diagramming program because that's what I always do, I may be neglecting another approach that does a better job of demonstrating the design concept. Paper prototypes or animated PowerPoint slide transitions, while "less sexy" than polished diagrams may describe the design idea better.

Just one more philosophical reflection before you dive into the practical stuff. If I were to boil controversies about design methodology down into a single topic, this would be it. Our urge, as designers, is to get closer to the product, to be a craftsman who can effortlessly float between imagining and building. As products, production processes, and demand change, we create a greater disparity between the

You are...	Which means...	And your deliverables...
Completely integrated	There is virtually no distinction between your team and the client team. Other people throughout the company might not know that you come from a separate vendor.	Strictly follow the documentation standards inside the organization. They're branded.
Extending the team	You supplement the client's team, but you (for example) maintain your own email addresses. The client likely handles much of the internal interfacing, but you may participate in conversations with the client's stakeholders.	May or may not bear the brand of the client organization, but they do reflect your authorship of the document.
Peers	The client treats you as a peer, providing design critiques and expecting the same in return. They may keep you separate from their internal customers.	Bear the brand of your organization, and clearly define you as the author. They are self-contained stories, but they may not deal with the entire project as you're brought on to fight particular fires.
Consultants	The client brings you in for your expertise, but likely drives the document creation internally, soliciting your input and maybe creating a diagram or two.	May be indistinct as you are more a contributor to other deliverables, creating artifacts for the client to use in their own documents.
Doing production tasks	Your role is to provide assets as part of a larger production cycle.	May be indistinct as you are delivering specific assets outside the context of a particular document.

Table 1.4: Your relationship to the client team will affect the process and deliverables.

people who can think of good ideas and the people who can implement them. The urge to get closer to production encourages us to revisit our design processes, techniques, methods, tools, and communication mechanisms.

You're about to read about several different diagrams and techniques for assembling them into a story. These artifacts, little projects in and of themselves, are abstracted from the final product. Yet, while the final product may not reference them in the slightest, that product depends on these artifacts for its conception, design, and implementation. They are, therefore, open to interpretation, discussion, improvement, and evolution, to best meet the needs of the product and the team responsible for building it. The recipes herein are starting points and guidelines, ready for you to shape them with your own needs, your own circumstances, and your own experiences.

Design Diagrams

Part 1

Chapter 2

Diagram Basics

dī'·ə·gram (n.)

A picture describing an abstract or complex idea, usually describing a portion of a web site's user experience or summarizing the design problem.

Let's establish a foundation, a shared set of assumptions about creating design diagrams. Personas, site maps, and wireframes, three typical artifacts in the design process, could not look more different from each other. Yet their preparation, creation, and surrounding discussion have much in common.

This chapter lays a theoretical foundation from which you can build all the diagrams in the first half of this book and captures many assumptions made in their creation.

ANATOMY OF A DESIGN DIAGRAM

In the next five chapters, I'll use the same structure to describe each artifact. Each diagram is divided (conceptually, at least) into three layers. This doesn't mean that the deliverable should be actually divided into layers that you can peel away. It's a metaphor to describe how important certain information is to each document.

Layer 1: Essentials

This layer captures the most important elements of the diagram. If any of this information is absent, you would not even call the artifact by the same name. For example, one of the first-layer elements of a site map—the structure of a web site—is pages or templates. Without this element, it would be difficult to create a document that counts as a site map. (We're getting existential again, but if you're going to think hard about deliverables, you might as well go all the way.)

Layer 2: Elaboration

Some parts of an artifact elaborate on the basics, providing more detail about what lies underneath them. These second

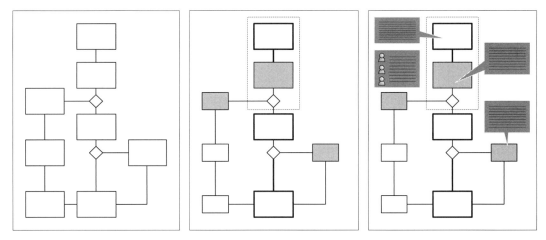

Figure 2.1: The layers of a design artifact may not be quite as literal as this depiction. Actual layers of information may not be so distinct. Use caution in embellishing your diagrams with too much information: As you add more information to a document, it becomes easier to obscure the main message of the document.

layer elements are not required but adding them can clarify the meaning or provide details relevant and necessary to the project. If you were to remove them, your artifact would still be valid but somewhat less meaningful. On a site map, embellishing a page or template using a style to distinguish those that are already in production from new ones is a second-layer element. You don't have to use every element described on the second layer.

Layer 3: Context and Connection

The specifics of a document's third-layer information really vary by document, but usually include elements that put the document into a larger context, drawing connections to other parts of the project. For site maps, this might include marking pages with dates to indicate when they will be launched, or highlighting those that require stronger content strategy.

Why Layers?

If you haven't produced much documentation before, you might be tempted to put as much information into your diagram as possible. This is not a good idea, and that's one of the reasons this book uses the layered approach. If you're unsure about creating an artifact, focus on the first-layer elements. This will get all the essential information. If you feel comfortable evolving the diagram, try adding one or two elements from the second layer. As you develop your own style of documentation, you'll cultivate a sense of judgment about what kinds of information you should include. You'll also get candid feedback from clients and team members.

The chapters that describe design artifacts all include an "Anatomy of…" section describing the elements of each diagram in detail.

CREATING DESIGN ARTIFACTS

Since the early days of web design, pictures have been the best way to document the abstractions design teams work with. While the activities that produce the diagram may vary, creating the artifact itself generally follows a similar process. That is, to produce personas, you first need to collect information about the web site's target audience. The activities for producing wireframes, on the other hand, are very different. In both cases, however, when it comes down to putting those ideas on paper, you can rely on similar processes.

Every chapter dedicated to an artifact includes a "Creating…" section, which describes how you can apply the general process explained below to that specific diagram. Note that the process isn't so much "first you draw a rectangle," but more "here are the things to think about before you put pen to paper." Or pointer to pixel, as the case may be.

Basic Decisions

Taking a few moments to think through the diagram's purpose, role in the project, and target audience can improve your efficiency in creating the artifact. Establishing the situation provides some focus. The other thing I do is make a list of all the content I want to include in the diagram.

Purpose

Every artifact needs a purpose. Ultimately, it will appear in a deliverable and needs to support the purpose of the document. Individual diagrams, however, need a purpose in and of themselves. This keeps them focused and ensures you're not just putting effort into busywork. The "Why communicate design" section in the Introduction explores some of the basic reasons why we make design artifacts. Here are some more concrete purposes, explored in greater detail throughout the book:

- **Capturing current state**: A description of how the web site (or some other element of the design problem) looks and works today.
- **Establishing the design problem**: A statement explaining what the design needs to do. There are lots of ways to express a design problem: in terms of user needs, indicating deficiencies in the current design, showing where key parts of a process are broken.
- **Presenting design ideas**: A depiction of a concept, an approach to solving the problem. Different artifacts are stronger at depicting different parts of the solution.

Timing

This book makes certain assumptions about when the design team might create each artifact, and the chapters appear in more or less chronological order. This isn't to dictate a process or best practice. It simply reflects the way most of my projects operate.

That said, deliverables are the result of activities. Project plans should specify tasks, not deliverables. They should say "design checkout process" not "create wireframes." Project plans are about what people need to do in order to achieve the project objectives: deliverables are a by-product of those activities.

Determine the appropriate deliverables once you've established the tasks required to meet an objective. If you've aligned the tasks based on dependencies (such as "we can't validate requirements without learning more about users"), you can determine the appropriate deliverables and their formats based on those needs.

Audience

Artifacts may require adjustments depending on who you're talking to. Typically, you might characterize the readers of your deliverables in terms of roles. Developers and engineers, for example, demand different information from other designers, project managers, and business stakeholders.

Great artifacts, however, account for more than just the audience's role. An intimate understanding of your project team helps you craft artifacts in such a way that will be most meaningful to them. It can help you determine which elements to leave in and which to take out. Here are some of the attributes you might look for. When you think about your team, are they:

- Detail-oriented or big picture?
- Abstract thinkers or concrete?
- Careful planners or impatient to jump in?
- Focused on text or visuals?

Content

Unfortunately, the book can't tell you exactly what to put in your diagram. The content depends on the specifics of your project.

Instead, each chapter provides examples of the range of content that might go in a diagram. For example, the site maps chapter discusses that site maps can represent specific pages on the web site (such as "About Us") or templates (such as "a product template"). But it won't tell you exactly what pages or templates to describe; that's up to you and the project team.

The process of determining appropriate content involves:

- **Abstraction**: How specific are you going to be about everything on the site?
- **Analysis**: What things did you learn by looking closely at the information you have?
- **Agenda**: What will best serve the design process in that moment? What do you need to move things further?

It's difficult to plan a diagram without knowing the exact data points. (Just like it's difficult to plan a web site without some insight into its content.) Making a list of the kinds of content you want to include is a good start, but expanding that list to describe specific examples of the content is even better.

Tips and Leveling-Up

Each artifact chapter also includes sections on tips for creating the specific diagram and ways to avoid its common traps. Here are some general ideas on the process I follow when putting any diagram together, and should serve as a starting point for any of the artifacts described in this book. The tips and skills sections in the artifacts chapters assume you're using some version of this process.

A rough process for diagramming

1. **Make a list**: Make a list of all the pieces of information you want to capture. You can start with a general category of information (like "page types") and then list out the specifics (like "product page, gallery page, product discussion page, product specifications page").
2. **Sketch first**: Create some pen-and-paper sketches first, capturing as many elements as possible. Your objective with the sketch is not to get all the details, but to give yourself a reasonable framework as a starting point.
3. **Share early**: Show the sketches to colleagues to get some feedback. Backseat your ego for these conversations. Good colleagues can offer a critique without getting personal, and their feedback is useful for your process: You need another set of eyes to help you determine if your approach communicates clear messages.
4. **Iterate**: One sketch is not enough. If you think you're ready to translate your sketch to a diagramming application, sketch it out one more time just to make sure you didn't miss anything.
5. **Explore a different approach**: I almost always build time into my process to explore a different way of presenting the information. After taking my initial concept through a few iterations to get it solid, I force myself to put it aside and look at the problem differently. One way to do this is to turn your initial assumptions on their head. For example, in describing a site's target audience I might focus on two attributes. To take a different approach, I may select two different attributes, or I may create a different set of relationships (like lifecycle) between the user segments. Your alternate approach may not be better (if it is, go with it!), but it may shed some light on your first one, giving you a chance to flesh it out or add some detail.

6. **Move stuff around**: Once it's in vector form in my drawing application of choice, I move the elements of the diagram around. This is especially useful for flowcharts, site maps, and concept models—any node-and-link type diagram—where the change in perspective can yield new insights.

7. **Color sparingly**: Some of the chapters offer ideas on how to apply color to the diagrams. Color is a dramatic way of highlighting differences: The contrast between a red thing and a blue thing draws the reader's eye almost immediately. It's a "heavy" technique for making distinctions and should be applied with the utmost care. When in doubt, stick with varying shades of gray.

8. **Use conventions**: Refine your visual language. The visual language is the set of shapes and conventions you've applied to the list of elements. At this point, you'll have a sense of where your visual language is working and where it's not working. Specifically, diagrams may be too busy to be readable, or may not convey a coherent story. When you refine the visual language, you're looking for opportunities to make sure the main messages are clear. You're also looking to strip away excess information—visual noise that doesn't hold much meaning or contribute to the story.

9. **Revisit inputs**: Check your work. Make sure you've got all the details expected by the others on the project, especially if the team expects the work to build on previous documentation (like requirements or user research reports). Comparing your diagram to those inputs can ensure you haven't missed any crucial elements. Earlier documentation can be a proxy for other members of the team; their questions and feedback will be drawn from their understanding of the project, which is presumably captured in these earlier deliverables.

10. **Label, label, label**: Never assume that elements of the diagram stand on their own. Better to over-label, especially in early drafts of the picture, than to assume your readers see things in the same way you do. Whereas color and line weight can be overdone, you can never have too much labeling. I look back on concept models that are less than two years old where I neglected to label the links between the concepts and I wonder, "Why did I link these two?"

TIP

Soliciting feedback on rough drafts

Your colleagues may be stumped as to the kind of feedback you need on a rough draft. You can draw from these questions to stimulate the conversation:

- What are the main messages you get from this diagram so far?
- What information do you think is missing?
- If you were making this diagram, what would you do differently?
- I was thinking about incorporating X (another data point or type of content). Do you think that makes sense? How would you do it?
- (If they know the client) How do you think Jane will react? What do you think she'll want to see?

Common diagramming traps

The "Creating Personas" and similar sections of each chapter end with some ideas on how to "level up" your skills for that diagram. These skills address risks specific to each diagram, but they are all drawn from the following:

- **Lack of planning**: Without spending some time considering the "basic decisions" described earlier, your diagram can spin out of control. A plan—even if you spend only five minutes on it—can establish focus and help you make design decisions about the diagram. A plan establishes a purpose, a timeline for creating the diagram, and a target audience. It can help you decide which content to include and which to leave out. It can help you decide what elements to prioritize visually and which to let recede into the background. It can help you decide when it's a good time to share the diagram and who can provide good insight into your early drafts.
- **No narrative**: This is a polite way of saying "hubris." Without any narrative, you expect your diagram to stand on its own. Consider delivering a diagram outside the context of a document a very special, very extreme case. Every diagram should be embedded in a document that can provide context, further description, and a rationale for the decisions reflected therein.
- **Too much information**: Without whittling down the amount of information you intend to include in the diagram, the visual language of the picture can overwhelm the message. Too much color, too many line weights, too many styles of type are all symptoms of trying to say too much with the diagram. If you can't communicate your message with less, consider removing some of the key points to help preserve focus.

CHALLENGES IN COMMUNICATING DESIGN

Following all these tips does not eliminate the challenges of communicating design. Putting ideas on paper is hard, especially in a new medium. Other forms of design have had years to perfect technique for capturing concepts (for example, architecture) but still face challenges when the rubber meets the road in implementation. Some creative endeavors (for example, dance) lack good conventions for documenting ideas. I appreciate our field's approach: borrowing and stealing where appropriate, but devising new approaches to design documentation where history has no model. Our medium has some unique challenges that make design documentation especially hard.

Earlier sections in this chapter attempted to address specific challenges—those that deal specifically with determining a purpose or the range of content in the deliverable. These challenges are broader, and perhaps can be characterized as those dealing with scope: what you should leave in and what you should leave out.

As-is vs. to-be vs. to-be-eventually

Most of my work these days is improving upon existing web sites and applications. Rarely do I get to design something from the ground up, and even if I do it is an attempt to improve on competitive products that came before.

In this context, a constant challenge is deciding how much you need to show the current state as compared to what the product should be. Sometimes my projects start with the assignment to design the ideal case, and then "tone it down" based on feasibility and other constraints.

While the complexity of these design challenges walks the fine line between frustrating and intoxicating, knowing what to put on paper is the bigger puzzle. Two possible ways to address this challenge:

- **Progression**: If you only need to tease out these distinctions during one part of the project timeline, you can create a progression of drawings that show the evolution of the product. This approach is great for setting context and helping people understand where subsequent design activities will focus.

- **Visual conventions**: If the need is ongoing, then each drawing should use the same convention for distinguishing states in every artifact you create. For example, you might use gray lines to recede current state and darker lines to push new design concepts to the forefront.

Detail and complexity

Designers vary widely in their ability to focus on details. Some designers are better big-picture thinkers, establishing an overall direction and sketching a few screens to set things in motion. Others are better at exploring the depths of a concept to hash out all the small design challenges awaiting at each interaction, business rule, and scenario. Designers produce documentation in alignment with their ability:

- **Documents without much detail** may not be actionable when it comes time to implement, or may not expose the range of risks associated with a concept. If the devil is in the details, the devil really likes different kinds of specifications: content direction, behavioral descriptions, state changes, display conditions, scenarios.
- **Documents with good detail** may be inappropriate at stages of the project when other team members are still trying to zero-in on the overall concept. These documents can easily lose the thread of the story as they get mired in the functions. They're harder to maintain and require careful bookkeeping around the version history.

One way to address this challenge is to divide your design team into two piles: detail people and big-picture people. Engage the big-picture people earlier in the project and then increase the participation of the detail people as the concept gets hashed out. If you employ this technique, keep these ideas in mind:

- Detail people can provide useful insights at the beginning of the project to head off implementation risks before they balloon.

- Big-picture people can ensure the integrity of the design concept later in the project.
- Both can work on the same document but should collaborate at the outset to make sure they establish a structure that meets both their needs.

Product and context

Experience is such a messy word. As our field tries it on for size, some of us like the fit, but some see it as too broad for what we do ("I'm just working on screens"). Others broaden their practice to accommodate the new label ("we design services, not interactive products"). Even if you know your focus and keep to it happily, you'll find yourself blurring the edges, asking yourself questions like:

- Should I include "offline" steps in this process flow?
- Why can't users have the same experience with the call center that they do with the online self-service application?
- Why should I design an application that assumes the data in the database is inconsistent, incomplete, and inaccurate? Shouldn't we clean the data first?
- How can I legitimately position the target audience as users with a one-dimensional relationship to the product?
- Why isn't the emperor wearing any clothes?

Well, maybe not that last one. But being a web designer today often puts you in the position of the little kid in that story. Building a web site exposes the ugly underbelly of an organization's operations. Building a web site with a user-centered philosophy forces you to cast a critical eye on all the different ways users will interact with the organization.

The challenge of communicating design is successfully drawing that line between what you can influence and what you cannot. Design deliverables must capture the design of a product while acknowledging that the context may not be optimal. They must provide a model for good design practices without alienating clients by calling attention to everything else they're doing wrong.

To walk this line, consider these approaches:

- Discuss the challenge at the outset with the project team. If you've identified the potential risk given the nature of the project, be sure to raise it with your stakeholders. You can acknowledge that your scope is focused on, for example, the web site, but that the user's experience encompasses many other aspects. Ask them how they would like you to handle these issues, and then raise the next bullet as a possible approach.
- Prioritize illustrating these risks as part of the visual language in your diagram. That is, if your assignment must focus on the web site, and not other aspects of the user experience, your deliverables can still recognize them. The diagram may not elaborate on these other aspects of the user experience, but it can highlight (a) where they overlap with the web and (b) potential risks that come with those aspects.

PRESENTING DESIGN

The second half of each chapter focuses on using the design diagrams, because even the best-looking flowchart or the most detailed usability report is meaningless outside the context of a project.

The majority of this section is dedicated to facilitating conversations about the design artifacts. Ultimately, this is the objective of any diagram—to stimulate conversation about the design problem, either illuminating the problem further or bringing the team closer to a solution. This happens through brain cells, not through diagrams. Diagrams, however, help get the conversation going.

To simplify the process of planning these conversations, the book provides a single framework for these conversations. Every artifact described can be discussed among the

project team using this same outline. The high-level agenda is presented and described here. Ideas on how to adapt the meeting structure appear in each subsequent chapter, so that you can tailor the agenda for the specific diagram.

Take pride in running a good meeting. It's almost better than preparing a good document—that feeling you get when people get up from a meeting and say, "That was a good meeting." You've ended early and you've made progress. These are the two things people look for in a meeting. Don't try to do anything more.

Discussing Design: The Basic Recipe

The philosophy here is simple: As the meeting facilitator, you are a journalist, not a joke-teller. Journalism puts the most important message at the beginning of the story and then elaborates on the details with decreasing priority. I should be able to leave a meeting within the first ten minutes and still have communicated my main points. (This might be extreme, but it is a good rule-of-thumb for planning agendas.)

Joke-tellers save it for the punch line. Designers might prefer a joke-telling format because they want their stakeholders to experience the impact of their efforts. The emotion and satisfaction that comes from telling (and hearing) a good joke is a tempting template for presenting designs. But it has no place in the business world: If a conversation has to end after the first ten minutes, you won't have gotten much past "A guy and a talking dog walk into a bar."

In the following recipe for discussions, steps 1 and 2 are necessary for setting the stage for the important information. The "punch line" is captured in step 3. If you had to, you could skip to step 3, filling in information from steps 1 and 2 as necessary. The point is that if you can't get past step 3, you've still communicated and possibly even discussed the key topics for the meeting.

1. Establish context

Start the conversation with a reminder about where things are in the project. Any conversation that's a "deep dive" on a particular aspect of the project risks losing the thread of the project as a whole. By telling a quick story at the beginning of the meeting, you can help project participants locate the site map in the overall project. With respect to a site map review, for example, you might say something like this:

> OK, we finished our content inventory—remember we went through the high points last week—and we've been analyzing all the content and have come up with a site structure. We'll look at that today. This site structure is just a draft, and we intend to validate and revise it over the next few weeks. This site map will establish the range of templates we need to design in the wireframing stage, up next.

To set context, you should:

- **Establish objectives for the conversation**: Somehow people think that bringing a document to a meeting automatically establishes an agenda and a purpose, but a meeting to review a document is no different from any other. To capture a meeting's purpose, creating a list of questions is perhaps the easiest technique. After all, you're bringing people together to discuss an issue and what better way to get the discussion going than with a list of questions? Remember that the deliverables in this book are tools to communicate ideas, vehicles for discussing them, not ends in and of themselves. Your purpose, therefore, shouldn't be focused on the document, but instead on the content.
- **Identify the key talking points**: Even if your purpose is to answer some questions about the web site design, the theme or key talking points can be to show stakeholders that you're getting conflicting direction from different areas of the organization. You don't need to keep this underlying message a secret from meeting participants, but it's important to recognize that while all meeting participants have a common purpose, they might not have a common agenda.
- **Remind participants of the design problem and/or design principles**: Take a moment to reiterate the project's objective in the form of a design problem. If you've established some principles that will guide the design effort, list these, too. This context helps people understand where the design effort begins and ends.
- **Inject users into the discussion**: Different artifacts will incorporate and focus on users in different ways. Conversations about documents that are further removed from discussing or describing users will benefit from reiterating key insights about the target audience. Draw a relationship between what you're about to discuss and what you know about the audience.

2. Describe visual conventions

Before laying out the main themes of the design artifact, you should help meeting participants understand what they're looking at. Describe the artifact in general terms, highlighting how you used particular shapes, for example, to represent different aspects of the design. You don't need to walk them through the entire document, but you should point out major concepts and explain the visual system— what each shape means, how you've grouped things together, and other elements that contain important meaning.

If your diagram includes a key, a box off to the side of the page that describes each symbol, you can use this to hit the high points. Good diagrams, they say, shouldn't require a key. But, frankly, I don't know who "they" are, and they're certainly not the ones in the room presenting the site map, flowchart, concept model, or whatever to your stakeholders.

3. Highlight major design decisions

"Major design decisions" constitute one thing: the important messages about the design work you've done. They could be:

- The direction you selected for driving screen designs
- The main takeaway from user research
- The underlying structure behind a site map
- The three or four key screens in a flowchart

To help identify this message, you can ask yourself this question, "When participants leave the meeting, what's the one thing I want them to remember?"

Some ideas for determining key messages:

- What's the most surprising thing about your design or your findings?
- What constitutes the most dramatic change from the current site?
- What presents the biggest design challenge?
- What are users most interested in?
- What is the one idea driving subsequent design decisions?

> **LITMUS TEST**
> ## Major Design Decisions
>
> A good way to check the effectiveness of your diagram is to compare the things you want to say about the structure of the site against the depiction in the diagram. Ask yourself, for each of my main messages, does the diagram adequately illustrate the message? Are any of the key messages buried or receded into the background relative to other data points?

Boil down the essence of your agenda into a handful of bullets and you also give yourself a focus for the meeting. Detours and distractions become clear because they don't deal directly with these messages. Details elaborated later in the meeting should support these messages.

4. Offer rationale and identify constraints

Having described the major design decisions, you can switch your attention to the details, elaborating on those key decisions. Just as we set context for the major design decisions, we should also set context for the details. This comes in the form of constraints. Reminding participants about the project's boundaries sets the stage by helping them understand the context in which you made decisions about the details.

There are always constraints in a design project. Your project may have them to a greater or lesser extent:

- **User research**: Designers who subscribe to user-centered design philosophy prioritize user research perhaps above all others. In short, user research yields a set of expectations—what users would like the product to do. As we produce design ideas, we can compare the idea to user needs. Doesn't address a need? The idea dies.
- **Project objectives**: Most of my work these days involves designing web sites to meet a specific business objective. Sometimes it's hard for me to relate the business objective to any other constraints, but that's the nature of the organizations I'm working for. The project is a small piece of a larger machine. Depending on the piece and the machine, failure of the part may or may not mean failure of the whole. Regardless, these constraints can sometimes seem arbitrary as they serve some abstract objective and not a concrete requirement driven by users.

- **Project parameters**: As much as we don't like to admit it, there are external (and again, seemingly arbitrary forces) that scaffold the design process. Most explicitly, these are deadlines that confine the range of activities we can perform in order to conceptualize and flesh out a design. Less explicitly, these may be the priorities of project stakeholders and other team dynamics.
- **Technical implementation**: Though technologists are fond of saying "We can make it do anything," the truth is that most design work happens in the context of existing systems. These existing systems come with capabilities and configurations that make some design ideas more feasible than others. The sometimes unspoken extension to the technologists' mantra is "We can make it do anything with sufficient time and budget."
- **Operational implementation**: Just as the technology provides a context for a design idea, so too does the organization that will support it. There are people behind every technology, having to provide support in everything from customer help to content updates. Without the infrastructure from an operational perspective, some design ideas will not be successful. To thrive, a design must acknowledge the organization that will support and maintain the final product.
- **Industry standards**: Otherwise known as "best practices," these conventions emerge after withstanding the test of time. Used widely on other web sites, such standards become constraints in so far as they establish a baseline from which other design decisions extend.
- **Organizational standards**: Establishing standards specific to the organization is a complex process with numerous benefits. Suffice it to say that from the designer's perspective, standards provide a range of starting points for solving problems. Positioning and integration into the design process is crucial; done poorly, these constraints come across as creativity-killers. (See Nathan Curtis's book, *Modular Web Design* for more ideas on establishing design standards in the organization.)

- **Design principles**: A good team will summarize their direction in a single theme or collection of bullet points. This direction is specific: "make it easy to use" gets eliminated as a principle pretty quickly, for example, because it isn't specific to the project and is common to all our projects. Instead, design principles are specific and meaningful to the team working on the project. They are means for making design decisions.

Design principles are, in a sense, a super-set of all other constraints. One way to look at them is that teams compose design principles when they want to boil down everything they've learned from all the other constraints.

These constraints can also provide a rationale for making the decisions. They limit the range of choices you can make in design by establishing criteria for those choices.

One challenge you might face in this part of the process is having to provide a rationale against well-entrenched assumptions. Examples include:

- A new way of thinking about users against a marketing segmentation model used for years
- A new flow for an application that doesn't align with internal processes
- A site structure that eliminates some content on the current site

It's swimming against the tide in these scenarios that tests a designer's mettle. There's no single solvent that will magically erase these challenges. To prepare for these conversations:

- Come up with three reasons why this approach makes sense
- Make a list of all the criticisms you might face and prepare responses
- Role-play with colleagues who are both familiar and unfamiliar with the project team

- Brainstorm a list of potential risks for the approach
- Brainstorm a list of potential risks for other approaches

If you're still wondering why it makes sense to discuss rationale and constraints prior to the details of the artifact, the simple truth is that discussing these topics will yield more productive outcomes. They:

- Teach you what's most important to the project team
- Force you to have a solid rationale for design decisions
- Help you clarify project constraints
- Help you refine your design ideas to make them airtight

5. Point out details

The conversation is now ripe for spelling out the details. This is where individual chapters will have the best specific advice: The details for each artifact vary dramatically. One challenge is how to describe a detail. My favorite approach is one I learned from Edward Tufte at his all-day workshop way back in 1999:

Particular-General-Particular (PGP): Select details that illustrate the main talking points from step 3, earlier. One theme or message constitutes a "general." Point out a detail that refers to this message, reiterate the message, and then point out a second detail that supports it. Using the donation flows from the Flowcharts chapter, one might apply the PGP model like this:

> In order to donate time in addition to money, users will follow this secondary flow that captures their activities of interest and availability. We take them to the secondary flow because the project objective is to create a flexible donation application accommodating multiple forms of giving while keeping financial donations extremely simple. Another example of this is donating supplies, which again relies on a secondary flow to capture the types of supplies and delivery information.

A second challenge is determining which details to focus on. Most deliverables contain more than 30 to 60 minutes' worth of conversation (and thankfully few project teams agree to regular 120-minute meetings). The key messages from step 3 should be your guide in determining which details to highlight, but this may not be enough. After all, most of the design decisions should rely on the principles described in step 3. Consider prioritizing details that:

- Reflect user needs
- Vary dramatically from the current state
- Present significant risk to the project
- Require further input from the project team

6. Communicate implications

Designers are responsible for anticipating the risks that may be associated with their ideas. This isn't to say they should censor themselves, but they should be able to predict (to varying levels of detail) possible problems with the design. Implications, typically, fall into one of three categories:

- **Design**: Design ideas lead to further design challenges. Consolidating the functionality of half a dozen desktop applications into a single web-based app is a design decision that leads to countless design challenges. Designers should be able to anticipate these problems and estimate a level of effort for addressing them.
- **Technical**: Just as lines on an architectural blueprint translate to walls in reality, lines on a site map or wireframe translate to bits of code. Some things are easier to build than others, and designers should be able to enumerate potential challenges facing the implementation of the design.
- **Operational**: A web site doesn't stand on its own. Depending on the scale, 10 to 10,000 people may be on the hook to maintain the site—producing content, updating pages, responding to transactions. Designers may not be able to predict the level of effort for these activities, but they should be able to help organizations see where their current operations will not support a new design concept.

Like in step 5, previously, the implications will be particular to the type of diagram and the specifics of your project.

7. Solicit feedback

There are three ways to engage participants in conversation about the ideas in the presentation: wait until the end, take questions during the presentation, or format the discussion as a brainstorming session.

In order to...	Set up your meeting by...	And watch out for...
Save feedback for the end	Highlighting the portion of the agenda where others will be able to contribute.	People getting antsy during the meeting. Despite your best efforts, people may have something they need to get off their chest.
Solicit feedback during	Introducing the range of topics on which you need feedback.	Rabbit holes that lead to a lot of conversation but not a lot of decisions. These may be worthwhile, but come with sacrificing time and potentially other topics that would be more productive.
Facilitate brainstorming	Describing the parameters of the brainstorming, including the key questions that need answers.	Losing steam. Brainstorming can be hard. Come prepared with more material than will fill the time slot so you can reinvigorate the conversation with new challenges.

Table 2.1: Approaches for soliciting feedback, timing, setup, and what to watch out for.

Each approach modifies the logistics of the meeting but not the intent. Whether the conversation is more of a dialog, a free-for-all, or a lecture with Q&A, the end result is the same—meaningful feedback on the work presented.

All three approaches may rest on the same principles, however: there are specific aspects of the deliverable for which you are seeking feedback, and there are particular questions you have about those aspects. You may require input on the whole picture, but kicking off feedback in terms of "what do you think" doesn't empower meeting participants to make worthwhile contributions. In planning the meeting, break down your needs like this:

Aspects: Get participants to focus on different components of the artifact. A component may be a region of the drawing (the header of the wireframe), or a set of similar objects (all the nodes on the site map that represent templates).

Questions: Once you've identified all the different aspects of the diagram you need help with, generate a list of questions. The chapters suggest questions derived from the following list of types, as well as others more specific to each individual artifact. These are listed in order of increasing difficulty to answer:

- **Is this correct?** In short, you want to know if the ideas presented meet the need. One way to do this is to present multiple options and ask the participants to discuss them.
- **What's missing?** As much as we hope our site maps accommodate every piece of content and our wireframes address every functional requirement, we frequently leave something out. For each aspect, you can generate specific questions about what might be missing. A general "Anything missing?" question is a good start, but may not be enough. Try to be more specific, as in, "Can you think of examples of content that wouldn't have a place in this site map?"
- **What does this imply?** Design concepts will have an impact on the work of other team members. It may put them on the hook to do some difficult coding or rewrite lots of content. Make sure you get them to think about how the design concept impacts them.

A final thought on feedback: Be careful to solicit feedback on the ideas represented by the artifact, not necessarily the artifact itself. While it would be nice to create a perfect site map, it doesn't help anyone to create a perfect diagram depicting an imperfect site structure.

8. Provide a framework for review

By this point in the conversation, you've hopefully recorded the feedback received and identified specific tasks for particular people in the meeting. This record (the meeting minutes, for lack of a less antiquated term) is a measure of the value of the conversation. Quantity isn't everything here. Judge your meetings on the utility of the discussion, the amount of movement on the project, the clarity of the assigned tasks, and the extent to which you've covered your agenda.

If gaps remain—if you didn't get to discuss everything you needed to—consider assigning homework. Offline reviews are essential if the design documentation is too massive to review in a single conversation. If this is the case, use step 7 (solicit feedback) to construct a model of the kinds of input you need. In that part of the conversation, your intent isn't to get feedback on everything in the document, but instead to provide an example of the kinds of feedback you need throughout.

In this stage of the conversation, as you reiterate the notes and tasks you captured, also remind participants of this framework. Get people to focus on three or four aspects of the diagram or deliverable, and ask one or two questions

You can...	But be sure to...	And watch out for...
Show it right away	Tell meeting participants that you'll walk through the diagram slowly if this is the first time they've seen it. If you're reviewing a second or third iteration, don't skip step 1 (establish context)—things may have changed a bit since you last met with the team.	Participants diving in with comments anyway. Don't get sucked into their reckless ways! Thank them for comments, but indicate you want to do a bit of context-setting to make sure you're all considering the diagram from the same vantage.
Save it for step 3	Show an excerpt or sample visual language in step 2 to help people understand the conventions.	Frustration or impatience that you're not showing the document right away.
Send it before the meeting	Include a cover letter that highlights a few items in the document people should look for. Send it with the meeting agenda so participants know what to expect during the conversation.	Participants still showing up unprepared. Just because you send it around doesn't mean everyone will have read it in detail. Don't sacrifice parts of the agenda where you walk through the document just because you sent it around before the meeting.

Table 2.2: When to reveal the document, some factors to consider.

about each of those things. Provide a solid deadline. Communicate implications (schedule, most likely) if you don't receive their feedback by the deadline established.

Adapting the Basic Recipe

So that's the basic approach to discussing design artifacts. Of course, it's just a framework; you should feel free to adapt as necessary for your situation. Here are some ways to modify the basic agenda to suit your needs:

- **Emphasis**: In the context of a meeting agenda, emphasis refers to the amount of time you spend on one portion. If people in the meeting are familiar with the diagram format and participated in the design work, you may give these parts of the meeting cursory treatment and spend the bulk of time on rationale, details, and feedback.
- **Order**: Though the order of the basic agenda is purposeful—putting the most important stuff up front and building later sections on the foundation established in earlier sections—you do have some flexibility. For example, you might combine context-setting and rationale to identify some constraints as driving the design. If people are already familiar with the deliverable, you might move "framework for review" to the beginning to clarify what it is you're looking for, both at the meeting and thereafter.
- **Elimination or reduction**: The basic meeting agenda is set up to eliminate redundancy, while providing ample opportunity to establish and reinforce a set of key messages. On the other hand, if you have less time than you anticipated, you might just focus on spelling out the big ideas. I'd be hard-pressed to say which sections can be eliminated; subsequent agenda items build on those that come earlier. I strongly recommend against eliminating any of the sections completely. Instead, consider reducing less important sections to a sentence or two, acknowledging them without elaborating on them.

Meeting Challenges

Even the best-planned meetings can go off course, losing the thread and taking participants further from the purpose. Facilitating design meetings means maintaining a firm grasp on the direction of the conversation. Watch for these challenges:

Loss of focus

Discussions might venture into tangential topics, taking detours that don't advance the design or serve the purpose of the conversation. You can:

- Put the agenda or objectives on a whiteboard at the start of the meeting. This makes the inanimate object the bad guy when you point to it indicating that the topic is out of place in this conversation.
- Jump in, cutting off tangents before they get too far, and capturing it in a visible place. Participants will feel like the topic has been heard. Be sure to subsequently capture these points in the meeting minutes and don't forget to follow up with them in subsequent design activities.
- Let the tangent run its course. Though it might not serve the purpose of the meeting, distracting topics may be relevant or otherwise important. If I judge a distracting topic too important to put aside, I'll let the conversation explore it for a little while. If it appears as if some people are interested in the topic while for others it will be a waste of time, I'll jump in with a "is now a good time to talk about this?" to make sure we're all willing to spend some time on it.

Excruciating detail

While not tangents, per se, digging so deep into the details as to get completely lost down the rabbit hole can also be counterproductive. You can treat these as you would tangents—redirecting, capturing, or letting it play out. At the same time, while a tangent may be a topic irrelevant to completing the design work, digging into the details usually is not. Two additional approaches: Suggest a separate meeting (or extend the current one) to deal with that detail; or suggest an alternate venue, asking participants to supply their comments on the details via email instead.

There are times when mind-numbing detail in a meeting may be unavoidable. Sometimes, what it takes to get to a project's conclusion is walking through every annotation on every page with all the key players in the room. If your project team is allergic to this approach, an alternative would be to give the document a detailed read and provide comments electronically.

Uninspired feedback

Lack of useful feedback from participants means the facilitator isn't working hard enough. There can be any number of reasons why the feedback isn't substantive, but to help increase the value of the conversation, the facilitator should:

- Clarify the story
- Ask better questions
- Dig into undeveloped feedback
- Give people something controversial to react to

No follow-through

You won't be able to see this problem during the meeting, but it can sap value from even the most productive conversations. After the meeting, all the value is lost because there hasn't been any follow-through. To make sure the meeting successfully leads to the next step in the project, you should:

- **Capture action items**: Make a list of all the things people promised to do during the course of the conversation. Flag items that are dependencies with your tasks so people understand what might delay your deliveries.
- **Reflect feedback back to participants**: Make sure you understand the feedback by restating it for project participants.
- **Send revisions as soon as possible**: Though this will be between you and the project team, I find the sooner I send revisions, the easier it is to keep the project moving forward.

Inviting the wrong people

Invite the minimal number of people possible. Nothing ruins a meeting more than people who won't have anything meaningful to contribute or take away from the conversation. Too many bodies at the table can make a meeting lose its focus or get caught in the maelstrom of competing agendas. Too many bodies can be difficult to manage, and difficult to steer through to the meeting objectives. Let's face it, sometimes you need to be honest with yourself about whether you're one of these people. Perhaps I'm jaded: I happily delegate conversations to other people and say, just send me a copy of the meeting minutes.

Meeting with new people

If you've never met with the participants previously—new project team or client, for example—the first conversation can be daunting. Without knowing the style of the team or the personalities of the individual players, planning a good conversation can be challenging. You're just not sure what kinds of tangents to expect, what the tone of the critiques will be. You don't know how comfortable people will be providing feedback or where and how to nudge them.

I'll let other books and web sites give you tips on ice-breakers and get-to-know-you games. These are great, and set a nice tone for the project. Here's something else I do: Make sure to bring another team member to the conversation. Their role will be to participate, but also to observe the players in the meeting, capturing some informal notes about them. Afterwards, compare observations and establish some strategies for preparing future meetings. Two examples:

- **The awkward silence**: In one instance, we realized that no one liked providing feedback out loud. Asking questions about the work we showed produced nothing but nods and one-syllable responses. Ultimately we learned that two different business units made up the team and they didn't want to reveal too much information to each other. We asked them to start providing feedback offline, which we could then compile.
- **The lack of preparation**: In another instance, a team couldn't give us feedback during the course of the conversation. We later learned that though we sent them the document a day in advance of our review meetings, they didn't have time to look through it. We ultimately established two shorter conversations: one to walk through the document and the other for them to provide feedback.

Letting your ego in

Even if you can manage all these other risks, the honest truth is that you may be the biggest problem the meeting faces. Facilitating a conversation means relinquishing control over one part of the design process and assuming (a different kind of) control over another.

Owning the design sometimes means letting it go, letting others into the process, and helping them find a voice to make a worthwhile contribution.

Relinquish	Embrace
The need to make every design decision.	The satisfaction of getting everyone to have his or her say.
The need to judge every suggestion, especially if leading a brainstorming meeting.	Capturing contributions in an actionable way.
The personal attachment you have to the design concept or the documents you created to explain the design concept. Feedback isn't personal.	Getting people to elaborate on vague feedback.

Table 2.3: To leave your ego at the door, you need to embrace a different kind of control.

TIP

The Airing of Grievances

Once you know what your own agenda is, think through the agendas of everyone else who will be in the room. You can refine your message and your agenda by imagining all the questions you'll be asked. For example, in politically charged projects, every person may see certain pieces of content or features as the highest priority. They may come to a discussion needing to get these things off their chest. Instead of listening to you or participating in the conversation, they'll spend the whole meeting thinking about their own agenda items.

One technique for dealing with this situation is to give people time at the beginning of the meeting to air these issues. Usually, they're not as controversial as imagined, and if you lead with a more comprehensive outline, you have an excuse to move past any unnecessary discussion. Having diffused the pent-up politics, you can move along to the main purpose of the meeting.

Virtual Meetings

Many of my clients—even the ones based near me in Washington—are comfortable using online collaboration technologies. More often than not, this is our venue for discussing design documentation. While we don't get to be face-to-face, online collaboration technologies afford us other advantages.

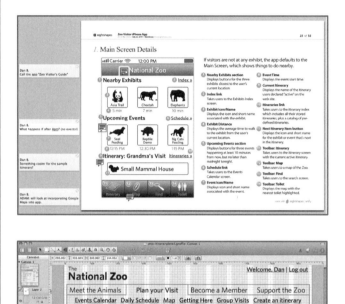

Figure 2.2: Using electronic tools to reproduce the in-person meeting experience. In this case, I'm annotating a deliverable with the built-in "sticky notes" function as meeting participants make comments. With screen-sharing, everyone can see that I hear their feedback.

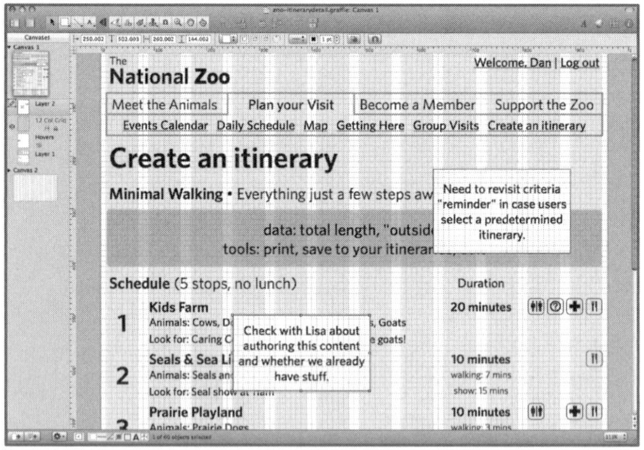

Figure 2.3: Capturing comments on the fly in the wireframe file itself. The same idea applies here, demonstrating that I hear comments and feedback, and responding to them as participants make them. If you can't make changes to the wireframe or diagram itself, you can embed text fields with comments.

Too Many Meetings

Everyone has busy calendars, so make sure you have a good reason for getting together before sending an invitation. Assemble a quick agenda and see if participants could address the purpose of the meeting "offline," sending comments through email. Better yet, send the agenda around via email and solicit feedback, asking, "Do we need to meet to discuss this stuff?"

Of course, everyone has too much email, too.

The pre-meeting meeting

I don't mind admitting to you that I've used the phrase "pre-meeting meeting." Yes, I feel a little unclean each time I do. Frankly, some meetings are big enough and important enough to warrant a little more planning, and that's often best done in person with a few key stakeholders. Presenting a new design concept or a discussion that's going to last more than an hour is like a doing a talk at a conference. The audience is smaller, the venue likely has better carpeting, but it requires a great deal of preparation to make sure you tell a good story and get the best out of the meeting participants. Topics to cover in the pre-meeting meeting:

- **Objectives**: Make sure everyone agrees on what they want to get out of the meeting.
- **Content priorities**: Decide which topics you'll cover first, and which topics are OK to sacrifice if you run out of time.
- **Timing**: Decide how much time to dedicate to each topic.
- **Potential risks**: Do a bit of role-playing to surface tangents, critiques, or distractions that you might not otherwise expect.

CONGRATULATIONS

You're done with basic training. If this chapter felt a little abstract, it's because it isn't focused on any one particular artifact, diagram, deliverable, or document. Instead, it's meant to lay a foundation for the next five chapters, which expand, elaborate, and break this starting point. The next section of the book (Part 2: Design Deliverables) takes these diagrams and shows how you can use them in the context of a larger document.

This chapter describes techniques that will become meaningful and practical in the course of working on actual deliverables. It's like scales for a musician or knife technique for a chef. They are the fundamentals you need to internalize to improve the efficiency and effortlessness in making design deliverables.

EXERCISES

1. This book describes five diagrams, ones that I use day in and day out in my work. But these aren't the only diagrams created as part of the design process. Find a diagram not addressed in the book (and it doesn't have to be part of the design process) and see if you can break it up into layers. What are the essential parts of the diagram? What parts of the diagram could be safely removed without losing the essential meaning?

2. The meeting framework suggested in this chapter should work with any design deliverable. Take an artifact from your portfolio and compose a meeting agenda based on the basic framework. You'll have to imagine the meeting participants: is this an internal design project or a review with stakeholders who haven't yet seen the design concepts? Review the agenda with colleagues or a study group and determine if there is a better structure for telling the particular story in the diagram.

3. Take a diagram from your portfolio and think about the process you used to put it together. Write down the steps you took, identifying where you brought in other people and where you iterated on the diagram. Compare your process to the one described in the Creating Design Artifacts section of this chapter. What did you do differently? Are there things you would have changed about your process? What can you do to make things more streamlined without sacrificing quality?

Chapter 3

Personas

pər·so'·nəz (n.)

A summary representation of the system's intended users, often described as real people. Any project can have one or more personas, each representing a different kind of audience for the system. Also known as: user profiles, user role definitions, audience profiles.

PERSONAS AT-A-GLANCE

If you need a way to talk about your users in meaningful terms, look no further than personas. They provide a framework for describing the target audience in a way useful to design projects. They bring the audience to life and serve as the voice of the user throughout the design process.

Purpose—What are personas for?

Personas focus design activities by helping the team prioritize system features and content that best support the audience. They summarize design research or frame user requirements. Use personas before engaging in a deep design project to:

- Capture the organization's understanding of the target audience to help drive design
- Provide a means for prioritizing a long wish list of system features

Audience—Who uses them?

Since ultimately personas help direct and inform design decisions, the design team is the primary audience, although stakeholders may weigh in on their creation, and engineers may find them useful for providing context for their work.

Scale—How much work are they?

Creating personas can be a project in and of itself. In some cases, personas become an ongoing project—a means to summarize a perpetual research program. On the flip side, you can generate a list of useful roles for guiding the design process in the space of a brainstorming meeting. The overall scale depends on at least four factors:

- Activities: What steps are you taking to generate the information for the personas?
- Detail: How much information do you want to pack into each persona?
- Breadth: How much of the site are you addressing with these personas? Is it one area or is it the whole thing?
- Stakeholders: How many people want to be involved with the creation of personas? Lots of cooks could mean a more complex process.

Context—Where do they fall in the process?

The design team generally prepares personas before doing a detailed design project, since personas capture requirements, provide context, and frame the design challenge.

Personas describe a site's target users, giving a clear picture of how they're likely to use the web site, and what they'll expect from it. Personas have become a popular way for design teams to capture information about customers that directly impact the design process: user goals, scenarios, tasks, and the like.

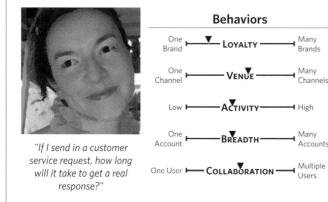

Rachel Berry • New Online Banking Customer
Long-time customer, recently started online banking

"If I send in a customer service request, how long will it take to get a real response?"

Behaviors

One Brand	◄ LOYALTY ►	Many Brands
One Channel	◄ VENUE ►	Many Channels
Low	◄ ACTIVITY ►	High
One Account	◄ BREADTH ►	Many Accounts
One User	◄ COLLABORATION ►	Multiple Users

Objectives

- Feel **confident** in security of funds and personal information
- Feel in **control** of finances
- Wants to learn about **relevant banking products**, especially for retirement and saving for college
- **Check and dispute** transactions
- **Move funds** from one account to another
- **Pay bills**

Concerns

- "Am I doing the right thing with my money?"
- "If I send in a customer service request, how long will it take to get a real response?"
- "Is it easy to dispute a discrepancy on my account?"
- "How do I set up a new payee and recurring payment?"
- "Can I use the web site to stop payment on a check?"
- "How do I set up a new account?"
- "How do I set up regular downloads to Quicken and make sure that link is working?"

Scenarios

- **Resolving Disputes**
  Rachel set up automatic bill payment with her regular expenses. Rachel gets a notice from PEPCO that last month's bill was unpaid. She logs into online banking to check to see that the payment went through, and noticed that it has. She uses the customer service contact form to send the bank a message inquiring about the transaction, including the transaction number. Rachel will do the same with the electric company, but she hopes to hear from the bank within a day.

- **Reporting Fraud**
  Rachel has several accounts at the bank, including a checking account, a money market account, and a credit card. Rachel notices some suspicious charges on her credit card bill. Rachel logs into online banking and hopes to kill two birds with one stone by informing the bank of the suspicious charges and explaining that she won't be paying the full bill. She expects the bank will respond, clarifying their policy on disputed charges.

- **Managing Accounts**
  Rachel just got her annual bonus and she wants to set that money aside for a short period of time, so she wants to create a new CD (certificate of deposit, a short-term interest-earning savings account). Rachel thinks she should be able to create the CD and seed it with money from her checking account, all online.

Background

Rachel is in her early 30s, married, and a new mother. She is taking some time off from work for the baby, and is using some of that time to get their finances "in order." Since she's spending more time at home and has more at stake, she's finally gotten into online banking to give her more control over the finances without leaving her laptop.

Figure 3.1. A pretty detailed persona.

Good personas make everyone happy. They give design teams an effective, accessible way to describe user needs and stakeholders a common language for talking about their customers. Personas mean that no one on your team will have to say, "I think our users want this" or "If my mom were a customer she would want that." If done well, they paint a multidimensional picture of the audience in terms that allow design teams to evaluate the effectiveness of their designs. Personas are also useful for getting stakeholders to agree on the composition of the target audience.

Personas aren't born from nothing, sprouting like Aphrodite from the designer's head. Instead, personas are typically the product of research into the target audience, and the complexity and level of detail depends on the available information. Research techniques vary from surveys and market research to interviews and ethnographic methods. There are shelves of books and articles on the best research techniques, but the purpose of this book is to describe the best approach for capturing and effectively communicating all that information.

There's no standard format for personas across the industry, and different gurus have offered different approaches. Regardless of what approach you select, personas should have a couple of things in common: expressing what users need and what they expect.

INTRODUCING PERSONAS

Personas describe a fictional person who aggregates common aspects of a particular user group. The person is described in terms of typical behaviors, their objectives, and what they might expect from a product like the one you're working on. These descriptions range from bullet lists to paragraphs of prose. Some designers will use diagrams to show ranges of needs or behaviors and where particular personas fall on those scales.

At their most detailed, personas paint richly detailed descriptions of a system's users, creating a quasi-biographical portrait of a composite person, based on research data. Others simply offer a brief sketch of each type of user. Over the course of this chapter, we'll discuss the merits of these various approaches, and how to tailor your personas to the needs of your particular project.

Personas have been a hot topic in the web design community since they were introduced several years ago. Whether or not you agree with the particular methodology and application of them or not, you certainly have gobs of examples online to draw from.

Personas represent distinct groups of people. How you come up with these groups is the topic of stacks of books on personas. In general, your process might fall into one of three categories:

- **Data-driven**: After deep analysis of the data, certain patterns emerged, driving you toward these particular groups. You can use the key data points to identify the persona.
- **Institutional**: These groups align to the way the organization typically talks about the target audience—just be sure to verify that they also work for your current purpose.
- **Procedural**: The persona roles are based on the customer lifecycle. You can develop personas that reflect the primary task in different stages of the lifecycle.

Challenges

Understanding users in the name of design is (I think it's fair to say) fraught with controversy and obstacles. Preparing the summary of such work might seem straightforward, but it, too, comes with its share of difficulties. It's easy enough to make people up, but summarizing what you actually know about your audience can be tough.

Figure 3.2: Todd Zaki Warfel's persona format has been refined over the years. The combination of quantifiable dimensions with more humanizing descriptions yields an artifact that serves as a solid foundation for design. You can find the original templates here: http://zakiwarfel.com/archives/persona-templates/

- **Incomplete information**: Personas summarize the target audience. Your understanding of that target audience can come from a variety of sources, but ultimately, you may not have access to the information you need to compose a persona. Addressing this challenge follows one of two strategies: seek out the information or use personas as an opportunity to highlight the lack of information.
- **Legacy customer information**: Another common pitfall in building personas is dealing with companies that have done business successfully for years without formal documentation of their customers. They may have informal ways of referring to different customer groups, which may not be relevant to your efforts. Part of the persona process is helping organizations learn a new way of talking about their customers.

any artifact, they are burdened with helping to move the design project along and getting the design team to communicate about the project. To many designers, however, personas are responsible for being the voice of the user throughout the design process. Herein lies the source of all these challenges: absent actual users of the system, the design team must be the voice of the user, and personas should serve as a constant reminder. There is no way for a single artifact to encompass the nuance of a persona, even in the specific context of design. People have a better chance. We may have them clearly pictured in our minds, but sometimes we need a document (like a persona) to keep us pointing in the right direction.

ANATOMY OF A PERSONA

The main choice you'll be making as you construct your personas is how much information to include for each one. Generally, there are three layers of detail to consider. The most basic personas will only include the first layer, while the most elaborate will flesh out all three layers.

- **Actionability**: Like any artifact not directly related to documenting the design, it can be challenging to ensure that personas are truly useful to the design process. They have the annoying habit of ending up on a shelf. If you're creating personas to be a tool for the design team, they need to contribute to (if not drive) the design process. It can be challenging to zero in on a format that does this successfully. One way designers have adapted personas is to make them a little less backstory and a little more "behavior focused." Reducing personas to their essentials gives designers the focus they need without losing any of the value.

Ultimately, personas are design tools—inspiration, reference, parameters, and constraints all rolled into one. Like

Layer 1: Establishing Requirements	Layer 2: Elaborating Relationships	Layer 3: Making 'em Human
Name	Concerns	Personal Background
Key Distinguishing Feature	Scenarios	Photo
Descriptive Dimensions	Quotes	System Features
Objectives & Motivations		Demographic Information
Source		Technology Comfort

Table 3.1: The elements of a persona may be prioritized into three layers. You can get away with just using first-layer elements. Adding data points from other layers can create more robust personas but will require further information-gathering.

Layer 1: Establishing Requirements

Personas can be rich with data, but these elements are the foundation for the greatest practical applications. They establish and frame user requirements.

Name

Personas are summary representations of people. People have names. Therefore, your personas should have names, if for no other reason than to make it easy to talk about them with other project participants.

- **Real names**, like those you'd find in the White Pages, are useful because they create a vivid picture, something real for stakeholders to associate with their customers. Real names turn formerly abstract conversations into more concrete ones.
- **A role- or purpose-driven name** can keep project participants focused on the important issues—goals, motivations, needs. Either way, the name should be short and distinctive, even when describing the purpose: "The Learner," "The Infrequent Customer," "The Worrier," "The Multiple Account Holder," and "The Competitive Researcher," for instance. These names describe what's bringing these particular user types to the system in the first place by focusing on purpose and objective.

Real names and role names are not mutually exclusive. Feel free to use both.

You can name personas based on the process you used to create the personas:

- **Data-driven**: Use key data points in the name of the persona.
- **Institutional**: Use the same names used by the organization today.
- **Procedural**: Use names that reflect the primary task in different stages in the lifecycle.

Key distinguishing feature

What makes this user group different from the others? Summarize the persona in a sentence or two to help other people understand what makes them special.

In Figure 3.1, the distinguishing feature of the persona is that she is a recent convert to online banking, though she is otherwise familiar with the bank and its products.

Descriptive dimensions

Ultimately, you want to communicate what users **know**, what they might **do**, and what they want to **achieve**. Even when not using explicit personas, I still employ dimensions whenever I need to characterize users.

Dimensions are individual scales that represent a range of possibilities for a single aspect of a person. By using scales to describe user groups, you have a simple mechanism for comparing personas. You can also identify which areas of each dimension are NOT represented among the groups. Such dimensions might include:

- **Knowledge**: The user's familiarity with particular aspects of the relevant domain.
- **Tasks**: The range of activities users choose to perform. The scale might reflect a quantity, or it might reflect two different extremes.
- **Interests**: The depth of focus users have on different aspects of the relevant domain.
- **Characteristics**: The degree to which users exhibit specific behaviors. Unlike tasks, these are passive, where people are not making conscious decisions or trying to accomplish something.

Not every dimension will be on a less/more scale. I created a persona for an online gaming site with "Platform" as a dimension. That is, a dimension that answered the question, "Where do people play the games?" Some personas were strictly online gamers. Others played on a variety of platforms.

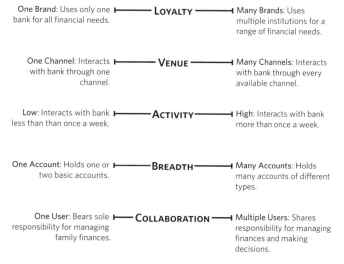

One Brand: Uses only one bank for all financial needs.	**LOYALTY**	**Many Brands:** Uses multiple institutions for a range of financial needs.
One Channel: Interacts with bank through one channel.	**VENUE**	**Many Channels:** Interacts with bank through every available channel.
Low: Interacts with bank less than than once a week.	**ACTIVITY**	**High:** Interacts with bank more than once a week.
One Account: Holds one or two basic accounts.	**BREADTH**	**Many Accounts:** Holds many accounts of different types.
One User: Bears sole responsibility for managing family finances.	**COLLABORATION**	**Multiple Users:** Shares responsibility for managing finances and making decisions.

Figure 3.3: Dimensions describing behaviors.

ALTERNATE APPROACH
Dimensions Only

I've always been wary of elaborate narratives to describe users. As an interaction designer, I need to get into the user's head from a cognitive perspective. I could never be convinced that knowing demographic information, domestic circumstances, or other anthropomorphic idiosyncrasies was crucial to this.

So on more recent user research projects, I've avoided narratives altogether and focused on behavioral dimensions exclusively. My deliverable wasn't, therefore, a stack of abstract people like "Sarah the New Customer" or "Harry the Experienced Online Banker." Instead, I've analyzed data to establish a set of scales describing the range of behaviors, knowledge, circumstances, or concerns.

Objectives and motivations

The artifact should include a set of bullets listing the persona's goals within the scope of the system. Typically, these goals may be expressed as what users want to get out of interacting with the system, but the goals may also reflect what users want from the organization, or what they want in general. For example, objectives for someone using a banking web site might be:

- Compare different types of mortgage products
- Apply for an account

Note the verb-object construction of these objectives. Like the descriptive dimensions, they express an action and the relevant information associated with the action. Such expressions are easy to parse relative to interactive systems, because they can directly translate to features.

Source

The best personas are born out of an intimate knowledge of the target audience, often through an ongoing user research program. Many teams, however, must create personas from a more limited set of inputs.

Treat your personas as individual research papers. Be sure to annotate (with footnotes, for example) citing the source of each data point, even if that source is an internal brainstorming session or the opinion of the CEO or VP of marketing.

Layer 2: Elaborating Relationships

With the basics in place, consider adding more information to elaborate on the relationships between the personas and the web site.

Concerns: What they care about

One way to clarify the relationship between users and the web site is to establish what concerns will influence their experience. Keep in mind that a customer's experience extends beyond the web, or a single session of using the site. There are a few ways to express concerns, and they're not mutually exclusive.

Features aren't specific functions or types of content, but characteristics of the experience itself. Examples:

- Sensitivity to privacy
- Focus on task at hand
- Implication that trustworthy humans are "at the other end"

The persona can include **questions** from the user's perspective, and reflect the kinds of things they're thinking about before, during, or after using the web site. Examples:

- What's the easiest way to get an update on my account information?
- I just refinanced my mortgage. How can I make sure I send the payments to the right place?
- How quickly do customer service representatives respond to email?
- If I do something online, will the people at my local branch know about it?

Within the context of the web site or the overall experience, a persona can characterize users' typical **pain points**. These are the areas that tend to give people the most trouble. Perhaps they're not equipped to deal with certain aspects of the experience or (more likely) the experience is not set up in a way to make things easy for them. You can express pain points as in these examples, and quotes are really useful for this:

- **Importing account information from other institutions**: "I know they're not going to let me tie in information from my mortgage lender."

- **Knowing what to do in case of a potential dispute**: "Ugh. Electric company is saying they didn't get the check and I have no idea how to contact the bank to find out."
- **Understanding the disposition of a customer service email**: "I sent them a message 3 days ago. Where the heck is it?"

Finally, genuine quotes from users allow the project team to raise issues they might otherwise avoid. Sometimes, a criticism or concern steps on too many egos, but deflecting the source minimizes the discomfort, and allows the team to have an honest conversation about it.

Scenarios and circumstances

Scenarios are more-or-less realistic scenes that set the stage for an interaction between a web site and a user. They allow project participants to picture the use of the system beyond the system itself, helping them understand how the system fits into their customers' lives.

Scenarios also help project participants identify what information users might have in-hand when they approach the site. For example, a user checking on flight status information should have the flight number, but may not in every scenario. They help the project team understand the range of decisions someone needs to make and the kinds of outputs they're expecting.

A part of the design process frequently neglected is how people use the information they get out of a system. From the system's point of view, it's "spit out some bit of information and the process is complete." But this is rarely the case for the person using the system. The information is a trigger for making a decision—"the flight is delayed, so I might miss my connection" or "my package still hasn't shipped, so I'd better call customer service."

A simple scenario consists of at least five parts:

- **Context**: The starting point for the scenario, identifying the user's location or situation leading up to the scenario
- **Trigger**: The event that caused the scenario
- **Action**: What the user did to address the scenario
- **Inputs**: What information the user must have to address the scenario
- **Expectations**: How the situation should change to meet the needs of the user

Scenarios can represent **extreme circumstances**:

> Melissa is out shopping when her credit card is declined. Upon returning home, she visits the customer service URL on the back of the credit card to determine why the card was declined. Melissa expects to see instructions on how to access her account and from there how to determine why the card was declined.

Scenarios can represent **circumstances unique to particular users**:

> Nathan is a small-business owner looking to set up payroll through the same bank that has his business checking and savings accounts. He emails his small business contact at the bank to inquire about payroll and hopes to get some quick instructions on setting it up.

Finally, a scenario can represent a **typical circumstance within the context of a specific user** group:

> Sarah is a new college student and is getting a checking account for the first time. She knows her Social Security number, but has no other information. She's expecting to go to the bank tomorrow to tell them what kind of checking account she wants to open.

Remember: A persona will likely include more than one scenario.

Quotes

Using quotes from users adds a personal touch without the distraction that comes with additional layers of personal detail. A good quote can be very evocative of how a user perceives his or her relationship to the web site. You can use actual quotes from your research participants to remind stakeholders that this information has a foundation in research.

Examples:

- "I don't mind researching banking stuff online, but I'd rather do all the transactions in person."
- "These days picking a checking account is like trying to pick a toothpaste. Have you seen the shelves of toothpaste in the grocery store?"

Layer 3: Making 'em Human

The first two layers contain all the essentials and more for describing users, but you may find the following data points useful for creating a real picture of your target audiences. These can make personas an easier pill to swallow for team members who haven't worked with them before.

Personal background

Personal background information can flesh out the user and make the persona more accessible to stakeholders and designers. Such information can include "day in the life of" descriptions or an overall relationship to the task at hand. In the case of our college student, for example, Sarah's personal background may indicate that she's never been good at managing money and her parents did not prepare her well for dealing with budgets and bills.

The personal background information is an opportunity to tell a story about the user, but it transforms the persona from a summary set of needs to a real—albeit fictional—person. On the other hand, too much information can be distracting.

Photograph

The cherry on the persona sundae is a photograph. Like personal background, a photograph can help stakeholders stop thinking about their customers as a singular anonymous mass and understand that they are people with particular needs. As a practical matter, a photo can represent the persona, an easy way to bring the persona to mind.

On the other hand, photographs often come with risks. Using photos of actual users taken during research activities, for example, may present legal problems. Be sure to secure permission from research participants before using their pictures in any materials. Of course, there are plenty of stock photography sites that can provide good images for this purpose. A Google Images search on "headshot" presents an abundance of material.

System features

System features spell out the site's content as it applies to the motivations of your personas. You may already have a sense of the features and content the site will include. In this case, you can align these elements with the persona's motivations to show which features will help users meet their needs.

Often, this process makes it much easier to spot the features that do not support any user needs, which will help the design team justify removing these features from the system.

By the same token, laying out the system features in this way will help designers see if some motivations do not have any features to support them. Stakeholders then learn where they should invest resources to ensure that their customers are getting everything they need.

Demographic information

A holdover from its predecessor, the marketing segment, demographic information is meant to describe the whole category of user, detailing, for example, the range of ages each persona might include.

By including demographic information in the persona, however, you are mixing genres. The persona is meant to be a summary representation of a group of users—a description of a single user (whether concrete or abstract) that best represents a set of needs. A persona should be described as a "35-year-old woman," for example, rather than as a "female, between the ages of 35 and 50." The purpose of a persona is not to describe the tendencies of a group of people defined by age, sex, race, and income, but instead to describe the behaviors of a specific person who represents a class of needs and goals.

Technology comfort level

This bit of information is a favorite among first-time persona builders, but the real value of this information is its implications. A user's comfort level with technology should be translated into actual needs. Knowing that some people have never used the web to shop before, for example, does not necessarily help the design team. On the other hand, knowing that a particular user group will still seek contact with a human because they do not feel confident in giving certain information online does have a direct impact on the design.

CREATING PERSONAS

The hard part for personas is figuring out how to format the information (of which there is always too much or too little) in a way that's most useful to the design team.

TIP
Existing Labels

An organization may have an existing vocabulary to talk about their users. Typically, these labels are derived from market research and have limited value as a design tool because they don't distinguish people by behaviors or tasks. You can still reference these labels to help stakeholders understand how personas relate to the audience as they understand it.

Basic Decisions for Personas

Creating personas, like any project, can spin out of control if not appropriately constrained. Understanding where, when, and how you'll use the personas (as well as who is going to use them) can help keep the endeavor focused.

Purpose: The role of personas

Whether you've already conducted user research, are just about to, or can only rely on existing institutional knowledge, establish a reason for creating personas. From an information-gathering perspective, this will help focus your efforts, but it will also drive what to include and what to leave out in the personas themselves. There are three reasons for creating personas:

- **Framing requirements**: If you're presented with a stack of requirements written in jargon and from the system's perspective, reframing those requirements from the user's perspective can help. The source of those requirements may be user research (translated into insights for design), but ultimately you're still establishing a framework for the design activities.
- **Validating design**: Instead of driving design, you might build personas as a tool to help validate your design decisions. In this case, the personas need to help you answer the question, "Does the design successfully meet the needs of this user?"
- **Hypothesizing research**: In recent user research projects, I have created personas as a starting point that gives the team something to talk about and provides a basis for testing. Generating a set of personas through internal brainstorming yields a set of questions about our target audience—perfect for establishing a research agenda. In conducting subsequent research, we gather data to validate the model.

Timeline: When personas happen

Ideally, personas come at the beginning of a project. They can supplement other documents that establish project requirements or—in a pinch—stand on their own.

Most of the user research projects I've been involved with culminate in a set of personas. While we have a general understanding of the products they'll be applied to, we're not necessarily teeing-up a specific design project. So, there are two circumstances in which you'll create personas:

- **Stand-alone project**: As a separate project, you've got dedicated funding and perhaps a longer timeline in which to create personas. The challenge is that you may be creating personas outside the context of a specific design problem because they will be a tool for use in multiple future design endeavors.
- **Precursor to design project**: Incorporation into a specific design project creates some constraints both positive and negative. While a limited budget may prevent analysis paralysis, it can also force you to compromise the development of the personas. On the other hand, creating personas with a design challenge clearly stated can yield a more targeted result.

At the beginning of a project, you may find yourself in one of two different situations:

- **Existing web site:** In the more typical situation, you already have a list of the kinds of content and functions available in the system. This list exists because you're redesigning an existing system or the stakeholders have a wish list of features. In this case, including these features in your personas will help put them in context.
- **New web site:** In the less typical situation, you are creating a new system from scratch and have only preliminary ideas about what kinds of features to include. This situation impacts persona design because you can only summarize what you learned in research: what motivates the users in different scenarios.

Audience: Who's looking at the personas

With an understanding of the position in the project, consider who will be using the personas. Personas capture a particular breed of requirements, and every project participant needs to make sure his or her work addresses those requirements. For that reason, the format for personas need not vary by audience. Still, some areas of the personas will be more useful to some project participants than others.

ALTERNATE APPROACH

Framing Personas as Questions

Although designers have used personas in their work for more than a decade, personas are still relatively new for many clients, customers, and stakeholders. If you're introducing the idea of personas by introducing the actual personas, you may run into some resistance. People unfamiliar with personas may question their value, or even get defensive. After all, most clients believe they are experts on their customers.

To help other people understand the value of personas, you can create personas from lists of questions rather than lists of user needs, thereby testing how much stakeholders really know about their customers. Questions about the user's experience, for instance, can trip up stakeholders who don't really know anything about their customers. "Which is more important to users, product summary information or product technical specs?" is one example.

It's often just as revealing to phrase questions as if addressed to the user about his or her experiences, asking, for instance, "What information do you use to decide whether you'll buy a product?"

Both kinds of questions show how the users themselves—and not internal stakeholders—must drive design decisions.

ASK THE EXPERT

*Tamara Adlin,
President and Founder,
Adlin, Inc.*

DB: What is the best starting point for a persona?

TA: *I bet you thought the answer to this was going to be "data." Surprise! It's not! The best starting point when creating personas is to ask, "What are your measurable business goals?" If you don't have clear business goals that are blessed by the exec team, personas will fail. In fact, clear goals aren't just a 'starting' point. They're a "don't even try personas unless you have them' rule.*

Sometimes this means asking the most basic question of all, which is, "Why did you start this business? Someone had an idea to satisfy some need for some set of people. What WAS that idea? And who was it going to satisfy?" If you ask this question, and you get a solid answer that everyone agrees on, you've achieved a major goal of any persona effort, which is to get everyone on the same page and speaking the same language.

As someone in charge of documenting things, it's now your job to record these areas of agreement and create a glossary of the standardized language. The personas are a major part of that new glossary: they are the nouns. Interaction design is about creating verb-driven experiences for those personas.

What about data? The truth is, personas are NOT all about data. Most companies are drowning in data already, and collecting more is not your first step. Instead, collect and organize all the assumptions that are impacting the product design process. After helping everyone see the confusion in the organization, and creating personas to help achieve clarity, you must then create materials that:

- *Remind everyone that lack of clarity existed (because everyone will forget any problem once it's solved).*
- *Convey the critical information about the personas.*
- *Tie the personas, and the priorities of the personas, back to the business goals.*
- *Remind people that the business goals come from the execs.*
- *Help people understand how to use the personas to achieve the business goals.*
- *Describe what you are offering in terms that will resonate for the personas (for each persona, what are you offering that no one else can, and why should I care?)*

Tips for Polished Personas

You could hand in a short stack of pages that represent your target audience and be done with it. But your research no doubt includes some extra details you'd like to share. Or perhaps you've done some analysis on how these target audiences relate to the business overall, or to each other. By bookending the personas with a little extra detail, you create a self-contained package of essential information.

Create a summary of the personas

Because personas can represent a significant departure from the institutional conception of the target audience, stakeholders may be caught off guard by diving into the details of the first persona right away. To ease them in, you can use an overview that describes the personas at a high level.

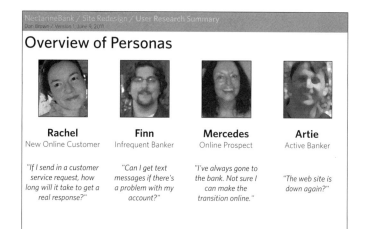

Overview of Personas

Rachel — New Online Customer
"If I send in a customer service request, how long will it take to get a real response?"

Finn — Infrequent Banker
"Can I get text messages if there's a problem with my account?"

Mercedes — Online Prospect
"I've always gone to the bank. Not sure I can make the transition online."

Artie — Active Banker
"The web site is down again?"

Figure 3.4: A one-page summary of personas can help give people a sense of the range of users in the target audience. This is also a nice device for kicking off a presentation on user needs.

Some elements you might include on this summary page:

- Name and role
- Picture
- Sensitizing quote
- Highest priority (what is the user's chief concern or need, or most important tasks)
- Reference to internal segmentation label (to help stakeholders cross-reference with existing vocabulary)

One of the following suggestions may yield a diagram that can be useful for the summary page.

Illustrate relationships between personas

Depending on your segmentation model, the personas may have relationships to each other that are worth describing to your stakeholders:

- **Progressive relationships**: Some sites expect a natural progression of users from new customers to seasoned customers and will treat each stage of growth differently. You can incorporate these relationships into the personas themselves, or on a summary page.

Prospective Online User · New User · Regular User · Advanced User · Exclusive User

Figure 3.5: Showing users' transition from one persona to another can help clarify the varying relationships someone might have to the web site.

- **Hierarchical relationships**: In your set of personas, some personas may be "parents" of others. For example, the New Customers group may include two subgroups: First-Time Customers and Customers New to Online Banking. Showing these relationships can be useful if, for example, most of the users have the same set of needs but there are dramatically different scenarios drawing two groups of users to the site.

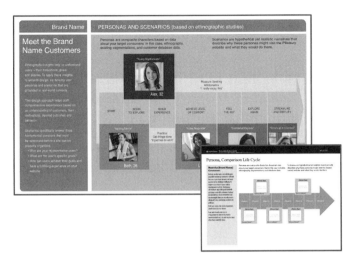

Figure 3.6: A more elaborate timeline can show how users' interactions with the web site change over the course of a lifecycle. Courtesy of Will Evans (http://semanticfoundry.com). Shown with the version created for EightShapes Unify, deliverable templates produced by my firm. Learn more at http://unify.eightshapes.com.

Because personas can be so new for your stakeholders, though, persona relationships may be more trouble than they're worth. If your stakeholders are already skeptical about personas, adding detail and data to the mix will not help them answer the question "So what?"

Facilitate comparisons between personas

Perhaps what matters more than how the personas are derived from each other is how they are different from each other. Highlighting similarities and differences can help establish a prioritization for requirements.

Show contrasts in needs, concerns, or tasks: Regardless of how you represent needs or concerns—a list of functional requirements, system features, or more abstract design principles—they can serve as a basis for comparing personas.

You can compare personas using tables that show which personas have which needs. Figure 3.7 is a table with simple yes/no checkmarks to indicate whether a persona has a particular need or not.

	Prospective Users	New Users	Regular Users
High responsiveness	N/A	✓	✓
Contextual help	N/A	✓	
Tutorial promotions	✓	✓	
New products promotions	✓	✓	✓
Push notifications	N/A		✓

Figure 3.7: A simple needs comparison indicates only whether a particular persona has a need or does not.

If your personas represent a more nuanced range, or you are comparing across design principles, your table can show those nuances. Figure 3.9 is a table using a device to indicate the relative level or importance of a task for each persona.

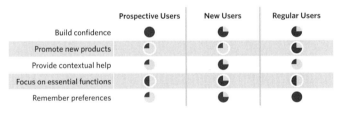

	Prospective Users	New Users	Regular Users
Build confidence	●	◕	◕
Promote new products	◔	◕	◕
Provide contextual help	◔	◕	◔
Focus on essential functions	◑	◑	◑
Remember preferences	◔	◕	●

Figure 3.9: Comparing design principles across personas, this table uses circles with shaded pie pieces to indicate where the priorities are. By the way, those quarter, half, three-quarter, and full circles are called Harvey Balls. I'm not making that up.

Tables highlighting similarities and differences are ripe for showing additional data points, using other symbols or changes in color or value:

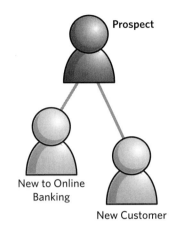

Figure 3.8: Hierarchical relationships between personas may be shown by physically linking persona icons together.

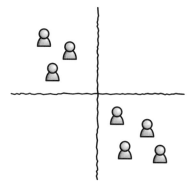

Figure 3.10: Using dependent dimensions, personas only end up in two quadrants, indicating that the variety among personas is limited to one dimension or that you need to find another way to compare them.

- **Availability of content or feature**: You can show whether the site already has the information or functionality to support the persona's need. Perhaps the organization can't support the need at all. Alternatively, a particular need may be common to two personas, but the organization may be able to support the need for only one of the user types.
- **Opportunity for user research**: If you don't know whether a user group exhibits a particular trait, you can highlight this in the table as a "best guess" with room for further research.
- **Elevate two dimensions**: Using a 2x2, you can show how personas compare across two dimensions. Picking the right dimensions is key, and you should focus on those that.
- **Have a true range**: The dimensions should have a range of values, not just yes or no. For example, "frequency of usage" is a good dimension because you can imagine something between "all the time" and "not at all." On the other hand, a dimension like "user type" with "home" at one end and "business" at the other doesn't imply any intermediate values.
- **Are independent of each other**: Dimensions that are dependent won't show any more than two user groups. In other words, if every user ends up in one of two diagonally opposite quadrants, they really only vary along one dimension. For example, with the dimensions "how much does the user pay attention to finances" and "complexity of interactions," you might realize that people who don't pay a lot of attention to their finances don't use complex interactions in online banking. In this case, users really only fall at two ends of a scale.
- **Are meaningful to designers**: Finally, the dimensions must have some meaning to the designer, the person who will be using this information to construct an experience. The venue for doing banking (online, ATM, phone, teller) may be interesting, but for the designer of the online banking experience, not highly relevant.

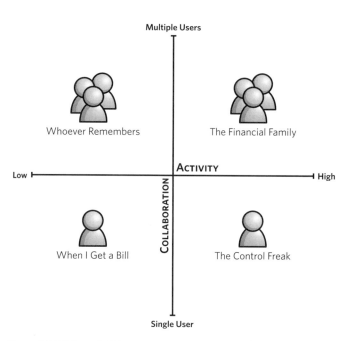

Figure 3.11: Using a 2x2 to compare personas can highlight major differences between them along key dimensions. This visualization won't dig into the subtleties, but it can help clients see what the major concerns are among their target audience.

With such a comparison, you paint the personas with broader brush strokes. Unlike the comparison tables in Figures 3.7 and 3.9, a 2x2 lacks the detailed inventory of priorities. The value, however, is showing stakeholders and designers what makes users different on a more fundamental level.

Show mental models

A mental model is one of two things:

- More generally, a mental model refers to a user's conception of the domain, usually related to content and structure. You might say, "A user's mental model of online banking centers around the concept of an account." You can use a concept model for this (chapter 4) and embed it right in a persona.

- More recently, mental model refers to a specific diagram created by Indi Young in her book *Mental Models: Aligning Design Strategy with Human Behavior*. With this technique, you compare user tasks, activities, and expectations with content, functionality, and other features of the site.

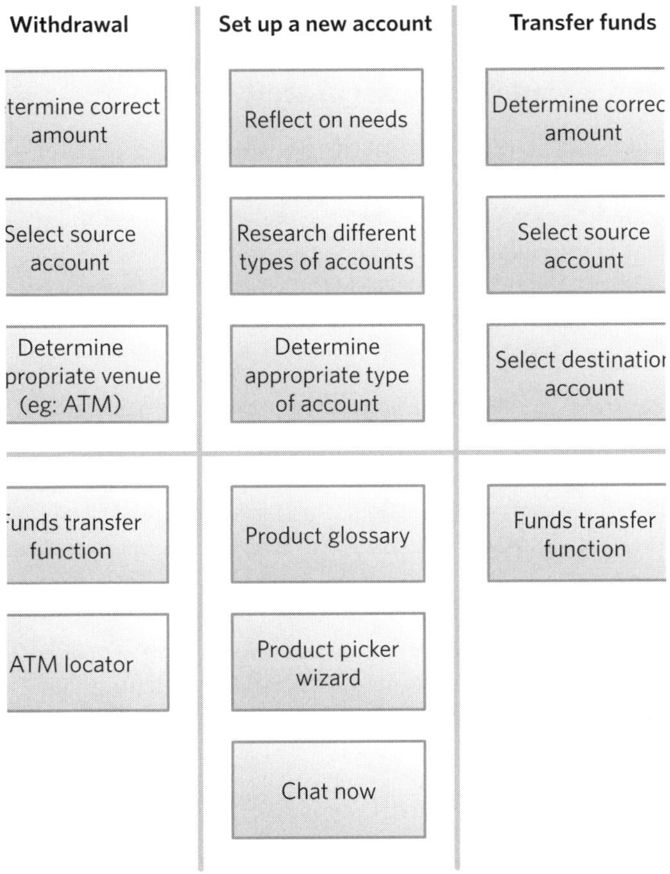

Withdrawal	Set up a new account	Transfer funds
termine correct amount	Reflect on needs	Determine correc amount
Select source account	Research different types of accounts	Select source account
Determine propriate venue (eg: ATM)	Determine appropriate type of account	Select destinatio account
unds transfer function	Product glossary	Funds transfer function
ATM locator	Product picker wizard	
	Chat now	

Figure 3.12: Mental models align user needs with content and features. User needs go above the line, divided up by tasks. Content and features from the site appear below the line, aligned with the needs they support.

One objective of user-centered design is to align the design of a system with the user's mental model. Regardless of how you illustrate them, incorporating the user's

mental model into personas can be a powerful way to focus designers on what really matters.

Level Up Your Persona Skills

Personas are pretend people that can really spark the imagination. While this can yield useful insights as you study data from user research and other inputs, it can also be a dangerous rabbit hole. Concocting novellas about your users can be fun, but it usually diminishes the purpose of personas: to be a useful design tool. Here are some things you can do to avoid slipping into Wonderland.

Incorporate actionable information

The value of personas is measured only by how useful they are during the design process. It's easy for the enthusiasm of project teams to wane as they enter the throes of wireframe revisions and prototyping. The importance of understanding your users, however, never diminishes and a misunderstanding can rear its head when you least expect it.

For design decisions that arise in the eleventh hour of the design phase, personas come in handy because they guide these decisions, avoiding the kind of completely random, bleary-eyed shots in the dark so frequently associated with these moments.

For these reasons, it's important not to forget about personas once user research is complete (which is, alas, all too easy). To avoid relegating personas to a dreary life on the shelf, there are a few things you can do:

- **Make cameos in other deliverables:** By incorporating the personas into subsequent deliverables, for example, you show how they support design decisions down the road. You might incorporate them into a site map, for instance, to show how certain categories were escalated to meet the needs of particular user groups. For

Figure 3.13: A persona trading card can be a useful tool in brainstorming meetings (each participant gets a card) while still appropriate to hang up in a cubicle.

wireframes, you might include the headshot of the persona representing a particular segment and suggest how a person from this segment might react to the wireframe.

- **Create posters:** One trick some user experience professionals use is to print the personas on large posters and tack them up around the office. (This would have been inappropriate during the author's tenure at the United States Postal Service, where the only people tacked up on post office walls were wanted in several states for larceny and fraud.) If this is what it takes to keep users top-of-mind for your project team, suck up the Kinko's printing costs and break out the thumbtacks.

Designing a poster is very different from designing a research report. Even if you create one-page cubicle hangings on standard office paper, you'll want to design them so people can glean the key points at a glance.

- **Create trading cards:** Alternatively (though perhaps no less expensive than printing posters) is creating a set of trading cards that represent user personas. Like posters, the format of trading cards forces you to boil a persona down to essentials. Print up a pack for every member on the team and make sure they bring them to brainstorming meetings.

ALTERNATE APPROACH
No Research? No Problem!

Even if we believe that user research is required, budget or time constraints might make it infeasible. This situation occurs more often than we like to admit. If you have not conducted a study yourself, you can leverage whatever third-party research is out there and create personas from this. The documentation in this case needs to include caveats indicating that this analysis is based on incomplete information. Also, you might use the personas in this case to make a case for some primary research.

Reference your sources

Although this is really a methodological risk, it deserves some discussion, because you can't make a persona without something to base it on. Sourced deliverables hold more weight, and team members generally appreciate the personas more if they understand where they came from.

Represent reality accurately

Though it's tough to admit, it's possible that our personas do not accurately reflect the customers. This could be a methodological issue—like the one earlier where there wasn't enough data to construct a complete picture—or a documentation issue, where the way you've chosen to display the results from the research does not accurately capture the users.

From a documentation perspective, you can lose sight of reality through too much abstraction: taking the results of user research and smoothing them over so much as to lose the nuances of user behaviors, objectives, and needs. It was this concern that led me to stop creating personas as groups of people, and focus more on ranges of behaviors—a trend I have observed throughout the industry. By starting with the names of personas, your inclination is to match findings with those invented roles, instead of letting the data speak for itself.

Keep personas lean

Background stories, photos, and real names are nice, but they can distract from the purpose of the personas. Stakeholders may focus instead on these details, which don't speak to need or motivation and which ultimately do not provide any relevant information to the project team. Keep an eye on the time as you flesh out the demographic details of your users and decide how much you want to spend on this part of the persona.

PRESENTING PERSONAS

Personas are people—abstract summaries of people, but people nonetheless. You are hosting a party. These people are guests. Introduce them. Remind your guests of honor (the stakeholders) how they might know them and what they have in common—perhaps even why they invited them in the first place.

The users of the system will have goals that support the goals of the stakeholders. As host, your job is to show them how these apparently divergent interests have something in common.

Establish a purpose for meeting

The primary reason I discuss personas with the project team is for clarification. When we've got a "complete" persona in front of us, it's still only a partial picture, and the project team probably has a lot of questions.

As a tool in the design process, personas may not have conversations dedicated to them, but they may play a role in subsequent design reviews. In this case, the purpose is not to discuss the personas themselves, but instead to talk about the design in the context of the personas.

Finally, you might need to discuss personas even before you've had a chance to make them because you need to "sell the idea" to your project team. If, historically, they haven't worked with personas or user research before, you might need to convince them it's a good idea.

Discussions to clarify personas

In this type of meeting, your team members and stakeholders are there to ask questions and provide input on the personas. This meeting occurs after you've created a draft of the personas. There are three main topics when clarifying personas:

ASK THE EXPERT

DB: What makes a great persona?

TA: Personas should help you clarify the questions and needs that customers have, and these should be the first elements in the "conversation" between the customers and your web site. We've all had the experience of going to a web site to try to buy a pair of socks, and arriving only to have that same site yell "Look at this sale on chandeliers!" or "Did you know we also carry puppies?!?!" Personas remind us to listen before we start yelling about the things we think are so cool and valuable about our companies and products.

Tamara Adlin, President and Founder, Adlin, Inc.

Persona documents should include the following:

- Alliterative, descriptive name that's easy to remember (Susie Shopper, Robert Ripple-Effect)
- Quote (something that sums up the persona's perspective, like, "I'll look everywhere for the best deal")
- Business priority (from the executives!)
- Short description (2–3 short paragraphs that tell us who this person is)
- Persona's questions in his or her own terms
- Answers to those questions in terms he or she will understand
- "Oh, by the way" statements about what we can offer the persona that he or she might not even have thought to ask for.

  For example, if we know people are likely to show up looking for socks, but we really think they should be interested in our cool flip-flops:

  Question in persona's own terms: Do you have socks?

  Our answer: Yes! We have socks, right over here, and they are great socks.

  Our "oh, by the way" statement: Socks are indeed wonderful, but don't you find it gets expensive to keep buying socks? We have these cool flip-flops that will last forever, and you'll never have to buy socks again! Come check them out!

  You'll be surprised how helpful it is to script the elements of the conversation before you start trying to design an experience.

- **Clarification of institutional knowledge**: Prior research or insight about users may feed persona creation. If this is the case, the people inside the organization are, for better or worse, the experts on users. In a feedback meeting, you're validating that you've captured the institutional knowledge adequately. If you're advocating for additional user research, these meetings might also highlight gaps in the institutional knowledge.
- **Interpretation of research**: Feedback on the content of the persona itself may be inappropriate if the stakeholders or other team members did not participate in the research. You may have to push back on suggestions to change the personas when the suggestions have no basis in the research you did. The team members may, however, offer different interpretations of the data, which could call your conclusions into question.
- **Prioritization**: User research can give you insights on what the target audience needs, but only the business can prioritize those needs relative to their operation. Just because something is important to users doesn't mean it's necessarily important to business. Successful products find themselves mediating this tension. That said, as you work with stakeholders to prioritize personas and their associated needs, your role is to be an advocate for users, ensuring that their needs are not lost in the effort to limit project scope.

Because user research or information-gathering methods may be (or appear to be) subjective, these meetings can be controversial. Participants may wonder why their particular interpretation of users is "incorrect." To help position the conversation and personas appropriately, your meeting should incorporate these messages:

- **Personas should include information to drive design**: It can be tempting to "gold plate" personas with all kinds of embellishments. As facilitator, your job is to keep the conversation on track. An occasional diversion into the culinary preferences of a particular audience segment might be fun, but ultimately you're building a tool for doing design.
- **Agreement is paramount**: Since personas form a foundation for understanding users and driving design, it's crucial for the design team to internalize this knowledge of the users. If they don't agree with it, they won't internalize it. Your methods may vary, but I recommend leaving information **out** if people on the team don't agree with it. At the very least, we leave it as an open question. What good is a constraint or a requirement if you don't know it to be true?

Personas in design reviews

If they're useful, personas will appear throughout the design process to keep efforts focused and on track. In design review meetings, the project team walks through the latest incarnation of the design. During these conversations, you can use personas to smack down scope creep or justify a design decision. The section "Using and Applying Personas" later talks about how to incorporate them into design documents themselves, but you can reference them even if they're not explicitly represented in subsequent deliverables.

Some key messages when bringing up personas in a design review:

- **Primary user requirements**: The personas erected a set of requirements that helped drive the design. Remind stakeholders of what main requirements came out of the personas and how those drove the big ideas of the design. Walking through a design means showing how themes resonate throughout the design, and personas can frame those themes.
- **Criteria for design decisions**: It may be challenging to draw anything beyond a broad stroke between personas and the design, but occasionally there is a clear connection between a portion of the design and the personas that inspired it. Be sure to point out these specific connections.

- **What's changed**: Subsequent user testing or user research may have moved the needle on the personas. If they need to be updated based on new information, be sure to acknowledge the change, but don't get distracted from the design review.

Selling personas

Getting project stakeholders to commit to creating personas is no easy task if they're not convinced of their value. A big part of selling an idea is making the idea palatable, which might mean adjusting your methods to fit the project into parameters established by the stakeholders. When discussing the potential of a persona project, I focus on these messages:

- **User needs drive design**: In the inaugural issue of *Want Magazine* (wantmag.com) Peter Merholz, president of Adaptive Path, said in an interview, "The thing we can't manufacture is needs." As designers, we can't tell people what they need. You must help stakeholders understand that design can't happen in a vacuum, and that great design happens in the context of well-defined constraints. The ideal constraints are an understanding of user needs.
- **We need more detail about users**: Organizations with existing conceptions of their target audience tend to paint them with broad brushstrokes. They describe them in terms of demographic groups when what is needed are descriptions in terms of behaviors.
- **We don't see the information we need**: Existing research usually includes reports on focus groups or surveys, and the questions are generally not directed at how people will use the web site or product. Typical market research seeks to understand what users want, not how they behave.
- **We don't research for research's sake**: Conducting user research and preparing personas should be in the service

of a design project. It's difficult to establish meaningful objectives for personas if they will exist outside the context of a specific product or web site.
- **A bare minimum**: Stakeholders unconvinced of the process may yet allow a bare minimum. For my projects, I try to arrange an interview or two with someone who the team identifies as the best proxy for the user, like a customer service representative or someone responsible for conducting market research. In this conversation, venture this as a possibility and show an example of the kind of output you expect.

In a buy-in meeting, different participants will look for different things.

Business stakeholders	want to know that the time and resources dedicated to building these personas were worthwhile; need to be shown that the personas represent customers who make sense in the context of their business
Designers	need to see that personas provide a useful set of criteria for making design decisions, which they'll later be able to trace back to elements of the personas
Engineers	want to see that the needs and requirements in the personas will lead to realistic and buildable systems

Table 3.2: Getting buy-in from different team members means reassuring them in different ways about the value of personas.

Adapt the basic meeting structure

A conversation surrounding personas can still follow the basic structure established in the Introduction.

You might discuss the personas in order of priority—in other words, by order of their importance, their value, or risk to the company. Or you might choose something like a "family resemblance" presentation, where personas are discussed in related groups. Finally, some people will describe the steps taken in creating their personas, in a chronological account of how they came to be. Table 3.3 provides some suggestions for how to determine the right order.

When you need to...	You should...
Translate user needs to system requirements Validate the design objectives relative to users	Describe each persona separately in order of importance Introduce the meeting by describing the criteria used to prioritize the personas
Explore potential overlaps between personas	Describe the range of behaviors exhibited by users and then show how personas map to those needs
Help team members understand how you created the personas	Summarize high-level findings at the beginning, then walk stakeholders through the process of gathering data that fed the personas

Table 3.3: Present personas in order, but the order is up to you.

1. Establish context

Kick off a persona meeting by explaining what role personas play in the design process. Even if you have two or three conversations to talk about the results of the user research or analysis, reminding participants what drove the endeavor in the first place helps solidify the context.

Then, describe the sources of information that fed the persona creation:

- For **primary research**, sketch out the methods and techniques, the number of users you engaged, and where you are in the analysis.
- For **informal research**, spell out what activities you have been able to accomplish and what constraints are keeping you from more extensive user research.
- For **secondary research** or **interviewing user proxies**, inventory the sources you read or the people inside the organization you spoke to.

2. Describe visual conventions

While a persona may not have the visual complexity or nuance of other diagrams, you should still provide a tour of a typical persona, pointing out the major areas of information. If you use visualizations in the persona to identify aspects of their behaviors, be sure to explain these, too.

3. Highlight major design decisions

A persona may not have "design decisions," per se, but the parallel here is the overall segmentation model. Take a moment to answer the question, "Why did you divide up the personas in this way?" Recall that there are three main ways for roles to emerge (data-driven, institutional, procedural) so you might use one of these concepts to drive the discussion.

During this part of the conversation, you can also introduce any summary diagrams that describe the relationships between the personas.

4. Offer rationale and identify constraints

If necessary, you can elaborate on the research methodology used to drive persona design. While research techniques can provide a rationale for the personas, be careful:

- **Don't spend too much time on methodology**: While you may be proud of the research plan and execution, the team needs you to cut to the chase (whether they realize it or not). A description of research methodology isn't to set up to the personas as a punch line. It's inserted in the discussion to help participants frame the result.
- **You may have to justify the justification**: Describing any form of research opens itself up to methodological attacks. Sometimes, project participants think that just because it's called "research" you'll have the time and resources to control every variable.

- **Acknowledge that user research is an imperfect science**: I almost always indicate that research is a design tool, and that its primary purpose is to help me, the designer, get into the shoes of users. I don't need to know every detail about their lives, and sometimes a good quote is all it takes to trigger an understanding of their position.

5. Point out details

You didn't spend too much time on 1 through 4, did you? Good because, this is where you dig into the personas themselves. The next section "How to Describe a Persona" talks about narrating a persona description in great detail. The challenge here is finding a way to discuss all of them in the space of 30 minutes. There are two approaches to structuring this section:

- **Priority order**: Articulate your criteria for prioritizing the personas. Start with the most important and work your way through each of them, spending less and less time. Perhaps use the "soliciting feedback" portion of the meeting (step 7) to get input on the priority. This approach is ideal when you have more than four personas and they're unrelated.
- **Family resemblance**: Instead of presenting each persona separately, you can drive the discussion around the characteristics used to describe the personas. Identify all the attributes up front and then describe how each persona stacks up against each one. You can then do deep-dives on personas that best illustrate each "family."

If your persona effort yielded a behavior model, not a set of individual personas, you can instead describe each dimension, its extremes, and where most users in your research fell along the dimension.

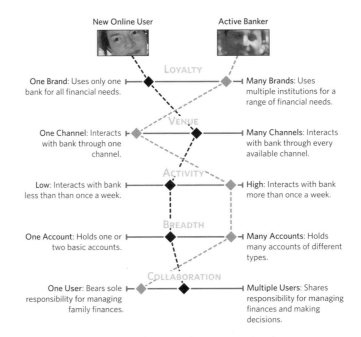

Figure 3.14: Linking dimensions together, you can show how one user group maps to each of the behaviors in the model.

6. Communicate implications

It's time for the rubber to meet the road. The personas yielded insights about how to design the product. During this portion of the meeting, describe the main conclusions that will be driving the design. You might identify:

- **Common requirements or design principles**: Collectively, the analysis of user needs will yield a set of basic requirements for the design exercise. These can be broad or narrow. Broad: "Users are generally coming to the site to accomplish two primary tasks." Narrow: "Make sure to highlight three primary benefits at the top of each product page."

- **Challenges from conflicts**: Any group of personas will likely yield a set of requirements that may have some inherent conflicts. One persona may prioritize one thing that another deprioritizes, for example. If your analysis has zeroed in on these conflicts, you can point them out and highlight the challenges facing the design process.
- **Unrealized opportunities**: Analysis on the personas may yield insights into the product design that the stakeholders had not anticipated. In short, you might get some ideas for the products.

7. Solicit feedback

As with any conversation about a design artifact, discussing personas means getting good feedback from the project participants. Establish a scope (what it is you need feedback on) and the kind of feedback you need. For personas, scope can include:

- **Segmentation model**: You might ask, "Based on what you've heard, how would you cut up the audience differently?"
- **Prioritization**: "I've listed these personas in order of importance based on how closely their needs align with the business objectives. Would you prioritize them differently?"
- **Behavioral dimensions**: "In our analysis, we focused on three key behaviors or attributes—loyalty, focus, and collaboration. Are there other behaviors you think are important?"
- **Descriptive elements**: Position feedback on personal attributes in terms of their impact on the design process. "I know the picture and biographical information is to help the persona come alive, but clarifying those aspects might help design activities."

8. Provide a framework for review

To make the meeting actionable, establish specific questions you still need feedback on. If you couldn't get to all the topics in the soliciting feedback step, it's worth articulating those in the meeting minutes as outstanding items.

To provide a more concrete framework for review, you can leave meeting participants with a homework assignment, answering two questions:

- **If you could ask our users anything, what would you ask them?** Questions produced in response will help you determine if the personas can paint a clear picture of the users in the heads of team members.
- **What is the single biggest design challenge you face?** Responses to this question will help you determine if the personas can provide direction for this challenge.

(Yes, you should ask these questions before endeavoring to create the personas, as they will help guide the research.)

How to Describe a Persona

Regardless of how you structure the meeting, at some point you'll need to describe a persona. The manner in which you describe a persona to someone on the team is going to vary by the nature of the personas themselves. Fully fleshed personas can be treated as characters with elaborate backstories, while role-based personas won't lend themselves to simple narratives.

Personas as people

Table 3.4 presents a simple pattern for describing a persona.

Characteristic	Description	Example
Name and/or role	The label used to refer to the persona	"This is Sarah, she represents our 'new customer' group."
Primary concern and objective	In one sentence, what's top-of-mind for the persona relative to the site.	"Like any user of a financial site, she's concerned about privacy and security. But the main obstacle for her is transferring all her information from other online financial services she uses."
Source	In a couple sentences, describe how you got this information. If through user research, be specific about the methods and the kinds of people who contributed to the understanding of this user.	"A lot of this information came from the survey we took of people who are not current users of your site. That survey covered 1,500 people and about half can be described with this persona. We embellished a bit in some areas to make Sarah seem more human."
Backstory	Optionally give a little information about circumstances or demographic information.	"We might think of Sarah as mid-30s, has a family, experienced with the web. Even though she's 'new,' she's been managing the family finances for a few years. She's considering your bank because she's heard great things about the online service."
Top three characteristics or scenarios	Pull these right off the persona deliverable, providing some elaboration as necessary.	[This will be kind of long. Layers 1 and 2 have examples of these.]
Contrast with other personas	Take a moment to compare the characteristics or scenarios you just described to another persona. The contrast can be useful to illuminate what makes this particular persona important.	"Sarah's different from 'online banking newbies,'" in that newbies may already be customers of your bank, but not yet using the online service. The 'explore online features' scenario we just discussed is shared by both, but Sarah's going to be looking for somewhat more advanced features."
Primary concern reprise	Repeat the primary concern as a way to tie up the presentation and reinforce the main takeaway for the persona.	"So the key thing to remember is that though Sarah is labeled 'new customer,' she's hardly a newcomer to online services, and may have deep experience with online banking."
Questions?	Solicit questions from the participants.	"What else can I tell you about Sarah?"

Table 3.4: Personas as people.

Personas as characteristics

With a more modern approach to personas, where user requirements have not been anthropomorphized to the same extent, the structure of your presentation needs to change. Instead of walking through each persona individually, you will present the range of behaviors or other characteristics that define the target audience. Recall that in this approach, you've identified half a dozen or so characteristics and represent them as ranges. Table 3.5 presents a pattern for describing each dimension.

This framework also works when you're using the "family resemblance" meeting structure. Instead of describing extremes or intermediate values, you can indicate what

TIP

Separate Design Implications

It can be easy to slip from persona description to design implication. ("New customers find feature X important, so we want to prioritize it on the home page.") Though it's perhaps best to separate persona descriptions from design discussions, if you find it unavoidable, make sure you clearly delineate the two. You can demarcate design statements explicitly so as to avoid making promises that down the road prove to be poor design decisions. At the same time, you can translate the desire into a meaningful requirement: "Feature X is a high priority item and we should reveal it prominently on the site."

Figure 3.15: By whiteboarding a characteristic you can embellish your explanation with emphasis on the extremes and intermediate values. It offers ample opportunity to show examples.

Characteristic	Description	Example
Name	The label used to refer to the dimension	"One of the ways your customers distinguish themselves is loyalty."
Description	A two-sentence description of the behavior	"Loyalty describes the commitment users have to their particular financial site of choice."
Extremes	Short explanations of what the extreme versions of this behavior look like	"At one end you'll have people that do all their banking through one site, and at the other people who visit multiple sites to do their online banking. There may be different reasons for their spreading things out."
Examples of intermediate values	Pick 2 to 3 random points along the dimension to describe nonextreme behaviors.	"You can imagine someone closer to the 'one site' end who does most of their online transactions through their main bank, but visits other sites–like credit cards and investments–infrequently. There's also the person who does a lot on two main sites (say checking and investments) and hits a few other sites as necessary."
Relevance	Highlight areas of the dimension that are the "sweet spot" for the site. Be sure to explain how to established that strategy.	"We're going for web-savvy people. We know that they likely already use some online financial tools and are worried about bridging the gap between those tools and your site. We should focus on this half of the dimension extreme, where people already use more than one tool."

Table 3.5: Personas as characteristics.

different intensities refer to. In other words, if you're mapping personas against a set of dimensions with a "moon phase" chart, you'll need to describe what someone with a quarter circle is relative to someone with a full circle.

Avoid newbie mistakes

It's just as hard to mitigate the following risks as it is to recognize that they're happening. Generally speaking, make sure you know what you want to get out of a presentation and be cognizant of the things that will prevent you from achieving those goals. This section describes some common meeting pitfalls.

Personas impact design

We've all been here: You're walking through your personas and your audience is not engaged. They ask no questions and provide no feedback. When faced with this risk, you must:

- Make it clear what the *potential impact* of personas is not only on the final product, but in their work on the project downstream.
- Offer examples of the *kinds of design decisions* you might make based on the personas, especially where the lack of personas will make deciding upon a direction more challenging.
- Show the people involved how *user needs translate into real design* decisions. Also useful is to have some counterexamples in your back pocket. Show how a lack of user direction made your favorite bad web sites the way they are.

Personas are design tools

Like the team assigned to create the personas, the people reviewing the personas may likewise become absorbed with the details behind the fiction, such as a photo or a user narrative. By spending too much time on age/race/sex/home-life conversations, you miss the notion that this person can be anybody, and that what makes them relevant in the context of your system is how they're going to use the outputs and what they will put into it.

In this situation, you can use a tangent to springboard into a more relevant scenario. You can redirect the conversation, attempting to "zoom out" of the irrelevant detail to show what the larger impact might be. Sometimes, I let these conversations peter out, to let the participants get it out of their system. This is a good "teachable moment" to help stakeholders understand what the focus of persona development should be: a design tool.

Make use of research

The purpose of a persona is to avoid conversations that begin "I think the users want…" or worse, "What I would want to see…." One way to avoid this is to distribute copies of the research results before the meeting. This allows you to point to them and remind participants that the personas are a friendly way of summarizing data from your research. While personas discussions shouldn't be overwhelmed by in-depth methodological descriptions or explanations of your analytic process, you can use an overview of the research technique and results to kick off the conversation.

Anticipate methodological criticisms

This book isn't about method and technique in conducting user research, but well-formatted personas can trigger such questions because they paint a vivid picture of the target audience. Disagree even slightly with a stakeholder on the nature of that target audience, and the first thing they'll do is question the methodology. Even when they have no particular beef with your findings, if some stakeholders haven't been along for the ride, they may question the validity of your approach. Though frustrating, these are important questions. If you can address them successfully, the personas will be more legitimate.

As with any meeting where you expect a challenge, the best thing you can do is anticipate the range of critiques you might get and prepare a response. Some typical critiques:

- Number of users
- Kinds of users studied
- Recruiting
- Lack of research
- Data-gathering technique

Facilitate corporate culture change

Stakeholders may gravitate toward talking about the users with the old mindset, with an institutionalized way of segmenting them that is irrelevant for designing the web site (for example, distinguishing international and domestic customers). To mitigate this risk you can:

- Remind stakeholders that for the purposes of this conversation, personas are the preferred means for talking about users.
- Indicate that the value of personas is that they represent user requirements as a set of needs that impacts the system design. Indicate that your intent is not to invalidate the old segmentation model, which might be useful for other activities in the organization.
- Provide readily accessible translations from old model to new by referencing common labels for the segments in the new model.

USING AND APPLYING PERSONAS

Personas are a great way to capture user needs, but they cannot stand on their own. Ideally, your personas must fit into the overall design process.

Personas provide a means for:

- **Prioritization**: Which features and content are most important

- **Validation**: Whether to include a feature
- **Completeness**: Whether anything is missing

Personas are both abstractions and summaries. They don't address every nuance of every user group or every system requirement. They depend on a segmentation model, a way of grouping customers that can also bias those user needs. Done correctly, personas should give the team a language for talking about users that focuses on actual user needs. They should also provide a structure for capturing requirements and for involving users throughout the design process.

Personas and Design Documents

Personas are a great way to interject rationale into the design decisions captured in these documents, just as they are with strategy documents. With a persona, you have a set of requirements embodied in a single label, like Amanda or New Employee. If you've used personas throughout the life of a project, you can utter these names to any member of the team and instantly call up a set of needs and scenarios without having to describe them one by one.

In each of these deliverables, you can use persona names to show how particular design decisions support particular user needs. Even if you don't spell out the connection (and if your personas have become well entrenched you won't have to) by simply including the label near the relevant design element, you demonstrate that the user needs played a role in making that decision.

Personas and the Design Process

Without personas, there is no common language for talking about what users want. Project participants with particular agendas may try to squeeze unvetted ideas into the design by saying things like, "Users really want to see…" or "This content is more important to users." They may even be able to rationalize it with some common-sense explanations, like "The pricing information is most important because users make decisions to buy based on price," or "Password requirements for user accounts should be very strict because our users want to protect their personal information." Without personas, you're likely to hear things like "If my mother came to the site, she would not understand any of the jargon."

Not everyone will agree. Or, worse, everyone will agree because they can't offer a rationale for disagreeing. It's easy to imagine competing explanations that are equally plausible. Conversations like these go nowhere and lead to designs no better than those conceived in a vacuum.

Personas help make users real people

In creating personas, the design team creates a common language with which to talk about end users and what they need. They also give you an out: If team members start speculating about users, you can stop the conversation, point to the personas, and refocus the conversation around what is known.

Personas help keep the design effort focused

Vacuous claims about user needs can lead to scope creep. They can lengthen project timelines by encouraging development of features that are not supported by user needs. They can lead to unnecessary compromise. Referring to the personas can help avoid these pitfalls.

Personas help organizations internalize user-centeredness

Some practitioners tell stories about organizations incorporating personas into all aspects of their businesses. Like any

Diagram	How to use personas
Concept model (Chapter 4)	Since it articulates the concepts that form the foundation of the system, the concept model may not draw on personas for requirements. On the other hand, personas can help demonstrate that the concept model successfully accommodates all user needs. Embedding personas adjacent to the model emphasizes the relationship between the site's underlying structure and the user needs.
Site map (Chapter 5)	Show how different areas of the information structure cater to different user groups. Alternatively, correlate user needs with information areas by calling out needs instead of persona names.
Flowchart (Chapter 6)	Like site maps, flow charts allow you to show how structural decisions directly support user needs. Alternatively, you can show how the user changes after going through the process.
Wireframe (Chapter 7)	Use the personas to put yourself in the user's shoes and react to the screen structure. Photos or avatars of user personas with thought bubbles can show how different user groups might perceive and react to the content priorities on the screen.

Table 3.6: Incorporating personas into other diagrams can be easy since personas can act as commentators on the design approach.

tool, the adoption and use will be driven by the organization's willingness and your ability to create something that fills a real need. People throughout organizations are hungry for knowledge about their customers; personas can provide not only this knowledge, but a framework for talking about customers.

Ultimately, the purpose of a persona is to help the design team make decisions about design. The persona takes as input observations about users and structures those observations in a meaningful way. Whether the organization of data is called a "persona" or not, without any framework the design team is working with a collection of observations out of context. They do not know whether some observations were limited to particular kinds of users, less important than others, or pure flukes.

By providing structure, we can identify priorities that facilitate decision making, not confine it. Constraints without structure are easier to ignore, because they're harder to incorporate into the decision-making process and can lead to meaningless design.

EXERCISES

1. Describe three scenarios for yourself doing a typical activity. Use a favorite hobby or an everyday task. Your scenarios should try to include context, trigger, action, inputs, and expectations for each one. In cases where you can't explicitly state one of these scenario descriptors, be sure to note that.

2. Erect a persona around these scenarios for this particular activity. Start with key behaviors from these scenarios and identify others. Select a few other elements from layers 1 and 2 and flesh out the persona. Remember that you're creating a tool for designers to help them design something to support this user group for these scenarios. Give the persona a name that describes its relationship to the activity.

3. Identify a contrasting persona who participates in the same activities but would be characterized by different behaviors. Give this persona a label that (a) describes its relationship to the activity and (b) sufficiently contrasts it from the first persona. Flesh out this persona if you wish.

4. PewInternet.org is a nonprofit research group that studies online behaviors. Pick a study from their web site and use it as a basis for a set of personas, as if this was the research report provided by your client. The purpose of the personas is to summarize the research. Identify the range of behaviors described in the report. Devise a set of personas and come up with distinguishing characteristics for each one. Find ways to capture nuances from the report in a more visual way in the personas. Highlight interesting data points, and if the report captures quotes from subjects, be sure to include those. (If the report already segments the users in a particular way, explore the possibility of a different segmentation model.)

5. Look at the list of possible methodological critiques on page 59. How would you modify your personas to address each critique?

Chapter 4

Concept Models

kän'·šept mä'·dəl (n.)

A concept model is a diagram that shows the relationships between different abstract ideas. You can apply the concept modeling technique in a variety of circumstances to explain different aspects of a web site. Also known as concept maps or affinity diagrams.

CONCEPT MODELS AT-A-GLANCE

Concept models describe structures, how different ideas relate to each other. The format doesn't prescribe particular kinds of relationships, nor does it assume any specific types of ideas. As an artifact of the web design process, it can capture the range of different kinds of information to be represented on the site.

Purpose—What are concept models for?

There really is only one reason to create a concept model: to understand the different kinds of information that the site needs to display. This structure can drive requirements for the page designs, helping you to determine how to link templates to each other. With the structure ironed out, you might also use the model to help scope your project—determining what parts of the site to build when.

Audience—Who uses them?

Use concept models for yourself. Ultimately, they are the most selfish, introspective, and self-indulgent artifact, a means for facilitating your own creative process.

Scale—How much work are they?

You can spend as much or as little time as you need, but it can be difficult to predict how much time to dedicate. The effort here isn't creating the illustration, but dissecting the various information that constitutes the site.

Context—Where do they fall in the process?

Concept models are tools for helping you to frame the design problem, so build them at the beginning of your process. Of course, you might realize late in a project that you needed to spend more time uncovering the site's underlying structure. Further along in the timeline, concept models can help provide context for existing design work.

Format—What do they look like?

Concept models are, at their heart, circles connected by lines. Such a simple format lends itself to some embellishment to highlight different kinds of concepts and relationships.

In addition to communicating ideas, design artifacts help you, the designer, work through difficult problems. Putting a structure on paper, sketching a screen layout, or summarizing user needs can all help you find new insights and new inspiration. I won't pretend to understand the neuroscience behind this. All I can tell you is, from experience, whenever I think I can neglect this part of the process I'm proven dead wrong.

Concept models swing more toward the personal side of the spectrum than perhaps any other diagram in this book. It is the diagram I most often keep to myself, rarely sharing it with clients and occasionally not even other team members. It is one of the first diagrams I build, almost immediately as I start familiarizing myself with a project's requirements. It helps build my comfort level with a project's scope and the related *domain* of information.

DOMAIN The sphere of information related to the project you're working on.

I transition concept models from hand-drawn sketches to vector art faster than any other diagram. Putting them into a diagramming application lets me manipulate their structure and content quickly, allowing me to see the ideas in new ways.

What ideas? What is it that a concept model helps to envision? Web sites have underlying structures: More than just navigation menus, a site's skeleton is the collection of stuff that makes it what it is. Imagine taking the concept of "article" or "story" away from CNN.com. The site would be fundamentally different.

Type of Site	Fundamental "Stuff"
News	Stories, topics, departments, authors
Intranet	Assets, people, events, product sales support
Commerce	Products, departments, account, wish list
Product marketing	Product descriptions, product comparisons, support, services

Table 4.1: Different kinds of content that typically appears on sites.

The complexity of web sites is not just in the level of interaction they permit, but also in their sophistication in dealing with the underlying information. The role of the concept model is to help designers iron out the structure for that information. Through modeling the concepts, designers learn:

- How to link content together
- How to expose content at different areas of the site
- What kinds of information should be associated with each concept
- The kinds of interactions users might expect with different kinds of information
- The relative priorities of different kinds of content or features
- The concepts that will serve as central "home" areas of the web site
- Which concepts will provide a context to view other kinds of information

INTRODUCING CONCEPT MODELS

A concept model follows the format of a few other diagrams in this book—shapes connected by lines. In this case, the shapes (sometimes called *nodes*) represent concepts. The lines represent the relationships between the concepts. Both site maps and flowcharts belong to the same family, but concept models are, in a sense, a superset. They don't prescribe a particular type of relationship or presume a particular type of node. Table 4.2 differentiates between concept models and site maps around some fundamental characteristics.

The one constraint on concept models is that the nodes are nouns and the connections are verbs. Each node-link-node combination can read as a sentence, as in:

Concept Models Are Diagrams.

Site Maps	Concept Models
Represent hierarchical structures	Represent all kinds of relationships
Have a clear beginning, but no clear ending	May have neither a clear beginning nor ending
Illustrate how content categories relate to each other	Tell a story about the site's underlying concepts (which may or may not be content categories)
Presume that nodes represent particular pages or templates	Make much broader assumptions about what nodes represent

Table 4.2: Contrasting concept models and site maps. How do concept models differ from site maps? Let me count the ways...four. There are four ways.

It's not much of a constraint; the format offers much flexibility, which cuts both ways. Sometimes it can be hard to determine what to include in the model and what to leave out.

How Concept Models Help: A Short Preview

Concept models fill a void between requirements and design, between stating the problem and solving the problem. Designers must internalize the design problem. Somewhere between "getting into the user's shoes," recognizing technical constraints. and understanding the business context there is a need for a unified vision of the product. A concept model establishes a consolidated, holistic view of what the thing is, what it does, and who it helps.

Concepts in the model translate to different parts of the site. A concept model can help determine your strategy for establishing templates, components, modules, navigation, *metadata*, and the underlying structure of a content management system. It can provide insight into the range of interactions users will need to perform. Short, right?

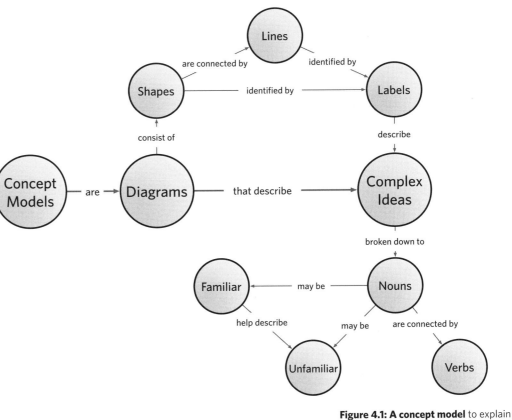

Figure 4.1: A concept model to explain concept models. I thought you might like the recursion.

METADATA A collection of information that describes other information. The distinction between metadata and the data it describes is becoming increasingly blurred.

Stephen P. Anderson ,
PoetPainter, LLC

ASK THE EXPERT

DB: What is a concept model?

SA: Concept models are pictures that simplify complex information. How? By modeling relationships through visuals and words.

I'm careful not to specify a particular form—a concept model can be anything from the "nouns and verb" bubble maps to Venn diagrams to complex infographics (such as the famous Napoleon's March poster). I'd even consider familiar business tools like swimlanes, matrices, and process diagrams to be concept models.

I do distinguish between concept models and other things like narrative explanations, graphical notetaking, charts and data visualizations. All of these tools help people think and communicate, but concept models are exactly that—a model of some difficult conceptual idea. This is very different from capturing notes—even visual notes—in real time, or visualizing statistical data. Concept models represent a particular viewpoint on how different pieces of information might relate to each other.

INTERLUDE
A History of Concept Models

Concept models are not unique to web design or even software engineering circles. According to Wikipedia, concept mapping was developed by Joseph D. Novak at Cornell in the 1970s as a learning tool. It has since been subsumed into other formal methodologies, including the Unified Modeling Language, a system of documentation techniques for software engineers.

One of Novak's basic tenets was that learning involves incorporating new ideas into existing ones—that when we learn something new we do so in the context of stuff we already know. For the purposes of web design and underlying structures, the important thing is to help the project team understand how parts of the business (stuff they already know) will be incorporated into the web design (new ideas). The simplicity of a concept model makes it ideal for communicating these notions.

For more detailed history, and for some good comparisons to other techniques, check out the Wikipedia entry http://en.wikipedia.org/wiki/Concept_map.

A rose by any other name

Someone once asked me how concept models are different from affinity diagrams. Affinity diagramming is an exercise to help a group of people identify similarities across a broad set of qualitative information, like observations during user research. Affinity diagramming is like any other grouping and prioritization activity—meant to consolidate a range of information and identify patterns. Beyer and Holtzblatt use affinity diagramming to consolidate observations from their user research technique, contextual inquiry, and identify new insights about the target audience.

Which sounds a lot like concept modeling.

Affinity diagrams don't follow the exact format I describe here, which is based more on Novak's concept mapping work (see sidebar on History of Concept Models). Beyer and Holtzblatt put a strong emphasis on consolidation through categorization and grouping, whereas my concept models don't necessarily revolve around a hierarchy.

Concept modeling is not unique to web design, nor is that the only name for this activity. Explicitly connecting ideas through visualization is a technique that comes in many flavors. I can only urge you to find the flavor you like best, or, like Ben and Jerry, invent one that suits your taste… er… style and approach.

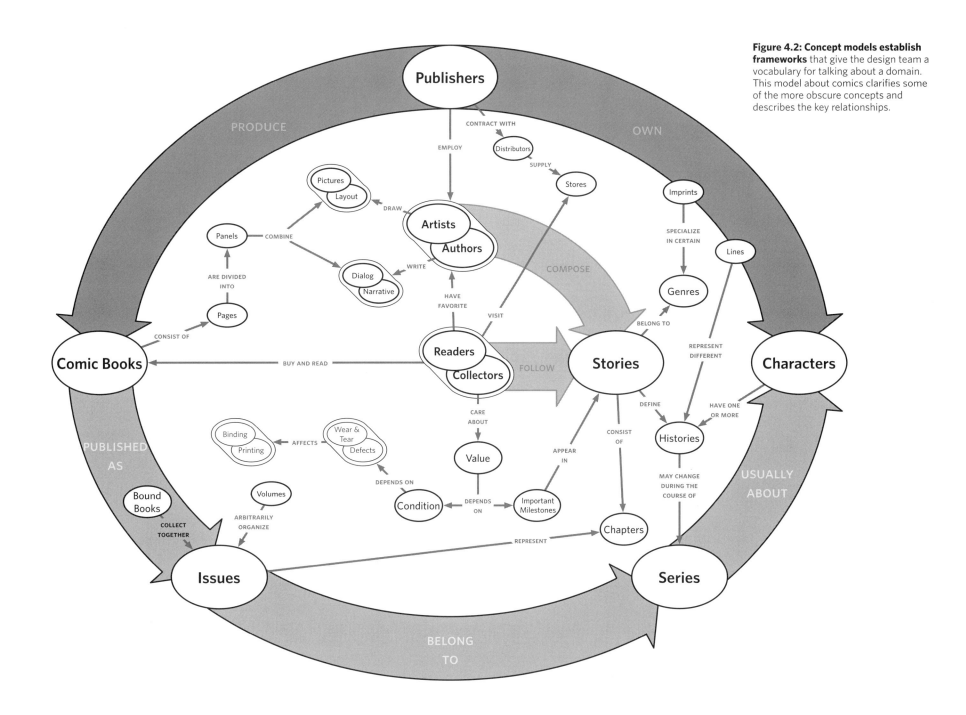

Figure 4.2: Concept models establish frameworks that give the design team a vocabulary for talking about a domain. This model about comics clarifies some of the more obscure concepts and describes the key relationships.

Comic Books

I love comics, a fact widely known in my personal and professional circles. In 2009 I was introduced to a couple of guys, Ben Scofield and Nick Plante. They also love comics, and we got together to try to reinvent the online comics experience. We didn't get too far, but I did a bit of concept modeling to help me wrap my head around the complexities of the architecture of comics.

Comic books are an interesting domain because they bring some unique dimensions. For example, the character (like Superman or Spider-Man) is the franchise. Spider-Man can appear in multiple series. This means there are multiple storylines (sometimes intersecting, sometimes in completely different universes) involving the same character. (TV actors can appear in one and only one series at a time, right? The occasional crossover happens, but we assume that the character remains exactly the same in all appearances.)

Authors and artists play a large role in reader preference. I'll buy a new comic by Ed Brubaker, just like I'd buy a new novel by Elmore Leonard. The prominence of the creator in movies perhaps has equal weight, but not in television. When was the last time you watched an episode of something because so-and-so wrote or directed it? On the larger comics franchises, writers and artists rotate. Brubaker wrote *Daredevil* for a few years but has since moved on. Readers may drop a series because their favorite writer or artist is no longer working on the book. (Admittedly, the new team on *Daredevil* has kept up the pace and tone set by Brubaker, so it remains in my monthly stack.)

Comics also appear in multiple formats—single issues and collections. There is also a substantial corpus of non-superhero comics (sometimes called graphic novels). All these nuances yield a set of concepts with complex relationships that make your intranet look positively flat.

Even if you're not into comics, the examples should still be meaningful. I don't geek out too much (that may be the last you hear of Spider-Man and Daredevil), and the concepts are directly relevant to most kinds of entertainment: movies, television shows, music. They should be, therefore, pretty accessible.

Challenges

Because it's an artifact to facilitate your thought process, the challenges with concept models—more than any other artifact—have to do with getting out of your own head:

- **Analysis paralysis**: There's nothing more absorbing than fiddling with a model. Whether you go back and forth on the diagram's layout or engage in an endless internal debate on the right structure, you can lose sight of its purpose. Ultimately, you don't need to get everything "right," you need to get it "right enough." Take your deliberations far enough to help you move to the next step. Have a good sense of the range of templates you'll need? Then stop messing with the line weight on your connections and move on!

- **Practicality**: Even if you bookend your thought process effectively, you might create a document that doesn't effortlessly take you into the next stage of the design process. Any good artifact must further your thinking, whether in understanding the problem better or creating a meaningful design to address the problem. Concept models are inherently fussy and force you to dwell in abstract concepts. The result can easily be an output with no obvious next step. Knowing when to stop (see "analysis paralysis") is key, but knowing what's going to offer the most utility is also important.

- **Perspective**: Like other artifacts, concept models depict a slice of reality, telling a story about how things are or ought to be. Unlike a flowchart, for example, a concept model has no clear protagonist, no obvious perspective. Put another way, two people creating a flowchart of the same process will come closer to each other than two people creating a concept model of a set of ideas. As self-indulgent as concept models can be, your models can be more successful if you incorporate multiple perspectives—or at least acknowledge that there may be several different ways of looking at the world. Perspectives can influence which concepts you incorporate and how you describe the relationships between them.

The previous challenges may rest on one central challenge: Concept models are, out of necessity, an abstraction. They don't talk about things, they talk about *kinds* of things. They don't represent the physical manifestation of any content or interface element. Their elements don't necessarily directly translate to parts of the interface. They remain at the highest possible levels of content, not digging into the dirty details of what goes where.

I've almost convinced myself to stop doing these things. Potential lack of practicality? Risks to the project plan? Abstract thinking? That can't be fun for anyone. And yet, I find myself turning to modeling project after project. As a tool for design, they help me start to shape structures, if only in the most basic way. As a tool for understanding, they help

me gain insights into a particular domain to get the lay of the land and to give myself a starting point for design. Drawing pictures, even quick ones to lay some groundwork, yields more fruitful design work than simply starting with screens.

ANATOMY OF A CONCEPT MODEL

Concept models illuminate domains of information, subjecting them to structured classification and relationships. The advantage of a concept model is that it doesn't force a hierarchical relationship among the domain's concepts. To be effective, the concept model must be clear about what's included and how the concepts and domains all relate to each other.

This section discusses the layout and style of concept models. Subsequent sections discuss choosing appropriate concepts and some of the weird things that happen when we try to boil the world down into circles connected by lines.

Layer 1: The Basics	Layer 2: Added Complexity	Layer 3: From Model to Illustration
Nodes	Styles	Amplify a comparison
Links	Backdrops and grouping	Find a metaphor
	Branched relationships	Concepts as backdrops
	Indirect object relationships	Simplify the story

Table 4.3: Three layers of concept models and the components of each.

Layer 1: The Basics

With concept models, we have two basic building blocks to work with: nodes and links. The format for a concept model suggests only that the nodes represent nouns and the links represent verbs describing the relationships between them.

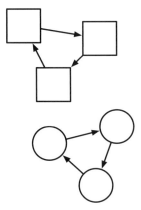

Figure 4.3: Nodes should be circles. Squares just don't connect well.

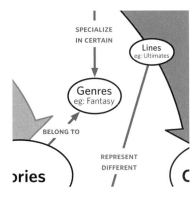

Figure 4.4: Give your concepts specificity, under the main concept of "Genres" a specific example is given—"Fantasy."

NOUN Person, place, or thing, but you remember that, right?

Nodes

Use circles to represent nodes. The advantages of circles:

- **They're easy to connect with each other**. Without sides (or with infinite sides, depending on your relationship with Euclid), it's easy to attach links to a circle. A line that connects to a circle's center is clean and easy to understand. The same thing with a square or other shape can be inelegant and yield "visual noise" that could confuse the diagram.
- **They don't crave a grid**. Four-sided shapes want to live on a grid. Circles don't need a grid to ensure legibility and visual appeal, which means they can get close to each other pretty easily, and you're not dependent on layout to convey a sense of hierarchy. A nice corollary to this is that aligning circles to a grid is a powerful communication device. Without doing anything besides lining them up, you can imply a particularly strong or central relationship.
- **Squares and rectangles imply screens or pages**. This may be appropriate in some instances—when your concept model actually represents a network of templates—but if you're laying conceptual groundwork, circles are good for concepts.

Label your circles. A couple of tips:

- **Remember, these are the nouns**. The next section covers how to choose appropriate concepts.
- **Use the plural**. It's easier to craft appropriate verbs in the links, and the purpose of these concepts is to generalize about the domain of information. Plurals don't require an article ("a", "an" or "the"), making it easy to construct sentences.
- **Specificity is good, but use examples in a subtitle**. Note that the sample concept model uses "Genres" as the main concept and "Fantasy" as the example.

Links

Use lines to represent the connections between nodes. In concept models, the links always have directionality. That is, they're always read as one-way from one node to another. Always label your links; I always regret it when I leave them off. Some ideas for good labels:

- **Remember, these are the verbs**. They should describe the relationship between one concept and the other by describing how the one acts on the other.
- **Avoid "to be."** This isn't a Strunk and White–like grudge against the passive voice. "To be" implies belonging, a hierarchical relationship. It doesn't illuminate the relationship. You're using a concept model because the relationships between the concepts are more interesting than a series of nested categories.
- **Avoid wishy-washy modifiers**. If you try to hedge your relationships by using "may" and "might", your whole model will be one giant apology. A good concept model is like good writing—authoritative and confident. Readers understand implicitly that not every relationship will hold true in every instance.
- **Avoid constructing multinode sentences**. You might be tempted to concoct a chain of relationships to create a more complete picture. (The next layer talks about how to deal with more complex relationships.) Generally speaking, I try to keep my node-link-node relationships self-contained. Although it's important to capture the complexity of reality, it's more important to create an artifact that serves the design process. Standing at any node, you should understand how it relates to the concepts around it, outside the context of concepts two or more degrees away.

A set of nodes and their relationships may break this last rule, but only when they represent the "backbone" of the domain—the essential theme that ties everything together. The section Creating Concept Models describes different starting points and basic structures for concept models.

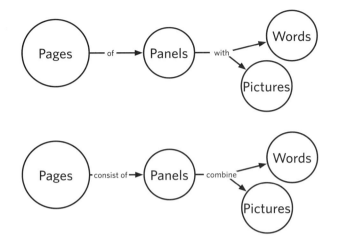

Figure 4.5: The challenges of multinode sentences: They lack of immediate context. Though the bottom version feels a little disjointed, the reader can start at any node and apprehend a complete thought. Using prepositions alone, in the top example, doesn't illuminate the concepts.

Layer 2: More Detail

It won't take long for you to run into severe constraints with the simple concept models described with layer 1 elements. Indeed, reality frequently demands richer visualizations. The devices in the second layer extend basic

node-link-node relationships to afford us more power in describing these complexities.

Distinguishing nodes with styles and backgrounds

Not every concept in your model is necessarily weighted the same. Some concepts are more central to the story. Others are more important to emphasize. Further, you might identify patterns in the nodes that are not immediately apparent from the relationships between them. You might want to highlight that some nodes represent people while others represent physical objects. In the case of the comic book model, for example, I could distinguish between concepts that allow me to classify and identify comics and those that have to do with the business of comics.

Determining appropriate distinctions and groupings will be discussed in Creating Concept Models, a few pages ahead. There are a few techniques for styling nodes to highlight the differences between them.

Similarly, you can use the same techniques to style the links between nodes. Of course, styling links has different implications. (See Table 4.5.)

Size

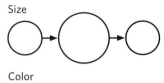

Color

Value

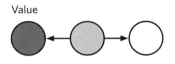

Line Weight

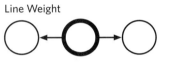

Background

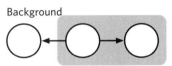

Link Styles

Figure 4.6: Differently styled nodes and links, even just using circles, fills, and lines, offer a lot of flexibility to communicating differences.

Use...	To show or highlight...	Be careful of...
Size	Importance	Hampering your ability to lay out the diagram effectively. Too many different sizes can make it difficult to create a good layout for the diagram.
Color	Additional relationships	Using more than three or four colors. Too much color can distract from your message and make your diagram look inelegant. Adding one color to an otherwise black-and-white picture is ideal to call readers' attention to something specific.
Value (how intense the color is)	Importance	Oversaturating individual nodes. Too much contrast can be distracting. Remember the principle of the "smallest effective difference," from Edward Tufte. The difference between two nodes doesn't need to be dramatic.
Line weight	Importance	Making it difficult to follow the relationships. Increasing the line weight of nodes can make it hard to perceive the connections between nodes, as all the lines start to jumble together.
Backgrounds	Additional relationships	Backgrounds can be useful to group together related nodes, showing how they're related at a more macro level without drawing explicit relationships between them. That said, make sure that in an effort to use a background you don't compromise the overall layout of the diagram.

Table 4.4: Techniques for showing nodes, how they are similar or different in a concept model.

Use...	To show or highlight...	Be careful of...
Line weight	Importance	Obscuring the nodes. Large connecting lines can make it difficult to discern the nodes themselves. This may be acceptable if you want to emphasize the relationships. Generally, however, I compensate for the size of the node with making the color more washed out. I usually use only one line weight, unless I've crafted a "value proposition" model with a central sentence. In this case, the connecting line is substantial to establish it as the foundation of the model.
Color (for links)	Specific sets of relationships	Using more than two or three colors. There may be a set of relationships that you want to call attention to. Typically, this is a chain of three or four nodes that tell a story-within-a-story. I use fat arrows with a distinct color to call attention to these. Readers may not know what to focus on if you use more than two of these devices.

Table 4.5: Techniques for distinguishing types of links between nodes in a concept model.

How much is too much? Readers need to know where to start and what to focus on. They need to come to a particular conclusion. Judiciously applied, styles can enhance the model's ability to tell the story. But too many can further confuse the issue.

In the comics model, I used the heavy arrows around the perimeter to establish a framework for the whole diagram with the main relationships connecting the primary concepts.

The branched relationship

Sometimes, when I get down to the leaves of the tree, so to speak, describing the smaller details of a model, I'm capturing various facets of those small concepts. A single concept is linked to several smaller ones that, in and of themselves, serve only to describe the larger concept. Identifying unique relationships to each of these smaller concepts may be more trouble than it's worth.

Enter, the branched relationship. A single label identifies all the links between the larger concept and the smaller ones. It looks somewhat different: instead of a single line between the concepts, the larger concept has a line that branches and the label sits on that single "trunk" or at the intersection of all the branched lines.

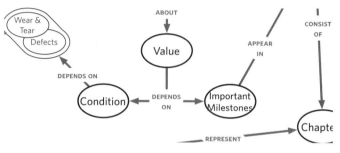

Figure 4.7: A branched relationship connects one concept to two others with the same verb. In this case, the value of a comic depends on two things—its condition and important milestones in the story.

There are any number of reasons why you might use this approach, but two specifically come to mind:

- The smaller concepts are descriptive of the larger concept. In this case, it's useful to identify specific aspects, perhaps because you want to highlight particular properties of the larger concept.
- The smaller concepts represent various possible states or conditions for the larger concept.

Direct and indirect objects

The grammarians among you might start to wonder about the simplicity of sentences based on noun-verb-noun. The domains you'll be modeling will likely demand more complex relationships. Breaking down the language of a concept model, the two nodes act as a subject and object: Subject acts on object.

This may be appropriate for most relationships you need to describe. In some instances, however, the relationship makes sense only with the addition of an indirect object.

In my own models, I've found that central ideas need to appear throughout the model. They, in a sense, mediate relationships between other nodes. In our running example, concepts like "Comic Books" and "Stories" are central concepts that may be indirect objects in many of the other relationships.

In some cases, you can change the perspective to frame the same relationship in a different way:

Sellers sell comic books in Stores ->

Stores [are] owned by Owners

In other cases, you can phrase the verb to swap the object and indirect object:

Distributors distribute comic books to Stores ->

Distributors supply Stores (with comic books)

Such an approach is grammatically and stylistically questionable, but appropriate for the purposes of the model.

If you find you can't effectively describe a relationship without mentioning another noun, consider embedding it in the link's label. You can give it a distinct color, matching the color of the original concept.

Layer 3: From Model to Illustration

You can stop at layer 2. Seriously, if you don't take your model beyond circles and lines, that's OK, especially if you're not likely to show it to anyone else.

But if you're anything like me, you sometimes want a little more. You want a meaningful picture that's fun to look at. If your project allows (or you have nothing better to do on the weekends) you might take some time to refine your model.

There's no easy way to teach this in the space of a few pages, but here are some techniques that I use to refine my models.

Amplify a particular comparison

Successful diagrams let readers compare ideas. You might pick two concepts, or two groups of concepts, and massage the visualization to show the similarities and differences between them.

REFINE Taking a diagram from bare bones to a polished illustration.

Figure 4.8: Comparing the business and the consumption of comics. This comparison emerged as I was evolving the model, distinguishing the experience of comics (bottom arc) from the business of making them (top arc).

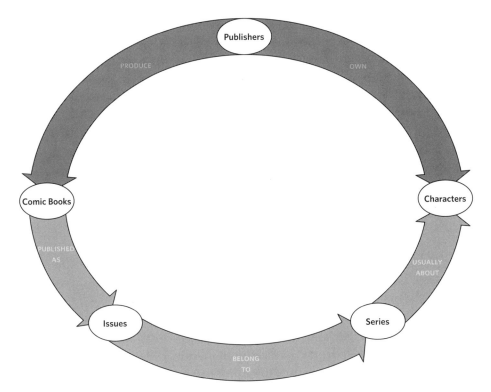

Find a metaphor

Like a concept model, a metaphor is a way of organizing relationships between ideas. By using a metaphor, we're mapping one domain to another and making inferences about the target domain based on knowledge we have about the mapped domain. In a less abstract way: When comparing arguments to battle, I'm mapping the elements of an argument (participants, discussion) to elements of

battles (opponents, fighting, winners and losers). This comparison frames the concept of an argument in a particular way, and implies certain conclusions.

Look through the key relationships in your concept model. Is there one set that lends itself to a visual metaphor? Starting with that foundation, extend the metaphor to encompass other concepts in your original model. How does the metaphor explain relationships to other concepts?

Figure 4.9: Transforming simple models into beautiful illustrations is a hallmark of Stephen Anderson's work. Driven by a small handful of concepts, Stephen elaborated the basic idea—a definition of user experience—into a visual metaphor that drives the point home. You can learn more about Stephen's work at poetpainter.com.

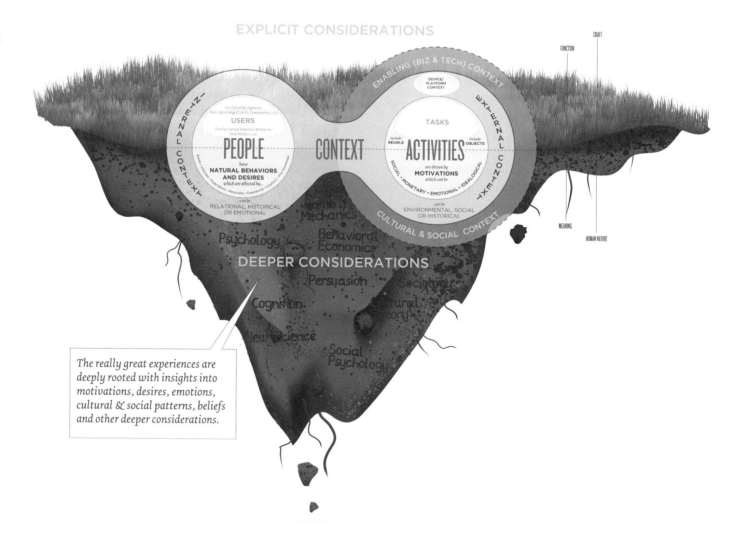

Concepts as backdrops

A mature model will have a number of midsized concepts. Ideas that are crucial to the story, but serve as a bridge between the central ideas and the meaty details. Instead of using these concepts as a bridge, have them recede, using them as a backdrop for the more detailed concepts.

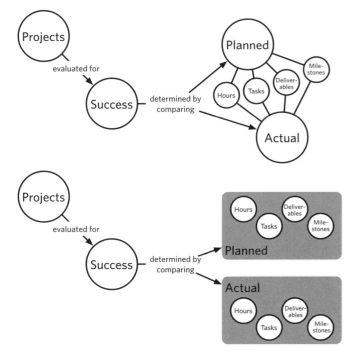

Figure 4.10: Receding concepts into backdrops can add depth to the model as well as communicate simple relationships with less visual noise.

Simplified story

Another technique to facilitate the transition from circles and lines to something more sophisticated is to strip out some concepts. With a smaller number of concepts, you can focus on showing the relationships between them instead of describing them through labels.

There are two ways to get to a simpler story:

- **Focus on one part**: A good model can show how seemingly unrelated things have important connections. That said, the conceptual leap from one end of your diagram to the other may not be the central part of the story. To generate a more visually appealing illustration, you can zoom in on one part of your model. This may yield one or two concepts serving as the central focus, and you can show how the more detailed and specific concepts relate to them.
- **Focus on higher levels**: Starting with the model's primary concepts, keep only those nodes that are one or two degrees away, shaving off everything "lower" in the model. With trimmed details, the model becomes easier to shape into a picture. You can play up certain relationships and identify other visual devices for describing the major concepts. As you zero-in on how to tell the high-level story, you can decide whether it's appropriate and feasible to incorporate the stripped-out details.

CREATING CONCEPT MODELS

Diagramming concepts can lead you down pretty abstract, esoteric, and sometimes unproductive lines of thought. A little planning goes a long way, at least by making some basic decisions about purpose, audience, and content. These will give the model focus and ensure you're not spinning.

Basic Decisions for Concept Models

Sometimes I don't know the answers to the following questions when I start modeling the concepts behind a new project. It's a useful exercise for me, and I've become reasonably responsible about not getting pulled too far down the rabbit hole. That said, once the model is underway and I've got a better sense of range and scope, I also start to frame up what role the model will play on the project. Either way, as the model starts to form up, answering these questions can help give you a sense of focus.

SPINNING When "creative efforts" are more effort than creative. Also known as analysis paralysis.

What is the purpose?

In design, the purpose of high level conceptual thinking is to inform the entire process. At different stages of the design process, the conceptual model will serve different purposes. The chief purpose of a model is, in my mind, to answer the question, "What are we dealing with here?" It seeks to illustrate and frame the range, scope, and depth of the things we're interested in.

While the answer to that question may shift and settle over the course of the project, its boundaries generally remain intact. The answer to that question, however, contributes to all the other decisions you and your team will have to make throughout the process. At the beginning, you might use a model to comprehend a new domain. As you get underway, the decisions might be about what's in scope and what's out of scope for the project.

Even the simplest concept models can help. I created a very simple model at the start of a project to help clarify some overlapping concepts (Figure 4.11).

Who is the audience?

"Well, that didn't go so well." So said my colleague Chris as we came out of a meeting where I presented a concept model to a group of business stakeholders. Boy, was he right. They just didn't get it. Unless a model is fleshed out and highly illustrated (and perhaps even if it is), you'll struggle to get any meaningful response. Table 4.6 explains why.

The section up ahead that deals with presenting concept models can give you some ideas on how to fine-tune the model depending on whether you need to show it to a client or not.

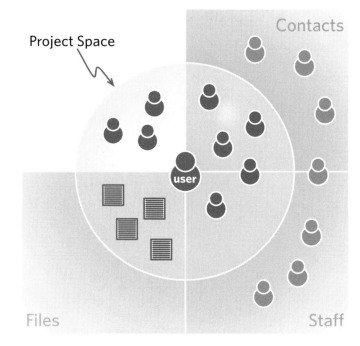

Figure 4.11: To help inspire new ways of thinking about the product, I created this concept model to better understand all the different moving parts. It's a pretty simple model, but it was enormously useful in clarifying the relationships. Note how this model completely evolved from circles-and-lines to more of an illustration.

Concept models...	and people generally...
Represent abstract concepts	Like talking about concrete things
Don't directly relate to aspects of the web site	Can't picture how it affects the design
Present familiar concepts in a new way	Find that uncomfortable
Introduce new concepts and structures	Have trouble putting new ideas into context

Table 4.6: Concept models can be difficult for people to understand.

Generally speaking, I create concept models for myself. If I need to solicit input from someone else, I'll package the diagram to tell a specific story. Here are some things you can do to facilitate such a presentation:

Since people generally...	You should...
Like talking about concrete things	Lace your model with examples
Can't picture how it affects the design	Embed implications by highlighting templates or components that emerge from the model
Find new perspectives on familiar ideas uncomfortable	Rationalize why you're shifting the perspective on otherwise familiar concepts
Have trouble putting new ideas into context	Be prepared to tell a story about one or two new concepts to help people understand why they're important

Table 4.7: To make concept models more accessible, consider tapping into people's strengths.

It's a big investment, so I always double-check that I have the time and budget and ask myself, "What feedback do I want from this person? Is this the best way to get that information out of them?"

What should you include in the model?

What makes a good node? Four things should drive whether you end up including a concept in the model:

- **Important to users**: Through primary or secondary research, you will learn what ideas are central to the users' experience of the site.
- **Important to stakeholders**: Interviews and requirements-gathering with stakeholders will reveal which ideas are important to them. These ideas are central to an organization's conception of success.
- **Meaningful landmark**: Some concepts provide a useful way to link other ideas together. They serve as a central point or bridge two concepts.

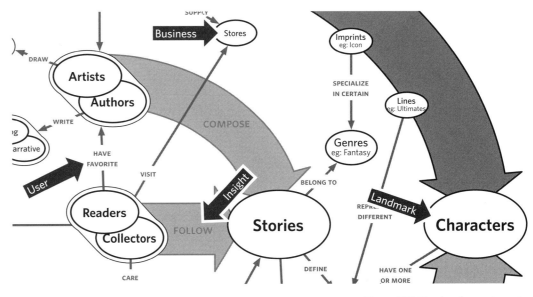

Figure 4.12: Good nodes are important to users, important to the business, provide a contextual landmark, or offer an insight.

- **Offers insight**: As you elaborate on your model, you may identify additional concepts that can help illuminate the underlying domain.

After you have a first draft of your model, you can also try to bring "bad" nodes to the surface—concepts that don't substantially contribute to explaining the domain. One way to do this is to pull out common words, concepts that are so broad that outside the context of the model it's hard to determine what they might be talking about.

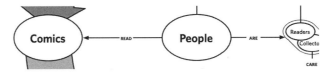

Figure 4.13: Common words are good opportunities to prune the model. One early version of the comics model included the concept "People," which was easy to eliminate.

The links between nodes should all strive for greatest interest and appeal. You should seek out relationships that:

- **Highlight the active**: Use active verbs that describe how one concept affects, influences, or otherwise changes another.
- **Evoke interface actions**: Assuming all the concepts will translate eventually into information on the web site, all the links could reflect the various actions users might perform. While not a necessity, the exercise lays groundwork for doing subsequent design work. If you subscribe to the idea that all interactions with data can be reduced to CRUD (create, retrieve, update, and delete), here are some verbs that relate to each of those actions:

Create	Retrieve	Update	Delete
Generates	Displays	Changes	Removes
Yields	Explains	Affects	Cancels
Produces	Represents	Depends on	Eliminates
Defines	Values		
Composes	Appears		

Table 4.8: Relationships in concept models may try to highlight the same sort of connection over and over again. These nuances, however, can have a major impact on the design process. "Create" could refer to something generated or yielded passively, as a by-product, or something with much more intent, like "composes".

How you should lay out the model?

Concept models start out messy. As you clarify the story and insights start to emerge, you may want to clean it up. The insights you learn should drive how you structure the model: They should tell you what concepts and relationships to prioritize.

My models tend to fall under one of three typical structures. These structures may be useful starting points once you've had a chance to move the concepts around the page a bit.

Note that it's rare for me to start with one of these structures right off the bat. In my initial models I do not prioritize any concepts. Only after I see how the story emerges do I zero-in on one of these approaches as appropriate for providing a framework for the model.

Tips for Crystal Clear Concept Models

It's not too hard to get some initial ideas down on paper, especially if you're familiar with the domain. But if you don't know much about it, you might get only a few nodes on paper before you get stuck. Here are some ideas for getting, you know, unstuck.

Structure	Description	Use for...
Hub and spoke	One concept rules them all. A central node from which everything else branches off.	Defining a single, central concept. Implying a site structure starting at a home page.
Diad, triad, quad	A core collection of two, three, or four concepts defines the primary structure. Everything else branches off that.	Acknowledging the importance of a handful of concepts and showing how they serve as landmarks for an information space. Structuring a site around a few different "views."
Value proposition	Three or four nodes forming a single sentence serve as a backbone for the rest of the diagram.	Stating a singular purpose, vision, or theme for the project and showing how other concepts support the theme.

Table 4.9: Three basic structures for concept models. Each has its own place, and may be a useful starting point if you have no specific ideas on how to initiate the model.

Do your research

Flesh out your understanding of the domain by reading up on it. Nothing gives you more nouns and verbs to draw upon than a few comprehensive, detailed descriptions of the business.

When I started an 18-month contract at the wireless division of the Federal Communications Commission (FCC), it was clear I knew nothing about the business. While the FCC's web site was a good starting point, I also sought out other web sites that cater to the same target audiences. This afternoon of surfing gave me enough fodder to build up a model. Ultimately, the model was never shared with others, but was a good tool for me to become comfortable with the various players and underlying business model.

User research is even better. Transcripts of interviews are rife with concepts that are important and meaningful to users.

Look under the hood

If you're stuck, pick a node and ask yourself, "What else can I say about this concept?" Unpack the concept, forcing yourself to be as specific as possible. If you need more specific questions, pretend you're interviewing a person (not a circle) who knows about the concept or the domain.

One of the jargon words used in talking about comics is "mythology," which informally refers to a character's backstory. Because many popular characters have been around for decades, and have been subject to so many interpretations, there are multiple mythologies for some characters. This idea is difficult to model.

Some questions I asked myself about the "mythologies" concept in order to arrive at a more detailed model:

- What makes one mythology different from another?
- How do storytellers deal with multiple mythologies?
- What other concepts are affected by a character's mythology?

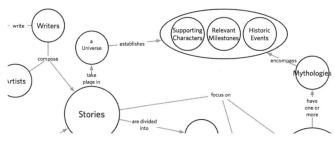

Figure 4.14: Some details emerge only after forcing yourself to unpack a concept. In this early version of the comics concept model, I elaborated on the concept of a "mythology". While it didn't make it into the final model, I did keep "relevant milestones".

FCC The organization in the U.S. government that regulates telecommunications and broadcasting

In elaborating on this concept, I knew there was a relationship to another key idea—a universe. In short, one way to resolve competing or conflicting backstories is to place different versions of the same character in parallel universes. (And people wonder why comics aren't more mainstream.)

It was difficult for me to think of a specific verb that created a relationship between Mythology and Universe, so instead I tried to think of concepts that "mediated" between them. This helped me flesh out this part of the diagram.

If you can't generate answers or find them through research, capture the questions in the model itself. When you get to interview an expert, these questions can guide your agenda.

Move stuff around

If you have dozens of concepts, it may be challenging to find a central focus for the diagram. The best way to elaborate on the model, focus it, and find insights in the relationships is to move the nodes around. This might seem like an oversimplification, and a very mechanical way of iterating on the model. By moving concepts around, however, you can test out new kinds of relationships, explore positioning relationships in a new way, and zero-in on gaps in the model.

Build up then tear down

Since it's difficult to picture the end state before you start a model, err on the side of too much information. Include concepts that may not be entirely relevant. Link a concept to as many others as you can. Your page will be covered with circles and lines, but starting with too much is part of the creative process, giving you more opportunities for insight. You'll have to cut things out ruthlessly when it comes time to clean up the model, but the pruning process can also lead to insights.

To **reduce links**, look for triangles (Figure 4.15). Three interconnected nodes can indicate that one of the relationships is redundant. Eliminate the relationship between the two less important nodes, focusing on the relationship between the important node and the ideas that support it. Alternatively, identify a chain of nodes that tells the simplest story.

To **reduce nodes**, eliminate words that are so common they are merely a convenient mechanism for bridging to other concepts. In an early version of the comics concept model, I used the concept "words" to encompass the different kinds of verbiage in a comic book–dialog, narrative, thoughts, and so on. Since I was already using the concepts "scripts" and "writers," "words" felt unnecessary.

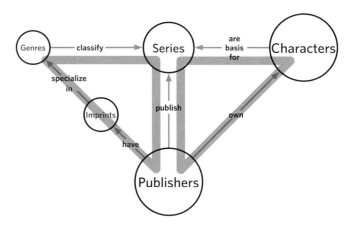

Figure 4.15: Reducing triangles from three connections to two can help clean up the model. Looking for triangles (like these from an early version of the comics concept model) can reveal opportunities to consolidate and focus the model.

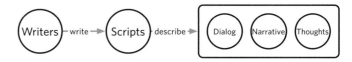

Figure 4.16: Redundant words make for good opportunities to simplify the model. Though writing a script is an accurate depiction of the comic authoring process, it may not be essential for planning the user experience. Of course, if one of the requirements for the project calls for allowing users to download scripts, it would be worthwhile to keep this concept in.

Level-Up Your Concept Model Skills

It can be easy to spin in circles (ha ha) with a concept model. Here are some things I watch out for:

Convergence: Everything wants to link to one concept

Though the hub-and-spoke model is a perfectly good way to represent how a central concept is the foundation for a series of interconnected concepts, the hub shouldn't be the *only* concept everything links to. A model with a hub and one level of spokes without much more doesn't help readers understand the rich array of relationships that drive the concept.

If you find yourself wanting to make statements about the same concept over and over again, a concept model may not be the right tool to describe the domain. Then again, you can try a couple techniques to breathe some life into the diagram:

- **Take the central concept out**. I know: crazy, right? When I find myself unable to express any relationship without linking to the central concept, I take the concept out and treat it as an assumption for all the other relationships. This helps me focus on the relationships between the concepts.
- **Use a value proposition structure**. Value proposition links three or four concepts together in a sentence, like "**Concept models** are **diagrams** that describe **complex ideas**." Treating this as your central theme (instead of the single concept) gives you more opportunities to explore detailed concepts.

Keep the concept in perspective

You may be tempted to define life, the universe, and everything with a concept model. Once you get the hang of noun-verb-noun, your inner 18th-century philosopher will be clamoring to be let loose on the world. Why shouldn't you be able to represent everything as interconnected circles?

Ultimately, you're trying to explain a domain. Serving only yourself, the concept model doesn't need to unearth the deepest assumptions. A model for readers will only be undermined by too much information.

There's no litmus test to see if you've gone too far, but practice shows that most of my models include no more than a couple dozen concepts.

Keep the model practical

Stay three or four steps ahead as you're constructing the model. You don't want to censor yourself to the point of eliminating every concept. But you also don't want to take your concepts down to the building blocks of life. Ask yourself these questions as your put the model together:

- Is this concept relevant to the target audience?
- How important is this concept to the business?
- Which relationships would the target audience prioritize?
- Can I imagine how these concepts will be turned into elements of the interface?
- Can I imagine some user research that would help me validate these concepts?

Answer "no" to any of these questions and you might be pushing into the realms of the impractical.

A concept model in the design process is like salt in a recipe: it sets the stage for a broader palette of flavors. Too much, and you'll overwhelm the rest of the ingredients. To remain practical, a concept model has to just provide a foundation for inspiring, informing, and establishing context in the design process.

PRESENTING CONCEPT MODELS

First things first: Ask yourself, "Do I need to share my concept model with team members or stakeholders at all?" If you're using it as a tool to get things straight for your own purposes, or with a small team, this may not be a formal deliverable: It will never see the light of the conference room. It may be more responsible to shield your stakeholders and other team members from this kind of document if it operates at a level of abstraction that would be difficult for them to comprehend without concrete examples.

If you decide that the concept model includes ideas that are essential for understanding the overall approach, think about whether you need to show the entire model. Is there an abbreviated version you can put together that boils the ideas down to just what's needed as prerequisites for the rest of the design? Alternatively, if the model yielded an insight or specific conundrum, you might assemble a separate diagram describing just the small piece.

Presenting a concept model means telling a story, putting the concept model into a context that team members and stakeholders can relate to. Your story needs to be grounded in reality, and this section describes several ways to do this.

Establish a Purpose for Meeting

The presentation should be driven by the purpose. With concept models, there are usually only two reasons why you'd present them: to prepare participants for more in-depth design discussions, or to hash out the model itself.

Preparing for design

One reason for presenting a concept model is to lay a foundation for the design, prepping the meeting participants for a more detailed discussion about the user experience. These meetings usually start out with, "I know you're eager to dig into the design, but there are some basic concepts we need to clear up before we do."

We could use our comics concept model (or a portion of it) to describe the design team's assumptions in designing the web site's interface. Those assumptions include answers to these questions:

- What are the most important categories of content?
- How do other types of content relate to those most important categories?
- What kinds of functions might users expect?

These kinds of meetings have at least one of these three key messages:

- **This is a useful exercise because…**: Be sure you understand how the concept model fits into the design process and where you're going with it next. Prepare a simple rationale for doing the concept model, and refer to it when the meeting loses focus.
- **Some initial design principles or requirements**: Pull out a few of the insights and use these as themes or talking points throughout the discussion. These insights should be positioned as design principles or guidelines: They are boundaries and constraints that help the design team focus their efforts.
- **Some remaining questions about scope**: Highlight the areas of the model that remain unclear, or which called into question the scope of the project. The model may have revealed dependencies that would make the established scope challenging. The model may have identified additional requirements not yet incorporated into the thought process.

Analysis of the concept model may have yielded some initial ideas about design—which content will get its own templates, what the information priorities are, a metadata model. If you're confident about your design decisions, you can use these as themes in the meeting. Otherwise, use them in the Communicate Implications section of the agenda.

Modeling together

The other reason to put a concept model in front of team members and stakeholders is to collaborate in its construction. In this case, rougher models are better because they lend themselves to feedback and discussion. It's important to come to a consensus about the underlying structure that supports a web site's user experience because it drives so many subsequent design decisions.

As described previously, concept models can help at any point in the design process. Building them collaboratively does not change this. You may come to an impasse in the design process, a clue that there's disagreement about the underlying assumptions, and use that as an opportunity to take a step back and facilitate a brainstorming meeting to flesh out the basic concepts.

In these meetings, establish three key themes:

- **Our focus is the scope**: That is, the purpose of the exercise is to establish the boundaries of the domain. We want to get our arms around everything that may be relevant to the design problem. We can always remove concepts later.
- **Our interest is in what's missing**: Participants should focus less on what's there and more on what's not there. They need to help identify concepts that may be important—even tangentially—and contribute to the overall picture of the domain.
- **Abstract thinking is hard**: Reassure participants that thinking about an information space in this way is not easy to do. We're thinking about the web site not just as a series of building blocks, but as a series of templates. Some templates can represent so many different things that their structures look so far removed from the actual content as to be of questionable value. This is OK, and it can be hard to wrap your head around.

The meeting structure following assumes you're preparing for design, not modeling together. If the purpose of your meeting is to present a skeletal structure for the concept model and engage participants in fleshing it out, you might skip steps 5 and 6. In these portions of the agenda, you provide details (you don't have any yet) and communicate implications (which would be premature).

Adapt the basic meeting structure

The basic meeting structure from the introduction is ideal for concept models. As you delve further, you are uncovering more details. Keep an eye on meeting participants; they may start to lose the thread if you get too abstract. In this case, you've reached the end of the useful life of this meeting. Wherever you are in your agenda, transition to soliciting feedback and defining next steps.

Refresh your memory on the timing of sharing diagrams (Table 2.2 in the Diagram Basics chapter). With concept models (perhaps more than any other diagram) timing is important because stakeholders' unfamiliarity with the models may add unnecessary challenges to the rhythm of your story.

1. Establish context

For concept models, which may occur early in the project, set the stage by explaining how this technique contributes to the design project. You can use this time in the meeting to clarify the parameters and boundaries you considered in putting the model together. Also provide a high-level description of your process—what sources you used, what it took to put the model together, and what you were attempting to capture in the model.

You can show the model, or the high-level version of it, when you conclude your context-setting introduction. This will set you up for the visual conventions, coming up next.

2. Describe visual conventions

Describe the model at a high level, first. The fact that the diagram consists of circles connected by lines may be self-evident, but it sets the stage for you to dig into the specifics.

If you've kept your model simple, limiting the range of styles for nodes and links, you may not need to say much more. If you've used a more elaborate set of styles, describe the types of contrasts those styles are meant to show.

3. Highlight major design decisions

It's now time to dig into the model. There are three broad descriptions you can offer before getting too deep into the details:

- **Overall structure**: Indicate the three or four main concepts that constitute the main pillars in the concept model. Describe the relationships between them, and how they form the main structure that supports everything else.
- **Unifying theme**: Describe the underlying story in the concept model. For example, the theme for the sample concept model is the two sides of the comics business. Models using the "value proposition" structure (see Table 4.9) have their theme stated clearly.
- **What's in and what's out**: Distinguish the boundaries of the domain. This description is especially useful if you're trying to zero-in on scope, and you need to clarify that you've left some things out of the concept model on purpose.

Before moving on, this is a good opportunity to show the value of the model by describing insights that came from creating it. Some of these insights might include:

- **New concepts essential to the experience**: Through your research or brainstorming, you might have identified a concept that is a useful piece of information for users, or is a category that unites several other concepts together.
- **New relationships between concepts**: Concept models represent your priorities very clearly. Through modeling a domain, you make specific choices about what concepts to connect, and some of these links may represent a new spin on the information space.
- **New perspectives on the experience**: In creating the concept model, you may have stumbled upon a new idea

for structuring the overall user experience. This may be a new navigation scheme or a new way to arrange the content templates.

4. Offer rationale and identify constraints

Meeting participants might still be noncommittal about the concept model, not sure why they're talking about circles and lines when (clearly!) there are bigger issues at stake. Use this portion of the meeting to reiterate the purpose of the model, how it fits into the project, and what you hope to get from the conversation.

Use this time during the conversation to describe research you did to feed the model. Indicate what sources you used to generate lists of concepts and identify potential connections between them. Such discussion may trigger ideas from participants on other places you can look to flesh out your understanding of the domain.

5. Point out details

Describing concept models in excruciating detail is useful only if you expect to get meaningful feedback at those deep layers. There's no need to hit every circle in the diagram unless you only have about a dozen concepts. Otherwise, use this time to point out a few of the detail areas:

- **Novel concepts**: If you've added any concepts that stakeholders might not expect to see, dig into these and be explicit about where the concept came from and why it's important.
- **Insights**: Assembling the concepts in this visual format may have yielded unexpected insights. Describe these areas of the concept model.
- **Challenges**: To transition to the next part of the agenda, you can draw participants' attention to areas of the model that imply difficult design challenges.

6. Communicate implications

For concept models, where the rubber meets the road is in how the model will lead to design. Most of this chapter is dedicated to creating the model in the context of a design project, so hopefully you'll have some ideas about what you're getting out of the model. At the very least, you should be able to describe at least one of these things:

- **A better understanding of the domain**: But merely saying that you understand the domain after so many hours of putting together a concept model is a bit of a letdown. Be sure you have something else to share.
- **A better understanding of the target audience**: Better, but why didn't you do personas?
- **A prioritized list of requirements**: This is good. The concept model helped you prioritize areas of the project: which parts of the site you're going to work on first. Why? The concept model told you to do it.
- **A list of potential challenges**: This is also good, and it shows you're thinking ahead. The concept model helped you identify relationships that will be difficult to communicate, concepts that will require lots of links, or processes that are not straightforward.
- **An inventory of possible screens**: This is best. The concept model yielded a set of concepts and relationships that helped identify a list of screens that you need to design for the user experience. It provided a foundation for the site's underlying structure.

When discussing concept models, you may need to jump ahead to this section: people may just want the bottom line. With concept models the conclusion is, "So how does this impact the design?" And there's no reason to save the implications for last if they represent the most important conclusions from your work.

7. Solicit feedback

You're interested in getting input on four things:

Concepts	Am I missing any concepts?
	Do any concepts have more or less prominence than I was expecting?
Connections	Am I missing any important connections between concepts?
	Are there connections between concepts that are redundant or unnecessary?
Themes	Did I get the overall story right?
	Is this a good characterization of the domain?
	Do I agree with the overall story of the concept model?
Implications	Do I perceive any other challenges?
	Does the list of templates align with my expectations?
	Does the sense of scale align with my expectations?

Table 4.10: A structured look at feedback helps ensure you get what you need.

8. Provide a framework for review

The next steps after a concept model discussion are all you, the design team. I can't think of an instance where I sent off a business stakeholder or developer with homework to review the model. It's an introspective tool, and we've let others in to see our thought process, maybe to validate it in real time.

But the lack of context when reviewing it "offline" would make it difficult for others to provide meaningful feedback (unlike a flow or site map or wireframes, which are more concrete).

Instead, clearly state where you're going from here.

Avoid newbie mistakes

Even the most concrete concept models can confuse participants. Unless they can draw a parallel to something in the real world, they may not understand exactly what they're looking at. And even if they do get it, they may not care.

Potential response 1: I don't get it.

Some people may just not get it, especially if the concept model dabbles in the really abstract. Models can represent categories of categories or tiny little blocks of data or information about metadata (which is information about information). They can use slight variations in visual conventions to represent different abstract ideas (arrows for navigation, arrows for transporting data, arrows for indicating semantic relationships). For people who are used to looking at spreadsheets, or the simple infographics in *USA Today*, these diagrams can be exhausting.

Before going into a presentation where you think you might get this response, boil the concept down into three sentences. If you're not getting anywhere with the diagram, whip out those bullet points. As you watch your meeting circling the drain, these three sentences can be a lifesaver, giving participants the essential message without belaboring the diagram.

The key here is to not make them feel dumber than they already do. To that end, you might say something like: "Why don't you take some time to digest this and give me feedback in a couple days? This model is important because it creates the overall foundation for our design work. While you're looking at it, keep the following three things in mind. (Insert your summary sentences here.)"

Potential response 2: So what?

Even if the meeting participants get it, they may not realize why it matters. You have two possible strategies in this situation: Try to show the connections between the model and the design, or simply cut the meeting short.

Cutting the meeting short is always an embarrassing and difficult tactic, but sometimes you have more to gain by avoiding conversation than forcing it. Since concept models tend to be highly abstract tools for designers to get their thoughts in order, the stakeholders may have little to gain by going through it.

Again, the key here is to not make them feel stupid. Try saying something like: "I think I've gotten everything I need. I appreciate your time. We'll take this feedback and incorporate it into the design. If you have further thoughts, let me know. Otherwise, the next time we talk we'll start to show you some of our design work."

Ending the meeting is a last-ditch tactic, and you should only use it if it's clear the stakeholders or other team members aren't interested in engaging at an abstract level.

APPLYING CONCEPT MODELS

Though potentially highly disposable, concept models can also have a long shelf-life to help drive ongoing design activities.

Providing Context for Other Deliverables

Once the model is complete, I'll stick it at the front of other deliverables. They provide a nice visual for stuff that usually comes at the beginning of the document: what is the problem we're trying to solve, what principles drove our design decisions, what is the relationship between the site's audience and content, what is the scope of our design project.

This is only meaningful if the concept model actually provided specific inspiration for the remainder of the document. Perhaps the model helped you identify what screens to build or seeded the idea for the site's navigation strategy. If this is the case, the model can help tell that story as well. Besides the diagram itself, you might include some narrative text or at least three to four conclusions ("key takeaways") drawn from the model.

On subsequent pages of the document, the model can provide more specific context. You can miniaturize the diagram, scale back the color, and use deeper saturation to highlight the relevant area of the model for each wireframe or persona or what-have-you.

From Model to Screens

If point A is the concept model, what's point B? Where do you go from here? Ultimately, concept models should frame a domain such that you have a good handle on the range and depth of information the web site needs to accommodate. If you're having trouble making that leap, from model to screen design, here are a few ideas to get you started:

Concepts as screens

Any node in the model might be a good starting point for designing screens. Pick one and decide how the web site should represent that concept.

Remember that nodes represent abstract concepts, generalizations across swaths of information. The "issue" concept in our comic book model can represent one of many different examples of a single issue of a series. Therefore,

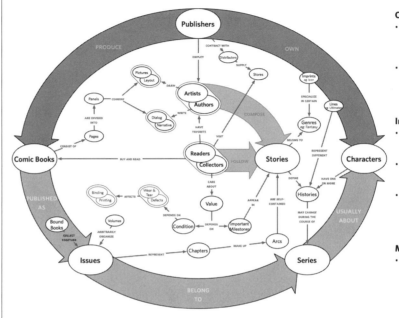

Figure 4.17: Identifying the insights gleaned from a concept model is one way to establish a set of design requirements. In this case, the page from the document also acknowledges what's missing from the model.

the screen we design to represent "issue" is a template or container: It has spaces in it to display information about a specific instance of the concept.

Some nodes adjacent to the concept you picked relate to it in some way. Your screen should show how users might navigate to that kind of information. How do users, for example, get from a single issue to a page about the whole series? How do users get from a single issue of a series to a page about related series? How do users get from a single issue to everything authored by the issue's writer? Or everything in the series authored by the issue's writer?

INSTANCE A single example of a concept.

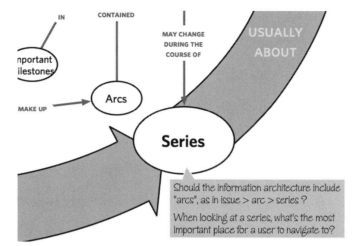

Figures 4.18: Questions about navigation, embedded in the concept model itself, provide a powerful way to (a) highlight the relevance of the model and (b) provide a mechanism for focusing discussions.

Concepts as metadata

Some nodes are descriptive, providing details about the concept. Issues have numbers. They are a chapter in a story arc. They might have a summary of the plot. All of these are potentially useful pieces of information, but not enough to serve as navigation mechanisms (they don't bridge to other concepts). Nor are they substantive enough to yield pages in and of themselves. Yet the concept model helps us see that they need to be represented on the main screen somehow.

Models to inspire structures

In the previous examples, we've considered the concept model to be the basis for the site's underlying architecture: Each of the major concepts translates to a template; the links between the concepts correspond to links between the templates. Site designs, however, may not be translated so literally from a concept model.

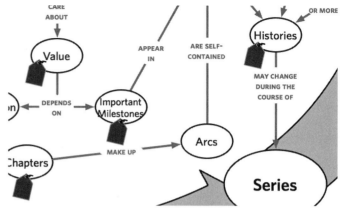

Figure 4.19: Some concepts make good metadata elements. In this version of the model, candidate metadata elements have been marked with a little tag icon.

For a recent project, I created a concept model that helped me look at the domain in a new way. Instead of designing a site structure driven by content type, I suggested designing templates based on lifecycle. To be specific, everything that passed through the system, regardless of its format or content, went through a similar lifecycle. The target audience wasn't concerned as much about format or content as they were about where something stood in the lifecycle: that was the factor that changed the decisions they made.

Can we do this for the comic book model? Does it suggest any other ways for structuring the information in a meaningful way? The model reveals some potentially useful structures and contrasts:

- **Reading vs. collecting**: These two activities are more than just use cases; they represent different relationships to comics. What's worth exploring is whether they can be served by the same web site and where the web site should be split to accommodate these two distinctions. Does an "issue" page template need separate tabs to display two different kinds of metadata? Do readers and collectors browse for comics differently?

- **Character timelines**: Working through the concept model helped me establish a clearer picture of the relationships between a character, its "mythology," the ongoing story lines, and the continuity between all of them. This is a situation unique to comics, especially mainstream comics. A single character can appear in multiple books at the same time. Most readers care about which story line represents the "canonical" history of their favorite character. Could we design an interface that focuses on character history and show the relationships between those timelines and the published issues?

Relationships as interactions

Finally, you could look at the relationships between concepts for inspiration on interactions. Verbs in the model may directly translate to actions users can take on the site. They might inspire functions or features you hadn't considered. They might shed light on the requirements.

These four techniques are hardly mutually exclusive. Picking one as the means for driving design does not mean the others won't offer equally useful inspiration.

CONCEPTS MATTER

Imagine a concept model, designed for a news publishing service, that describes the anatomy of a news story. It shows how the news story is composed of different kinds of information, the metadata attached to a news story, and the different types of news stories displayed on the site.

The concept model establishes a vocabulary for talking about the structure of these stories, and how they might be formatted in different ways on different parts of the site. The front page will have short teasers. Subject category pages might have longer teasers and a couple of features with longer introductions. The design team gives all these data points distinct names so they can talk about them easily:

ASK THE EXPERT

DB: How do you use concept models?

SA: A good concept model makes sense of something complex—it gets everyone saying "I see what you mean!" That's it. Beyond that, effectiveness depends your intent. The posters I create are primarily for me—to make sense of things like "What makes an experience?" or "What's involved with becoming a consultant?" In fact, I'm currently working on a concept model to make sense of all the varieties of artisan cheeses!

On just about every client project, I use this same kind of visual thinking. If there's a complex discussion that gone on for more than 10 minutes (or several emails), I find that even a basic sketch is invaluable to framing and facilitating a product discussion. In these cases, what is drawn on the whiteboard may be enough, or I may clean it up a bit in Apple Keynote if needed. But, full-blown infographics are rarely required except where an idea has a larger or extended audience.

I've also created concept models explicitly to persuade people to think a certain way—to justify a particular course of action or shape how people think about a subject. In these cases, visual metaphors are quite powerful tools. Things like icebergs, canyons, trees, and other conceptual metaphors—once that relationship is established—are difficult to argue with!

*Stephen P. Anderson ,
PoetPainter, LLC*

short summaries, headlines, subheads, long summaries, main body, extended body, and many others.

For all the effort put into this terminology, it may never be exposed to the end user. Its purpose is simply to facilitate the design process, to come to a common understanding of how the underlying concepts relate to each other. It is through the final design that the people using the site are intended to understand these concepts. Ironically, the design needs to be more effective than the concept model in communicating them.

And yet, many designs couldn't get off the ground without some kind of conceptual model. This won't change anytime soon, and with web-based systems becoming more complex and richer in their interactions with users, concept models will be more critical than ever to the planning process. Web sites whose navigation systems rely more on searching than browsing, or that depend on organic growth with content contributed from users, or that simplify information delivery through syndication, will require more conceptual designing up front. The concept model may become a more central tool in the process of designing web sites.

EXERCISES

1. Pick one of the following "systems" and create a concept model describing it, but don't use the word itself in the model. The challenge here is separating the system from the processes associated with the system. For the library, for example, your model shouldn't be a step-by-step description of how to check out a book. Instead, it needs to provide an overview of all the different things that make up the library and describe the relationships between them. Even if you can't use the name of the system, you can use nouns and verbs that evoke the system.

Bicycle	Checkers
Text messaging	Library
Stand mixer	Guitar
Movie theater	ATM

2. Show someone else your concept model and see if they can guess what system it describes. Once you have that out of the way, practice walking through the model and soliciting feedback.

3. Create a model like the one for comics for your favorite medium (television cop dramas or sitcoms, a specific genre of music, period literature, children's books, and so on). Don't be afraid of getting too specific. One of the most memorable models I've seen mapped different varieties of dance music, showing not only the relationships between them but the beats per minute along a scale. Your model should describe the experience of the medium from as many angles as possible, but you may decide to limit the depth. (Do you really need to talk about camera operators or technical consulting in the production of a television show?)

4. Use the model to map out a web site (or other product) that supports, enhances, or commercializes the experience of the medium you selected. Identify two or three approaches for designing and structuring the site, inspired by the concept model. Your approach need not be elaborate. Instead state in a few sentences (or with a picture) how you intend to architect the site: What are the main templates and navigational mechanisms? What is the range of content you'll support? What kinds of things will users be able to do? Reference the concept model (perhaps through color coding?) to provide a rationale for your approach.

Chapter 5

Site Maps

sīt' măp (n.)

A visual representation of the relationships between different pages on a web site. Also known as a structural model, taxonomy, hierarchy, navigation model, or site structure.

SITE MAPS AT-A-GLANCE

Site maps represent the hierarchy of information on a web site. The nature of that hierarchy varies depending on the project. Also, site maps increasingly represent page types or templates in addition to (or instead of) specific pages.

Purpose—What are site maps for?

A site map shows how all the information on a web site fits together. It provides the project team with one view of how the site will be constructed. It helps:

- **Clarify information hierarchy**: Site maps give the project team insight into where different pieces of content "live" and how they're classified.
- **Establish a navigational backbone**: While a site may have multiple navigation mechanisms, a site map can describe the primary structure that helps users browse.
- **Facilitate content migrations**: Mapping content from an old site to a new one can be tedious, and a site map can help ensure nothing falls through the cracks.

Audience—Who uses them?

- **Designers and developers**: The project team will be interested in how the site fits together, how people browse content, and how the site handles content that can live in multiple categories.
- **Project managers**: Site maps make an excellent planning tool, playing a crucial role in establishing scope.
- **Stakeholders**: Navigation can be fraught with political and design controversy, and site maps allow project teams to work through these issues.

Scale—How much work are they?

With the right inputs, a site map can take a day or two for the initial draft. But a site map is the kind of diagram that needs constant tinkering. New requirements or insights usually mean moving a box here or changing a label there. In this way, site maps can be a "live" document for the duration of the project.

Context—Where do they fall in the process?

At the beginning, either to establish what a new structure will look like based on an audit of the content, or to create an "as-is" picture of the current structure. A view of the current structure can help diagnose navigation problems or identify gaps.

Format—What do they look like?

Generally speaking, a site map consists of shapes representing different areas of the site, connected by lines. The lines generally show hierarchical relationships between the areas of the site but may show other kinds of relationships as well.

Designers and information architects use site maps to represent the hierarchy of information on a web site. Site maps generally illustrate "membership" relationships, where an item lower on the map belongs to an item higher on the map.

While site maps only approximate navigation pathways, readers generally understand that people have multiple ways of accessing content at the lower levels of the hierarchy. Since external search engines allow users to bypass upper levels of the site altogether, the pathways on a site map may be better representations of how to navigate *up*.

Site Maps Are Content!

Throughout this chapter, I'll draw a clear line between site maps and content. A preposition-heavy definition would read: A site map is a depiction of the structure of content on a web site.

So, what is content? The word *content* evokes the stuff that CNN.com and WashingtonPost.com and WikiPedia.org are made of—static, long-form "articles," maybe with pictures. Of course, content can be other stuff, too. Table 5.1 describes different ways of thinking about content.

Formats	Audio, video, tabular data, prose, form fields
Topics	Product information, support information, entertainment, performance reports

Table 5.1: Content, it's what's for breakfast. On the web.

ORG CHART A diagram describing the hierarchy of a group of people.

GLOBAL NAVIGATION A menu of options available from every page of the web site.

For the purpose of this book (though you're welcome to use it elsewhere), let's define content as:

Anything accessible on the web that helps people learn, understand, or make a decision.

Let's also append this corollary definition:

Content is anything on the web that can be linked to anything else.

Besides distinguishing the web as a publishing medium, linking is what gives content a structure beyond itself.

Design Artifacts vs. Online Tools

By the way, just to be clear, these design artifact site maps are not the site maps you find on web sites themselves. Some sites include a "site map" that acts as an index of all the content. While they may be similar in some respects, the design and construction of a site map that someone is meant to use is very different from preparing an artifact in the course of a design project.

INTRODUCING SITE MAPS

Site maps have become common artifacts in the design process, and even people who have never before seen one in the flesh recognize what they convey.

This basic site map (Figure 5.1) shows a site map, somewhat evolved from the typical org-chart format. It shows three levels of navigation beyond the home page and is very specific about the categories of information. On this site, for example, you understand that the Freezer product category lives inside Large which lives inside Appliances. The gray ring "orbit" around the home page indicates which elements are available from the site's global navigation.

Site maps can be more abstract, too. While this one shows literal pages and literal categories, some site maps focus on the structure of the templates that comprise the site. If site maps get too abstract, however, they will stray into the realm of concept models. In my mind, there remains a pretty clear distinction between them, described in Table 5.2.

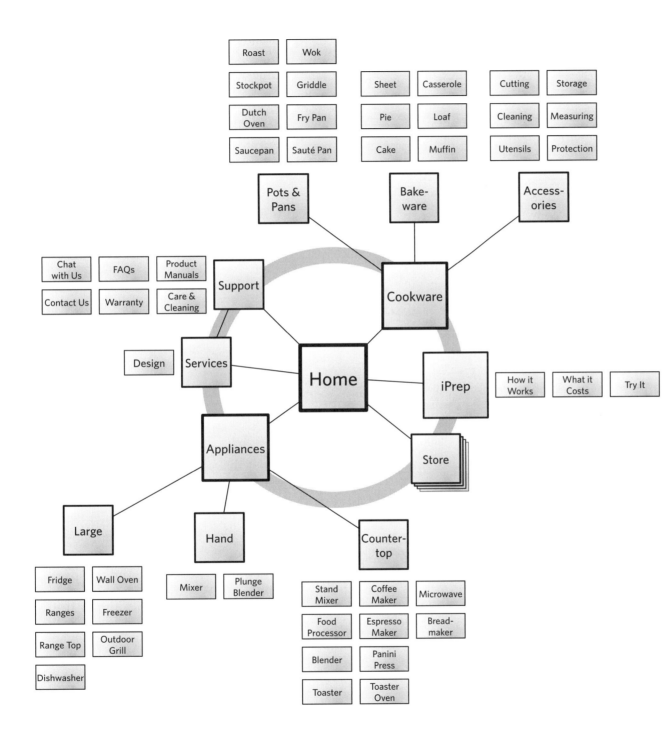

Roast | Wok

Stockpot | Griddle | Sheet | Casserole | Cutting | Storage

Dutch Oven | Fry Pan | Pie | Loaf | Cleaning | Measuring

Saucepan | Sauté Pan | Cake | Muffin | Utensils | Protection

Pots & Pans | Bakeware | Accessories

Chat with Us | FAQs | Product Manuals

Contact Us | Warranty | Care & Cleaning

Support | Cookware

Design | Services

Home | iPrep | How it Works | What it Costs | Try It

Appliances | Store

Large | Hand | Countertop

Fridge | Wall Oven | Mixer | Plunge Blender | Stand Mixer | Coffee Maker | Microwave

Ranges | Freezer | Food Processor | Espresso Maker | Breadmaker

Range Top | Outdoor Grill | Blender | Panini Press

Dishwasher | Toaster | Toaster Oven

Concept Models	Site Maps
Describe a complex concept	Describe a web site hierarchy
Use "concept" as the basic unit of currency	Use web pages as the basic unit of currency
Have ambiguous starting and ending points	Have a very clear starting point
Show semantic connections between ideas	Show hierarchical connections between pages

Table 5.2: Comparing concept models and site maps, both are node-and-link structures but they describe different kinds of relationships.

Challenges

Most designers and information architects are not only familiar with site maps, but have used them extensively. The challenges with site maps lie in their ability to scale to accommodate larger and more dynamic sites.

This latter case is important because it also covers situations where each piece of content has multiple locations, where the user can reach a single piece of content through any one of many different pathways. The site map may suit content in a particular set of relationships, but the dynamic nature of the web means that these relationships are not exclusive. It can be important to establish a set of primary categories for the content on the site, but the major risk is that other team members will think that the navigation is static.

- **Demand**: Because it's an artifact that people recognize and have seen before, clients may insist on your creating a site map, even building it into the project contract. They may appreciate the elegance and simplicity they've seen in other site maps, and their ability to show the big picture. As a seasoned designer, you may recognize that a site map is not appropriate for a particular project.
- **Structural reality**: With web sites becoming more dynamic, the notion of one page "belonging" to another is

becoming an increasingly antiquated concept. The meaningful relationships between content may not be hierarchical. Content may "live" in multiple places on a site, and users may get to that content in many different ways.

- **Navigation vs. hierarchy**: Even if the information on the site is hierarchical, the challenge with a site map is simultaneously implying how the site's navigation works. Primary categories in the content hierarchy may not directly translate to one of the site's navigation mechanisms.
- **Detail**: A site's complexity is also reflected in the nuances of the content, which may be lost in a broad-brush diagram like a site map.

NAVIGATION MECHANISM A menu or other interface element on the site that lets users browse content.

TIP

Three Levels Maximum

If you need to communicate more than three levels of structure, consider breaking the site map up into several diagrams. While you might be able to show four levels in a pinch, anything more than that will be difficult to communicate effectively on a single page.

ABOUT THE EXAMPLES

The Apple of Kitchens

My recent work has involved looking at the information architecture of very large marketing web sites—designed to sell or describe products, along with the various services and "solutions" that come with such an endeavor. If you want to test your mettle as an information architect, redesign the web site structure for one of the Fortune 100.

Besides exercising my IA chops, this work has exposed me to the range of challenges around marketing a broad and deep catalog of products. Such portfolios are challenging because there are lots of ways to categorize products, lots of ways to combine them, they target lots of different kinds of customers, and they meet lots of different needs.

For the examples in this chapter, I married my experience with large marketing web sites with something I love—cooking. Hardware for the kitchen rivals the tech and consumer electronics industries in terms of quantity, range, and depth. So, I gave myself a simple assignment: What if Apple had gotten into the kitchen business instead of the computer business?

These challenges sometimes boil down to answering the question, "Should I be doing a site map at all?" For sites that consist of information that people will consume in some way, a site map is indispensable because it allows the design team to create a model for the structures that hold that information. It facilitates the rest of the design process because it allows the project team to deal with broad categories consisting of multiple pieces of content rather than every individual piece of content. This is especially true for design projects involving migrating an old site to a new structure, where the big picture of a site map can help ensure that everything has a place.

ANATOMY OF A SITE MAP

At its most stripped down, a site map is a collection of web pages with connections between them. The additional layers of a site map can help create a more specific understanding of the structure a site map is trying to communicate. Layer 2 includes information on different types of pages and links, while layer 3 includes further context—the basis for structuring the site as shown in the map.

Layer 1: Must-Haves	Layer 2: Elaborating Pages & Links	Layer 3: Further Context
Pages and templates	Page details and distinctions	Project management and planning
Links	Grouping pages	Editorial and content strategy
Layout	Additional connections	User needs

Table 5.3: Layers of a site map, building from basics.

Layer 1: Boxes, Arrows, and Little Else

At its essence, a site map is a collection of shapes connected by lines. The shapes represent different pages on the web site. The lines can be structural, showing how users navigate through the information hierarchy.

Pages and templates

The nodes in a site map correspond to pages on the site, but even simple site maps sometimes show more nuance:

- **Just a page**: The basic unit of currency in a site map is the page. Pages are typically represented by a square or rectangle, and sometimes by a circle, and they are always labeled with the name of the page.
- **Group of pages**: A node on the map represents a set of pages that share some function or purpose. Of course, your site map can include both individual pages and groups of pages, in which case it should clearly distinguish between them.
- **Asset**: Your site map may include things other than HTML pages, specifically downloads of other file types. If you're keeping your site map basic, you can differentiate these kinds of downloads from regular pages by including the file type in the label—for example, "Company Overview (PDF)." If you decide to make your site map more elaborate, as described in layer 2, you can differentiate between these different formats visually.
- **Category**: Finally, a node may represent an entire area of the site. More than just a group of pages, a node on your site map can represent an entire section consisting of many, many pages. This works well when you just want to present a general structure for the entire site at a very high level. A site map using areas, rather than groups or individual pages, can act as an introduction to a much more complex site map or set of maps.

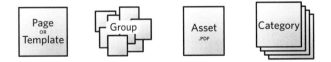

Figure 5.2: The nodes of a site map can include various nuances of a "page," each giving the reader a slightly different impression of how the page works. Regardless of the meaning you assign to each type of node, be sure to apply them consistently.

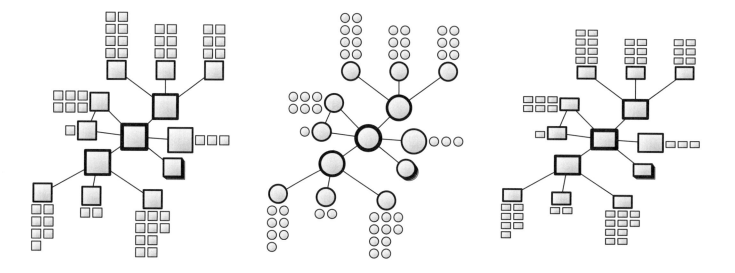

These days, however, most pages on a web site are generated "on-the-fly" combining content from a database with a template. Site maps generally reflect the relationships between those templates. To distinguish between a unique page and a template page, I generally visualize templates with a "page stack."

My tastes go through phases, but I generally represent pages on a site map with squares. At the lower levels of the site, these become rectangles to save space and accommodate longer labels. You can also use rectangles or circles.

Shape	Best for...
Square	Site maps that don't necessarily conform to a grid and most of the nodes are templates. For some reason, squares look more "template-y" to me.
Rectangle	Site maps that conform to a grid.
Circle	Site maps that are really concept models. :-) I use circles when the map is an evolution of a concept model or when the map represents a much higher level of abstraction: all groups of pages instead of individual pages.

Table 5.4: Different shapes for nodes in site maps can be good for different situations. Whatever you do, be consistent and try not to use more than one shape.

Finally, the labels on the nodes should correspond to the page name or page template. It's best to err on the side of using user-facing labels. That is, the site map should use the names of the pages that users will themselves see on the live site. When labeling templates, however, this isn't possible: Users will never see the name of the template. Instead use the content type.

Links

The links between nodes are deceptively simple. There's a lot going on behind the connections between the pages and templates of your site. The main decision you need to make is whether you're showing hierarchical relationships or navigational relationships:

- **Showing hierarchy**: Typically, site maps represent only the parent-child relationships between pages on a site. They show which pages "belong" to others. Linking one page to another shows that that page has a more narrow focus on the same topic. While this relationship also implies navigation, it tacitly acknowledges that there are numerous ways to browse to the pages.

- **Showing navigation**: When mapping sites with a less rigid hierarchy of content, the map can show the primary ways to travel between major destinations.

While I'm wary of geographic metaphors applied to the web, in this case a comparison to urban landscapes can help clarify the hierarchy/navigation distinction. In answering the question "Where is the Washington Monument?" you might say:

> The Washington Monument is on the National Mall in downtown Washington, DC.

This describes a hierarchical relationship between regions in Washington, DC. But you can also answer the question this way:

> The Washington Monument is a ten-minute walk from the Smithsonian metro station on the orange and blue lines.

This describes a navigational relationship. It indicates where the Washington Monument is based on how to get there.

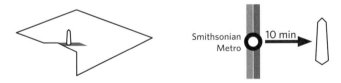

Figure 5.4: Hierarchy vs. navigation described through a geographical metaphor.

Generally, connections don't need labels on a site map because every link represents the same thing: belonging. Where you want to distinguish between different kinds of belonging, you can use different line formats.

Layout

The site map's layout—how the nodes and links are placed on the page—is crucial for communicating a site's structure. Site maps that show hierarchy should be laid out to reinforce those relationships. Usually this means aligning the nodes to a grid and laying them out top-down. When a site map is meant to emphasize navigation, strict adherence to a grid is less necessary.

The advantage to org-chart-like site maps is that they are easy to understand because they follow a convention of sorts. On the other hand, they don't show a lot of detail, and this format can take up a lot of space on the page. If your site map means to communicate strict hierarchical relationships between the content areas, an org-chart approach is your best choice. The layout reinforces the hierarchy and readers can look at any node and immediately ascertain where it sits in the overall structure.

If the site map's emphasis is instead navigation, or the hierarchy is less strict, consider a layout that isn't confined to a grid. A diagram more like a concept model communicates the inherent complexity of the relationships between the information. A web-like layout is appropriate when the structure:

- **Operates at a higher level of abstraction**: Site maps capture templates or content types, not individual categories or pieces of content.
- **Emphasizes the hierarchy of content types**: Templates relate to each other differently from topical and subject-driven categories. Some templates are "parents" to others when they contain a basic layout or structure that is adapted by "child" templates.
- **Describes navigation between templates**: Such pathways are not necessarily hierarchical in nature, but instead might follow more of a hub-and-spoke model.

Figure 5.5: Comparing layouts on site maps that show (a) strict hierarchical relationships and (b) not so much.

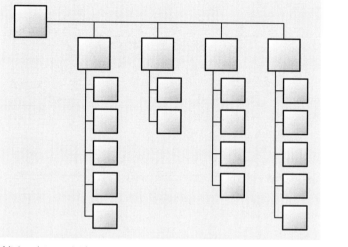

Aligned to a grid

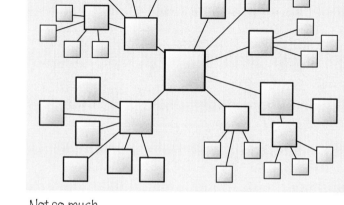

Not so much

With a looser layout, however, you need to make sure you enforce the hierarchy with other visualization techniques. Moving central pages to the middle of the page and increasing the size of the primary categories can cue readers on where to start. You may have to take a moment to familiarize your project team with the new approach. Use an example or two to show how this format changes the emphasis of the site map without completely abandoning hierarchy.

Layer 2: Elaborating on Pages and Links

Rectangles connected by lines can say a lot about the structure of a site, but your situation may call for more detail. Layer 2 builds on the basic structure created by the boxes and lines to elaborate on each.

Page details and distinctions

Your project may require supplying some detail about each page or providing some distinctions between them. One of the most common:

- **Existing vs. new**: Site maps may aid projects to update web sites by incorporating new information while leaving the old mostly intact. In this case, before-and-after site maps might be less useful than a site map showing how the old stuff fits into the new stuff. (Or the glass is half full, your choice.)

Some other useful distinctions:

- **Global navigation item**: Your site map needs to show hierarchy, but you also want to clarify what items belong in particular navigation mechanisms. Marking a node as "appears in global navigation" or "appears in product navigation" can help readers understand the browsing tools as well as the underlying structure.

- **Template types**: Different areas of the site may support different content but rely on the same templates for displaying that information. Site maps can visually distinguish the nodes to indicate which templates are in use.
- **Administrative or management issues**: While some organizations are more dynamic than the information on their web sites, it can be useful to depict the relationship between the content and the people supporting it. Administrative and management issues can include ownership, timing, or frequency of updates.
- **Partial pages or page elements**: In some instances it can be useful to show that a component appears on a page. Too early in the design process and it might be difficult for you to represent the details of page contents on a site map. In this case you can represent a page element as a node as well, changing the shape or other stylistic element to distinguish it from a full page.

So, how to distinguish? Table 5.5 shows various techniques for describing the differences between nodes.

Use caution with these styles. My site maps never use more than two or three stylistic distinctions, and I always apply them sparingly. Too much variety in line weight, for example, can have the opposite effect: It creates too much visual noise to let readers make useful distinctions.

Grouping pages

Even though site maps show categories through hierarchical linking, there may be other useful ways to group pages together. Here are three common cases:

- **Page pools**: Sometimes links on a category page are drawn from a pool of content. For example, the site map has a pool of white papers to draw from. The link between the category page and the pool shows that the category may link to one or more pages in that group. You could do the exact same thing with a page stack icon, but visually a pool may be easily linked to many different categories. It also communicates that from a hierarchical perspective, these are a set of interchangeable pages.

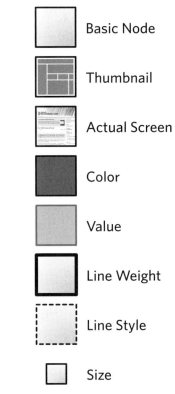

Basic Node

Thumbnail

Actual Screen

Color

Value

Line Weight

Line Style

Size

Figure 5.6: Applying styles to a node can distinguish it from its peers.

Use...	In which you...	Which is best for...
Thumbnails	Put small thumbnail sketches of a page layout in place of the square or rectangle for the node	Distinguishing between different kinds of templates or page layouts
Actual screens	Put a small screenshot of the page in place of the square or rectangle for the node	Highlighting the distinction between existing and new screens Also, for displaying an as-is site map
Color	Change the color of a node	Differentiating nodes by type or breed
Value	Change the value of a node (where value is the degree of lightness or darkness of a color)	Differentiating nodes by importance
Line weight	Make the lines around some boxes thicker than others	Differentiating nodes by importance
Line style	Make the lines around some boxes dotted	Showing which items are in or out of scope or distinguishing between new and existing pages Using nodes to represent page elements or partial pages
Size	Adjust the size of the box	Differentiating nodes by importance or emphasizing the hierarchy in non-grid-based site maps

Table 5.5: Embellishing nodes in your site map can help clarify functions or properties of different pages.

ASK THE EXPERT

DB: What makes for a good site map?

DS: A good site map has four attributes: it has good content, is easy to understand, uses the appropriate form, and is simple.

Content is the most important part of a site map. No amount of perfect alignment or sexy typefaces will help if the content of the site map is poor. And that means your information architecture must be good—your categories must be sensible (both for the users and the content) and use clear, descriptive labels.

Good site maps can be understood even when you aren't there to explain them. Even though you may explain them to the client initially, other people will need to look at them later on. Good site maps have:

- *just enough annotation or explanation to anticipate people's questions, without swimming in detail*
- *a legend to explain the different shapes, colors, or icons*
- *additional detail in some sort of supporting document (particularly for complex sites)*
- *examples of how the site map will be represented via navigation in the final site.*

The form of a site map is also important. For a simple hierarchical site, a simple hierarchical diagram is appropriate. For a database-driven product site, a document that lists out metadata for each object may be best. For a large hierarchical site, a big spreadsheet will be easier to create, read, and maintain. For complex sites, all of these may be needed.

A good site map is also simple. It has just enough information to communicate exactly what you need to communicate, and no more. Focus on what it needs to do, and do that well.

- **Functional groups**: You can group pages that relate to each other because they serve some common purpose.
- **Contextual groups**: A collection of pages can capture some external context, like being intended for a particular set of users or managed by a particular part of the organization.

So, how do you group nodes on a site map? Draw a line around 'em! Or, for the more subtle among you, use a backdrop. An enclosing shape allows you to represent links to the group as a whole, rather than having to link to individual pages. Sometimes I create a mass of pages to do the same thing.

Figure 5.7: Grouping nodes on a site map involves enclosing them with a box, circle, or irregular shape. You can use a line or a lightly shaded backdrop. You can also just create a mass of pages.

You might have noticed that pretty much any of the distinctions you might make at the "node level" you could also make by grouping the nodes. The value of visually grouping pages together is that they can be treated as a unit, at least from a hierarchical perspective. Individual white papers may be managed differently inside the organization, but from the perspective of the site's information architecture, they can be treated the exact same way.

There are any number of ways to group pages visually, but the key concern from a design perspective is to avoid confusing groupings with links. The visual conventions you use to group pages, therefore, should be subordinate to the links between them.

Additional connections

Site maps that primarily show hierarchy may need to depict other important relationships. Layering an entire navigation system on top of a hierarchy is challenging and likely unnecessary. But showing some important navigation links can help complete the picture of the user experience, especially in light of some of the ways we've embellished nodes.

Other links you might consider:

- **"Also linked from…"**: Web sites will be rife with cross-linking, and showing every possible link is pointless. But there can be value in highlighting particular links. (Figure 5.8, annotation 1)
- **Context-setting link**: Sometimes, you might be designing—and therefore depicting—only part of a web site. Showing pages that may be out of scope for your current project can help set the context for the in-scope pages. I tend to make these nodes and links recede (lighter values). They're there to answer questions like, "How do I get here from…?" (Figure 5.8, annotation 2)
- **Connecting to groups**: Links don't have to occur between specific pages. In this case, the site map shows a link to the group of pages, indicating that every page in the group is linked, without showing multiple lines. (Figure 5.8, annotation 3)
- **"Appearing in…"**: Some of your nodes may represent partial pages or page components. Though these nodes should be formatted differently, using a differently styled connection will also clarify that the link isn't exactly navigational or hierarchical. (Figure 5.8, annotation 4)

Layer 3: Providing Further Context

The information in the last layer takes readers outside the user experience and provides context for the site's structural information. "Context" refers to other aspects of the project, from content and editorial strategy to business objectives and technical constraints.

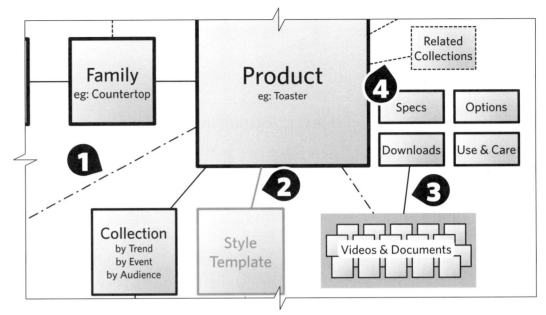

Figure 5.8: Beyond hierarchical connections, there are other kinds of links you can use in a site map. This portion of the basic site map shows all four approaches: also linked (1), context-setting (2), groups (3), appearing-in (4).

Besides applying styles to the shapes themselves, there are a few other techniques for supplying more information about the pages in a site map (Figure 5.9):

- **Annotation**: Sometimes, it's easiest to simply embed a note right next to the node. I use a distinct typeface and color, though the style will depend on the purpose of the note. Pointing out problem areas, I'll use red text.
- **Little tabs or corners**: If you can use a short word to distinguish nodes, you can embellish the node with a tab or corner to label it. I like this approach for classifying nodes by content type or template type.
- **Icons**: A little more intrusive than either of the other two techniques, a small icon is useful for distinguishing nodes based on page type or user need. I'd also use icons to highlight pages from an administrative perspective, distinguishing them based on project phase or priority.

Source:
site.com/aboutus

Annotations

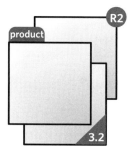

Tabs & Corners

Icons

Figure 5.9: Additional information about a node can be embedded using annotations or little tabs. Use these techniques consistently—a tab, for example, should always represent a template type. Also style them appropriately. If annotations are meant to point out problems, use a distinct color.

The context you provide in a site map depends on the purpose of the map. Be sure you consider how you'll be using the site map (see "Purpose and timing" in the "Basic decisions" section later) before adding all of the following data points.

Project management and planning

Site maps make great project management tools, especially when you need to look at a big picture and determine a plan of attack. Site maps offer an overview of the landscape and a chance for project participants to move their pieces around to focus on specific territories. (Be grateful it's taken me this long to milk the metaphor.) Project management considerations include:

- **Priority**: Which areas of the map will you pursue first?
- **Order**: How do areas of the site correspond to phases in the project?
- **Ownership**: Who is responsible for different areas of the site?

Content and editorial strategy

Site maps make great conversation pieces between information architects and content strategists (if your team makes such a distinction). Where information architecture focuses on the structure of the experience, content strategy focuses on what people find in that experience. The site map is a tool for making decisions about content, both right now and from here on out:

- **Emphasis**: What's the most important thing on this page? The content strategy will need to specify how to prioritize content. Prioritization can be topical (which kind of content) or thematic (what do we need to say).

- **Updates**: Another way to distinguish pages is by the interval of their editorial lifecycle. Areas of the site requiring more frequent updates get one color and those that are static get another.
- **Source**: An ideal label for content migrations, the source of the material can be added as an annotation with the specific URL.

Content strategy is an emerging discipline, becoming more formal as the web matures into a robust medium for large-scale publishing and consumption. As the needs of content strategy become more structrured and specific, you will need to reflect and document these needs in the diagram.

User needs

Illustrating a relationship between the site's structure and user needs can provide a rationale for the approach defined in the site map. Some site maps show the relative importance of different pages based on how well they address the needs of the target audience. A more robust way to capture nuance between different groups in the target audience is to mark pages based on their importance to different personas.

CREATING SITE MAPS

Knowing the parts of a site map can only take you so far. This section describes how to put them together.

Basic Decisions for Site Maps

The simplicity of site maps makes it tempting to dive right in without careful planning. Like any design diagram, however, a little planning goes a long way. Who will use the site map and how they'll use it can make a huge difference in its final format.

Purpose and timing

A site map shows one of two things in the design process:

- **As-is state**: A site map showing what the structure of the site is today. Frequently fraught with notes and exceptions that highlight the organic growth of content.
- **To-be state**: A site map showing the target information architecture for the site. If building a site from scratch, the emphasis here may be rationale–why this structure makes the most sense. If migrating an existing site, the emphasis will likely be on mapping the old content to the new structure, pointing out potential gaps.

A site map serves several purposes on a project, and these are not mutually exclusive:

- **Depict a navigation strategy**: A navigation strategy answers the question, how do users get from one area of the site to another. Navigation strategies describe one or more systems for browsing content on the web. A site map can help zero in on appropriate strategies by showing the range of content and desired pathways between them.
- **Illustrate a classification strategy**: A classification strategy establishes a framework for categorizing information. Those classifications yield a structure for content to live in, and a site map can help you visualize the resulting architecture of a categorization scheme.
- **Validate a content strategy**: A content strategy describes what content you're going to use where. It operates within the framework established by the site map to optimize delivery of content appropriate to the anticipated target audience. Like a content migration (see next bullet), a content strategy can use a site map to see all the gaps it needs to fill.
- **Facilitate a content migration**: In a content migration, a web site is being moved (in part or in whole) to a new structure. The reasons for doing so are myriad and

usually slightly irrational. A site map helps this process by allowing you to map old content to new content.
- **Diagnose any of the above**: By depicting the site's structure in its current state, you can gain insights into current problems (and strengths) of the navigation, classification, and content strategies.

The inherent big picture-ness of a site map makes it an ideal tool for the beginning of the design process. It sets the stage like a concept model does, but (done right) will provide even more actionable input into the design. (Concept models are useful for establishing an overall approach, but don't necessarily provide meaningful design principles.)

Audience

The message behind a site map is relatively simple, which means there isn't much nuance based on who you're building it for. Designers, developers, and project stakeholders all expect the same thing—a document that establishes site structure, site navigation, and page priorities.

Content development

Before committing the site map to paper, you may find it useful to create a list of all the pages you want to capture in the document. This approach allows you to think through each data point you might want to capture for each area of the site—how important it is, what type of page it is, or any of the other distinctions mentioned in layers 2 and 3.

If you're using the site map for one of the specific purposes just discussed, Table 5.6 identifies ways to embellish the diagram.

Regardless of what you call them (pages, templates, what-have-you), the nodes on a site map represent discrete parts of the user experience. They are recognizable chunks of the

If you're using the site map for...	Consider highlighting...	By adding...
Navigation strategy	Which categories appear in which navigation mechanisms	Coded bullets or icons to distinguish each navigation system
Classification strategy	How different kinds of content will be classified using a metadata framework, faceted classification, or some other technique	Coded bullets or icons showing which facets or meta-data elements apply to which templates
Content strategy	Content examples	Annotations listing example content, especially those that might be controversial
Content migration	Where the content comes from in the old site	Annotations listing categories or URLs from the old site

Table 5.6: Embellishments to site maps should be driven by the purpose of the diagram.

site that are responsible for presenting information, as well as informing users of where they are in the structure. It can be easy to lose sight of this when you're pushing boxes around a page.

A crucial decision for each node is the level of abstraction. This is a tension between two extremes: Is the node purely structural or is it a specific piece of content? Does the node represent, at one extreme, any category of product? A broad category of product? A very specific category? Figure 5.11 shows how a single concept (refrigerators) can be expressed in three different ways, at three different levels of abstraction.

The decision is ultimately one of design: The information architect's job is to figure out the range and depth of templates required to create a meaningful experience. But this decision cascades to the deliverable: How do you successfully convey the purpose of a category through the visualization?

Though more and more, I find my information architectures operating at a higher level of abstraction, there are two risks:

INSTANCE Used here to mean an example of an abstract category.

- **Exceptions**: Instances of a category may have exceptions. So, while Refrigerators maps accurately to the abstract structure, a category like Accessories might not.

- **Additional documentation**: Even though the abstract site map might successfully describe the site's underlying structure and template system, you may need additional documents to specify the exact content. What are the exact categories, subcategories, and products? A spread-sheet (or something) accompanying the site map will help flesh out the picture of the user experience.

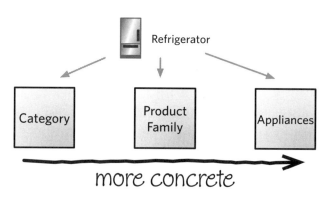

Figure 5.10: Levels of abstraction may seem like just another information hierarchy, but what this diagram shows is that you can describe the same collection of content (refrigerators) in a few different ways. Any one of these labels ("category" "product family," or "appliances") is a legitimate label describing the same group of objects. Ranges and toasters could also be described with these labels. At the same time, the labels you select have dramatic implications on the overall design of the site.

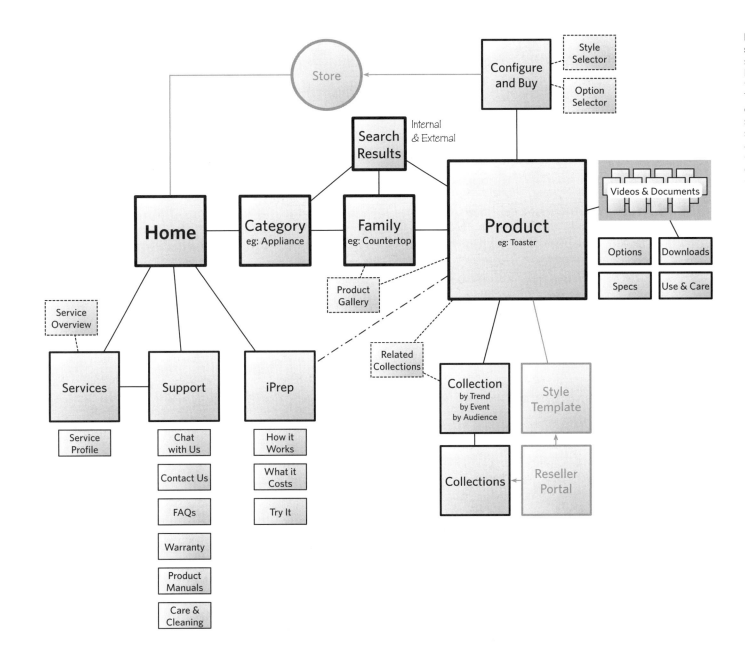

Figure 5.11: Rendered as an abstract structure, the sample site looks substantially different. The emphasis here is less about "what lives where" and more "what's the structure of the experience". Though the site map references specific content, it does so by way of example, showing what kinds of content are represented by different templates. The links are more nuanced because templates (pages at a higher level of abstraction) can relate to each other in more subtle (and more numerous) ways.

ASK THE EXPERT

DB: **What makes site maps hard?**

JM: *The challenge to making a great site map is finding the balance between clarity and richness. A simple tree structure is the clearest way to communicate with stakeholders—every page has one place and one parent, like an outline. I always start with the tree if I can. But what web site actually follows a strict tree anymore? Inevitably, the web experience is more nuanced and interconnected than a simple tree, so the site map needs to communicate key organization or navigation patterns too.*

In addition, the site map usually exists to tell a bigger story than where the pages sit in a content management system. More often than not, the site is broken in some way and a site map is the clearest way to communicate the underlying problem.

This bigger story can be told by layering color, positioning, and other cues on top of the basic tree to convey key attributes. For me, the exact combination of attributes is different each time, but generally falls into these groups:

- *user navigation*
- *traffic*
- *content management*
- *project scope*
- *content type*

To tell the web site's story, I sometimes have to try several combinations of attributes to find the right set. I often take a step back and try to explain it to a coworker. This forces me to communicate the story verbally and confirm that my site map supports it. Was the basic structure lost? Do the additional layers paint a clear picture? It always takes a few iterations to find the right balance with a complex site or a subtle story. Having someone to bounce ideas off of always helps me find that balance.

Tips for Stellar Site Maps

The basic org-chart format for this artifact is adequate, and if this is your first site map, that may be the easiest approach. After you create a few site maps, however, you might begin to see some inadequacies with such a strict layout. These tips can help you move beyond the rigid presentation of site maps.

Isometric layout

One trend in site maps is to use an isometric layout. In an isometric layout, the diagram creates a sense of perspective by skewing the angles on the nodes. (A picture is worth a thousand words here.) Nodes are placed behind each other to show them receding backward. This depends on keeping to a grid, therefore reinforcing the sense of hierarchy. Isometric layouts are best when:

- **Showing hierarchy**: Navigational layouts, which may not easily conform to a grid, can be challenging to represent with isometric site maps.
- **Showing as-is states**: You can use screen-grabs for the nodes to show the hierarchy of existing pages. With the challenges of labeling nodes in an isometric site map (see Figure 5.12), it's best to use recognizable pages that don't require extensive labeling.

In isometric site maps, labels generally appear outside the node. The shape of the node (a skewed rectangle) makes it difficult to include legible labels. Arranging the nodes "behind" each other leaves less space on the node to put a label. You can label nodes by moving the label outside the shape, but this takes up more room.

Figure 5.13 shows that some diagramming applications don't let you skew the text to align appropriately to the isometric grid.

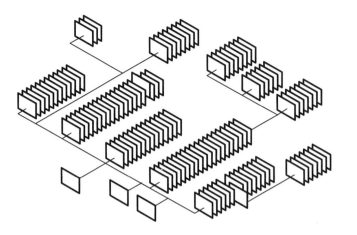

Figure 5.12: Isometric layouts for site maps are useful for communicating a strict hierarchy.

That said, isometric site maps are great for showing *quantity* and *groupings*. They are powerful tools for communicating existing challenges of managing content.

Visual language

In short, create a stencil of your favorite site mapping shapes and use them over and over again.

A stencil will help you be consistent across different artifacts and within a diagram. It will force you to make difficult (but good and important) decisions about what to leave in and what to leave out. It's not about constraining your creativity, but focusing it on devising the most effective symbols for your stencil. The stencil will then reinforce your set of visual conventions and guidelines.

The most effective way to develop a visual language for your site maps is to make a list of everything you need to describe in the diagram. After prioritizing this list, you can identify how to represent each kind of information.

TIP
More Isometrics

The single best source of learning more about isometric site maps is the book *Mapping Web Sites*, by Paul Kahn and Krzysztof Lenk. They provide a range of excellent examples.

My firm released templates for creating isometric site maps as part of its EightShapes Unify documentation system.

Large maps

One way to tame an unruly site map is to break it up across several different pages. Separating each logical section of content onto a different page makes the map easy to understand because each page is more or less self-contained. A cover page can show how all the smaller site maps fit together.

Level-Up Your Site Mapping Skills

As web sites become more complex and dense with information, it will be more difficult to capture all that information in a simple two-dimensional map.

Keep connections simple

Though it can be tempting to show all the different connections, keep your site maps to only showing the ones that help communicate structure.

Decide what links you must represent based on the purpose of the diagram and the overall structure of the site. In either case show only those links that communicate the essential structure.

ISOMETRIC Creating a sense of perspective by angling elements in the diagram.

STENCIL A collection of shapes used to create specific kinds of diagrams.

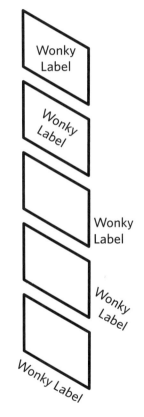

Figure 5.13: The challenges for labeling nodes in isometric site maps.

Stencils in Diagramming Apps

Most illustration tools—like Microsoft Visio or Omni-Group's OmniGraffle—allow you to save individual shapes in a stencil so that you can reuse them. Once you have a visual language that works, there's no point in reinventing the wheel.

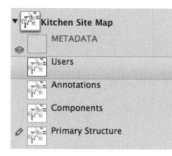

Figure 5.14: OmniGraffle's layers make it easy to show and hide different parts of the drawing.

Minimize distinctions

Web pages come in all shapes and sizes, despite your best efforts to put them in nice little buckets. As described in layer 2, a site map can make many different kinds of distinctions between pages, from the behind-the-scenes technology to additional layers of information architecture to project management issues. You may be tempted to pack as much information in as possible—after all, it's a special feat to communicate lots of detail in a little space. On the other hand, this can make your site map dense and clumsy.

One way to show additional information about the pages is to create multiple versions of the site map. Some tools offer features to make it easy to (literally) layer on different kinds of information. Most diagramming applications have a layering function that allows you to hide or show different parts of your drawing. Regardless of how you make it happen, you can create different versions that show different aspects, so one version might focus on the technical issues and another on the editorial issues.

Oversimplifying

You can also go in the other direction, showing too little information. Watch out for:

- **Missing content or categories**: It may seem unlikely that you'll leave out entire sections of the site, but it happens. Focusing on other higher priority or more visible areas can leave others falling through the cracks. If you're responsible for the site map, you're likely to be responsible for making sure that doesn't happen.
- **Missing distinctions**: Showing how pages differ from each other is a crucial piece of information for planning sites. If you're struggling to capture all the distinctions, leaving some out is a good inclination, but you don't want to leave too many out.

- **Missing links**: Most of my site maps incorporate the assumption that users can pretty much get from any page to any other page. Depicting every one of those links is, therefore, unnecessary. But to show only one kind of linking may be doing your structure a disservice.

How do you avoid leaving out too much? A couple techniques:

- **Make a list** of everything you think you could include in the site map and ask the people who will use the diagram to prioritize. "Look, there's a lot going on here. Is it more important for me, at this stage of the project, to distinguish between content templates or content ownership? I don't think the diagram will support both."
- **Check and double-check** your work against the source material. Have a content inventory? Is there a place for everything on the content inventory in your site map?

PRESENTING SITE MAPS

A site map can communicate a site's structure effectively, but it contains complex and sometimes controversial information. The only way to work through these issues is through a meeting. Or two.

Establish a Purpose for Meeting

Most of the site map–specific meetings I lead or sit through are attempting to answer one of two questions: "What's here?" and "What's missing?" (Table 5.7 describes ways to position a site map in these meetings.)

Providing a lay of the land: What's here?

In the introduction to the site map, your role is to play tour guide. Like any good tour guide, your job is to, in a sense, personalize the landscape for the people on the tour. At the same time, you need to communicate what makes this particular structure unique. And you thought the hard part was walking backwards.

An introduction has a few key messages:

- **Unifying theme**: This is the singular vision that led to the design of the structure. For site maps describing as-is architectures, your unifying theme will not be design vision as much as key insight. "In putting the site map together, we realized that though most of the organic growth occurred in the products section, lots of good content was added to solutions, too."
- **Important landmarks**: Certain aspects of the architecture are going to be more important to meeting participants. These landmarks satisfy some need that's important to the stakeholders, but also serve as a means for illustrating the unifying theme. They can also be a bridge for drawing participants' attention to another aspect of the architecture that has been neglected.
- **What's changed**: If this isn't the first time you've shown the site map, your overview of it isn't an introduction as it is a version history. As you present each evolution, your message is "We heard your feedback and here's how we responded."

For the sample abstract site map in Figure 5.14, here are the key messages I might use in an overview meeting:

A "lay of the land meeting" may happen several times over the course of a project. You may have new stakeholders who require a tour. Equally likely, the emphasis of the meetings will change from providing an introduction to showing how the structure has evolved over the course of your work.

Validating approach: What's missing?

Once stakeholders are familiar with the site map, they become crucial reviewers. In some cases, you'll discuss the site map with people who are more familiar with the

Unifying theme	The site preserves a "conventional" approach for classifying kitchen items, but affords opportunities to layer on additional browsing mechanisms.
Important landmarks	Besides the key structural elements—category, family, and product—the structure includes a "Collection" template for ad-hoc groupings of products. Note that we've started including some out-of-scope items like the Reseller Portal just so you can see how the overall structure accommodates those features.
What's changed	Since the last time we looked at this map, we've added in two things: some of the details around the content outside the product hierarchy and components displayed on these templates. These are represented with dotted lines, like the Product Gallery component attached to the Family and Product templates. You'll see what the Product Gallery component looks like in the "Sitemaps and Wireframes" section.

Table 5.7: Different ways to position a site map in a meeting introducing the artifact.

content and site requirements than you are. They will be able to identify where the site map does not align with content. You're looking for two kinds of gaps:

- **Where does X go?** The project team needs to understand how a particular piece of content fits into the overall architecture.
- **What do you expect to go here?** The project team needs clarity on what content will fit into a particular category.

You may show up to the meeting with questions of this ilk. You might leave the meeting with an inventory of questions like these about particular pieces of content. The purpose is different from an introductory meeting: You're seeking some movement from the current state of the site map to something better, more refined, more complete, more detailed.

In these kinds of meetings, the tone must reflect two messages:

- **This is just the beginning**: There will be lots of opportunities to validate the site maps as the project progresses. I usually use such a message to help set people at ease, noting they will have other opportunities to provide input. BUT…

Donna Spencer ,
Information Architect,
Maadmob

DS: I don't always show my site maps to clients and I've recommended that other people don't either. I used to do it, but more often than not they were met with puzzled looks. And if I didn't get puzzled looks, I'd get a barrage of questions when the clients first saw the navigation design—questions that should have come up at the time they saw the IA.

What was happening? My clients didn't know how to interpret the site map. It was an abstract diagram and they had never seen anything like it before. They didn't know what to think, what to focus on, and what to ask. Most importantly, they didn't know how to extrapolate what they were seeing to a built web site or intranet.

So how do you avoid this?

- *Understand your client: Learn about your client's previous experience with site maps. Find out whether it's the first time they've ever received one or whether they have seen many. If they've seen many, find out which ones they liked and understood best.*

- *Explain in person: Don't just send a site map diagram via email. Present it to them—face to face or remotely, whichever makes sense for you.*

- *Go through it step by step: Don't just show them a full diagram. When you are explaining it, step through it section by section. Explain what each is about, how you came up with it, and the alternative options that you decided not to keep.*

- *Put it in context: Show how the site map relates to the finished site. If you haven't designed the navigation for your current project, show how previous site maps you've designed related to the navigation. Show that there are lots of ways to eventually represent a site map.*

- *Wait: Wait until you've designed the navigation and pages, and show the client both at the same time.*

- **This is a crucial step** for ensuring we're building from a solid foundation. While "this is only the beginning" takes the pressure off, participants also need to understand that their inputs need to be correct. Decisions at this stage can not be arbitrary.

If you uncover critical missing components which slipped through, and the site map review brought this to light, then your meeting has been a success.

Adapt the Basic Meeting Structure

The generic meeting structure described in the introduction requires little modification for site maps. Here are some ideas on how to tailor the sections for a site map discussion.

1. Establish context

At the beginning of the meeting you help participants understand where you are and where you're going:

- **Project context**: A site map, while providing concrete information, can feel very abstract to participants, and it can be easy to lose the thread of your design process. By telling a quick story at the beginning of the meeting, you can help project participants locate the site map in the overall project.

- **Users**: Context also means reminding the team who the users are and why they're coming to the site. For each type of user, provide an overview of their needs and hint at how the structure supports them. You'll have ample opportunity to dig into these details later in the meeting. If user groups have been prioritized, start with the highest priority group. If not, you can start with the user profile that represents the most common tasks or scenarios.

2. Describe visual conventions

Before digging into the details, make sure meeting participants understand the format of the site map. Explain the visual conventions you used, and pay particular attention to the distinctions. From the participants' perspective, every box represents a page. So, if you've gone out of your way to distinguish the boxes, take a moment to confirm that the people in the meeting know what those distinctions mean.

3. Highlight major design decisions

With a site map, the major design decisions are generally structural—what categories you chose and how you connected them. In this part of the meeting, your job is to point out the important decisions you made about the structure. These could include:

- **Unifying theme driving the structure**: Structural themes can describe why the primary categories were selected. They can highlight novel ways of classifying content or navigational connections. They can be expressed as an objective, as in "In addition to supporting people finding just the right oven, we wanted to create a structure that let you create meaningful groups of products outside the context of the merchandising hierarchy."
- **Significant changes from the existing site**: Entire areas have been moved whole-hog elsewhere or renamed.
- **Surprises**: Items got categorized in areas that you wouldn't likely expect, but ultimately have the best rationale.

There are other decisions reflected in this diagram. For example, your site map may specify the range of templates needed to support the site, or may be specific about which templates apply to which pages.

4. Offer rationale and identify constraints

No doubt the best rationale for structural decisions stems from the people using the content. If you have insight into how they go about finding the information on the site, use this to justify your design decisions.

There are, of course, other constraints that might drive design decisions on a site's structure:

- **Technical constraints**: It can be hard for a designer to understand developers when they say, "We can't put that content there." Still, legacy content management systems (homegrown or otherwise) often impose constraints on how content is structured. Acknowledging these in your meeting is important, but it's equally important to focus on the technology, not the people responsible for the technology.
- **Political constraints**: More challenging to point out, but important nonetheless. In this case, you've categorized or linked content because of some political issue in the organization. You are not empowered to sort out these issues within the organization itself. And while it's perhaps expedient to avoid naming names, it is important to acknowledge that the constraints yielded a design different from what you would recommend.

Be sure the meeting participants leave understanding why you chose to make certain critical decisions, and why and where you were constrained to make others.

5. Point out details

The purpose of this section of the meeting agenda is to dive into specific examples. Contrasted with the "major design decisions," which describe the design in a more thematic way, this portion of the conversation should illustrate those themes with specific examples. For site maps, these details include:

- **Connections between content**: Though these will be self-evident from the diagram itself, you can point out some good examples of how content is linked.
- **Classification and labeling**: Point out some of the categories and the labels you've chosen for them. Describe what content fits in this category.
- **Template choices**: If the site map indicates what templates are in use, be sure to point out an example of each. In addition, inventory all the templates that are needed to build the site structure specified.
- **Exceptions**: Draw participants' attention to any part of the site structure decisions strays outside the design principles, standards, or vision.

The objective here isn't to cover every box and every link, but use good examples to describe the range of design decisions you made.

6. Communicate implications

Every design decision has a downstream impact on engineering and on the business as a whole. Those communicated in site maps are no exception, and for site maps describing a new direction, you should be prepared to enumerate:

- **Content gaps**: In meeting business and user needs, the new structure may demand new or revised content. Stakeholders need to understand that launching a revised structure also means updating and filling in content.
- **Dependencies**: Crucial to project planning, dependencies on a site map show which areas of the site affect others. Especially if you're talking about the process for building a site, presentation should point out where particular areas of the site will need development earlier in the project.

- **Template changes**: Whether you're adding some new templates to the mix or making significant changes to existing templates, the engineering team will need this information to understand the scale and scope of their work.
- **Operational impacts**: New structures mean new spaces to fill. The structure you designed may create an ongoing need to generate new content.

As-is site maps will yield the same implications, just in a different time frame. You can use the site map to talk about the current downstream impacts of having such a structure. This conversation can be a useful input to project planning, especially if you're using an as-is site map to discuss how changes to the structure might impact other areas of the organization.

You can communicate these implications in conjunction with the details (in the previous section "Pointing out details"), but prior to transitioning to "Soliciting feedback," upcoming, you should recapitulate the big ones.

7. Solicit feedback

To get the most effective feedback from meeting participants, you need to establish scope and then break your questions down into two categories.

The scope of feedback establishes constraints on the discussion: It can be easy to wander off into every crevice of the site structure. The site map provides a framework for getting feedback, but you need to direct participants' attention to the important elements. For a site map, these might include categories, content, labeling, connections, and template selections. (See Table 5.8.) You can direct attention to any or all of these, but be explicit as to why you're focusing on some aspects, but not others.

As described in the introduction, soliciting feedback means asking two kinds of questions. Here are those questions mapped against the different areas requiring feedback.

	Did I get this right?	What's missing?
Categories	Is the current content categorized correctly?	Can you think of any content that would not have a place in these categories?
Content	I've suggested adding content to some specific areas. Does this content seem appropriate?	Is there any content that should be incorporated into the site map that isn't?
	I've shuffled some of the content. Does it make sense where it is?	Have we addressed all requirements (or user needs or business objectives) with the content here?
Labeling	Do these labels make sense?	I've just put a placeholder in here, but we need to brainstorm possible labels for these categories. (In other words, don't leave any labels OFF, just acknowledge you've used placeholders.)
	Do these labels adequately capture the content of the category?	
Connections	Are there links here that should not be here?	Is there anything that should be linked but is not?
	I've connected these pages. Do you have any concerns about those links?	
Templates	I've divided content into these six content types. Do you anticipate any problems with creating and maintaining these six templates?	I consolidated the content types for simplicity's sake. In going from eight to four, did we lose anything?
	Do you think these templates are appropriate for this content?	
	I've guessed what templates you're using today based on the site audit. I was particularly concerned about X, Y, and Z. Did I get those templates correct?	

Table 5.8: A framework for soliciting feedback on site maps asks two key questions about five aspects of the site structure.

8. Provide a framework for review

Getting people to review abstract diagrams like site maps on their own time can be challenging. Giving them a means for doing the evaluation can help ensure you get the feedback you need and they're not faced with such a daunting task.

At the close of the meeting, the minutes should:

- **Capture the scope** of what people should focus on. For example, please review labeling and connections for areas A, B, and C.
- **Make a list of remaining questions**. Try to be specific, like "Does 'Appliances' need to be expanded to clarify that it includes both large and small products?"

- **Establish a realistic deadline**. For internal reviews of site maps, one to two days is sufficient. For most of my clients, two to four days is a feasible turnaround on a site map.

Ultimately, the point is you should not conclude a meeting with "Please get me additional feedback by tomorrow." You must provide a set of questions to give them some direction for their feedback.

Avoid Newbie Mistakes

Site maps are rife with opportunities to get off track in a meeting. Every box is another rabbit hole. Stakeholders may direct their attention to the wrong part of your map (labels are particularly tricky). You might also face a situation where site maps surface some organizational politics.

Getting stuck on labels

A question for the philosophers: If categories don't have labels, are they really categories? As designers, we understand that a category can represent a collection of content and the label can be tentative. A label on your site map refers to a category, but it may not be the exact wording you use on the site.

For some conversations about site maps, the labels are out of scope. That is, we've acknowledged they're tentative, we're not interested in nailing those down at the moment, and our primary concern is getting the structure right. (Can a structure even be right without labels? You're welcome to tape the philosopher's mouth closed.)

Thinking of the structure before you hash out the labels is a perfectly legitimate approach and process. But to meeting participants, the labels can be a distraction. Still, if this is the worst thing that happens during your meeting, consider yourself lucky (as discussed in the next section).

To mitigate this risk, build the site map to make the labels look like placeholders, or include a note on the site map.

Figure 5.15: Labeling options when you haven't zeroed in on an exact label.

When people argue about labels without any real foundation for validating their choices, meetings lose steam and take on a competitive atmosphere rather than a collaborative one. You attempt to redirect attention by writing label ideas on the whiteboard, saying:

These are all great ideas. I've captured them on the whiteboard so we can consider them at the end of this meeting if we have time. If we don't, labeling is the main agenda item for our next working session.

The politics of hierarchy

Creating a structure for a web site brings out the worst in organizational politics, which is why so many web sites—especially in the early days—were organized around corporate structure. To validate the design of a new structure, you may need to bring all the different players to the table. With teams consisting of people from every part of the organization, everyone frowns at seeing "their" content buried deep in the site while someone else's content is at the surface.

Your skills as a facilitator will be challenged. The introduction to this book describes some general techniques for dealing with conflict in design, but here are a few specific to site maps:

- **It's not your content:** The desire to "own" something in an organization can overshadow the true need. In this case, while different people may be responsible for creating, managing, and updating the content, it really belongs to the people using the content. If the content is not presented in a way that's meaningful or legible to them, it doesn't matter who "owns" it.

- **Contrary to vision**: A good design process will establish a purpose or vision for each page. This singular summary of what a page is "supposed to do" can be a powerful mechanism for weeding out requests that don't contribute to that vision.
- **Not everything can go on the home page**: Stakeholders may wonder why everything isn't linked from the home page. Your explanation needs to clarify that burdening the home page with a link to every piece of content (or every area) will yield an unusable home page.
- **Users don't enter through the home page**: Reminding stakeholders that at least half the entry into their site comes from search, not from visiting the home, can encourage them to think broadly about the role of the home page.
- **There are multiple navigation systems**: A good navigation strategy includes multiple mechanisms for browsing the site. A single navigation mechanism (say, "topical navigation") can not realistically provide access to every area of the site.
- **Here's an example**: Use examples (both good and bad) from around the web to show what happens when content and structure don't play well together. While a web site can't tell us everything about the design decisions behind it, we can speculate about how it came to be.

It can be easy, as a designer, to dismiss organizational politics: All you can do is point out the problems, not solve them. You're a designer of products, not a therapist. As described in the first chapter, politics can be an obstacle to project completion or a catalyst for compromise. As the designer you can position yourself outside the fray (align yourself with the product or with the target audience, either works for me) and facilitate the process to do what's best for the project.

USING AND APPLYING SITE MAPS

Site maps, inherently big-picture views of the project, provide ample opportunity to use them throughout the design process.

Planning Projects

Planning a web site project means, among other things, determining "what will we work on and when?" Site maps figure into this dialog by helping you see the range of possibilities. They can help you zero in on scope because they let you physically draw circles around the areas of the site you will work on.

SCOPE The "what" of what you're going to work on.

NAVIGATION STRATEGY The collection of mechanisms for browsing a web site.

> ### *ASIDE*
> ### *Planning Documentation*
>
> Are site maps special? Are they the only ones that can be used for planning? They are certainly not the only artifact useful for planning, but they offer some advantages over flowcharts and concept models:
>
> - **Concept models**: A good candidate for planning, but sometimes they don't tie concepts—circles on the diagram—to specific areas of the site. A plan is useless if you can't be specific about what you're working on.
> - **Flowcharts**: Flowcharts generally reflect a self-contained process. While you may choose to leave some things out—phasing different portions of the flow—a flowchart doesn't necessarily provide a comprehensive picture of the site. This big picture is necessary to talk about the site in chunks.
>
> Site maps themselves can fall flat as planning tools if they show only a portion of the site (as flowcharts often do) or they map out something besides specific pages (navigation categories, for example).

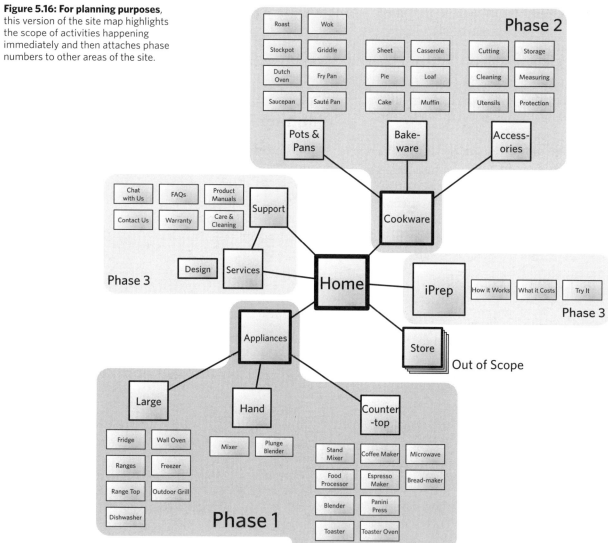

Figure 5.16: For planning purposes, this version of the site map highlights the scope of activities happening immediately and then attaches phase numbers to other areas of the site.

Adorn a site map with dates or phase numbers, and you can show the "when" portion of planning questions. You can use color to distinguish between "what we're doing now" and "what we're doing later."

Planning depends on, well, dependencies. Being able to identify all the moving parts and how moving one affects others is important for establishing a plan. Dependencies determine order and scope: what you need to build when and how much needs building in any given portion of work. Site maps illuminate dependencies by literally drawing connections between areas of the site and templates.

While a site map won't automatically provide an answer on what you need to build first, the diagram provides a good basis for brainstorming with the team about dependencies.

None of this conversation changes if the site map describes an as-is state. As-is site maps also provide opportunities to describe the phases of the project or identify dependencies.

Site Maps and Wireframes

You can use site maps with other diagrams to show their relationship to the site structure.

If you do nothing else, at least number the boxes on a site map and use the same numbers to identify wireframes (or whatever you're using to describe screens). Even a simple inventory like this can help with project execution, ensuring that you've designed every screen and addressed every dependency.

Site maps can become a visual element in other parts of your documentation to communicate context visually. Miniaturize the site map, place it next to wireframes elsewhere in your deliverable, and highlight the relevant box, as in Figure 5.17.

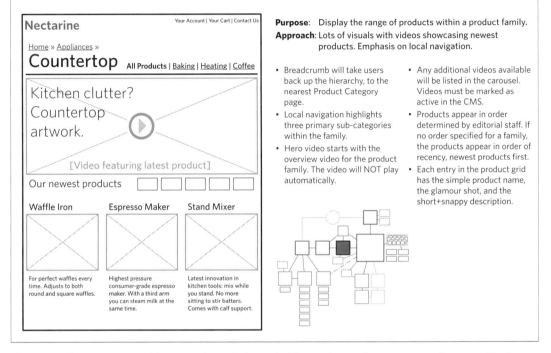

Figure 5.17: Site maps can provide context for a wireframe. In this sample page from a user experience specification, a simplified, miniature site map evokes the structure established in the larger version. Simple contrast differentiation can highlight the relevant box.

THE WEB'S CARTOGRAPHIC CONUNDRUM

In the first edition I dismissed site maps as a dying artifact—too static and too rigid for the emergent web. They (those site maps) are laughing in my face now as they remain a diagram I use again and again.

They have evolved, no doubt, to keep up with the changing nature of the web. I tend to favor a more abstract version of site maps: one that emphasizes templates over specific content or even categories. My site maps today are shorter lived, too, providing a means for jump-starting the design process.

I hereby change my assessment of site maps: They remain useful blueprints for mapping out web projects, especially in conjunction with other artifacts described in this book. That said, the web continues to evolve, and site maps will need to find ways to keep up.

Parallels between the web and physical space continue to obscure the potential of the web. A "page" on the web continues to lose coherence as a discrete location. Site maps can enforce this metaphor, to the detriment of functionality.

Nathan Curtis, in his book *Modular Web Design*, envisions the design process as creating a collection of Lego-like bricks. Page templates are convenient ways of arranging these bricks (what he calls "components"), but content meets structure at this component level. Is it feasible for information architects to continue designing at a page level when it's the representation of structures at a smaller level that really matters?

Finally, can site maps deal with trends around social networking and user-generated content? Such newer technologies permit a looser relationship between a site and its content. Some web sites have little predictable structure; this it true, for example, of sites that act as repositories for user-contributed content.

Increasing reliance on the web as a publishing medium. Increasingly complex transactions. Greater traffic of content. More nuanced exceptions within content strategies. Innovations in classification techniques and strategies. And perhaps most significantly, a dramatic increased comfort level with users of complex structures. Designers are taking advantage of the medium in new ways every day. Is the site map up to the challenge?

I've had my doubts. Yet the site map remains a useful artifact for conceiving structures. Every one of those challenges relies on some underlying structure in its solution. They rely on establishing a set of connections between real parts of a product. Concept models will provide an understanding of the domain, but once you start linking together screens, content, interactions, or features, you're creating a more concrete blueprint—a site map—for the web site.

EXERCISES

1. Sit in a public place with clear boundaries (I'm in a Starbucks as I write this, for example) and make a "site map" of it. (I could imagine doing this in a playground, too, but be careful sitting on a bench, scribbling in a notebook, in a place with lots of kids.) What is the range of "content" in the place? What are the different areas people go to? How are they connected? Focus your effort on the place, such that the site map describes a browsing experience. You're not trying to describe a domain of information, like you would with a concept model, or a series of steps people perform to accomplish a task.

2. In the site map from the previous exercise, add further layers of information—perhaps user types, or a classification for different kinds of areas. Since you're observing in real time, consider including some sense of frequency. (Customers step up to the coffee bar frequently, but rarely peruse the shelves of Starbucks-emblazoned paraphernalia. About a third of the customers stick around at a table, while the rest take their caffeine to go.)

Chapter 6

Flowcharts

flō' chärt (n.)

Flowcharts visualize a process, usually centered around a specific task or function. For web-based processes, flowcharts often represent a series of screens that collect and display information to the users. Also known as flows, user flows, process charts.

FLOWCHARTS AT-A-GLANCE

Flowcharts describe how people complete tasks. A flowchart may not reveal all the details of the interactions, but it does offer a comprehensive view of the user experience for a particular objective. The objective can be high-level, like researching cars, or more specific like establishing a user account.

Purpose—What are flowcharts for?

Use flowcharts at the beginning of your process to understand:

- The kinds of tasks you need to support through the web site
- How different people work together to accomplish a task
- What happens to information after it has been entered into the site

Use flowcharts during the design process to:

- Describe the series of screens people see to complete a task.
- Show an overall application framework—the collection of screens that defines the range of functionality in a web-based application.

Audience—Who uses them?

Every member of the project team will use the flow.

- For developers, the flow is an overview of the logic in the system, documenting each step in the process and the business rules linking them.
- Designers will use flowcharts to plan screen designs, understanding how to prioritize elements on the screens to communicate the process to users.
- User flows give stakeholders an early glimpse into the final product, so they can validate the approach from a business or operational perspective.

Scale—How much work are they?

These documents can be used at a broad level, painting an entire picture of how an organization interacts, or at a microscopic level, describing how a single person accomplishes a specific task. As with any other document, the amount of work depends on the level of detail and the amount of research or planning required. Even the simplest tasks can require a complex series of business rules to accommodate every situation, which must be documented for the flowchart to have any value.

Context—Where do they fall in the process?

User flows are flexible tools that can be used throughout the project to document different aspects of it. Business processes may constitute requirements for the system, and can be documented using a flowchart. Further into the project, the design team can use a flowchart to define how a particular function works on the site.

Format—What do they look like?

There are many different ways to illustrate a flow. The typical approach involves using a variety of symbols to indicate different steps in the process. Each symbol generally has a distinct meaning, and lines connect the symbols to show a person's progression through the process.

Flowcharts describe a conversation between users and the web site. The site asks for information, the user responds, and the site responds back. Users may express an interest in something they see, seeking to interact with it. Information and interest may be conveyed by any number of means—typing, uploading, clicking, dragging, speaking, hovering, gesturing, or any number of behaviors. Paths through web space must be planned, and flowcharts are the designer's tool for defining those paths.

Flowcharts must show progress and the give-and-take of information between users and the web site. They illustrate sequential relationships between steps in a process, leading to a particular outcome, like a checkout process or setting up an automatic payment. As the web becomes more sophisticated, supporting a broader range of tasks, activities, and processes, flowcharts must evolve to communicate the complexity.

INTRODUCING FLOWCHARTS

This is a pretty simple flowchart, but it demonstrates many of the basics. Note that, like a site map, it is a series of boxes connected by lines. This flow describes the process of making a donation to NEADS, an organization that trains assistance dogs for the deaf and disabled (see sidebar). To make a donation, users of this site must go through a series of steps, represented by the boxes. As they complete each step, they proceed to the next one, indicated by the line. Flows uniquely show forks in the path, usually driven by choices users made earlier in the process.

Stripped down, flowcharts look somewhat like site maps, don't they? Boxes connected by lines. But there are crucial differences between these two artifacts:

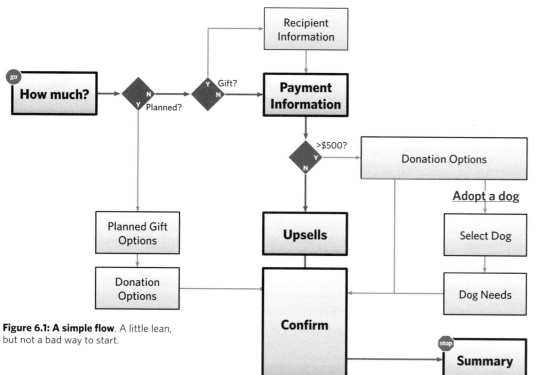

Figure 6.1: A simple flow. A little lean, but not a bad way to start.

Site Maps	Flowcharts
Represent hierarchical structures	Represent progression through time
Have a clear beginning, but no clear ending	Have a distinct beginning and ending
Illustrate how content categories relate to each other	Illustrate how users transact information with the web site or system

Table 6.1: Contrasting site maps and flowcharts, some basic distinctions.

Challenges

In trying to capture the exchange of information between user and site, you will face some difficult challenges preparing flowcharts:

- **Complexity**: Designers who have worked on large enterprise applications know that any piece of information supplied by users can trigger multiple processes, algorithms, and responses. Flows are useful for thinking through this complexity, but you may struggle to show the depth of some processes. On the other hand, flows that successfully capture the complexity of an experience may be illegible, burdened with too much information.
- **Completeness**: No matter how elegant, a flow can never truly represent reality. Designers must always leave something out because they are tasked with abstracting and generalizing an elaborate dance between people and web sites. As much as we'd like every process to be executed the same way every time, this just doesn't happen in the real world. Yet on most projects designers don't have an opportunity to spell out every scenario and every nuance. Usually, the range of nuanced scenarios is so great that it would be impossible.
- **Comprehensiveness**: Web applications grow more sophisticated every day. The simple give-and-take, transactional approach is useful for describing flowcharts, but oversimplifies what the web can do. A truly comprehensive flow shows how people accomplish a particular task in many different scenarios.

With an awareness of these challenges, you are now prepared to confront them. In some ways these three things are limitations of flows: There's only so much you can do in two dimensions. Flowcharts remain an effective tool for hashing out the transactional, interactive, and otherwise conversational aspects of user experiences. They open up a broader, more holistic view of the experience than individual screens can do. Yet they provide a more concrete representation of an experience than an abstract reference to "logging in" or "making a donation."

ABOUT THE EXAMPLES
Online Donations

The flows in this chapter describe the user experience of donating to a charitable organization. The organization mentioned in the examples is NEADS, based in Massachusetts. NEADS trains dogs to provide support and assistance for disabled and deaf people. A sentence from their web site sums up the mission simply:

These assistance dogs become an extension of their owners and bring security, freedom, independence, and relief from social isolation to their human partners.

Like most charitable organizations in the United States, NEADS thrives on donations, and the Internet has become a useful venue for promoting their work and soliciting contributions.

The diagrammed flows in this chapter show how NEADS might accept donations online. The specifics are, however, purely speculative products of my imagination, representing neither what NEADS does today, nor what they have planned (as far as I know). Their story, however, provides an interesting framework to explore the potential complexity of online transactions. And they have puppies!

For more information about NEADS (and to see pictures of puppies!), check out their web site at www.neads.org.

Layer 1: Must-Haves	Layer 2: More Detail	Layer 3: Further Context
Steps	Step distinctions	Triggers
Starting and ending points	Step details	Connections to other flows
Paths	Swimlanes and other groupings	User motivations
Decision points	Error paths	Screen identifiers
Name		Remaining questions

Table 6.2: The elements that make up a flowchart, in three layers.

Layer 1: Must-Haves

Other diagrams in this book follow a similar node-and-link format: shapes connected by lines. Flowcharts, on the other hand, must also show progress, directionality, and usually some kind of logic to direct users along the appropriate pathways.

Steps

The basic unit of measure in a flow is the step, a discrete part of the process that takes users closer to the objective. They are typically represented as rectangles.

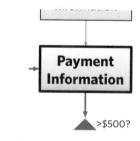

Figure 6.2: A step in a flow.

ANATOMY OF A FLOWCHART

A user experience flowchart must tell a story with the user as protagonist, and therefore must include a beginning, middle, and end. The middle shows all the paths the user may travel before accomplishing the task and reaching the end.

You might look at flowcharts, like all the diagrams in this book, as defined by three layers. The first layer includes all the essentials: Leaving one of these things out would likely change the diagram. Even the simplest flowcharts have everything in the first layer. The second and third layers contain additional information providing further detail and context. Whether to include them depends on your audience, your project, and your team.

Steps, for the most part, come in two flavors: solicit and collect, and respond and instruct. Solicit and collect steps ask users for information. This may be explicit, such as requesting payment information for a donation, in which a user must enter a credit card number and other data. Less-explicit information collection would be tracking user behaviors or watching for specific gestures. Generally speaking, when the system receives the information requested, users move onto the next step.

Once users supply information, they generally expect some kind of response. Respond and instruct steps in the flow show the consequence of the system reacting to the information supplied: validating a credit card number, showing weather for a given postal code, displaying detailed information about a selected item. Variations of this kind of step include clarification (asking users to refine their input) and instruction (helping users understand what to do next).

A flow can consist of any combination of these kinds of steps, and it is in this combination that we see the conversation emerge, the give-and-take between user and system to move closer to an objective.

Steps are represented as a shape (rectangle) with a label. Good labels for steps summarize in a couple words the purpose of the step: shipping information, login, search results. If you struggle to label your steps, give yourself more than a couple words, at least to get you started. Also consider using a verb-object arrangement, like "Collect Recipient Information" or "Change Settings."

Starting and ending points

A flow's first and last steps are pretty important: They show where users enter and exit the process and, because of that, they distinguish flows from other node-and-link diagrams. A flow represents a process, a transaction, and a transition from one state to another. Going through a flow, users go from not owning a book to owning a book. The starting and stopping points represent the head and tail of that arc and should clearly communicate that state-change.

Steps or Screens?

Throughout this chapter, I use *steps* and *screens* interchangeably, as if the basic unit of currency in a flow is either one. Reality is, per usual, more complex.

By *step* I mean any discrete activity that has its own beginning and ending and, upon completion, takes participants closer to the objective. "Get beans" is a straightforward step in the process of making coffee. It ends when the preparer has coffee beans. The complexity of the activity depends only on the circumstance. (For example, preparer's wife forgot to buy beans.) "Edit document" is also a step, but not necessarily in making coffee. As part of a content management flow, say, this step is much more complex than "get beans" and can be a process in and of itself.

A *screen* is a portion of the user experience, usually viewable in one scrollable browser window. In earlier conceptions of the web, it corresponded to a page, but this notion is increasingly antiquated. A screen, therefore, is what the user sees at any given moment in the context of your application. A modal dialog box appears overlaid on whatever the user was looking at prior to triggering the modal. It constitutes a screen because it is the focus of the user's attention.

Screens and steps may not line up one-to-one. A "step" in the process may consist of several screens. Alternatively, a screen may encompass several steps in the flow.

The latter becomes increasingly relevant as the notion of a single, discrete screen diminishes with the growth of the web's capabilities. Load a web address these days and you may never see that address change as more and more can be accomplished in a single "page."

I'm hard-pressed to articulate a single rule-of-thumb for what counts as a step. Better to err on the side of granularity. That is, nodes that represent smaller chunks are better. So, if you can break up "edit document" into review, annotate, deliver, discuss, and so on, so much the better.

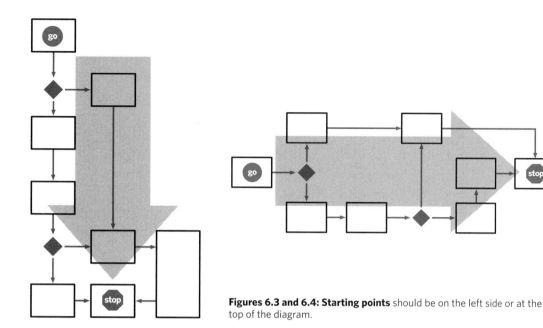

Figures 6.3 and 6.4: Starting points should be on the left side or at the top of the diagram.

Position (where the box appears on the page) and labeling (what you call the box) can visually distinguish starting and stopping points from other steps in the process:

- **Position**: Legible flows read from top to bottom and/or left to right. Bonus points go to flows that read from upper left to lower right. This puts starting points toward the left or toward the top and ending points at the opposite end. Some flows need to represent a hub-and-spoke experience: Users start at a central screen and jump to different areas to complete different aspects of the objective. In this case, positioning that starting step in the center of the diagram makes sense.
- **Labeling**: I like to highlight the starting and ending points beyond just the layout. This helps people read the flow because they know exactly where to start. These visual distinctions, as they jump off the page, can also help readers gauge the depth of the flow. Seeing how

many steps, paths, detours, and decisions there are between the beginning and the end can help set the tone for the flow's complexity. Figure 6.1 shows how the starting and ending steps have been embellished with icons for Go and Stop. These are green and red, respectively, which you would have seen, but we wanted to save you a couple bucks buying this book.

Flows may have more than one starting and ending point. Flows that support multiple groups of users, for example, may have separate starting points for each. In these cases, the diagram must make clear in what circumstances a person would start at one point rather than another.

The only other case where you may need to embellish your starting points is when a flow is a smaller process inside a larger one. Like the geographical map that points to some other location off the page, the flow's starting and ending points should indicate where users might have come from and where they will head next.

Paths

Most people are used to the convention of lines between shapes representing paths between steps. This common visualization says "Complete this step and move onto the next." What can make it difficult to understand is the overall layout of the flow. Paths constrain the layout, limiting where you can put boxes in relation to each other. Some basic guidelines for assembling flows:

Don't cross the streams: Paths that cross each other make the flow difficult to understand. Even if readers can parse your meaning, the overall impact of the flow is diminished when the basic story is not immediately clear. Instead, lay out your flow so that the paths don't need to cross.

Limit embellishment: Paths should be lines with arrowheads to show directionality. You can use other techniques to imply progress: I'm a big fan of tapering lines.

You can vary line weight, color, or style, but simplicity is paramount. If you must, use no more than two or three different styles of paths. Two is appropriate for distinguishing between the main path and secondary paths through the flow. A third line style may be used to show other transactions happening in the background—for example, data being deposited into a database.

Emphasize main structure: The paths should be laid out to get readers to focus on the primary structure. That structure may be a set of steps followed linearly to complete a simple task, or it may be a central hub of three or four screens from which the rest of the flow branches off. Either way, arrange the paths so that these structures jump out at readers. In looking at flows, readers want to understand where people start and how the task is resolved, and the main structure is crucial for this understanding.

Orthogonal lines vs. straight lines: In flowcharts, use orthogonal lines. They imply pathway connections rather than structural connections. Two steps are connected in a flow because they follow a sequence, not because they are related to each other in any other way: orthogonal lines communicate the nature of that relationship well.

Orthogonal lines also allow you to arrange steps and other nodes in the flow on a grid, which makes it easier to follow.

Flows may be labeled to show conditions or highlight changes in state, but we'll talk about these as part of layer 2.

Decision points

No process is free from conditions. Even the simplest processes require some "if…then" logic to determine which branch to follow. The sample flow tests for the condition, for example, of whether the donor is making a contribution on someone else's behalf, as a gift.

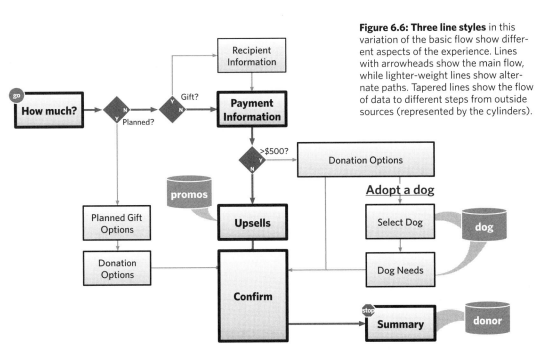

Figure 6.6: Three line styles in this variation of the basic flow show different aspects of the experience. Lines with arrowheads show the main flow, while lighter-weight lines show alternate paths. Tapered lines show the flow of data to different steps from outside sources (represented by the cylinders).

ORTHOGONAL: Meeting at right angles.

EXCEPTION
Breaking the Ghostbusters Rule

You may find yourself in a situation where you have no choice but to cross paths. This is not all that surprising: A flow attempts to represent complex processes in two dimensions. When a flow is so complex that it requires you to cross paths, use this as an opportunity to revisit the structure of the user experience itself and as an opportunity to revisit the documentation. Have you made the process too complex? Are there ways to simplify the experience? If not, you may want to look at the diagram itself, perhaps breaking it up into smaller segments. (See page 147 for more ideas on simplifying complex flows.)

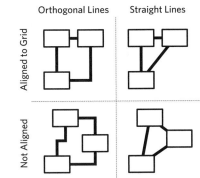

Figure 6.7: Connecting lines may be straight, with no angles, truly the shortest distance between the centers of the two shapes. They may be orthogonal, in which case they generally connect to a center point along one side of the shape. Shapes, for their part, may be aligned to a grid or not. This two-by-two shows all the variations.

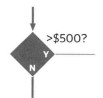

Figure 6.8: A decision point, expressed as a yes-or-no question, with each possible answer leading to a different path.

Figure 6.9: Stacking up the decision points in a revised version of the basic flow concentrates the logic in one area of the diagram.

These conditions are usually expressed as yes-no questions, like "Is the donation a gift?" The typical approach for representing a decision point, the diamond, is suited for branching flows based on the yes or no response.

Decision points don't usually explicitly represent elements in the interface exposed to the user. That is, the diamond that says "Gift?" next to it doesn't represent a dialog box in the interface that asks "Is your donation a gift on someone else's behalf." But decision points do describe conditions based on some user input. In the case of the sample flow, there is no indication of where users tell us whether the donation is a gift or not, but it is clear we need to collect that information somewhere.

Yes-no (or "binary") conditions are useful for thinking through the potential branching in a flow, but may not be ideal for communicating the user experience in a holistic way. Your use of decision points should be based on the purpose of the flow and your target audience. If it makes sense to represent conditions in this explicit, binary way, however, consider a couple guidelines:

Stack 'em up: I like lining up the decision points so that the branching logic is all focused in one place. This makes the story more explicit and can help facilitate understanding.

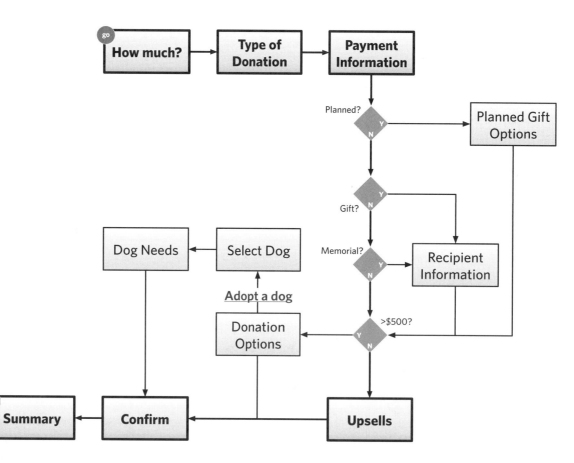

In this flow, we've addressed an additional requirement (letting users make a donation in memoriam) and recast the flow to line up all the decision points. The overall narration of the flow makes more sense: Determine type of flow, collect payment information, deal with potential exceptions, offer donation options, and then conclude.

Format decision points the same way: When you start playing with the decision points, you'll realize that you can phrase them to control whether a yes response or a no response yields the exception. For example, the condition determining whether the donation is large enough for giving users donation options may be expressed as either ">$500" or "<$500."

Throughout the flow, however, we have used yes responses to take users off the main process. Yes answers to "Gift?" and "Planned?" take users to additional screens to deal with those exceptions. Therefore, we formatted the "donation size" decision as ">$500," for which a yes answer yielded additional screens.

Some decisions can't be expressed in a word or two. Having the text of the decision float next to the diamond gives you room to articulate it however you see fit. Don't even try to fit labels inside the diamonds, even with short questions. The "Y/N" text works nicely in there anyway.

Beyond binary: Most logic can be expressed as one or more yes or no questions. The traditional diamond shape representing a decision point, however, has **three** spare vertices, right?

Although you don't need to take advantage of this, you don't need to limit your flow's logic to true/false. Decision points like this are relevant when:

- The flow is impacted by a **simple selection**: Users might select ground, two-day, or overnight shipping.

- The flow is impacted by three **possible situations**: Users might be logged in, not logged in, or recognized as previous users. (Web sites can use a cookie in the browser to capture whether users have been there before.)
- The flow branches based on a **quantity**: A search mechanism might show different interfaces based on how many results are returned.

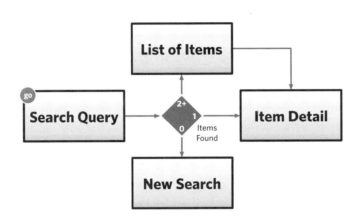

Figure 6.12: **Presenting quantity-based options**, this decision point escapes the constraints of binary yes-no logic.

Name

Finally, every flow should have a name. Names are crucial for every artifact—they give your readers a convenient way to refer to them. But a title for the flow should also summarize the objective described. To devise the name for the flow, try to answer the question, "What does this process let users accomplish?" Some good names include:

- New user registration
- Login
- Edit account preferences
- Make donation

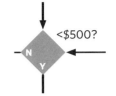

Figure 6.10: **Rephrasing the decision point** in this case has negligible impact on the readability of the flow, but watch for consistency and how the phrasing can affect the flow's layout.

Figure 6.11: **The diamond shape** permits flexible layout and offers several possibilities for a logical structure beyond true/false.

Layer 2: More Details

With the basic flow laid out, the primary opportunity to provide more detail is in the steps themselves. While layer 1 focused on simple distinctions (primary path versus secondary paths), elements in layer 2 describe more nuanced distinctions and details for each step.

Distinguishing steps

In a one-layer flow, every node looks like a rectangle. You might vary the weight and value of the rectangle to get readers to focus on the primary path, but most processes may be conveyed with this level of simplicity. You can amp up the distinctions if you find yourself dealing with multiple participants or processes that cross into different media. Flows can include external systems or make outcomes and milestones more explicit.

In all these cases, such conceptual distinctions require nothing more than simple visual distinctions.

Though flows are generally a series of steps to help users complete a task, there may be an implicit hierarchy in the steps. Changing the line-weight or color and shading of the rectangle, or the typography of its label, can help communicate this hierarchy. Such distinctions may be important to help your audience understand how to read the flow: where to focus their attention first. Here are some reasons you might distinguish steps:

- Some steps are more important, perhaps because they serve as a primary jumping-off point for several different flows.
- A flow may consist of one primary pathway and several secondary pathways.
- The flow may have required steps and optional steps.

WIREFRAME A sketch of a screen, showing its contents and structure, but lacking aesthetics or accurate layout. More on these in Chapter 7.

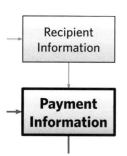

Figure 6.13: Some steps are more important than others, and this hierarchy should be reflected visually. Why? In this case the Payment Information screen is one everyone sees, whereas users see the Recipient Information screen only when they select the gift option.

Step details

Another natural evolution in your flowchart will be exploring what goes into each step. In elaborating on these details, you can liberate yourself from the tiny square to a larger area, in which to include various screen elements. There are four ways to provide further detail:

Functional notes: Before digging deeply into the details of each screen, I generally include some notes adjacent to the more important steps. These notes clarify the flow by offering insight on the things users will do in each step.

Notes should be brief, unstructured, and focused on describing behaviors and screen content that moves users through the flow.

Full screens: At the other extreme, you might dump a full screen rendering in the flow. There are various reasons why you might have full screen renderings on-hand:

- You've done some design work and are now stepping back to paint context.
- You're creating a flow of a competitive product.

So, if you've got screens, use 'em. These hybrid documents are sometimes called *wireflows*, combinations of wireframes and flowcharts. The utility of a wireflow over each of its genetic parents is indisputable: They solve deficiencies in each of the source documents.

Partial screens: Somewhere in between (but closer to "full screens") is to include crucial screen elements in each of the steps, but not in any particular layout. The rectangles contain a handful of fields or content elements, meant only to evoke the conversation between user and web site.

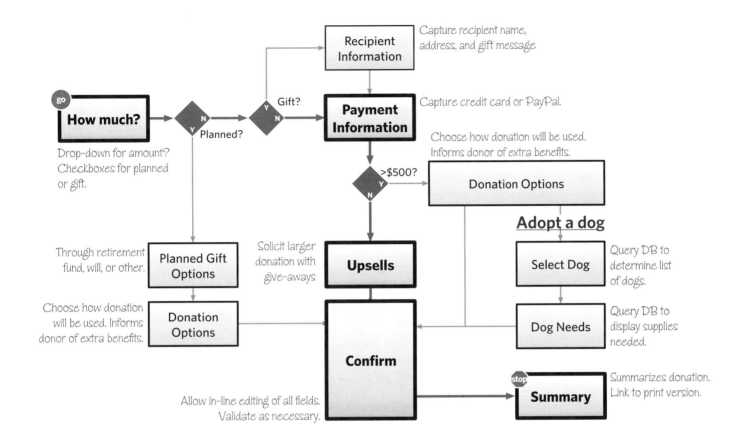

Figure 6.14: **Oh, man!** Someone wrote all over this flow. Darn handwriting typefaces.

[Flowchart annotations, reading top to bottom:]

Recipient Information — Capture recipient name, address, and gift message

Payment Information — Capture credit card or PayPal.

Donation Options — Choose how donation will be used. Informs donor of extra benefits.

How much? — Drop-down for amount? Checkboxes for planned or gift.

Planned? / Gift? / >$500?

Planned Gift Options — Through retirement fund, will, or other.

Donation Options — Choose how donation will be used. Informs donor of extra benefits.

Upsells — Solicit larger donation with give-aways

Select Dog — Query DB to determine list of dogs.

Dog Needs — Query DB to display supplies needed.

Adopt a dog

Confirm — Allow in-line editing of all fields. Validate as necessary.

Summary — Summarizes donation. Link to print version.

With this approach, the way to determine whether an element is important is whether it has an impact on the procession of the flow. For example, most of my partial screen flows sometimes do not include a submit button on the forms. Such an interaction is self-evident and doesn't contribute to the broad story.

Sketches or thumbnails: Another option is more abstract. In this approach screen elements aren't stated explicitly, but evoked through the use of geometry and labeling.

Again, circumstances driving the decision to use this approach may vary. It's useful, for example, if you're working with a preexisting design system and you can use these thumbnails to refer to well-understood page templates.

I once used thumbnails in a flow after I had already done some wireframing. In the situation, it wasn't necessary to show the detailed functionality of each screen, but I did want to show how all the screens stitched together in various usage scenarios. The design team had been looking at wireframes for weeks, and a simple thumbnail was all they needed to recall the screens.

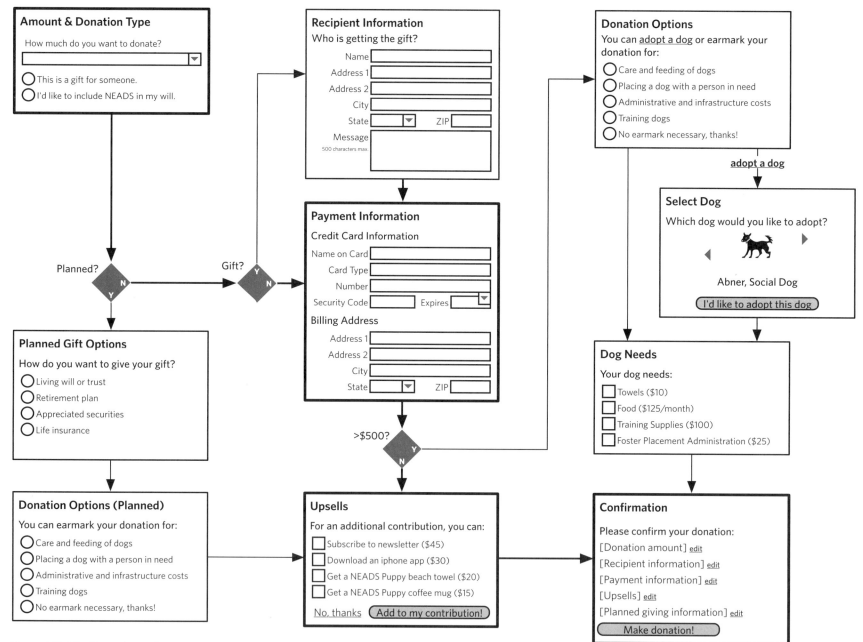

Figure 6.15: Wireflows, the terrifyingly beautiful love-child of flowcharts and wireframes, with partial screens. Each step in the flow shows only the essential elements of the screen.

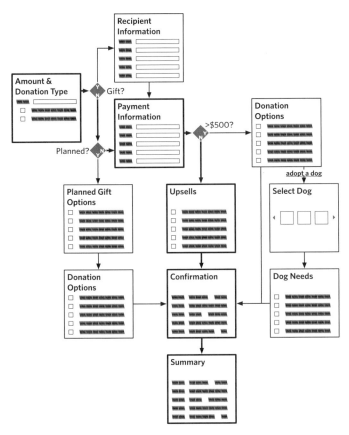

Figure 6.16: **Using thumbnails** instead of partial or full screens, this wire-flow evokes the structure and purpose of each page through symbolism rather than through actual content.

Path details

Paths do not afford as much opportunity to express details. Embellishing the lines too much can make the drawing difficult to understand. Also, with enough detail on a path, might as well make it another step, right? Still, there are two reasons I might add further detail to a path.

Triggers: A flow may branch based on a simple user action, like clicking a link. This branching is less about business rules and more about users making an explicit choice. In

these cases, a typical decision point is overkill. "Did user click 'add options link'?" makes perfect sense, but it is excessive for capturing the spirit of the interaction and may even bury the intent. You can label the line with text, formatted to look like a link, that shows what users need to click to trigger that path.

State changes: Sometimes steps have secondary consequences. Following a certain path may, for example, cause a cookie to be set in the user's browser. It may activate a particular indicator or change the status of a flag. All these secondary consequences are like mini-steps, but may be owned by someone (or something) other than the user. The purpose of the flow may not warrant a more in-depth visualization to capture these changes. (Designers who do require such detail in their flow might consider swimlanes, a technique discussed in the next section.)

Swimlanes and other groupings

Another way to elaborate on steps is to group them together. Steps may be grouped because they are performed by the same person. Perhaps a group of screens collectively represents a particular stage of the process—"macrosteps," as it were. The groupings may be more subtle: A screen may look different in different circumstances, and the group represents all the different "views" of the screen. I've used three different techniques for grouping screens:

Swimlanes: The elegance of swimlanes makes them an excellent tool for communicating the multiple roles involved in a process. Swimlanes form a backdrop for the flow as either broad rows or columns, with each row or column assigned to a different participant. Steps appear in the row or column of the participant who performs them. As paths cross into different lanes, the picture shows how several people work together to achieve the process's objective.

You can dedicate a column to the web site itself, showing tasks the system must perform in response to user

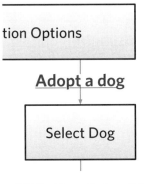

Figure 6.17: **Text formatted as a link or button on the path itself** can clearly indicate how users get to this part of the flow.

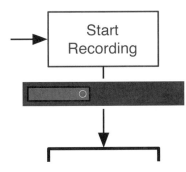

Figure 6.18: **State change.** OK, this isn't the donation flow any more. This is an excerpt from a flow describing the process for programming a DVR. It shows that when the DVR starts recording, an indicator light appears on the face of the physical device. The interface of the box goes through a state change.

actions. Until now, the "steps" reflect screens—or portions of screens—users interact with. Swimlanes afford designers the opportunity to make explicit online and offline processes.

Ultimately, however, the value of a swimlane diagram is to show how different people operate together. Frankly, I find them most valuable when trying to describe a business process (or how an existing process will benefit from a new participant: the web site). Typically, those processes come after users have interacted with the system in some way—how an order is fulfilled, for example.

Imagine NEADS creates a site that consolidates all the contributions people can make in one place. Users can donate money, time, or supplies all through one convenient form. (More on this later in the chapter.) This swimlane diagram shows what happens after a user has submitted a donation. Three different groups within NEADS would have to get involved:

Figure 6.19: Using swimlanes, this flow speculates about what happens when a donation is submitted to NEADS. It shows the business processes and the various parts of the organization involved.

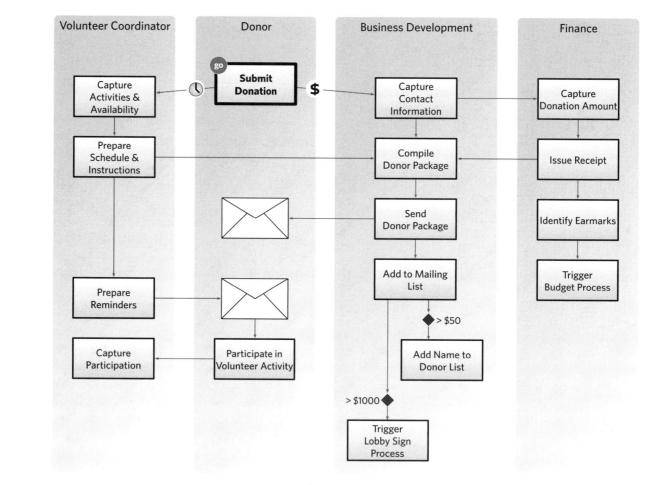

- Volunteer coordination, to deal with someone who wants to donate time
- Finance, to capture monetary donations
- Business development, which serves as "donation central," processing everything that comes in

Background fields: You can create backdrops for the steps in your flow, putting simple fields of color behind them to communicate a logical grouping. This approach is more appropriate for indicating that the collection of steps is related functionally in some way.

The donation flow, for example, might create four groups:

- Basic donation information
- Donation exceptions
- Donation options
- Finalization

It's worthwhile to create these groups if there's a need to speak of the flow in terms of these broader "macrosteps." Each macrostep might be documented separately, such that the main flow shows the overview, and a second, separate flow explores the details.

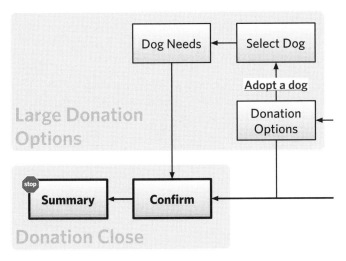

Figure 6.20: By labeling groups of steps in the donation flow, designers and team members have a way of referring to its four "macrosteps."

Styling the steps: Color and other style elements offer one approach to communicating logical groupings of screens. With a quick glance at a flow where boxes are color-coded, readers will immediately understand that similarly styled boxes are related to each other in some way. Color-coding can be challenging because the nature of those groups may not be readily apparent.

Typically, I use this approach when the differentiation between the steps is not essential to understanding the user's experience, but is useful from other perspectives, like:

- **Implementation perspective**: Some screens exist and need no modifications, some need extensive modifications, and some are new.
- **Slightly different implementation perspective**: Some screens use templates from the content management system and others do not.
- **Development perspective**: I want to strongly differentiate screens that appear in response to an error.
- **Architectural perspective**: There are two environments, and screens appear in one or the other—like before and after the user logs in.
- **Strategic perspective**: Some screens offer greater opportunities for selling ad space.
- **Usability perspective**: Screens throughout the flow may fall into different categories based on their objective or purpose.

Error scenarios

Error scenarios describe what happens to users when they do something that prevents them from completing the process. Perhaps they forget to enter information in a required field, for example, or they supply inconsistent information. You can document these on the main flow, showing what screens go through a validation process and the kinds of errors that might be caught. Error validation beyond simple field-level checks might warrant detailed flows of their own.

Flowcharts should visually distinguish between branching—taking users down different roads depending on the choices they make—and errors, which temporarily abort the flow. The kinds of decisions inherent in an error scenario may not need spelling out. In this sample flow, the validation routines are represented by a box and the possible errors as separate rectangles within it.

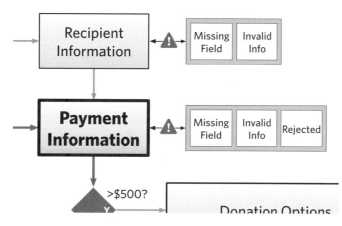

Figure 6.21: Validation errors, incorporated into this version of the flow, capture mistakes users might make during the course of completing the process.

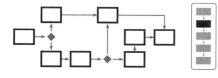

Figure 6.22: Establishing the overall flow at the beginning of the document allows you to set context. As you elaborate each step in the high-level flow with a more detailed diagram, incorporate a small version of the high-level flow to highlight where you are.

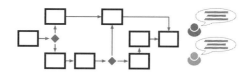

Figure 6.23: A quote from each relevant persona is the least you can do to ground your flowcharts. Make the characters' reactions honest but meaningful relative to their relationship to the flow. "I can't figure this out," isn't helpful. But, "I've donated to other organizations, and this process is confusing," is better.

Layer 3: Further Context

Your flow may contain an additional layer of information, showing how this user experience connects to other aspects of your project. Flows that are small segments of a larger experience or the output of substantive user research or the lead-in to a wireframing exercise all need connections to those documents.

Connections to other flows

The best way to simplify a complex flow is to break it down into smaller pieces. The "big" flow shows high-level steps. Each step should refer to a more detailed flow.

The detailed flow must show what came before and what comes after, putting more burden on the start and end points to communicate this additional context. Further, a mini version of the comprehensive flow, adjacent to the diagram showing the detailed process, helps set context.

User motivations

Nothing brings a flow to life more than injecting some insights from user research. The more you know about the people who will actually experience the flow, the more you can describe it in the context of usage.

You can express motivation on several levels, but with a complex flow it may be easiest to focus on the highest levels. Employ quotes (hopefully real, but fictitious with justification works, too) at the beginning of the flow to show why users might trigger it. A choice quote can help establish context and set readers' frame of mind when reviewing the flow.

Screen identifiers

If the steps in your flow correspond directly to wireframes, you can bridge the gap between them by assigning identifying codes—combinations of letters and numbers that uniquely identify the screen. By using these same codes on the pages of your document to describe the wireframes, readers will feel like all is right with the world.

Such universal harmony can come back and bite you on your karmic butt if any of the screens change. Add and remove steps here and there and your whole numbering scheme can be thrown off. You and your soul were warned.

Remaining questions

If you intend to solicit further discussion about the process the flowchart represents, you can embed questions about the flow in the document itself.

The flow might be, out of necessity, incomplete. It may include speculative decisions about the process, serving as a "strawman" to stimulate discussion. (Note design has perverted the definition of strawman. Normally, such an argument is a restatement of someone's position in such a way as to make it seem weaker.) Such an approach easily sets the agenda for conversations with stakeholders.

STRAWMAN A sample approach you put in front of the project team to generate conversation.

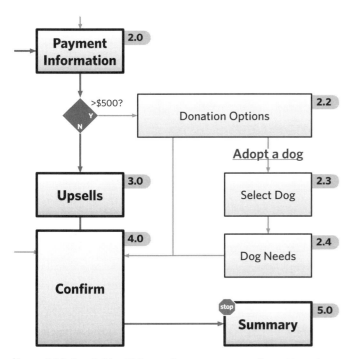

Figure 6.24: A code identifying each screen appears adjacent to each step in the flow. These handy codes will let you refer to the screens in other artifacts.

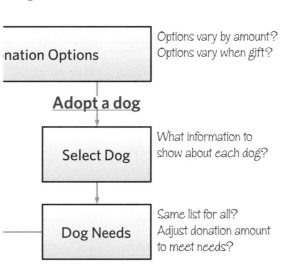

Figure 6.25: My job is really about asking questions. Asking the right questions of the right people can yield a wealth of information. Asking questions about specific design concepts can be even more powerful. Since design diagrams are meant to facilitate conversation, you might as well embed your questions right into the document.

Chris Fahey,
Founding Partner and User
Experience Director,
Behavior Design

CREATING FLOWCHARTS

When you are sitting down to begin a flowchart, where do you begin? You face some initial decisions about the content and format of your flow.

Basic Decisions for Flowcharts

The elements of a flow are pretty straightforward. Their simplicity and pre-existing conventions make them easy to understand yet offer a lot of flexibility in the overall presentation. Like any diagram, flows present countless opportunities to do too much—try to tell too big a story, show scenarios for too many users, or describe multiple levels of abstraction. Purpose, audience, and content all help keep flows focused.

What is the purpose?

A flow's purpose is not the task or user objective it shows. Sure, the purpose of a flow is to communicate such a story, but the role of the diagram in the project should drive its composition. Like any deliverable, a flowchart must in some way contribute to the progress of the project. If you can't describe how the flow moves the project forward, you probably shouldn't be doing the flow.

Like the other visualizations described in this book, flows have two primary purposes (see Table 6.3):

- **Capturing design decisions**: Flows can represent how a site will behave. That is, it can show the outcome of a creative process—one that sought to establish the best possible approach for supporting a particular task or set of tasks. In this case, the flow might go through multiple revisions as you refine the approach, clarify the design problem, and incorporate new ideas. At the tail end of such a process, the flow will provide context for subsequent design work.

- **Reflecting as-is understanding**: Flows might also be useful for describing how the site behaves currently. As such, this visualization can facilitate conversations about what it's not doing today that it needs to be doing. In short, flows describing as-is processes are tools for learning more about the design problem. In this case, the flow may take a broader view, describing not the site's current user experience, but the current business process that a new site must support. Describing a business process is another way of stating the design problem.

The purpose of creating the flow may be more specific.

Use your purpose to drive the decisions about the content and format of your flow. Every flow must have layer 1 elements, but elements on layers 2 and 3 are optional, and should be supported by how you intend to use the flow.

You should be able to draw a clear connection between the content in your flow and the flow's purpose. More details on the content decisions you should make in creating a flow appear in the upcoming section, "What does it show?"

Capturing Design	Reflecting As-Is
Getting buy-in from stakeholders on your approach	Ensuring you understand the business process before designing a web site to support it
Sharing a design concept with other members of the design team	Describing the baseline user experience so you can show the improvements in your design approach
Finalizing the user experience to transition into screen designs	
Evaluating different approaches before committing to a particular direction	Showing how a new feature or process will map into or align with existing features

Table 6.3: Zeroing in on a more specific purpose for your flowchart. Many of these purposes are similar to other design documents.

How does it fit into the process?

With respect to methodology, the key decision for a flow is whether it comes before or after screen designs. For the most part, you'll do a flowchart before you design screens: They provide an easy way to work out the overall structure and make it readily apparent what screens you need to design.

Project plans should allow for sufficient time to revise the flowchart. The mere act of documenting a process on paper (and showing it to others) can trigger new ideas of what the process should be. Even after you begin designing screens, you'll likely revisit your flow, adjusting the approach based on information that surfaced throughout the design process.

There are circumstances when you'll create a flowchart even long after you've been working on screen designs.

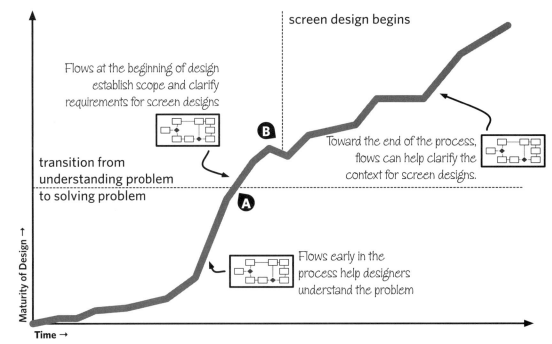

Figure 6.26: Your design efforts will make two key transitions. At (a) the design team switches from "understanding the problem" to "solving the problem." At (b) the design team switches from sketching out high-level concepts to digging into the weeds. Flows can play an important role before, during, or after either of these transitions.

In this case, the flow provides context after the fact. The flow isn't describing anything new—with the screens designed, the overall experience is already in place—but instead it's helping to explain it. This can help the people reviewing your screens understand how they all fit together.

Who is the audience?

Second only to purpose, the target audience for a flowchart drives its content and composition. Really, purpose and audience work together to influence the approach. Generally speaking, with respect to flows, different audiences have different priorities:

Business stakeholders	Does the flow adequately reflect and/or address the core business problem?
Other designers	Does the flow effectively communicate relative priorities, so I know how to design other aspects of the site?
Developers	Is the logic in the flow comprehensive, and does the flow illustrate every possible scenario?

Table 6.4: Different audiences have different priorities. This is what makes them different audiences, right?

The challenge will be dealing with multiple audiences. When there's no clear priority, I always focus on the developers. Get the logic and structure right, and the rest will follow.

What does it show?

The layer descriptions described earlier provide a detailed account of the kinds of information you might include in the flow. Steps, decision points, paths, and other elements represent a template, a collection of Lego bricks you can use to construct your flowcharts. There are less tangible decisions you need to make, too:

- **Scope**: A broad scope shows an end-to-end process, not just making the coffee but everything from growing the beans, to transporting them, to roasting them, to selling them. A narrow scope shows a thinner slice of the process. Your scope may already be defined based on the need.
- **Abstraction**: Even with the scope defined, you can talk about the steps in the process at varying levels of abstraction. In this case, abstraction represents the distance from tangible reality. It's the difference between describing people's thought processes for making donations and the actual screens they see and buttons they push. Early in the design project, you will create more abstract flows to help you understand the process the web site

will support. As the project progresses, your flows will become more concrete as you focus more on the specific screens and interactions.

- **Detail**: How much can you say about each step? Highly detailed steps are explicit about the kind of information collected or the kinds of tools used (in the case of a business process). Highly detailed steps can identify the exact information to be displayed back to the user. A flow's purpose should identify how much detail is required, implying, for example, how much you need to say about a step in order to meet the need.

With these decisions nailed down, the purpose defined, and the audience identified, you can make a list of the things you want to show in your flow. Sure, you're going to describe a process through steps, paths, and decision points, but every diagram is more interesting when it shows a contrast, when it tells a story with multiple layers. Will you show how different users use the flow differently? Will you show how the new user experience will seamlessly integrate multiple legacy systems? Will you draw a parallel between an online and an offline experience? Use this list to help plan your flow. Sketching some ideas first, you can see how you might wrap in some of your other elements. You can also prioritize your messages to avoid overburdening the visualization with communicating too much.

There are countless opportunities to say something more, but the best stories are meaningful because they reflect the context in which they're told.

How is it structured?

Designing the flow itself is beyond the scope of this book—the structure, pace, and sequence of your flow are up to you and the subjects of many books, articles, and workshops on interaction design. Caveat out of the way, two structures seem common enough to warrant further elaboration. These structures are patterns, really—typical approaches that provide reasonable starting points for thinking through a process.

In the words of Morpheus, this is going to feel a little weird.

Exclusive flow: In this kind of flow, users face one or more gates where each option takes them on a specific path. It's called exclusive because the paths are separate from each other: Taking the red pill means not taking the blue pill.

Visually, exclusive flows will have one or more decision points linked together to identify the appropriate path. In the illustration, there is a separate path for each kind of donation: gift, planned, in memoriam. What's distinctive is that each path ends at the same place, the next step in the process.

How do you know if you've got an exclusive process? If you can describe it as "users can do A or B, but not both," that's an exclusive path.

Inclusive flow: The other kind of flow is where users can select multiple options, and they'll follow the paths for all the options selected. It is inclusive, because it's possible for users to select all the paths. Figure 6.29 is an example.

Figure 6.29 describes a new experience for donating to NEADS. Users can elect to donate money, time, and/or supplies. Because they can do one, two, or all three of these things, the paths connect up to the next decision point. Selecting a financial donation does not preclude me from selecting a volunteer activity.

You're now leaving the Land of Logic—population, your headache. As visual thinkers, we might find it frustrating to delve into this kind of mind-numbing work of ORs and ANDs. Design, however, thrives on patterns, simple recipes for thinking through a design problem and providing a starting point for new approaches.

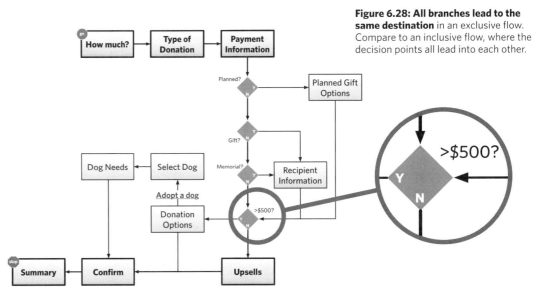

Figure 6.28: All branches lead to the same destination in an exclusive flow. Compare to an inclusive flow, where the decision points all lead into each other.

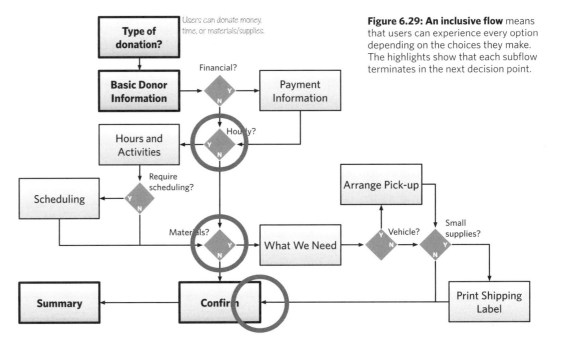

Figure 6.29: An inclusive flow means that users can experience every option depending on the choices they make. The highlights show that each subflow terminates in the next decision point.

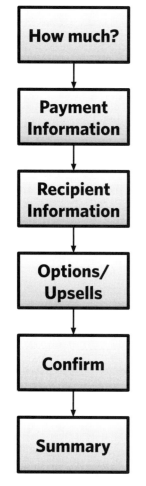

Figure 6.31: Nascent flow. When I bring the flow into a diagramming application, I start simple.

Tips for Fantastic Flowcharts

Having established the overall context—what for, for whom, and what to say—you can do several things to make sure your flows are easy to build and to understand.

Start with crucial landmarks

Every flow starts with a handful of boxes connected with lines. Do this with pen and paper to lay the groundwork, and let the flow start to take shape in your head. Crucial landmarks are the primary steps or screens in the process. This initial cut for me is always a series of half a dozen boxes running vertically or horizontally. Sketching these out first, I'll do subsequent passes on the flow, annotating the boxes or throwing in smaller boxes on either side.

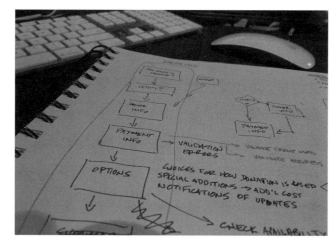

Figure 6.30: All my flows start like this. Just be sure to label everything. You don't want to come back to it later and forget what you were thinking. Sometimes I get so intrigued by a layout or approach I forget to label things, opening myself up to some cheeky remarks about the state of my neurons.

At some point, that first sketch becomes too difficult to read, it's got so much going on. Further iterations elaborate the flow, inserting the new steps and decision points. The shape of the flow is not yet formed in these early stages.

Your aim at this point is to get all the information down on paper: What are all the steps and decisions in this process?

Keep the layout simple

Transfer your sketches to your preferred illustration or diagramming application. Lay the steps and decision points out on a grid. This will make it easier to follow the logic and insert backdrops for grouping steps together.

Identify a visual language

Establish a consistent set of shapes and graphic conventions to use in your diagrams. Even if the subtlety of their meaning is lost on your readers, the consistency will facilitate understanding.

Fortunately, flowcharts have been around for a long time, and come with established conventions. Many people are familiar with these conventions, and they are as reasonable a starting point as any for constructing a flow. The simple geometry offers lots of opportunity to embellish the conventions, injecting your own style and meeting the needs of your diagram.

A visual language implies a grammar, a predictable set of rules to help people interpret your diagrams. The visual nuances identified earlier—line weight, color, shading, value, and typography—are powerful differentiators. Apply them in ways that illuminate the important distinctions in your flow:

- Primary path vs. secondary paths
- Standard steps vs. steps in error scenarios
- Existing screens vs. new screens
- User 1 vs. user 2
- User task vs. system task

Know what distinctions you want to make before defining your visual language and assign these graphical variations after you've identified them.

Simplify complex flows

Complexity comes from trying to do too much. When your flow starts to lose cohesion and when people don't "get it" just by looking at it, you need to simplify. First, however, you need to diagnose what's wrong (see Table 6.5).

Perhaps the best way to simplify a flow is to eliminate explicit decision points. Stop your sputtering. Not 10 pages ago, I was telling you that decision points were essential to a flow. Note that I said "explicit" decision points. There are ways to communicate the logic of a flow without a little diamond.

Here is that "exclusive" flow a bit tidied up. What I did:

- The flow now consists of a single stack of steps, which makes the process easier to follow.
- Decisions are not represented by explicit and discrete nodes, eliminating visual elements that might distract from understanding the story.

I had to cheat one thing. Note the thick black line in the middle of the flow. This is to account for two decisions that happen back-to-back: what kind of donation and the amount of the donation. With no intermediate step between them, I need a way to show that these decisions happen sequentially. This technique is actually something used in Activity Diagrams in Unified Modeling Language (UML), a collection of diagrams describing software engineering designs. In that convention, though, this technique (called a "fork") implies two paths running concurrently.

The Situation	The Problem	The Solution
Too many options or scenarios	You're trying to tell too many stories in a single diagram. How many tasks does your flow represent? If it's a single task, can it be further segmented into smaller tasks?	Create a single flow showing how all the smaller segments stitch together. Then create separate flowcharts for each segment. The smaller diagrams should be explicit about how they hook into the segments before and after.
Too long a timeline	The scale of the flow is too big: You're trying to show too much of the end-to-end.	Break the flow up into meaningful chapters.
Too many user groups	While everyone is working toward the same objective, they have competing tasks toward that end.	Focus on one or two user groups and show touch-points with the others.
Too many secondary or error paths	Your flow has substantive branches or detailed error scenarios that clutter the diagram.	Abbreviate secondary flows and errors, perhaps by highlighting a few key screens in a background box.

Table 6.5: Hardly a comprehensive list of all the things that can go wrong with a flow, but a good place to start.

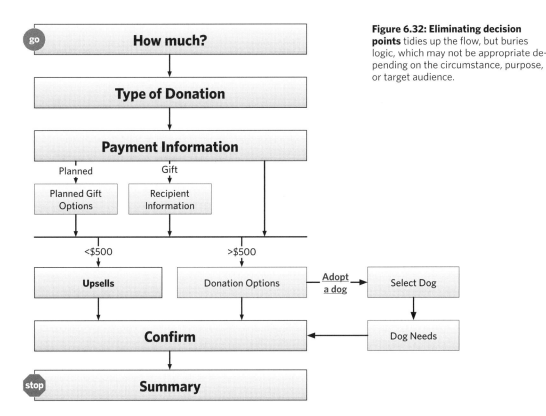

Figure 6.32: Eliminating decision points tidies up the flow, but buries logic, which may not be appropriate depending on the circumstance, purpose, or target audience.

Build frameworks

Web sites are looking and behaving less like a sequence of pages and more like applications you'd find on your desktop. Through this maturity, we find that typical point-A-to-point-B flows are insufficient for representing the range of features in our web applications. The screens making up our web applications can support more than one scenario at a time. A framework, therefore, is a network of screens that permit users to accomplish multiple tasks, or one task within the context of many scenarios.

With this approach, your flow might look more like a site map—a set of connected screens. What makes it more flowlike, in my mind, is:

- It represents a change of state (such as the transaction of a donation).
- It has a starting point and an ending point, though the framework may capture multiple starting and ending points.
- Its connections represent a progression through time, not through a hierarchy, taxonomy, or other series of categories.

Figure 6.33: A framework doesn't prescribe a particular starting point or ending point necessarily, but there remains a sense of progression. The relationships between the nodes aren't hierarchical in the sense of belonging. A screen that points to another screen isn't a larger category as it might be in a site map.

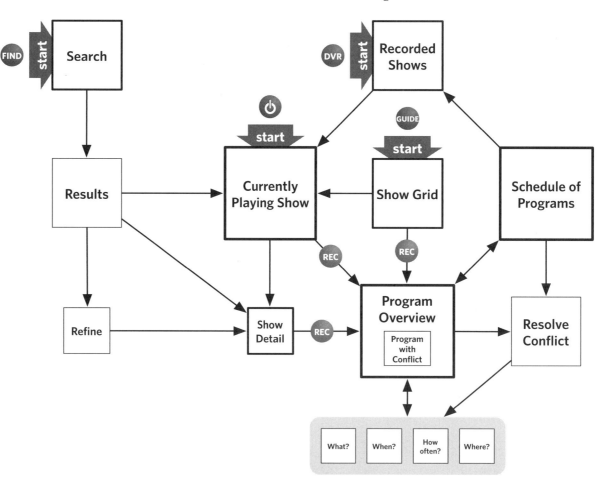

The donation flow isn't a good example for a framework. Though users may all have the same larger objective (helping the organization), the nuances in the flow are driven entirely by the user. Compare that to, for example, programming a DVR to record a television show. Although users control many of the settings, there are several other variables that can affect how they accomplish the task:

- Where and how they trigger the recording
- What else they have scheduled to record
- The nature of the show they want to record

Generalizing about this flow, processes that might lend themselves to a framework exhibit many of the same properties.

Processes that lend themselves to a framework...	For example...
Have multiple possible starting points for a single objective	When programming a DVR, users can initiate the process by browsing the show grid, conducting a search, or recording the show currently playing.
Focus on a single objective but can have multiple outcomes within that objective	A "program" can mean a show scheduled to record once, a show scheduled to record in episodes, or a show the user records right now.
Have variable inputs to the application logic depending on the starting point	Hitting "record" while watching the currently playing show yields specific data points (where, when, and what to record). Starting on the search doesn't provide as much information as a starting point for creating the program.
Usually follow a hub-and-spoke model, where the application is structured around a central screen or set of screens	I've structured the experience around two main screens: the one describing the program and the one with the schedule of shows to record. There are a number of secondary and tertiary screens, but those two constitute the central structure.

Table 6.6: A "framework" is a specialized kind of flow that works well for some processes. A framework relaxes some of the constraints of a flow. This table describes characteristics of a process that are better represented as a framework.

Telling the story with a framework can be complicated. You need to be able to show how the framework successfully supports all the possible scenarios. For most applications, this is impossible; no amount of research will be able to anticipate all the different situations the application will need to support. That said, research and stakeholder knowledge will be able to anticipate several crucial or frequent scenarios, and these are the ones you should show.

EXAMPLE
A Real-World Framework

As of this writing, I'm involved with a project for a major hardware manufacturer. We're designing an application to let people return defective hardware. The process needs to incorporate several variables:
- Type of return: Is the hardware under a service contract or under warranty?
- Service level: What type of service is available under the contract?
- Destination: Where is the part being shipped?
- Privileges: Who is ordering the return?
- Device: What hardware needs replacing?

And several more...

Instead of devising one flow to deal with each of the situations represented by these combinations of variables, the lead designer focused on creating a framework.

This framework represented all the major screens in the process: capturing the type of return, shipping information, and the device to be returned, among others. He created logical connections between these screens. The magic was showing how these screens worked together in different scenarios. For each scenario, he created a storyboard—a sequence of screens—showing how the framework supported the situation.

Level-Up Your Flowcharting Skills

Despite all your planning, you may still run into a few problems as you develop your flowchart. Here are some ideas about how to deal with them when they come up.

Capture all the details

The experience you are designing has a long way to go before it becomes a real web site. There will be, in other words, ample opportunity throughout your process to capture details that you miss at this stage. Still, wouldn't it be nice to know that you've identified the majority of little details that crop up?

Remember when you first conceived the flow? The whole thing didn't just pop into your head, ironed out and done. It was a gradual process, starting from a loose series of boxes that you elaborated over time. That elaboration included:

- Additional steps to capture additional information from users
- Single steps that you broke up into two or more steps
- Additional logic
- Branches to deal with unusual exceptions
- Branches to deal with users making errors
- Branches to deal with new features, introduced by stakeholders who forgot about them until they saw the first version of your flow
- Background system responses based on user input
- Sourcing the data
- Branches to deal with additional types of users
- And so much more.

Remember all those things? Right, so when you're looking for details, these are the kinds of things you're looking for. A couple techniques to help:

- **Get someone else to look at the flow**: Walk another designer through the diagram. Another pair of eyes may identify things you missed. More importantly, the act of narrating the flow to another person inevitably raises issues you hadn't thought about. The bonus is the new perspective your colleague brings. Bringing her experiences to bear on your work can raise issues you never thought about, and the ensuing dialog (always get her to clarify her feedback!) can also expose hidden issues.
- **Try to design the flow differently**: For almost every project I do, in the early stages I force myself to imagine a different approach. If I've zeroed-in on a linear flow, I force myself to imagine it using a hub-and-spoke model. If I've decided that users should complete the flow in a specific order, I try to create a flow in a different order. This pushes me to consider the flow from a new perspective and ask myself a new set of questions: Are these fields in the right place? Am I requesting the right information from users? Are there other errors they can commit here? The new perspective can help you ensure that you've addressed all the details on your original flow.

Express reality

Flows have a tendency to smooth over the natural variations between circumstances, giving the impression that every user will go through the same experience. Getting caught up in the details of the flow, you might start to see your users as automated repositories of information who simply spit out data when it's requested, rather than individuals who bring unique scenarios along with them. A few mitigation strategies:

- **Tie the flow to requirements**: Presuming that your flowchart is an incremental step in the design process after gathering requirements, you can make sure the flow addresses every requirement. While not perfect, such an approach does at least ensure you're internally consistent.

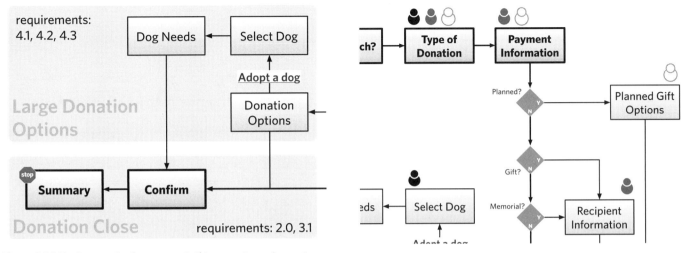

Figure 6.34: Replacement references — in this excerpt, requirements references (represented by the numbers) appear adjacent to the groups of steps. Apparently, the "Donation Close" macrostep addresses requirements 2.0 and 3.1.

- **Embed personas in the flow**: Putting users in the flow itself forces you to put yourself in their shoes. Represent them by including their avatars in the margin with some account of how well their needs are met by the flow. Alternatively, you can put small avatars next to steps or other parts of the flow, as in the illustration, to indicate whose needs they address.
- **Move on**: Don't get to the point where you're fretting about a flowchart. In most cases, the flow isn't the destination: it's a starting point. Use it to set the direction and frame up your initial ideas about the interaction, nothing more. Design is a process of continual refinement. Designers must use and discard tools like flows (and the other diagrams in this book), getting from them what's needed without expecting much more.

Figure 6.35: Steps in the flow are geared toward the needs of specific personas. Each persona is represented by a different shade of avatar.

Keep the document up to date

Flowcharts are hard to keep up to date because in the natural evolution of a design, they may be quickly left in the dust. Before worrying about how you'll keep your flowchart up to date, decide whether it's essential to do so. If you're using a flowchart to kick-start the design process, but not necessarily as system documentation, you may decide that going back and keeping it up to date after changing the flow may not be worthwhile.

Flowcharts that become part of system documentation (and there are still a few of us who need to do this) should be updated to reflect the most up-to-date experience in production. A couple of thoughts:

- **Keep it simple**: Highly elaborate flows are harder to update. You may be proud of how you layered in user needs with database calls and business rationale, but those details are not essential to system documentation. By all means, at the beginning of the project, tell the whole story. But keep a copy of the simple version of the flow, so you can work updates into that diagram.

- **Preserve the original**: The system documentation should include both the most up-to-date version and the original version of the diagram. Compromise happens, especially during the course of a technology project. The original may reflect a desired state while the design in production is a collection of compromises diminishing the user experience from the ideal.

PRESENTING FLOWCHARTS

Presenting flowcharts to team members and other project participants can be challenging because although they represent something concrete—the interaction between system and user—they do so in an abstract way. Your flow may not contain details like screen elements because you are focused on designing the interaction before the interface. At the same time, it's much easier to talk about the user experience with an interface in front of you; people tend

to provide better feedback on a wireframe or screen design. Building on the presentation framework from Diagram Basics (Chapter 2), you can adapt your meeting structure using the tips below.

Establish a Purpose for the Meeting

There are three main reasons to discuss flows: to evaluate the design of the user experience itself, to assess the experience in terms of technical feasibility, and to see if the organization can support the experience. In all three cases, you're trying to answer the question, "Will this work?"

Design feedback: Is this a good approach?

In one kind of meeting, your purpose is to validate the approach to the flow, where *approach* refers to the ordering of the screens, the logic behind the user experience, and the potential burden to the user. In a design review meeting, these will constitute your main messages:

- **Design principles**: The basic guidelines established at the beginning of a project which guide design decisions throughout the creative process. In this meeting, you should reiterate the main principles applied while creating the flow.
- **Requirements**: A definition of the design problem. For the purposes of this conversation, reviewing each and every requirement is unnecessary, but acknowledging a few key requirements that drove the design behind the flow is worthwhile.
- **User burden**: An assessment of how much effort users will need to make in completing the flow. Completely subjective, of course, but providing a sense of how much effort the flow will be can set the tone for the review, especially if the desire is to streamline the process.
- **Technical risks**: The implementation challenges introduced by the flow. In the context of this conversation, the purpose may be to help stakeholders understand the

When you need to...	Use a...	In which you...
Sensitize the team to the concept Get some initial validation on your direction Elaborate on the flow Get answers to some detailed questions	Design feedback meeting	Remind participants of the scenario Remind participants about the activities that came before, which should inform the design Explain how any prior work led you to some of your decisions Put the flow in the context of how people will use the system
Assess the implementation issues with your design	Technical feasibility meeting	Provide a quick overview of the flow Dig into the flow's complexities Describe assumptions or dependencies behind the flow
Make sure you're expressing the design problem correctly Assess the organization's readiness to support the flow	Operational validity meeting	Present a flowchart that describes a current situation or process Ask a lot of questions about what you got wrong and what's missing

Table 6.7: Choosing the right type of meeting for reviewing your flow.

associated risks. The following section describes a meeting whose purpose is to evaluate the implementation risks of the flow in greater detail with developers.

Technical feasibility: Will this work?

In this meeting, you're still validating the approach, but looking at it from the perspective of technical implementation. The development team needs to evaluate the requirements implied by your flows. They may look at the experience from several different angles, and have great suggestions on the design, too. In these kinds of meetings your messages are:

- **Underlying assumptions**: The flow may have some unwritten dependencies. (For example, the sample flows around donation assume that the underlying infrastructure can store certain pieces of information about users.) Developers will be able to suss these out, but it's helpful to bring them to the table.
- **Complex interactions**: Parts of the process that are especially complex, either from the user perspective (it puts a larger burden on users to successfully complete the process) or from the implementation perspective (lots of queries, database interactions, or decision points leading to potential pathways). Use these to frame the meeting, giving developers an opportunity to weigh in on how to overcome these implementation challenges.
- **What's new**: Developers, in my experience, are keenly focused on change—how a system is evolving. To that end, you should be able to explain the delta between what's in production today (or whatever the baseline is) and what you'd like to see happen.
- **What's important**: You should go into conversations with an understanding of priorities. In some circumstances, developing every flow exactly as designed is not feasible. So, know what the deal-breakers are, and work with the development team to make sure these can make it into the final product.

Operational validity: Is this right?

There are two kinds of conversations from an operational perspective, and the one you have depends on the kind of flow you created. One focuses on *alignment*: Does the flow accurately represent actual processes? The other conversation focuses on *impact*: How will the organization need to adapt to accommodate the flow?

Flows may place new burdens on the organization: There are implications to your design beyond how the user experiences the web site. Permitting users to submit a financial contribution and volunteer for an event simultaneously may force the organization to revisit how it processes these incoming donations. So, here are some themes you should emphasize during these meetings:

- **Discrepancies**: You may have knowingly departed from how things work today. Pointing these out should be a key theme in the conversation.
- **Operational burdens**: To the extent that you can predict what the organization needs to do in order to support the flow, you should point these out. (In the example flows, perhaps the volunteer coordination group is not prepared to handle incoming donations of time online.)
- **Sources**: You'll have ample time in the meeting to provide a rationale for your decisions, but be sure to reference your sources repeatedly. This isn't to implicate them in any wrongdoing (and you wouldn't do that anyway, right?) but instead to validate the accuracy of the content.

Adapt the Basic Meeting Structure

Because flows are little stories in and of themselves, it's easy to structure a meeting around them. By far the most effective meeting structure is the narrative form, in which you walk participants through the flow as if you were a user of the web site. There are a number of other approaches you can use, however, and you should select the structure that best suits your purpose and audience.

1. Establish context

To set the context for a conversation about flowcharts, describe situations—the scenarios addressed in the flows and the users participating in them. In this part of the conversation, you also establish the overarching theme and the design problem you were trying to solve. Be able to start the meeting with a single sentence or two that says what the flow is about:

- **The business objectives**: By organizing your presentation around a set of business objectives, you describe how a flow supports particular goals. For example, if one of the goals of the web design project is to double new customer registrations, you can show how the flow has been designed with this objective in mind.
- **The user need**: In conducting user research, you may have identified broad needs from the users, like "make

it easy to move from one function to the next" or "I need to share my information across different accounts." Whatever the need, you can show how the flow supports this. As with a business objective, making a user need the central theme of your presentation means you do not have to dig into every detail of the flow, but can instead simply point out the elements of the flow that support that need.

- **Technical requirements**: Far be it from me to advocate designing a system around technical requirements, but this message may be important to your stakeholders. In these cases, there is usually some overwhelming technical consideration that directly impacts the flow. Your theme might be something like, "The legacy system has a specific definition for a user account, so we designed the new flow to accommodate that definition." This isn't to say that the technical requirements drove the design. Instead, you're using the technical requirements to frame the conversation about the design.
- **Problem clarification**: Certain problems may seem intractable to clients or team members, and a flow can be an effective way to provide a solution or at least clarify the problem. For example, suppose your client says, "We have lots of disparate systems that all do the same kind of thing. Can we consolidate them?" Flowcharts can be a useful tool for documenting each system, or documenting what the systems have in common, and then structuring the conversation to determine an answer to the question.
- **Organizational implications**: Every online flow has some impact on the organization. As a new channel for sales, the flow impacts fulfillment and customer service. As a supplement to an internal business process—records management, for example—the online flow changes how people do business. You can use this impact as a central theme for educating people on the client side about how their jobs will be changing.

Figure 6.36: Donation flow, refer to this figure when reading Table 6.8.

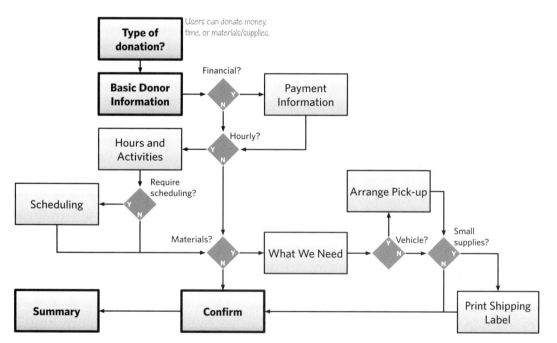

2. Describe visual conventions

Before diving into the details, make sure people know how to read a flowchart. I like emphasizing starting and ending points, and showing any visual techniques I might have used to highlight the main process.

If you've layered on additional information beyond steps, paths, and decision points, be sure to point out how you've captured this information—the icons and styles you might have used.

3. Highlight major design decisions

Describe the flow's main characteristics, including:

- **Interaction model**: Point out some of the distinguishing attributes of the interaction you used. Is this exclusive or inclusive? Is it a linear process with a few detours or is it highly branching? Is this a framework that allows for multiple functions? Is this a hub-and-spoke model or something more complex?
- **High-level process**: If you've chunked the steps into groups, used swimlanes, or identified a handful of steps as the primary path, these devices can help you describe the flow at a high level.

4. Offer rationale and identify constraints

Besides tying the design choices you made to the usual suspects (design principles, user research, industry standards, and so on), you can also reference any internal stakeholder interviews you conducted. This source is especially important if the flow depicts an internal process or a user experience for supporting an internal process.

For this theme...	I would introduce the flow...
User need	Users select the different ways they want to contribute to NEADS. Our research indicated they wanted to go to one place to do all their interactions with the organization. Let's say our "Dog Enthusiast" persona was doing a donation. She might have money, time, and supplies to donate. We collect basic contact information from her, then payment information. Since she's indicated she wants to volunteer time, we ask her to select activities that she'd like to do, plus times she's available. We then ask her what kinds of supplies she has to donate. Since she's just donating blankets, the system prints a shipping label. We confirm her donation and then provide a summary.
Business objective	You asked us to create a donation system that was flexible [that's a business objective!], such that it was efficient for users who just want to donate $25, and comprehensive for those who want to make a larger commitment. For users who just want to donate money, we don't make them click through lots of screens. For users who have more to give, we show them just the screens they need to complete their contribution.
Technical requirements	In creating the donation system, we started with the assumption that you were going to unite the various databases you have for your donors. We understood that the financial folks have a MySQL database storing most information about the donors. The volunteer people have an Excel file where they keep information about the various volunteers. The operations people don't have a formal database at all, just an archive of email. The purpose of this flow is to help with the consolidation of these data stores by putting a front-end on it.
Problem clarification	We put together a sample flow to illustrate the "best case" approach to how different areas of the organization might work together, presenting a "unified face." As NEADS interacts with different people about different things, it must be consistent, especially if one "customer" plays several different roles. Let's dig into this flow and see if it adequately describes the problems NEADS faces when interacting with customers.
Organizational implications	This flow describes how users will donate different things—time, money, or supplies—to NEADS, but as we walk through it I'd like us to think about what happens on the other end. We should be trying to answer the questions, is NEADS set up to handle incoming donations in this way? How does the organization need to adapt to handle a flow like this? We can then also look at the flow itself to see if it is the best approach for users.

Table 6.8: Different themes position the same flow in different ways, but still emphasize the same key points.

5. Point out details

Unlike some other artifacts, where describing the details entails pointing out a handful of important examples that illustrate key points, you can walk through a flow from beginning to end. The simplest approach is to first follow the "happy path," the primary pathway from beginning to end without any divergence:

- **To start**: Clarify the scenario before doing any walk-through, to help participants understand the circumstances in which users might face the flow.
- **For each step**: Describe the key points of information presented on that screen. Focus on the information that is displayed in response to user action or is essential for users to perform the next action.
- **For each decision point**: Elaborate on the decision and who's making it. Describe the criteria by which the decision is made.
- **To conclude**: Describe the disposition of the user at the end of the process—what has changed for them having gone through the flow. If any other artifacts have changed (for example, money has changed hands, databases have been updated, and so on), be sure to describe these changes-of-state as well.

You can use other approaches for walking through a flow:

When you need to...	Use a...	In which you...
Make sure the team members understand how people are going to experience the site	Narrative approach	Describe the flow as if you were actually using the site Be as specific as you can about the scenario and situation
Make sure your stakeholders are comfortable with the flow due to some overarching concern or issue	Thematic approach	Explain how the flow is structured around a central theme or two
Demonstrate comprehensiveness Account for multiple flows Take your description outside the context of usage or other themes	Inventory approach	Describe the range of flows you created Account for all the screens and logic in the flow

Table 6.9: Some approaches for walking through flows work better than others depending on the flow and the purpose of your meeting.

6. Communicate implications

Experience shows that the key metric stakeholders look at with flows is "How long will it take?" For better or worse, this is typically measured in clicks or number of screens. Most research shows that, in practice, users aren't as concerned with number of clicks as they are with confidence: They want to have confidence that they are getting to their objective.

So, for this portion of the conversation, besides the usual discussion of technical constraints and design challenges, you can also elaborate on:

- **Efficiency**: Describe how the flow is efficient for users, minimizing steps or pages, prioritizing interactions by dependency or importance to the user.
- **Additional requirements**: In constructing the flow, you may have identified additional requirements for the design.

Like other artifacts, flows communicate a design that will likely impact the organization's operations. Unlike other design decisions, however, the organizational impacts are pretty explicit in a flow. Use this portion of the conversation to hash out how the operations of the organization may need to evolve to support this new process.

7. Solicit feedback

When discussing a flow, I'm interested in these things:

- **Is the logic right?** Especially with complex flows, making the right decisions in the right order can be tricky. Putting decision points in the wrong order can yield unnecessarily complex flows, but they can also lead to flows that don't make sense to users or are not easy to implement. Getting the logic right means ensuring that the dependencies between steps don't lead to recursive pathways or dead ends. Since it's in the abstract, you may have to facilitate the conversation, speculating about what happens if you were to move a decision point earlier or later, and let stakeholders react to the change.

- **Are any steps missing?** Stakeholders may identify a range of things that are missing. Despite design trends, most organizations still deploy web sites with complex interactions that burden users with having to supply way too much information.
- **Is there a way to improve efficiency?** Cutting down the steps of the flow (as described in "Communicating implications") is a worthwhile objective. Use the flow to show how the project requirements demand a complex process. Suggest that expecting less commitment from users will yield better results. Take the opportunity to brainstorm about each step and decision point to identify ways to eliminate it or consolidate it with other steps.

8. Provide a framework for review

One of the things that make flows great is that they are meaningful to many disciplines on the project team. Take advantage of this multidisciplinary perspective when soliciting feedback:

- **Technologists and developers**: They have a strong logical bent and will have an intimate understanding of the underlying infrastructure. Ask them to identify any risks with how the process is structured or what the current technology platform will not successfully support.
- **Business stakeholders**: The best way to frame homework for the business stakeholders on your project team is to compare the flow to requirements. Business stakeholders heavily involved with the project will have an intimate understanding of the requirements. They can provide insight as to whether the flow misses any requirements or doesn't adequately address them.

Avoid Newbie Mistakes

There are two main obstacles to a flowchart meeting that could derail it. Your participants may struggle to picture the user experience because the flowchart is very abstract. The quality of feedback depends on participants' ability to envision the process, and if they can't do that, your meeting could end up being a waste of time. When they can envision the process, however, they may get lots of ideas you hadn't yet considered. You need to think on your feet to react to, accommodate, and potentially discourage ideas that fall outside of scope.

Make the abstract concrete

As concrete as the ideas in your flowchart may be, the document itself is an abstraction. Your meeting participants may not be able to offer constructive feedback because they can't picture the user experience. Knowing whether this is a risk or not depends on how well you know your clients. If you and your clients can comfortably have back-of-the-envelope kinds of brainstorming sessions, they may be prepared to deal with the abstraction of flowcharts.

If you don't know your client well enough to know whether the flows will be meaningless to them, it will become painfully obvious in the meeting. They might complain that they want to see screen designs or that they can't picture it. Worse yet, they might sit there, nodding and smiling as if they understand everything about the flow.

- **Build the flows together**: If you're quick on your feet, you can change your approach in the meeting, presenting the ideas in a different way. For example, it might be best to put the documents aside and build the flows progressively on a whiteboard. This way, the client can focus on one thing at a time, and ask questions along the way without the distraction of the documentation.

- **Shift focus**: On the other hand, you may realize that the clients' attitude suggests that you won't get anywhere in the current meeting. In that case, there's no harm in changing the focus of the meeting. There's no point in belaboring a document if it's not getting you or the project team what you need. Remove the document from the focus of the conversation and shift to a dialog or interview. Use the flow to remind yourself of the remaining questions or the key themes and design decisions. For the sample flow, you might extract these questions and design decisions:

Questions	Design Decisions
Should we give users predetermined amounts with an option to enter an amount of their choosing?	We broke up the process across several screens. Simple donations won't take any more than a few screens, just to collect contact information and payment information.
What if users want to donate "large supplies"? What instructions should we give them?	
Help me understand planned giving. What's involved? What information does the organization need?	We followed typical ecommerce best practices (like including a confirmation screen), but we feel like there may be opportunities to consolidate further.
What does the organization plan to do with donors who "adopt" a dog? How will you keep them apprised of the dog's progress?	
We haven't talked about issuing a receipt. Can you just email that, or do you need to do something via regular post?	The process will trigger "adopt-a-dog" options only if donors are providing more than $500.
Can you accept donations from international donors?	We would like to integrate planned giving with regular donations more closely, but need further input.
Can donors doing planned giving also "adopt a dog?"	

Table 6.10: Is the diagram distracting people in the meeting? Consider putting it aside and either asking some clarifying questions or describing some of the key design decisions you made.

- **Know for next time**: Knowing the disposition of your client may lead you to skip sharing the flows with them altogether—not a bad strategy if doing so would waste everyone's time. But, better to know this going into the

project. Carve some time out at early meetings to share some sample diagrams, things you've done in the past that might sensitize your client to what they should expect to see. At this stage, before you've invested any time in developing deliverables for the project, you can assess what's going to be most effective.

Stay flexible

Like many other design documents, flowcharts can open your team's eyes. Their exposure to the user experience, even in abstract form, can trigger ideas that did not occur to them earlier in the project process. Even though user flows are not very concrete, they may be more tangible and closer to the final product than anything that came before.

Imagine taking some of these sample flows into a meeting with the stakeholders at NEADS, the nonprofit organization soliciting donations online to support their assistance dog program. At the table are people from communications, from business development, from the volunteer coordinators, from the dog training group, and several others. Walk them through the flows, and the ideas are bound to fly.

> **"Let's do an iPhone app for donors, so they can get updates on the dog's training process."**

It wasn't something that came up during the requirements process, but it's something you need to accommodate.

> **"Let's let donors who sponsor an individual dog compete to see whose dog completes the training with a higher score."**

That was the business development guy. You wonder if the people in the dog training program appreciate putting a competitive spin on training. Still, perhaps introducing aspects of game design into the donor program could yield some interesting results.

"Let's set up Twitter accounts for individual dogs."

Eyebrows raise. And we need to get back on track…

These situations can be difficult because clients may not recognize why throwing new requirements into the mix at this stage can be risky. It can be difficult to see that a single new requirement can have a cascading effect, impacting other requirements and design efforts. In these cases, drawing the new requirements right on the flow can help demonstrate the associated risks. Of course, such an approach could backfire: proving that even the craziest ideas are feasible on some level.

USING AND APPLYING FLOWCHARTS

As just one of a series of possible deliverables, flowcharts should draw connections to other milestones in your project plan. They can reference work that came before. They can set you up for work that's to come. Here are just a few ideas of how flowcharts can be nestled comfortably inside the larger project structure.

Flowcharts for Planning

Planning a project requires understanding the big picture—the project's final destination and how your tasks and outputs contribute to it. A flow at the right level of abstraction (not too detailed) can provide that big picture, and therefore a backdrop for effective planning.

Flows used for planning should:

- **Avoid digging into too much detail on logic**: To use a flowchart for project planning, you need to layer in additional kinds of information, like milestones, phases, project teams, even cost.
- **Render the user experience to accommodate the project schedule**: Even if the long-term vision is to put all the donation options on a single page, showing this won't help envision the project plan.

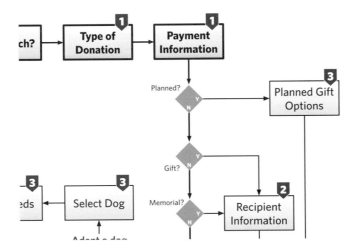

Figure 6.37: Yet another means for marking up steps, this time with mile-markers indicating in which phase the team will address the design. Implicit in this approach, perhaps, is a hierarchy of importance driven by engineering resources, budget, or something else.

Flowcharts and Wireframes

Earlier in this chapter, flows were elaborated to include screen designs. Called "wireflows," this approach combined the best of both deliverables. The flow describing interactivity and showing context united with the wireframes or screen designs to show the structure and purpose of each page.

Examples earlier in the chapter showed the boxes in flows replaced whole-hog with wireframes, screen designs, or thumbnails. But your wireflows could lean toward the other extreme as well, downplaying aspects of the flow and focusing more on the transitions between screens.

With less emphasis on the flow, the diagram looks more like a storyboard. The logic and multiple branches recede. The story is less about the overall picture and more about what users see in a particular circumstance, or in a particular transition. For the heck of it, let's see what a diagram with a more even distribution between "wire" and "flow" looks like.

FIDELITY How closely a wireframe or screen design resembles the final product.

With an even emphasis between the screen design and the flowchart, the diagram shows some branching with associated application logic, but it doesn't try to be comprehensive. It shows less detail on the screens, either by reducing the fidelity or shrinking the size of the screen. Both approaches sacrifice legibility in favor of showing more "flow."

Figure 6.38: Shifting the emphasis more to the screen designs means not necessarily increasing their fidelity or detail. Instead, in this case, it means stripping out some of the application logic and secondary pathways of the flow.

Figure 6.39 Some logic preserved. In this case, what happens when users provide a donation greater than $500. Still, some detail is missing from original flow, and we haven't completely subsumed the diagram with details about the screen contents.

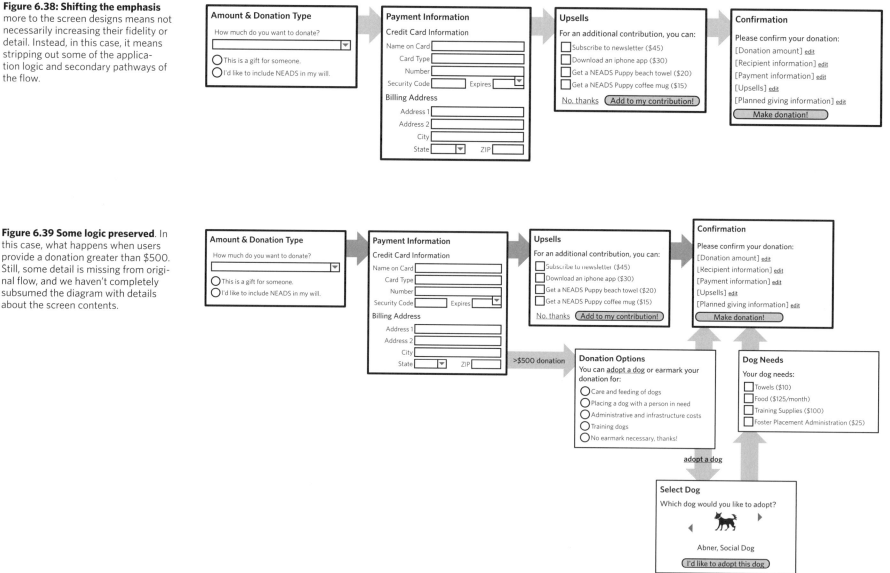

The Large Format Printer

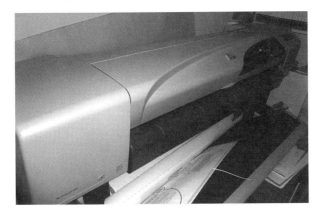

My pride and joy, the HP DesignJet 500.

A small confession: I love owning a large-format printer. Truth be told, my company owns it, which means I own half of it. (The yellow and red ink cartridges. Nathan got the black and cyan.) Knowing that I can print a poster any time I want makes me a little giddy.

Many of the compromises you have to make with wireflows fly out the window when you have more room on the page. You can size the screen designs to be legible and you can show the full range of logic in the flow.

Of course, the challenge with poster-sized deliverables is that they can be hard to work from. Poster deliverables aren't desk-friendly, so designers and developers who have downstream work have to walk back and forth between the poster and their computers.

That said, as a means for brainstorming with a group, posters have several advantages:

- Lots of room to write
- Posting it on a wall forces participants to stand up
- Posting it in a public place gets more people to look at it

*Chris Fahey,
Founding Partner and User
Experience Director,
Behavior Design*

ASK THE EXPERT

DB: *What do you think of wireflows?*

CF: *Love them. Wireflows are awesome for many reasons.*

- *They force the designer to make that correlation between actual product states and symbolic boxes-and-arrows in the flow. A wireflow makes it hard to fall into the trap of using the same kind of symbols and boxes for wildly different interaction elements, such as user actions, system actions, system states, external processes, data sources, and so on. By thinking hard about the screens and flows at the same time, the designer is forced to think about the transitions.*

- *Making wireflows for complex UIs is a great way to help slow down and loosen up the design process, delaying and even smoothing over the often-premature transition from high-level interaction design (flows) to page-level information and interface design (wireframes).*

- *You can whiteboard or sketch a high-level but still fairly comprehensive user experience using wireflows, without jumping all the way into making wireframes—but also without leaving mountains of design decisions vague and open for misinterpretation, which can often happen with traditional flows where a box usually contains only a few words describing the interface. If you kind of know what the interface represented by a flowchart box might look like, wireflows allow you to actually draw or sketch that interface right in the context of the flow.*

- *For mobile apps, or anything with a physically small interface, wireflows are hands-down the best way to completely document an interaction design. You need not create two different deliverables (flows and wireframes) at all.*

Flowcharts and Personas

One of the third-layer elements of flowcharts is user motivation. It can be useful to highlight what drives users to participate in the flow. You can "amp up" the presence of the user's thought process in your flow by combining it with personas.

This hybrid can ground your flows by articulating the relationship between the experience and the users. I call this technique "wireflow comics" because "wireflow graphic novels" was just too ambitious. In this case, persona avatars appear adjacent to each screen with a thought balloon expressing the user's reaction to the screen. These reactions can be:

- **Impressions**: A description, in the user's voice, of what they think they need to do on this screen based on its contents.

- **Expectations**: A description, in the user's voice, of what they think they need to do on the screen. This can be especially useful if the flow is meant to support an existing, well-entrenched business process.

Of course, this approach is very powerful if you use quotes from actual users. With that kind of data, you have an opportunity to demonstrate how the design addresses requirements, straight from the horse's mouth.

> *TIP*
> ## DesignComics.org
>
> I got the artwork for the persona from designcomics.org, a site developed by Martin Hardee. Besides people, the site includes free illustrations to create all kinds of comics for the purpose of design.

PERSONAS Artifacts that summarize user needs, behaviors, and objectives. (See Chapter 3.)

Figure 6.40: Combine a wireflow with personas and your design comes to life. Use the personas to flesh out the explanation of the experience. Or, as in this case, the personas can provide a commentary on what they're "seeing." In this way, this approach acts as a design tool, helping you think through all the nuances and details for the design. (Illustrations by ISD Group, available on DesignComics.org)

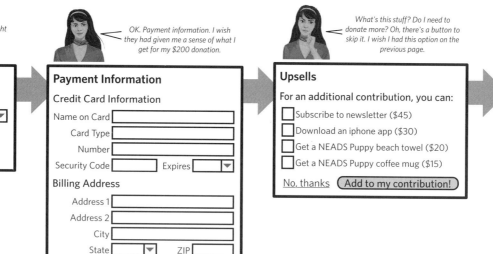
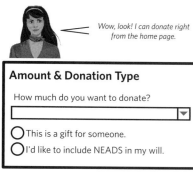

THE DEPTH OF PROCESS

In the early days of the web, sites were just repositories of information, where the structure of navigation was paramount. As the web evolves, permitting different types of interactions, designers and developers will need a means for planning and documenting these complex user experiences. Flowcharts will become increasingly important as web sites become more interactive.

But there's another aspect of the flowchart that makes it important to the design process. Internet technologies are playing an increasingly strategic role in business, becoming an essential plank in the customer communications and internal business operations platforms. Process documentation is crucial because the web changes the nature of interactions with customers and between colleagues. The flowchart allows us to get our heads around not just how people interact with the web site, but operations as a whole.

This isn't anything new—management consultants have been using flowcharts for decades to describe the internal operations of an organization. But with the web comes an unprecedented level of interaction between people and technology. The web does more than allow us to conduct business differently, it has changed the face of what business is. As work becomes increasingly focused on information, the kinds of interactions organizations have with their customers and the kinds of collaboration that take place between workers change dramatically. Workers are no longer cogs in a machine with specific tasks to accomplish, and customers are no longer held at arm's length with minimal impact on the organization and the work.

The web, as a business tool, forces us to think about how information moves in and out of the organization. The flowchart illustrates this experience.

The web, as a catalyst for change, forces us to rethink the roles of workers and customers, and their contributions to conducting business. In this case, the flowchart needs to operate at a higher level, showing how organizations must take advantage of and participate in these kinds of interactions. To accommodate this change, our notion of a flowchart must also change. Flow and process will never go away, but our assumption that flows are linear and made of discrete steps must change to recognize the evolution of business.

Moving to application design

Simple flows will remain useful for years to come. And by *simple* I mean diagrams conveying self-contained processes with a small number of steps and allowing users to accomplish single, discrete tasks. Even web sites that more closely resemble desktop applications will require such simple flows for a variety of tasks—authenticating users and setting preferences come to mind.

Web sites resembling desktop applications are becoming more prevalent. Some would argue that "desktop applications" are increasingly a thing of the past. Just as activities like banking and shopping and travel planning have moved online, so too are tasks related to word processing, spreadsheets, and countless business processes. This transition offers expansive opportunities for user experience designers: These applications can be highly interactive while networked, and blindingly responsive while being updated invisibly. Designers' tools must keep up. Can flows evolve to reflect the power now possible in online applications?

Flows will endure, because they are inherently flexible. They can be as abstract or as concrete as you need. They can be as rough or as formal as necessary. They can be produced in the space of an hour, and they're easy enough to understand to precipitate all kinds of useful conversations.

We will need to discover new formats that allow designers to communicate platforms—online ecosystems that support dozens or hundreds of tasks, like desktop applications today. These platforms also allow users to accomplish the same objective in numerous ways; for example, an online banking application accommodates severals ways of balancing a checkbook or different approaches for researching a home loan. And so flows won't show how users get from Point A to Point B, but instead how an informational ecosystem responds to a range of actions.

And yet organizations like NEADS will continue to use the web to collect donations. As much as these transactions can be commoditized, every organization has its own nuances, operational hiccups, and crazy marketing concepts. Putting these down on paper with rectangles, diamonds, and arrows will likely be the best way to communicate and elaborate on these ideas for years to come.

EXERCISES

Practicing flowcharts involves two things: learning about the details of a particular process and then translating that process to a user experience.

1. Create a flowchart for your morning routine, up through leaving your house. Incorporate the decisions you make about various inputs (like the day of the week or the weather).
2. Interview a friend or colleague about their work or hobbies. Identify a task and create a flow for a new application to support that task.
3. Transform the exclusive flow in Figure 6.28 into a wireflow, combining elements of the flowchart with actual screen designs. Decide how much of each screen you want to show. Decide how you want to lay out the flow and communicate logic with something less explicit than decision points.
4. Create a flow describing the experience for signing up to get an assistance dog. NEADS' current web site (www.neads.org) is pretty explicit about how the process works. Use your imagination to think of how they can use the web site to support this process. Your flowchart should use swimlanes to show the interaction between the customer (the person with the disability), the web site, and the organization.

Chapter 7

Wireframes

wī ər frāmz' (n.)

A simplified view of what content will appear on each screen of the final product, usually devoid of color, typographical styles, and images. Also known as schematics, blueprints.

WIREFRAMES AT-A-GLANCE

Wireframes describe the contents of a web page and their relative priorities. They help the project team envision the functionality and behavior of different screens, or more commonly, different screen templates. Most renditions of wireframes are laid out to look like web pages.

Purpose—What are wireframes for?

Wireframes can do lots of things. Ultimately, they help the project team establish the functionality, behaviors, and relative priorities of content on web pages. But in this way, they can kick-start the design process, help elaborate the functional details, and assess the feasibility of the design concept.

Audience—Who uses them?

In most web design cultures, if wireframes are used, they are touched by everyone on the project team. Developers use them to understand the site's functionality. Designers use them to drive the UI design process. Business stakeholders use them to validate requirements and ensure the design will meet objectives.

Scale—How much work are they?

Depending on how you use and implement them, wireframes can be a lot of work or very little. A small investment in wireframing standards, stencils, and tools can make even detailed wireframing very efficient. Ultimately, however, the time it takes to make a set of wireframes depends on how you use them in the design process. Using them only to instantiate a design concept can make them a relatively quick diagram to put together. Using them instead to drive detailed conversations about requirements and design can yield much longer timelines.

Context—Where do they fall in the process?

Ideally, wireframe creation begins somewhere between high-level structural work—like flowcharts or site maps—and screen designs.

Format—What do they look like?

Wireframes look like web pages devoid of most visual and graphic styling. Sometimes, you might prepare wireframes of portions of pages, rather than entire pages, in which case the wireframe will look like a slice of a user interface. Wireframes vary in their format from high-fidelity (looking a lot like a web page) to low-fidelity (looking like a bunch of rectangles).

Wireframes are diagrams based on the simple idea that you can best describe the interactions of screen-based products by removing any aspects of the design incidental to its behavior. A wireframe is, ostensibly, a simplified view of a screen, devoid of any aesthetic beyond the barest minimum and the most neutral. The aim is to focus the team's attention and encourage conversation about what a screen does, not what it looks like.

That's the theory, anyway.

In reality, wireframes remain one of the most controversial tools on your utility belt. Even within their narrow definition, there is a lot of wiggle room. Designers disagree on the role of wireframes in the design process, their ability to communicate behaviors, and what "barest minimum" aesthetic means. They disagree on how closely the wireframes need to align with actual screen layouts and how much real content a wireframe should show.

Now, a bit of advice from Dan the Dad, instead of Dan the Designer. Don't get baited into religious wars about wireframes or any design document. Know what you have available to you. Know the strengths and weaknesses of every tool. Apply the right tool for the job. Do you think Batman stopped carrying around grapple cables once he had a hang glider built into his cape? (Apparently, all my fatherly advice relies on comic book mythology.)

Anyone who tells you the design process is absolute doesn't make a living doing it.

INTRODUCING WIREFRAMES

Wireframes represent screens, or portions of them. They are meant to evoke what users will actually see when they use the web site. Figure 7.1 is a wireframe for the Zoo iPhone app.

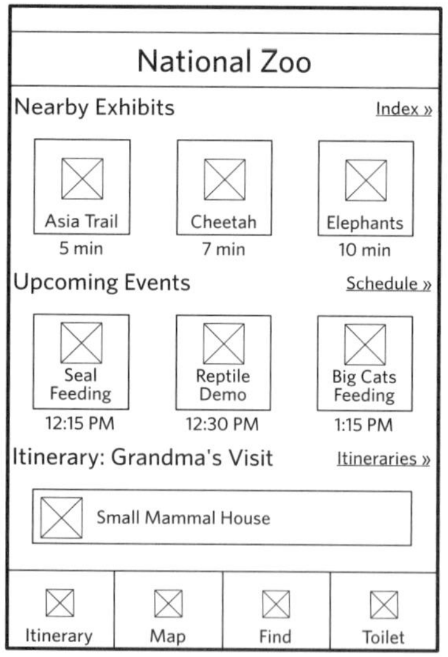

How is this different from the final design? Table 7.1 compares and contrasts the actual product with its wireframe.

Figure 7.1: A example of a wireframe for an iPhone screen.

Wireframe	Final Product
Devoid of color	Uses lots of color
Does not account for web-based typographic styles	Accounts for how type works online
Does not represent any particular aesthetic	Should evoke the Zoo's brand
Nonfunctional	Should do something when you interact with it
Displays placeholder content	Must support a range of actual content

Table 7.1: Comparison of wireframes and final product. Devoid of style, wireframes may seem like a waste of time. If you're not designing the page itself, what are you designing?

You might see these things as deficiencies, and some web designers think they render wireframes a useless tool.

If, to you, these deficiencies hamstring the design process you use, you can do things to overcome them. You can incorporate wireframes into a functional prototype, so that when users click on the buttons, something happens. You could use real content wherever possible, or create several versions of a wireframe to show how the design would support different content in different scenarios. You could use components for wireframes that more closely resemble the design standards for your web site, as in Figure 7.2.

But now let's talk about what wireframes can do:

- Provide a fast, easy way to present concepts for interfaces
- Focus on underlying logic, behavior, and functionality
- Enable rapid iteration on design concepts

Wireframes are a fast and relatively inexpensive tool for showing interface ideas. I can put together a deck of wireframes pretty quickly. At the very least, I can go from design idea to picture fast enough to keep pace with the creative process.

Since wireframes remove much of the aesthetic qualities of a design, they encourage the project team to talk about how a web site behaves, and everything that comes with that. Wireframes focus the team's attention on:

- The kinds of information displayed
- The range of functions available
- The relative priorities of the information and functions
- The rules for displaying certain kinds of information
- The effect of different scenarios on the display

ABOUT THE EXAMPLES

The Mobile Zoo

My family has become intimately familiar with The National Zoo in Washington, DC. Just a few stops away on the Metro and free to enter, it is an easy, inexpensive trip for us that doesn't have to soak up a whole day. It quickly became a favorite of my son's, and there are some months where we visit more than once.

The Zoo's newest exhibit is Asia Trail, which includes these adorable bears called sloth bears. In one visit to the Zoo last year, I recall standing in front of the sloth bear enclosure, pulling out my iPhone with the urge to learn more about them. Reaching for my phone has become a habit, and while I could have looked up sloth bear on Wikipedia, I knew I wanted more:

- The phone should know where I am in the zoo, and bring up the relevant exhibit right away.
- The information about the exhibit should tell me about these exact bears.
- The phone should tell me where I can go next or where (as is always the need) the nearest bathroom is.

The National Zoo iPhone app was born: in my head, anyway. The examples in this chapter have screens from this imaginary iPhone application. (Wireframing challenges remain consistent regardless of the size of the screen.) To demonstrate web page wireframes, however, I've also mocked up some concepts for a companion application on nationalzoo.si.edu.

Wireframes, despite their power, thrive only when supported by additional information. They tell a piece of a larger story, and must be incorporated into some vehicle for elaborating that tale. Like any thing representing something else, wireframes on their own leave room for interpretation. Combining them, the pictures, with words, closes this gap. This chapter focuses on the diagram itself, but toward the end of the chapter you'll see how to combine words with pictures.

Figure 7.2: Two buttons, both alike in dignity. A button in a wireframe can be plain, or it can start to inject elements to make it seem closer to the final design.

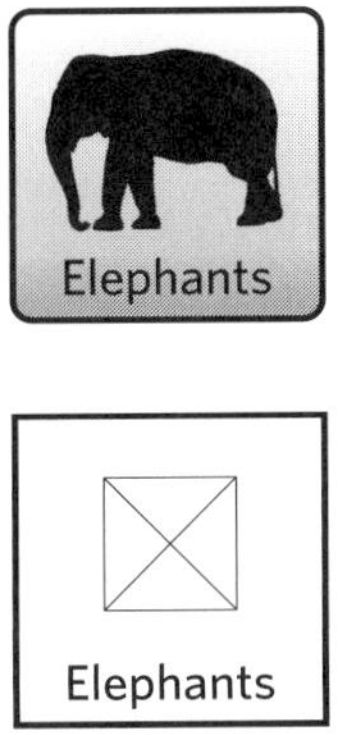

Challenges

To say that wireframes are the most controversial diagram in this book would be implying that the other diagrams are even remotely controversial. Wireframes are in a universe of controversy all their own.

The debate around the utility, value, and function of wireframes is healthy: It forces the design community to think deeply about the diagram and its role in the design process. Over the last couple of years, the case against wireframes has yielded two main criticisms. Unfortunately, these things are polar opposites, creating a tension that makes it difficult to determine the best wireframing approach.

Realism

Because much is sucked out of wireframes to keep them focused on what's important for their core purpose, the wireframes lack realism. Typically rendered in a vector-based drawing program (such as Visio, Illustrator, InDesign, or OmniGraffle), they don't reflect web-based layouts. A vector drawing can't emulate layout in a browser.

FRONT-END TECHNOLOGY
The HTML, CSS, and scripting that renders the user interface in a browser.

Wireframes, often flat drawings, don't effectively demonstrate interactivity. The web's modern front-end technologies allow a greater depth of interactivity in the browser itself, and a flat drawing can't show this. Carousels, in-page tabs, accordions, expanding panels, hovers, and other

devices are the mainstay of modern web UI design. (Wow, I feel old. "Kids, back when I was a web designer, we didn't have any of your fancy JavaScript tricks. AJAX? Luxury!")

Because wireframes usually describe templates, they need to demonstrate what real content will look like on the page. Logistical challenges aside (maybe the content hasn't been written) wireframes are mediocre at showing actual content.

Burden

To overcome wireframes' deficits, some designers try to push them closer to more realistic web pages. Wireframes at their heart answer two questions:

- What types of information go on the page?
- What are their relative priorities?

Presented with complementary words, wireframes can answer other questions about behaviors and business rules and states, but (in my mind) that's really a part of "what goes on the page."

But because wireframes look like real pages, we sometimes want them to answer other questions, like:

- What does real content look like on this screen?
- Where does the "fold" cut off this screen?
- What are the character counts for each field?
- How many pixels do we have for this image?
- Can we get these two things to line up?
- Can you round those corners?

Attempts to answer questions like these inside the wireframe will distract from the core purpose and misapprehend what a wireframe can do.

The real challenge of wireframes is knowing where their capabilities begin and end, and how much they can be burdened with addressing these concerns. This is not limited to the questions you just saw. As web design becomes more sophisticated, we will be confronted with new questions. Wireframes will not become obsolete (after all, a hand-drawn sketch is a wireframe), but we designers will need to assess whether they are capable of answering new questions.

ANATOMY OF A WIREFRAME

By understanding a wireframe outside the context of a laid-out web page, the central function of the diagram emerges: Wireframes describe the content of a web page and its relative priorities. In this case, "content" refers to anything users might see or interact with on the page.

These days, most wireframes represent templates, a framework for displaying similar kinds of information. When you design the product page of a web site, you're not designing a page for each and every product in the catalog. You're designing one template that might be used by all the products, or a reasonable percentage of the catalog.

The Zoo iPhone app has one template dedicated to exhibits, one for events, and another for animals. The Zoo has dozens of exhibits and events, and hundreds of animals, so these templates are reused to display this information.

Throughout this chapter, I'm assuming you're designing templates. I'm assuming that your pages are containers meant to hold content of a particular type. And this is where the anatomy of a wireframe begins: simple descriptions of what goes on the page.

Layer 1: Rectangles, just rectangles	Layer 2: Rectangles with form	Layer 3: Beyond rectangles
Content areas	Layout	Grids
Priorities and distinctions	Content for labeling and structure	Prioritization styles
Screen identifier	Sample content	Aesthetic elements
	Functional elements	

Table 7.2: Three layers, increasing in complexity and challenges.

Layer 1: Rectangles, Just Rectangles

Wireframes start with rectangles, carving out areas of the page or screen to dedicate them to different kinds of content. The most basic wireframe is a rectangle (the page) chopped up into smaller rectangles.

Content areas

A content area is a region of a page with a single, discrete purpose. You should be able to state the function of a content area in a sentence, maybe two, but no more.

- This area of the page lists recent headlines.
- This area of the page is where users provide their contact information.
- This area of the page identifies the purpose of the page, letting users know where they are on the site.
- This area of the page allows users to see what else is on the web site.

It's rare for a web page to contain only one content area. So the basic wireframe diagram will consist of several connected rectangles. Not all rectangles are created equal. There are several types of content areas you'll work with:

- **Structural areas**: Even though your site may use multiple templates, there will be some common elements across templates. On many sites, the header and footer remain consistent, regardless of what template you're looking at. Areas common across all templates generally establish an overall structure for the site.
- **Reusable or shared areas**: Even if a content area isn't repeated on every template, you may have some content areas that you want to use on more than one template. The exact content may vary from page to page, but the content area structures the information in the same way. A list of headlines is a good example, or a carousel at the top of some pages.

- **Unique areas**: Not every template will simply mix and match shared content areas—that would make for a boring site. Individual templates have a distinct purpose, and must display unique content to serve that purpose. In our Zoo iPhone app, the animal template shows a large photograph and "animal stats," content areas not used elsewhere in the app.

Rectangles should be labeled, to indicate their purpose. Structural areas will have unique names, like "global navigation" or "header." You can't have multiple "header" areas on a single page. Likewise, when you see "header" on different templates, you imply that the area appears the same on both, with perhaps only minor variations.

Reusable areas also have names to describe their purpose, but these might be repeated (a list of headlines may be used multiple times on a single template, for example) and further qualified to clarify the exact content appearing in that area.

The Zoo's web site has (in my imagination) a companion application to the iPhone app. On the web, you can download different itineraries to your phone. The site provides lists of itineraries that you can dig into and choose from. The starting page for this part of the web site actually has two lists of itineraries: one that displays the newest ones and one that displays the most popular. If I call that shared area "itinerary list," I can create a wireframe like the one in Figure 7.3.

Priorities and distinctions

Besides showing the content areas on a page, a wireframe has another job—to show the relative priorities of those content areas. One way to understand this is to think further down the design process, as the team is responsible for transforming wireframes into real screen layouts. The most important direction a designer needs in thinking about

Header
Navigation
Page Title

Itinerary Picker	Itinerary List: Popular
Itinerary List: Recommended	Itinerary List: Saved
	Custom Itinerary

Footer

the layout is "What's the most important information on the page?"

When designers create wireframes that evoke a particular layout for the page, they are really trying to communicate priority.

The simplest way to show this is to list the content areas in order, with the most important one first. You might not actually deliver wireframes to your client that are just lists of content areas, but such lists are useful exercises for planning wireframes.

You might be asking yourself, "Should I put the header first?" The header is at the top of the page, but is it the most important thing on the page? I've done it both ways,

listing the header lower in the page priorities to encourage the designers to truly think of the first item in the list as the main focal point for the page. I've also listed the header first to remind them that they have structural areas that are immutable.

On some projects, I use a format called Page Description Diagrams. This approach shows a visual ranking of content areas, but isn't quite as absolute as a single list.

Another way to address this is to define page regions—common areas of the page. Figure 7.4 shows page regions for the Zoo's itinerary app. With those regions defined, I accomplish two things:

• I communicate to the design team that the basic structure of the page has four basic areas: a header to identify the page, a main body to hold the essential content, a sidebar to provide supporting content, and a footer to anchor the page. Though described in a graphic way, they're really conceptual.

• I can prioritize content in each of these areas. Thus, the itinerary picker is the most important content area in the body region.

There are other pieces of information you might want to communicate about the content areas:

• **Their function**: Navigation, list, content, promotion, and so on

• **How they relate to web site operations**: Manual versus automatic content management, where the content is sourced from

• **Any issues related to project logistics**: For example, distinguishing content areas based on the phase in the project in which they'll be designed

At this level, showing only content areas without much detail, there's really only one way to distinguish them visually: through color. Assign each type of content area a different color. You can use these designations throughout the document to elaborate on the structure and function of the content areas. If purple always means navigation, it means readers of the documentation know that whenever they see purple, the document is describing navigation.

Screen identifier

Before leaving the barest essentials of wireframes, I'd like to talk about how to label the screen itself. Every template should have a name (because it represents a unique configuration of content areas). I like naming them based on the primary purpose of the page or the primary type of content on the page.

A sophisticated site may require that screens have further identification:

- **Variations**: A single function (like displaying product or animal information) may actually require multiple templates. The iPhone app, for example, may use two different templates for displaying exhibits—indoor exhibits and outdoor ones. The exhibit template has two variations, which may amount to some relatively subtle differences, but enough to warrant the distinction.
- **Codes**: For sites with more than a dozen screens, the design team will benefit from attaching codes to screens. These codes provide a convenient shorthand for referring to the screens, and provide a built-in approach for identifying variations.

Layer 2: Rectangles with Form

If you think you can't get away with a straight list of labeled rectangles for your wireframes, the second layer of elements forms up the page into something more recognizable. Tread into this layer with caution: making the structure of a page look like an actual page comes with risks.

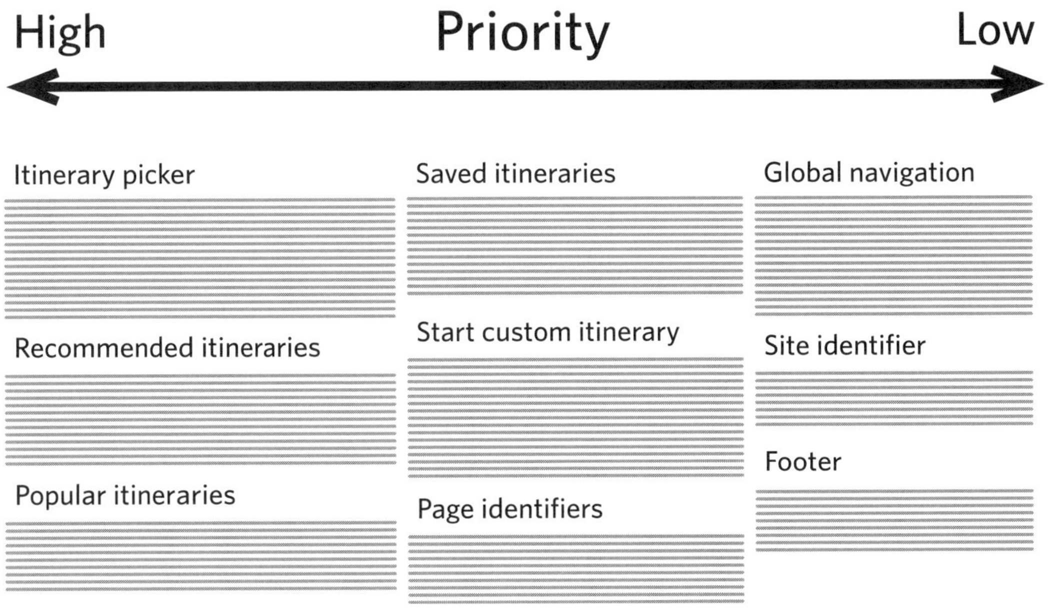

High　　　　　　Priority　　　　　　Low

Itinerary picker

Saved itineraries

Global navigation

Recommended itineraries

Start custom itinerary

Site identifier

Popular itineraries

Page identifiers

Footer

Figure 7.4: A page description diagram groups content areas into high, medium, and low importance. With such an approach, you can avoid having to put together an absolute list of most important to least important.

Layout

When you give the rectangles of a wireframe a layout to resemble a web page, the wireframe communicates more than just relative priority. The wireframe evokes what a web page could look like. The project team, looking at a wireframe with layout, still needs to make the leap from vector drawing to browser rendering.

Laying out a page means considering the height and width of the rectangles, because priority is communicated not just by placement on the page, but how much of the page the content area occupies.

Figure 7.5: Using the dimensions of
a rectangle to communicate priority.
The bigger the content area, the more
important it is, even if it is not very high
up on the page.

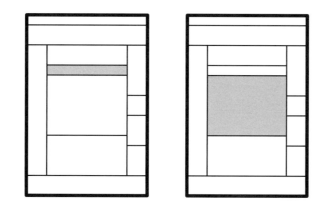

Working with Design Systems

Part of our work at EightShapes is giving design teams a set of wireframing tools that emulates their design system. By "design system" I mean the existing set of standard components they use to compose web pages. Such a system is typical of large, well-established web sites. Because these components have withstood the test of time and are flexible enough to be used in a variety of situations, the design teams can translate them into relatively accurate wireframe renderings. These wireframing components may be more accurate from a layout perspective because they're derived from existing, already-rendered HTML components. Wireframes created from scratch (new additions to the design system, for example) will not have that luxury.

A layout gives the project team better insight into your vision for the relative priorities of information on the page. It establishes a starting point for the design team to explore.

Don't put too much stock in a wireframe layout, though. Designing for the web means accounting for numerous other pressures (browser rendering issues, HTML standards, content of various lengths and formats, accessibility compliance, graceful degradation on the front end, and the list goes on). What might look good in the wireframe may not translate well to the web.

Content for labeling, structure, and instruction

Some of the words and pictures on a screen are not for consumption. They are, instead, wayfinding devices, helping users understand where they are on the site. Beyond navigation, they set expectations about the experience and provide instruction on how to use particular features.

In some instances a wayfinding label may vary depending on the kind of content displayed in the content area. For example, itinerary list is a content area used throughout the web site, but it comes with some business rules to define

which itineraries are listed. The header for this content area can't simply say "Itinerary List" everywhere it appears. Instead, the structural content is variable depending on the context.

You can use color to illustrate the purpose of specific kinds of text, specifically error messaging. Typically, this information is highlighted with red, an effective color for calling the user's attention to something important. (Red, certainly in Western culture, has come to evoke "danger.") Note that this color isn't meant to be ported directly into the final designs—you're not making an aesthetic decision. The color is merely meant to convey the function of the text.

Sample content

Incorporating real content into a wireframe is feasible, just so long as you do it in a way to support the purpose of the wireframe. Dropping a 1,000-word essay into a wireframe to show what the page will look like with a long article does the wireframe a disservice because (a) it assumes the wireframe does a good job of approximating the layout of the page, and (b) it undermines the purpose of the wireframe. (Dropping a 1,000-word essay in an HTML template, on the other hand, makes much more sense.)

This isn't to say that wireframes should be devoid of real content. In fact, the more real, the better. For most people on the project team, assessing the efficacy of a screen depends on their seeing real content. For example, people may be able to make the cognitive leap from seeing a page filled with "Title Goes Here" to the kinds of content that will appear there. On the other hand, seeing real content eliminates the need for them to imagine the experience.

If you're short of real content, you have several other options, described in Table 7.3.

Technique	Good for...	Not so good for...	Address
Dummy content Invented content that looks like actual content	Content with obvious formats (like addresses or phone numbers) such that readers recognize the purpose of the content without getting sucked into the content itself.	Copy or tabular data; it's easy to mistake these for actual data and sidetrack the conversation. To fill a table, you may need to repeat dummy content, or invent lots of different dummy content—both of which are distracting and time-consuming to the reader.	John Doe, 123 Main Street, Anytown, ST 98765
Symbolic content Strings of repeated letters or numbers to represent different fields; for example, 999-999-9999 for a phone number and MM/DD/CCYY for a date.	Tabular data, dates, information with recognizable formats (like phone numbers)	Prose, unless you want your entire wireframe to look like it's been redacted by the CIA	XXXXXXXXX XXXXXXXX, XXXXXXXX XXXXXXXXXXXXXX, XXXXXXX, XX, 99999
Labels Usually enclosed in brackets, a label provides a description for a field of content. Labels can include additional information about the field, like size and type. For example, [firstname—30] might represent a field that contains someone's first name and is limited to 30 characters.	Pretty much anything	Labels are nice and flexible and should be able to cover most sample content needs. The downside is that they may be difficult for a nontechnical person to interpret.	[FirstName] [LastName], [StreetNumber] [StreetName], [City] [State] [ZIP]
Greek/Latin Borrowed from graphic design, prose can be faked by using strings of pseudo-Latin text. (Some people call this "greeked" text and some people call it "latin," while others call it "lorem ipsum" or "lipsum" after the Latin words that typically come first.)	Anything that's typically rendered in more-or-less full sentences.	Lipsum in tabular data or to represent an address just looks silly.	Lorem Ipsum, dolorsit amet lorem, consectecur, st, 99999

Table 7.3: Representing data in wireframes can be challenging, especially with so many options available. Also, this is the only content in this chapter I took from the first edition whole-hog.

STATES The display variations of a particular interface element based on different conditions.

Once you start incorporating sample content into the wireframes, you can lose the borders around the content areas. With content, real or otherwise, the areas of the page become defined, even without a distinct rectangle shape.

There's one other way to represent content in wireframes—I give you the squiggly line (Figure 7.6).

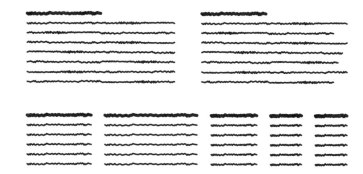

Figure 7.6: Representing blocks of content using squiggly lines inside wireframes. Depending on the scale of the wireframe, they can be used for most content so long as they're sufficiently distinguished from other lines in the drawing.

Squiggly lines are good for rough sketches. The weight of the line can give a good sense of the weight of the content. Squiggly lines, however, provide the least amount of context or direction. Unless accompanied by detailed annotations, the lines will be completely meaningless.

Functional elements

Wireframes can incorporate another kind of "content," interactive elements like form widgets. Showing these interface devices (Figure 7.8) evokes the range of behaviors exhibited by the screen, and establishes the range of inputs needed from users.

Like content, functional elements have varying levels of fidelity, and a reasonable starting point is the simplest rendition that evokes the widget.

While remaining aesthetically neutral, simple form elements also communicate the nature of the interaction, leaving open the possibility of other ways to accomplish the same function. For example, Figure 7.7 shows a version of the itinerary screen with a drop-down menu instead of a slider for the group size selector. Using a drop-down menu in the wireframe would have been legitimate, especially if I didn't have any particular idea on how to accomplish this interaction. Acknowledging the essence of the function (user must select one from a handful) allows the rest of the design team to weigh in on interface widgets that offer other advantages. Interactions go beyond form elements. Modern web design incorporates elaborate interface elements, some of which have not yet standardized on a particular format. Carousels are a good example of an emerging interface element that has yet to land on a particular approach. Table 7.4 has some guidelines for wireframing new elements like these.

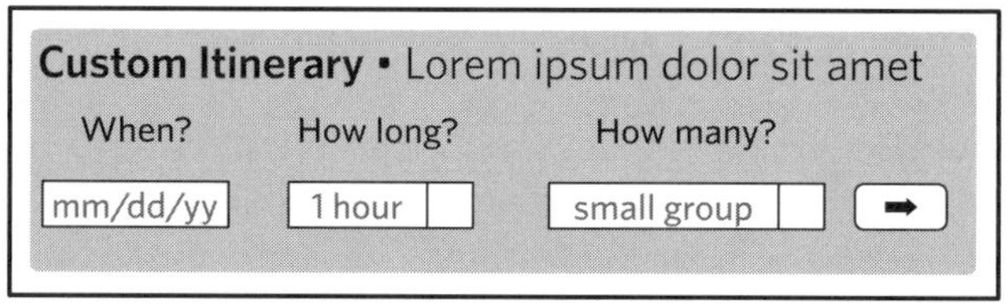

Custom Itinerary • Lorem ipsum dolor sit amet
When?
How long?
How many?
mm/dd/yy
1 hour
small group

Figure 7.7: Simple, standard form elements used to communicate interactions give the design team the idea behind the interaction and permission to explore other interface options.

You should...	For example in a carousel...
Be explicit in the range of behaviors offered.	Show that users can rotate the slides manually or jump to a particular slide.
Indicate how user gestures trigger behaviors.	Holding the cursor over a slide may show a tooltip with the name of the slide, so show the cursor on the wireframe.
Show the parts of the interface that react to gestures.	Incorporate an indicator to highlight which slide is active. Even if this doesn't make it into the final design, you want to be able to speak to how the component responds to user actions.

Table 7.4: Representing functional elements, for example a carousel.

Functional elements usually have more than one state. A link, for example, can be visited or unvisited. It can also have a hover state, what it looks like when the user holds the cursor over it. Tabs can be active, inactive, or unavailable. When communicating state:

- Make sure the state accurately reflects the scenario of the wireframe. Showing an active tab with incorrect content, or an unavailable tab that should always be available, will just confuse the project team.
- Don't use the wireframe of a screen to show all the various states of an interface element. Prepare separate, smaller wireframes for each possible state of an interface element like a tab set.

Like using red with error messages, there is a functional element that benefits from a little color in wireframes. Color links and other clickable items blue. Blue, for better or worse, is long-established as the color of hyperlinks—clickable things. Using blue for clickability helps you to focus on those elements when walking through a wireframe. You can overdo it, if there are a lot of elements users can interact with. In these instances, I use blue for things that trigger primary functions, or things that would not otherwise look clickable.

Layer 3: Beyond Rectangles

The elements in this layer polish your wireframe, but they are by no means necessary to the essential purpose of the wireframe. They may help align your screen concepts with other aspects of the design project, but they can also interfere with other activities, so apply them with caution. While they lend a certain polish to the wireframe, they also may distract from what you're trying to communicate with the diagram.

Grid

Grids establish a visual framework for aligning the various elements on the page. It is a concept long-entrenched in graphic design that has, due to CSS, become more feasible and more accepted among web designers.

The grid's role in wireframing is still emergent: Should wireframes use the exact grid used for laying out web pages? If the wireframe doesn't replicate the HTML/CSS grid exactly, should it evoke a similar layout? Should the grid be functional in nature (such as a "body" column and a "navigation" column), or should it be based on dividing up the page into equal regions (for example, eight columns)?

In graphic design, grids establish a proportionality between the elements that the human eye finds pleasing. It aligns elements on the page, and creates opportunities for visual tension by breaking that alignment.

Careful alignment of content areas in a wireframe cuts both ways: The wireframe itself is more polished and may do a better job in communicating priorities, but it also evokes an accurate web page rendition, which may be risky depending on the project team.

There is one other consideration: Grids make it easier to design. If your focus is less on graphic design and more on structure and content, a grid provides a useful framework for building wireframes. Like any concept from graphic design (contrast, white space, typography, and so on), grids in the hands of an untrained designer (present company included) can be applied irresponsibly.

For the web page examples in this chapter, I followed a 12-column grid, using a template downloaded from the web. Whether the final web pages follow this exact layout or not, the grid made it easy to create a polished, consistent wireframe.

Figure 7.8: Simple, wireframe-ready form elements establish the interaction and remain devoid of any specific aesthetic direction.

provided a convenient starting point for laying out the examples in this chapter. Even if the final design system doesn't use the 960 grid, the 12-column layout is easily translatable to other pixel-widths.

TIP

The 960 grid

Far be it for the web to standardize on anything, but one emerging best practice is the 960 grid. This pattern, which is—you guessed it—960 pixels wide, establishes a common starting point for a grid. Conveniently divisible, it also offers flexibility for web designers looking for a variety of column configurations. Visit http://960.gs for more information about the 960 grid and to download templates you can use in a variety of drawing applications.

Prioritization styles

Using placement on the page as the only way to communicate hierarchy, wireframes can become extremely dense. While the simplified aesthetic steers clear of making any decisions about style, it can backfire, making the page seem weightier than it really is. Typographic styles, grayscale, and moderated line weight can work in concert to explain the hierarchy of information on the page without committing you to a particular style.

Table 7.5 explains some of the prioritization styles I used in the sample wireframe from Figure 7.13.

I used...	to...	because...
Gray background	Distinguish the functional area from the rest of the content on the page.	Enclosing it in a bordered box would have created additional visual noise.
Font weight	Make the headers pop, and distinguish between the main header and an explanatory subhead.	The content in the headers is important for conveying the overall tone, but I want the designer to understand that part of the header is more important.
Icons	Convey to the design team what I had in mind for the functionality of the itinerary picker.	I had a specific design concept, and image placeholders wouldn't have conveyed it as effectively.
Font size	Imply a clear hierarchy of content.	Without the different sizes, the wireframe would look pretty mushy.
Gray text (inside the form elements)	Show that the form includes some sample text.	Sample text is a common practice, and I didn't want the text to be mistaken for user selections.
Underlined text	Show links.	It is the web after all.

Table 7.5: Function and priority conveyed through style help prevent the wireframe from becoming a tangle of lines and visual noise.

Some style in wireframes can emphasize the priorities and function, but be sure to ask yourself about the rationale for moving beyond simple rectangles. For example, I'm not sure why I rounded the corners of the background for the Custom Itinerary section.

Aesthetic elements

Aesthetic is like weather: It's always there, you just notice it more sometimes. The paucity of color, typography, imagery, and style in a wireframe does not mean it is devoid of aesthetic. Creating a wireframe means (in most cases) using the simplest, most universal aesthetic to avoid making any concrete statement about style. Minimizing aesthetics is a common practice in wireframing because it allows the project team to focus conversations on behavior, structure, and priority.

Some second-layer wireframe elements (structural content, functional elements) discussed the use of color. It's important to distinguish these uses of color. A wireframe may rely on color to help communicate the function or purpose of some element.

The kind of color we're talking about in the third layer is the color that's specifically attached to the brand. The National Zoo uses a forest green as the central color in its palette, and surrounds that green with some other earthy tones. The question we're asking here is whether to inject the wireframe with colors from that palette.

Incorporating a bit of style into a wireframe comes with risks (will the choice of type or graphic distract from the purpose of the wireframe?), but it can lend some authenticity.

CREATING WIREFRAMES

Even with the basics, there is still a wide range of what wireframes might look like. How do you pull all these elements together? Start with some basic decisions to help focus your efforts.

Basic Decisions

Usually, this section starts with the purpose, thinking about what you want to accomplish. In this case, however, I want to first explain the range of **content** decisions you can make before considering purpose and audience.

Scale: Pages or content areas

In describing the anatomy of a wireframe, I assumed that every wireframe reflected a complete page. This isn't always true. Some wireframes represent portions of pages. That is, you can create a representation of a single content area (see Figure 7.10).

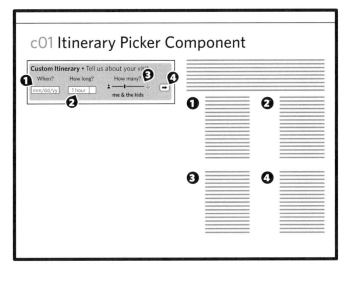

Figure 7.10: The scale of the wireframe refers to whether you're showing the whole screen or a portion of the screen. A smaller scale affords a greater level of detail about each function and an opportunity to explore all the variations of a component in the context of the component itself. On the other hand, the component may lose context being described outside its native environs: the web page.

TIP

Modular Web Design

Nathan Curtis's book *Modular Web Design* (New Riders, 2009) is the best source on taking a Lego-brick approach to designing web sites. Curtis explains not only how to treat web design in a modular way, but also the operational aspects of developing a component library for sophisticated design systems.

Designing the individual page components is useful if you intend to use the components again and again throughout the site (and why wouldn't you). It ensures consistency, and its efficiency trickles down to other parts of the design and implementation processes.

Of course, this approach requires that people looking at the component drawings can understand them outside the context of a screen. It can be challenging for the project team to evaluate the quality of a design if they're reviewing it piecemeal. Your design process may ultimately entail moving back and forth between designing screens and components.

From a documentation perspective, wireframes at either level (screen or component) face the same challenges and draw from the same techniques. Where the deliverable will differ is in the telling of the story: with wireframes of individual areas, the deliverable needs to state clearly how the components fit together, and how they might be incorporated into different screens.

When documenting a partial page, you should use a visual cue (Figure 7.11) to help people understand that they're looking at an excerpt.

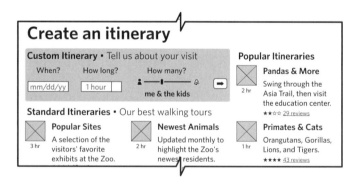

Figure 7.11: Borders around partial pages should include a jagged edge to indicate that there's more to the screen than shown.

Fidelity: How close to reality

As careful as the Anatomy section was in treating wireframes as virtually devoid of any style, some designers prefer wireframes that come close to a final design. This is known as fidelity: how faithful the representation is to the final product. A high-fidelity (hi-fi) wireframe looks more like the final version of the design, incorporating realistic graphic design elements. Low-fidelity (lo-fi) wireframes stick to the rectangles and labels.

A higher-fidelity version of the first wireframe in this chapter may introduce some rounded corners, some little icons, and some gradients, to evoke a genuine iPhone interface. Figure 7.12 shows what this might look like.

Figure 7.12: High-fidelity wireframes introduce some aesthetic elements. In this case, making the basic screen from the National Zoo app look more like a native iPhone user interface can help facilitate buy-in. With a gradient and rounded corner here and a clipart icon there, you have something higher fidelity.

Styling wireframe components can be time-consuming and depends heavily on the diagramming program you use. Some applications (such as Adobe Illustrator) give you lots of control over the style of the drawing objects. Others (OmniGraffle, MS Visio) give you fewer stylistic options.

But the decision to emulate the final design rests on other factors beyond the technical:

- **Purpose**: How does creating a realistic-looking web page contribute to the purpose? Some purposes (kicking around a new UI concept, for example) don't require such a close adherence to a final web design. Others (using wireframes for usability testing) would benefit from a more realistic rendering. The most typical usage of wireframes (documenting behaviors) likely won't need much in the way of style.
- **Consumers**: Who is the ultimate audience for wireframes, and how will they benefit from high- or low-fidelity wireframes? Lo-fi wireframes may seem inaccessible to inexperienced project participants. The flip side is that wireframes with too much style thrown in set expectations about the final design, a position the team might not be ready to take.
- **Project context**: Fidelity depends a lot on the nature of the project. Designing a brand new product within a large project team may benefit from the deliberate approach of a lo-fi wireframes: emphasizing a focus on functionality before getting to visual design. When repurposing existing components within a well-baked design system, there may be no reason not to use hi-fi wireframes.

Abstraction: How specific is the content

The content in the wireframe in Figure 7.11 has low abstraction: It uses realistic content, if not entirely accurate content. The content is specific and concrete. Readers of the diagram may ultimately struggle to understand how the template is generalized to other content, but the purpose of the page is made clear through the content samples.

Figure 7.13 shows the same wireframe but more abstracted: The structural content remains intact, but much of the content is replaced with text that is less specific and more representational.

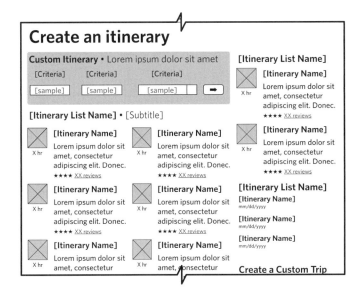

Figure 7.13: Abstracted content in a wireframe means swapping out concrete information with text that's more representational. Note the use of three different forms of sample content: labels (with brackets), symbolic (representing the time, number of reviews, and the dates), and Latin text (for the itinerary descriptions).

A more abstract wireframe can be difficult to visualize, but it does a better job in describing the functionality, behaviors, and states. It gives you a clear picture of which content on the screen is dynamic and which text is fixed. Abstracted content in wireframes is appropriate for functional specifications, when you need to explain a range of behaviors. More concrete content is better earlier in the design process, when you're trying to help the project team visualize the interactions.

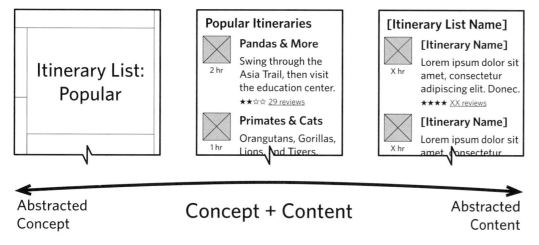

Figure 7.14: Abstracting wireframes can go in two directions. Abstracting the concept means taking out any sense of internal structure, but being relatively specific about the topic or focus of the content found there (left side of scale). Stripping out any real content but preserving the structure gives you a sense of the kinds of information (title, image, etc.) but no clear focus.

Depth: How many variations

If the surface of wireframing represents the barest minimum you can do to communicate the user experience, digging below it means elaborating to describe every last detail. The surface describes what happens in a typical scenario, and digging deeper reveals details about additional scenarios. The surface gives me the primary screens, and the deeper I go the more information I get about:

- **Secondary screens**: Screens that are not essential for understanding the user experience (a login, for example) but which need to be defined or the product will fail.
- **Variations at the page level**: How the pages might change in different circumstances. For a search results page, variations might reflect the quantity of results returned. Does the page look different with 1,000, 100, 10, or 1 result?
- **Variations at the component level**: How a portion of the screen might change in different scenarios. A global navigation element might look different when users are

or are not logged in. A form element might change when users commit an error.

Purpose

The four dimensions (scale, fidelity, abstraction, depth) give you a sense of the range of decisions you can make about the wireframes themselves. Unlike other diagrams, wireframes have a pretty concrete range. These four dimensions give us a lot to play with, and it's important to understand them before talking about the inputs into those decisions.

The main input into how to fine-tune your wireframes along these dimensions is purpose: What are you using the wireframes for? I usually come up with one of two answers:

- **Blueprints**: Document detailed functional specifications. The wireframes are meant to give developers every last detail they need to build the web site. The diagrams work hand-in-hand with annotations to elaborate on business logic, editorial guidelines, state descriptions, and behaviors.
- **Concept**: Capture an overall design idea. You will use the wireframes to solicit feedback on an overall approach— either on technical feasibility or whether requirements are adequately addressed—or merely to see if it's a good idea.

There is another purpose for which I might use wireframes: testing. My experience, for better or worse, is that I create a set of wireframes for blueprints or concept, and then the project team later decides to do some testing. We gravitate toward using the wireframes, a decision we ultimately regret because they weren't created for testing purposes, so they need to be edited heavily for that reason, adding realistic content, creating separate screens to address each scenario in the test, and linking all the screens together.

Audience

To be clear, when we talk about the audience for wireframes, we're talking about the people who need to use the diagrams, not (usually) the users of the web site you're designing.

Assessing the target audience for the wireframes means more than just understanding their roles on the project: Different people may be more or less comfortable with the inherently abstract nature of wireframes.

Tips for Wicked Wireframes

Effective wireframing depends on a little careful planning and preparation. You could write down a few lists or spend a few hours sketching ideas, but either way, don't start inside your diagramming application. Find a quiet spot with a pen and notebook and consider these tips.

Sketch first

It may seem obvious to start with a pen and paper, but a lot of web designers I know like to go right into a drawing application. Sketching out some initial ideas can help set direction and give you a starting point before firing up the application.

How much should you sketch? Different people do this differently, and as the technique goes through a bit of a renaissance in the web design business we get to see lots of different techniques. Here's what works for me:

For each iteration, I sketch as little as possible, but I do as many iterations as it takes.

For me, the point of sketching is to make sure I establish the basic framework for the page, solving the essential design problem. I'll do multiple iterations to explore different approaches, but I don't need to do a lot in each sketch

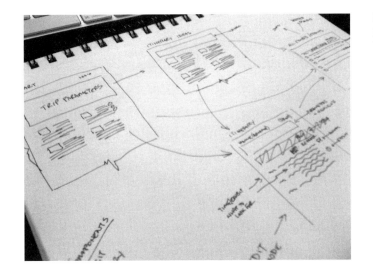

Figure 7.15: Sketching with pen and paper is an important step in the wireframing process.

to establish an approach. For me, sketching is about quantity, not about quality. It's a means to generate and evaluate ideas. I may do a few iterations on a single approach to hash out a few of the details, but I tend to save the heavy lifting on the details for the wireframes.

Establish a purpose for the page

Before even sketching a page, I ask myself, "What is the one thing this screen has to do?" Establishing a central focus can help drive the design decisions you make about the page, especially with respect to prioritization.

While the entire project constitutes a large design problem, each page is a small design problem in and of itself. There's no reason why a good practice (defining a vision) can't scale downward. You could do this at the component level, too. (Of course, the smaller you get, the easier it is to define a purpose.)

ASIDE
Sketches for Documentation

More recently, I've been scanning my sketches and dumping them into documents. This approach is especially effective at the beginning of the design process, when the concept is still rough around the edges. Sketches are inherently informal, and stakeholders may be more willing to critique or offer suggestions of their own.

Another approach some of my colleagues have tried is to render formal wireframes in a "sketchy" style, a technique that's simplified with some diagramming and illustration programs. (Adobe Illustrator has pencil-line brushes built-in, and you can apply these to any line in any PDF. Pretty handy.)

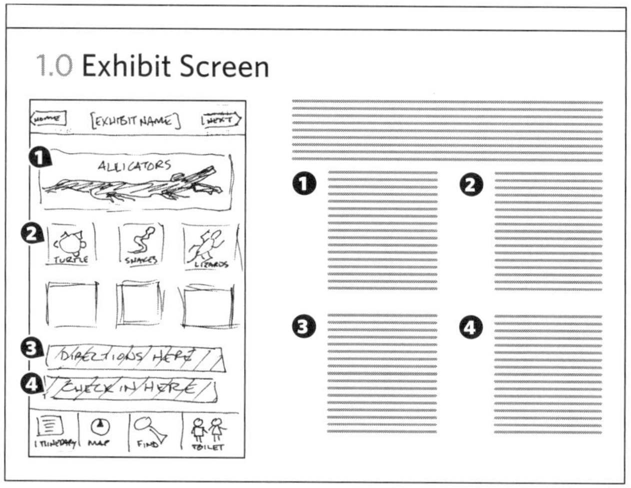

1.0 Exhibit Screen

Figure 7.16: Scanned sketches in design documentation allow you to put concepts in front of the design team faster without losing any context or additional descriptions.

Figure 7.17: Sketchy wireframes afford some of the same advantages of actual hand-drawn sketches, but translate easily into something more formal as the need arises.

Recall design principles

If your project entailed some discovery work at the beginning, you likely have a design brief with a fundamental direction and design principles. I like to recapitulate these in the margin of my sketchbook before I dig too deeply into a screen design. The mere act of writing them down again keeps them fresh in my mind and triggers good ideas in the part of my brain that designs web pages.

List page contents

If it wasn't clear from the Anatomy section, wireframes can be boiled down to a list of things on the page. Even if you can't turn in a list as your final deliverable, you can use it as a starting point. In addition to putting design principles in the margin of my sketchbook, I also make a list of everything I want to put on the page. Some things get circled as the most important things to include. For especially complex components, I'll create sublists to describe the priorities within a particular content area.

Use realistic scenarios

In the Zoo example, the companion web site includes a page that lists different itineraries, the List Template. This template is used in several different scenarios: when users conduct a search for a specific itinerary, when users provide a set of criteria for designing an itinerary, when users look at a list of their saved itineraries, or when users click a link that says "see more" or "see all." This List Template needs to do a lot.

It may be tempting to show the "every case" scenario. That is, all the possible configurations for the template in one wireframe. While this may seem useful, it can undermine the project team's understanding of the screen. The "every case" scenario may show all the possible elements, but it doesn't successfully convey appropriate behaviors.

Your wireframe should depict a single, realistic scenario (and the annotations should be clear about that scenario). If the template has several dramatic variations because it supports multiple scenarios, you should create a separate wireframe for each.

For example, the Zoo's List Template would use different components at the top of the page depending on how users got there. It might list search criteria, or it might display a toolbar for managing my saved itineraries. Instead of displaying both components (the "every case" scenario) in one wireframe, the document should include two versions of the wireframe.

Level-Up Your Wireframing Skills

The power and flexibility of wireframes affords countless opportunities to improve upon them, as well as our techniques for creating them. Here are a few we've been playing with.

Take a modular approach

With a modular approach, you treat wireframes as Lego kits, assembling screens from individual, shareable pieces. Creating wireframes means designing the individual pieces and then designing the page frameworks for those components. The components snap together in the context of a page template.

Headers and footers are common components. Navigation elements are common components. You can create a common component for interfaces that display particular kinds of content (videos, for example).

Thinking in these terms may be challenging if you're used to a more holistic approach to design. As you embark on your own journey to take a more modular approach, keep these tips in mind for your documentation:

- Components won't make sense if people don't understand the larger context. Lego manuals always start with a picture of the whole model, and your documentation needs to establish context by showing the components in action. Once the project team understands the context, they can have more meaningful conversations about how the component works elsewhere, or how a variation on the component might work in the same context.
- Components require a rigorous identification system. A web site consisting of half a dozen templates may rely on ten times as many components. Careful encoding of the components helps people using the library keep them straight, and ensure they're using the right one.
- Components have particular functions and are likely meant for particular page regions. In chapters 8 and 9 of *Modular Web Design*, Nathan Curtis describes how teams can break down page templates and classify components corresponding to typical page areas and features on a web site.

For example, the itinerary description shown in Figure 7.18 is used throughout the web site to summarize an itinerary.

Figure 7.18: This is a component, reusable throughout the web site. The content is just placeholder content, which I'd have to swap if I put the same component on a single page multiple times. Alternatively, I could replace the sample content with variables, like "[Itinerary Name]".

COMPONENT A portion of a web page that serves a specific purpose or function.

Establish styles

To ensure consistent use of typography, create a set of simple styles (like you might in a word processor) so that all your headers, all your body text, all your links, and all the other text elements are formatted in the same way.

If your wireframe makes use of other elements to communicate priority (like shaded rectangles), you can create styles for these shapes as well. Create a rectangle, select the "background field" style, and you can be sure that every background field in your document is formatted in the same way. (Even I forget to do this sometimes and find myself wondering, "Did I use a 4px rounded corner or a 6px rounded corner?" That gets me distracted because then I start thinking, "It's a wireframe! Who cares?" And THEN I start thinking, "They might not know, but I'll know, and then I won't be able to sleep." In short, styles prevent neuroses.)

Different drawing applications offer varying levels of support for styles. Most offer some way to store a set of style options and are generally sufficient for our wireframing needs. Learn your preferred tool backward and forward so you can take full advantage of its capabilities, ensuring that you become an efficient and consistent wireframing machine.

Create a library of elements

Most diagramming programs allow you to store shapes in a stencil or library. (Every application calls this feature by a different name. Of course.) Rapid and consistent wireframing depends on using the same set of elements. These can range from individual form elements to more elaborate configurations like a navigation bar or a set of common search fields or resizable image placeholders.

Lest you see these libraries as constraining, a few reminders:

- Elements in a library are starting points. Lists of headlines don't vary that much from one to the next, so having a standard format provides a quick and easy way to drop it into the wireframe.
- Elements are tried-and-true design conventions. Your value is not in reinventing a drop-down menu, but in how you use those elements to solve specific design problems.
- The purpose of a wireframe is to convey functionality as quickly as possible. By incorporating a library into your design process, you can create new screen designs efficiently.

Hold a design studio

If you're keen to take your sketching up a notch, consider a more collaborative approach. Design studios bring together the project team and engage them in a series of sketching exercises. This technique was introduced to me and my firm by Todd Zaki Warfel of messagefirst. It's a variation on well-established collaborative design techniques.

- **Outcomes**: Sketching studios generally last a full day, and at the end you'll have a stack of ideas to draw from. Studios definitely emphasize quantity over quality, but by bringing together a range of disciplines (not just designers) with varying perspectives on the project, you're bound to see a new idea or approach.
- **Structure**: In a design studio, participants break up into multidisciplinary teams. Throughout the day, the team creates sketches for two to four different scenarios. The studio facilitators describe the scenario and provide sufficient inputs (like descriptions of the target audience). Members of each team sketch different ideas, spend time discussing the ideas, pick a direction, and then do another round of sketching where they work together to create a single concept from their brainstorming.

- **Preparation**: As studio facilitator, you are responsible for a few things. You need to prepare the scenarios. This depends on having an intimate understanding of the design problem. Scenarios are most successful when they are specific, stating the user's situation and desired outcome.

How do sketching studios factor into design documentation?

- **Sketching = setting expectations**. By getting people to create sketches, they have a better understanding of the kinds of artifacts you will produce.
- **Scenarios = understanding context**. After people have thought through the scenarios to create their own designs, they will have a more intimate understanding of the context for the design concepts you present.
- **Collaboration = buy-in**. Participation in the design process creates a sense of ownership. Even if you don't use someone's idea, they will have been part of the process to explore design concepts and evaluate different approaches.

One nice side-effect of holding design studios at the beginning of the design process is the acculturation of the design team to reviewing screen concepts. When it comes time to review wireframes, they'll at least have some exposure to the process. Regardless of their experience, the next section provides some suggestions on how to present wireframes to the project team.

PRESENTING WIREFRAMES

"Presenting" may not be the right word. Because wireframes are perhaps the most tangible design artifact, they generate more conversation than any other diagram, and become a tool for collaboration on the design. Still, you're on the hook to facilitate those conversations, and that's the position the remainder of this section takes.

Establish a Purpose

The purpose of any wireframe review meeting is to discuss the user experience. If you're doing these diagrams more or less in the order described in this book, wireframes will be the first venture into a concrete view of the system. Depending on your process, wireframes will merit multiple discussions, and the tenor of those discussions will change as the design progresses from initial concept to detailed functional specifications.

Pitching a concept

Wireframes are fast, they are reasonably approximate, and they are meaningful pictures of user interfaces. They make, therefore, excellent tools for pitching a design direction.

In meetings where you're laying out the overall concept, you may have a small number of wireframes, just enough to provide a sense of how people will interact with the system. Your messages are straightforward:

- **Alignment**: Your wireframes should clearly trace back to the stated design problem. They should resonate with any design principles established earlier in the project, conform to requirements, and respect identified constraints and boundaries.
- **Complexity**: In telling the story behind the experience, a small number of wireframes, perhaps focused on the main parts of the user interface, may belie tremendous complexity under the surface. Your presentation needs to be honest about the challenges implied by your vision.
- **Remaining**: Eager project teams may latch onto the direction and think they can start building. (Heck, I make this mistake with greater frequency than I care to admit. My passion gets the better of my good judgment.) Your pitch meeting should come with at least a high-level plan describing what remains to be done; these initial concept screens are a good starting point, but more must be said before coding begins.

Wireframes make great sales tools. Even those lacking polish evoke the user experience in ways flowcharts and other diagrams can't.

Discussing the experience at a high level

The same set of wireframes you use for pitching a concept may be used to hash out the experience. In this meeting, you're evaluating the design against the established objectives, requirements, and constraints. You need to answer at least these questions:

- Does this approach address all the objectives? Use this meeting to solicit other pairs of eyes to compare the design approach to the documented objectives. For example, the objective of the web-based itinerary picker may be to encourage people to use the iPhone app, where the Zoo generates revenue through the cost in the iTunes app store. One criticism of the itinerary web site is that it doesn't do a good job in promoting the iPhone app, encouraging people to use and download it.
- Does the approach conform to design principles and good design practices? Looking at my itinerary wireframes after leaving them for a couple days, they seem really dense to me. This may be OK, but raising it in a review meeting, I would ask whether the approach aligns with the project's design principles or current trends in web design.
- Do we need to reevaluate the requirements? Seeing designs in the flesh may shed light on the design problem or the requirements in ways you could not conceive before having screens in front of you. The designer may have come up with an idea not reflected in the requirements (in the iPhone app, stating the user's distance from another exhibit in terms of minutes, for example).
- What's implied by this screen? Careful examinations of screen designs reveal new requirements through dependencies. In order to support the itinerary picker, for example, the team needs to create business rules for

generating an itinerary based on the inputs. While these concepts may have been identified in the requirements, the design makes them real, and the exact implications become clear.

These questions help the design team generate another version of the wireframes, refining the functionality based on these findings. At some point, however, in some processes, these conversations are not enough. The design team needs to dig in deeper to make sure they've dotted all the i's and crossed all the t's before turning the functional specification over to the development team.

Some teams stop wireframing here. Their processes allow for half-baked wireframes to serve as the catalyst for further design and development. For some projects, their scale, the configuration of the project team, the design culture, and other factors make multiple iterations of wireframes pointless.

Discussing the experience at a deep level

A deeper discussion ultimately boils down to stress-testing the design concept to see if it can handle the rigors of production. Such reviews get mind-numbingly detailed, and you get to learn who on the project team has the severest case of mild obsessive-compulsive disorder. Here are just a handful of deep-level questions the team might explore during such a conversation:

- **Have we addressed all possible scenarios?** A scenario establishes a set of conditions that affect the display of particular screens, and a good design anticipates all the possible scenarios. This is a multidisciplinary task. User experience designers can imagine all the weird scenarios created by usage, but only people responsible for technology and operations can anticipate a full range of unusual scenarios. ("What if database X is down but database Y is still running? What if there's no one available to answer a customer service call?")

- **Does the team have enough information to render a visual design?** Playing through all the scenarios may mean generating additional wireframes to show the full range of displays. Visual designers work in pixels, which affords much less flexibility in laying out a screen. They need a clear understanding of the range of possible displays so they can design a user interface that supports the functionality without breaking.
- **What content is needed in the interface?** Combing through the interface will reveal the full range of messaging and content it requires. Someone will need to generate final labels for navigation, instructional text, field labels, hints for completing forms, error messaging, confirmation messaging, and page titles, not to mention all the actual content on the site.

The truth is, you could do these kinds of reviews forever, spelling out the user experience in ever-increasing detail. How much is enough? In some cases, these deadlines are spelled out for you: A good project plan should establish constraints on when to transition between phases in the design process. If you're struggling to conform to a particular schedule, here are some warning signs that you're spending too much time reviewing detailed wireframes:

- **A wireframe has gone through more than three revisions.** This number may be five on especially complex systems, but look at the revisions on a single wireframe. Long revision histories generally point to unstable objectives or requirements, which means there's a deeper problem on the project.
- **You've reversed a decision more than once.** Let's use a drop-down. No, let's use a slider. Hmm, let's go back to a drop-down. Time to move on.
- **Key stakeholders no longer come to review meetings.**
- **You can't get through a full review in less than an hour.** After the first or second detailed review (which may take more than an hour), subsequent reviews should be relatively fast, nailing down specific questions or issues.

Some of these are, frankly, somewhat arbitrary measures of doneness. Spinning on a wireframe generally points to instability or lack of clarity elsewhere in the project, but don't let the wireframes become an excuse for not moving forward.

Adapt the Presentation

Running a wireframes meeting should be the same as discussing any other design diagram. The overall framework for these conversations—starting with the big idea and rationale, followed by details and implications—works well for all wireframe reviews. Regardless of whether you're talking about the user experience at a high level or in painstaking detail, starting with a lay of the land and major themes helps keep the conversation focused.

1. Establish context

Establishing context at the beginning of any design review means reminding the project team of where you are in the project and providing objectives for the conversation. For wireframe review meetings, you will also need to remind people about which screens you are reviewing today and what scenarios they belong to.

2. Describe visual conventions

For project teams who aren't used to looking at wireframes, provide a short introduction to the format. You can also use the whiteboard to make two lists: what you will and will not discuss as part of the wireframes.

During this portion of the meeting, you can also explain your decisions regarding scale, fidelity, abstraction, and depth. Helping meeting participants understand where the wireframes fall in each scale can also set their expectations about what they will and will not see. Note that you should use plain language to describe the wireframes; words like "scale" and "fidelity" won't mean much if people in the meeting haven't had much experience with wireframes.

Figure 7.19: Setting expectations about wireframes at the start of the meeting can help head off difficult conversations.

3. Highlight major design decisions

Before digging into the details of the wireframes, you can walk through them quickly. During the quick walkthrough, you can touch on:

- **Overall themes**: How would you characterize the major design decisions? What were the driving concepts behind most of the design ideas?
- **Key objectives, principles, or requirements**: What were the objectives and principles that were top-of-mind during the design process? What are the main requirements this design addresses?
- **Page purposes**: In designing the page, what was the central purpose you established for it?
- **Important design innovations**: What are the coolest parts of the design? What design decisions are you most proud of?

There's a lot of information listed here. Err on the side of brevity: The intent is to provide an overview, not an in-depth discussion. This section can be even more brief on subsequent reviews, and should instead summarize the main changes since the last conversation.

4. Offer rationale and identify constraints

You can use this portion of the meeting to highlight the significant challenges you encountered during the design of these screens.

If any design principles played a major role in driving design decisions for this particular set of screens, you can reiterate (and even capture on the whiteboard) these concepts.

5. Point out details

When it's time to dig into the details of the wireframe, use the approach in Table 7.6 as a starting point for structuring your discussion.

If you need a simpler framework to walk through the screen, consider this mnemonic: APU, area-principle-users. Focus on the *area* and describe its function. "Zoom out" and describe the *principle*, objective, or requirements that this area relates to, then zoom back in and walk meeting participants through the area as *users* might experience it.

6. Communicate implications

Any design decision captured in a wireframe will come with cascading implications. As described in the general approach, these implications can be technical (how will we build this?) or operational (how will we support it?). Functionality can be deceptively simple, requiring substantially more development or support than appearances would suggest.

Step	Describe	For Example (see Figure 7.20)
1	Reiterate the primary focus of the screen.	The purpose of the main screen is to help visitors understand what's nearby.
2	If meeting participants are familiar with the framework or general template, call their attention to it.	This screen follows the convention of many iPhone applications, with a title header and a toolbar at the bottom. This toolbar is used on most screens throughout the app.
3	Start with the area of the screen in the middle of the page, or the element that most directly contributes to the overall page purpose. If you're describing a screen as part of a user flow, describe the area of the screen that will help users initiate the process.	The screen is divided into three main areas: exhibits, events, and itinerary. In exhibits and events we show icons and titles for each of three that are nearby or happening soon. We also provide some information on how far they are (in the case of exhibits) or how soon they are (in the case of events).
4	Depending on the level of depth you want to discuss, highlight each field within the content area.	We've dropped icons in here, but I think it would be great to use real photos. Putting the distance to the exhibits in terms of walking time is pretty crucial, and my hope is that we can just store that information in the database so the app doesn't have to do any calculations.
5	For each field, describe the range of inputs users can provide, or describe the range of content that can appear.	For the events, we need to establish some pretty clear rules about which events to show. We don't want to show events that are happening next week. My assumption is that there's always something happening every day, so there will always be something here.
6	Describe any underlying business rules or application logic.	We need to iron-out the logic for determining which exhibits to show. It depends on the app recognizing the user's location, and that location being somewhere within the Zoo.
7	Narrate what comes next, helping meeting participants understand where this area of the page fits into the whole user experience.	Tapping on one of these would take users to screen 2.0 or 4.0, which describe the exhibit or event, respectively.
8	Repeat step 3 for each of the other main content areas.	(Provide description for the "itinerary" area of the screen.)

Table 7.6: Digging into details, how to structure your approach.

Figure 7.20: Refer to this figure for descriptions in Table 7.6.

Prior to the meeting, make a note on the wireframe where you suspect the most severe implications. Make a note of the most important functionality. During this portion of the conversation, ask participants to pay close attention to both of these. For suspected complex functions, you're confirming your suspicions and asking the experts to ensure that they account for the potential challenges. For the most important areas of the design, your intent is to validate the approach so you don't have to compromise the design later.

7. Solicit feedback

Contributions to wireframe reviews really run the gamut; sometimes participants can't stop talking (see "Avoid Newbie Mistakes," later) and sometimes they just don't say anything.

Don't take silence for complacency, agreement, or buy-in. There are a few different reasons why stakeholders don't jump in with comments, listed and mitigated in Table 7.7. Avoid "testing" meeting participants. Nothing discourages productive discussion like being made to feel like an idiot. Deflect any potential hurt feelings by bringing the user into the conversation.

Why they're quiet...	What you can do...
Misapprehension 1: They don't understand the functionality in the wireframe.	Ask if there are any parts of the screen that don't make sense, or ask if there are any parts of the screen that they think users will have trouble understanding.
Misapprehension 2: They don't understand how the wireframe fits into the overall user experience.	Wonder aloud if you've successfully accounted for every scenario and inventory all the different ways in which people might arrive at the screen. This gives you an opportunity to repeat yourself and spell things out in greater detail.
Hypersensitive: They don't want to hurt your feelings.	Remind everyone that the people you're trying to serve are the target audience. Bring someone to the meeting who doesn't mind criticizing your designs. Sometimes it takes one honest comment to open the floodgates.
Politics: They don't want to talk in front of other stakeholders in the meeting.	Schedule a second review meeting where people can share their thoughts after they've had time to digest. When I do this, I find people will happily send comments in email.

You could try to fix the corporate politics. Ha ha. |
| **Inexperience:** Providing design critiques is hard if you've never done it before. They may not know what to say or focus on. | Show up to the meeting with pointed questions about the design. Also bring examples of the kind of feedback you're looking for. Shooting down a comment because it's not in-scope for the conversation doesn't help if you can't provide a model for participants to follow. |

Table 7.7: Dealing with quiet meetings requires sensitivity to diagnose why people might be afraid to speak up.

8. Provide a framework for review

Inevitably, the depth and complexity of the design documentation in wireframes makes it difficult for all the details to be hashed out in a meeting. Giving stakeholders homework (and this is true for asking people to review the wireframes before a review meeting, too) requires specificity on what needs reviewing and what kind of feedback you want.

Typically, there are five things that you want from the project team:

- **Alignment with objectives**: What's missing from this wireframe that prevents it from meeting the project objectives?
- **Usability issues**: What parts of the interface design would users find most challenging?

- **Content and priority issues**: Is there anything wrong with the content as rendered or the relative priorities?
- **Functional issues**: What happens to fields A, B, and C in scenario X?
- **Feasibility**: What part of this design will be the hardest to implement, and why?

(Notice how I avoid yes/no questions, to prevent tacit assent?) To the extent you can ask these questions specifically and pointedly, you should embed them directly in the annotations for the wireframe. That is, open questions should be captured and highlighted in the documentation itself.

Avoid Newbie Mistakes

In this section, "newbie" might be the wrong word for the title. The mistakes outlined in the next few sections are made on every project by the most experienced designers. Ultimately, this part of the design discussion—somewhere between abstract and concrete, between problem and solution—is the hardest.

This section presumes that wireframing and graphic design are separate endeavors. In many web design practices, finalized wireframes are turned over to visual designers, who then interpret the structure and create a final user interface, incorporating other inputs (like a brand strategy). Likewise, the team may include people dedicated to writing content. It assumes that those content strategists will have deliverables over and above the wireframes.

None of the following tips matter if the right people aren't a part of the conversation from the outset. Getting them engaged is important, too. A developer sitting at the table even from the very beginning of the design process does you no good if he or she doesn't take the role seriously and provide substantial input into the design.

Set expectations about the purpose

In the context portion of the meeting (step 1), clearly state what you want to get out of the meeting. The rabbit holes described next don't make themselves: They come from a lack of focus, and a lack of facilitation.

As part of setting up the purpose of the meeting, you can call out the questions you need answered. Using the questions to frame the meeting helps establish the tone and focus at the outset.

With any rabbit hole, there are a few positions you can take:

- **Not discussing**: "This is out of scope for this meeting, and I need to get answers to these questions or we can't move forward with the design effort."
- **Table for later**: "These are really good points, but out of scope for this meeting. Let's capture them so we can discuss them later."
- **Let's hash it out (with consequences)**: "I don't mind spending time talking about this stuff, but we're going to lose ground on the wireframes. We may need to schedule another meeting, or I need to get feedback via email."

Getting back on track for any meeting is challenging, and often means you have to play the bad guy. While being a stickler for meeting agendas isn't the worst crime in the world, it can be frustrating for team members who see something more pressing.

Wireframes contain content and graphic design elements out of necessity, even if they're not trying to put a stake in the ground for either. Reacting to and discussing priorities and structure is difficult in the abstract. But the concession we make with wireframes to help people understand them (or even to solicit this kind of feedback on purpose) means risking conversations that diverge from the matter at hand.

The content rabbit hole

Even with a well-defined purpose, wireframe discussions can quickly lose focus. The primary culprit is meeting participants reacting to elements of the wireframe that are not really in question. Words (meaning structural, instructional, and sample content) is (a) something easy to react to and (b) something everyone has an opinion about.

Establish at the beginning of the meeting which content in the wireframes is in scope for discussion. You may have incorporated some real sample content to give people a realistic view of the page, but don't feel the need to dig into it.

Structural content (headers and navigation) and instructional content (field labels, error messages) may be in-scope. This may be a more challenging conversation to moderate: You may be more interested in addressing the tone and message of the content without digging into the exact words.

Should content ever be out of scope? Can you legitimately talk about a wireframe without talking about its content? A more nuanced view of what content is (there are different types and every wireframe reflects all of them to a greater or lesser extent) yields, perhaps, a less absolute position. Some content is always in-scope for a wireframes discussion.

The visual design rabbit hole

Wireframes are inherently visual, just like they have words. Both are generally unavoidable. In some ways, visual design is a more challenging distraction because it's difficult to reassure people that the things they're concerned about won't have an impact on the final design. People who raise issues about spacing or type size or whitespace have legitimate concerns—wireframes are just not the right place to work them out.

Structure, aesthetic, voice: Managing the overlap

If you take off your web design hat for a second and look at wireframes again, it seems weird to separate three things that make up experience. These elements—structure, visual style, and voice—are experienced as one.

One mistake you can make is to keep looking at them in separate and distinct silos. Your job as a designer is to shape the whole experience, and the nature of our medium means that sometimes you have to do that a little bit at a time.

Whether you bring this up explicitly in your conversations or not, do not forget to take a moment to think about the wireframes as a skeleton needing flesh and more to make it a true living product.

Dismissing feedback and getting defensive

Do not, under any circumstances, undermine the feedback provided by meeting participants. Establishing yourself as someone unwilling to discuss design ideas positions you as an obstacle. The organization will learn to route around you, cutting you out from subsequent design activities. I've seen this happen.

People don't mind being wrong, but they want their voice heard. Your role as a designer is to help them find that voice, discuss the ideas, and zero-in on something good. Your role is to help other people provide good feedback on design, to become better critics and to be productive members of the design team.

That said, making every design decision through committee debate or democratic voting misses the point of discussion. Design decisions need rationale, clarity, and alignment with a vision. Therefore design decisions should be driven by:

- A singular vision, hopefully held by a manager or director on the project, who is empowered to enforce that vision.
- A set of standards, established through testing and validation.
- Meaningful, relevant, and appropriate testing procedures.

Productive design conversations happen in cultures where at least one of these things holds true. The discussion becomes unproductive when designers rely on their "expertise" as the sole rationale for the design decision. Such environments are ripe for breeding defensiveness and arrogance. If you find yourself bumping up against other people who "just don't get design," take the responsibility to educate them, helping them contribute to the discussion. This is the only way to create design-friendly corporate cultures.

APPLYING AND USING WIREFRAMES

Wireframes' use does not end with creating and discussing them. Their value extends beyond realizing design ideas and facilitating conversations about user experience. You can employ them throughout the design process to elaborate on concepts, provide direction to downstream activities, and even as a vehicle for testing. Before you get to any of that stuff, though, get good at annotating wireframes: adding adjacent text to explain its behavior.

Annotating Wireframes

Like any other diagram in this book, wireframes cannot stand on their own. Though less abstract than a concept model, more tangible than a flowchart, and more specific to design than personas, wireframes are still representations. Wireframes, especially those rendered on paper, cannot capture the detailed behaviors and functions of an interface. Annotations help bridge that gap.

While there are many ways to annotate a wireframe, the tried and true method is using markers to point out important parts of the wireframe, and elaborating on details in notes on the side.

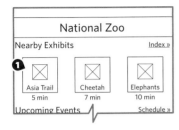

❶ Event button: Tapping this button takes users to the event details screen.

Figure 7.21: Tried and true wireframe annotations entail a number, a pointer, and a note.

In some cases, it's worthwhile to use a larger field to highlight an area of the wireframe. Even though you might have conceived of the wireframe as having specific content areas, these distinctions may be lost once the wireframe becomes more detailed. Your annotations may also only refer to a small piece of a content area, or they may refer to multiple content areas.

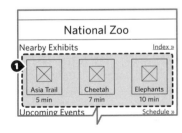
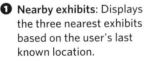

❶ Nearby exhibits: Displays the three nearest exhibits based on the user's last known location.

Figure 7.22: Delineate particular regions of the wireframe for your annotation using a larger semitransparent field,

Of course, the complexity of your wireframes could warrant some combination of these two approaches. One way to do this is to first annotate the large regions, then create separate pages in the document to annotate each component. Figure 7.23 shows what this might look like.

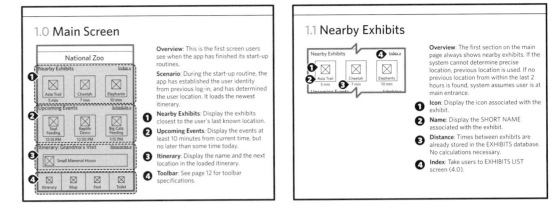

Figure 7.23: When simple annotations aren't enough, you may have to break up the wireframe to provide the right level of detail.

A modular approach works well here, giving you room to annotate the details of each component.

Wireframes themselves can vary along four dimensions (scale, abstraction, depth, and fidelity). Likewise, annotations may be measured by "weight," which refers to the level of detail. Light annotations are those that provide a description of the screen's functionality and behavior without digging into the details. Light annotations gloss over the various scenarios and don't provide a comprehensive view of all the different states a wireframe may display. Heavier annotations provide increasing levels of detail, to the point that they constitute functional specifications sufficient for driving development.

While you can drive the weight of your annotations, final assessment is up to the people responsible for building the site. The development team may require additional levels of detail, even if you feel you've provided heavy annotations.

There are four topics that should drive your annotations: overview, behaviors, content rules, and states.

Overview

A blurb describing the purpose and objective of the wireframe helps set context. Use the overview to boil the wireframe down into a single sentence.

But the overview can be more than just a single sentence, providing further context with some additional fields:

- **"Use when" and "don't use when" instructions**: As our design processes become more modular, our outputs become more about providing a set of Lego bricks that can be used in many different instances. Providing usage guidelines can help in subsequent efforts to determine whether a page template or a component can and should be used in different circumstances. For example, the itinerary long description component might specify that it should be used when displaying unfamiliar itineraries. It might specify that they should not be used in a sidebar itinerary list.
- **Scenario**: Describe the user's situation when looking at this particular screen. If the screen addresses multiple situations, spelling them out will help the development team. Focus on the portion of the scenario that sets context for the screen or could affect the display: log-in, user role, and where the user came from.
- **See also**: While maintaining references in a deliverable can be challenging, especially complex experiences may be difficult to document all on one page.

Behaviors

Annotations that describe how the interface changes in response to user inputs describe that screen's "behaviors." Consider these behaviors:

- **Links**: The simplest behavior annotation answers the question, "Where do people go when they click on this link?" The answer is generally a reference to another wireframe, or to some other page on the site.

- **Form elements**: Fields in a form require annotations to help people understand what is and is not allowed in the field. Text boxes may be annotated to indicate character length or validation criteria. Drop-down menus may be annotated to capture the full range of choices.
- **Form submissions**: Like links, these annotations answer the question, "What happens when people submit this form?"
- **Transitions**: With front-end technologies allowing more complex interactions, annotations sometimes have to explain transitions. For example, hovering over an itinerary produces a balloon with additional information. How quickly does the balloon appear? Does it just appear, or does it animate in? How long does it stay on the screen? If in scope for the wireframe, its associated annotations can answer these questions.
- **Other rules**: Some rules are specific to the particular interface. For example, in the itinerary picker, describing the behavior and states of the slider for choosing the size of the group may require rules not easily categorized elsewhere. (Does the slider move smoothly or "click into place?" How many different settings are there? Does each setting have a unique icon and label?)

Content rules

Back to basics: Wireframes define content areas in templates. Those content areas will contain similar kinds of information, but not necessarily the same information every time the site renders the page. Rules about content should describe the criteria used to select content for a particular area of the site, and provide some suggestions on the kinds of information displayed for the content. Some criteria you might use to specify rules about content:

- **Recentness**: From what time period should the system draw content?
- **Quantity**: How many pieces of content can be displayed?
- **Type**: Should content be specified from a particular type?

- **Topic**: Should content be marked with a particular set of keywords?
- **Other metadata**: Is this content from a particular author? Or, if a product, of a particular price range?
- **Usage and popularity**: Should the content be drawn from among the most trafficked?
- **Default**: If nothing matches the criteria you specify, what should be displayed?

Some of these criteria are more loaded than others. Usage and popularity depends on the site's tracking of that information. If the infrastructure has no means for capturing and interpreting usage information, it can't be a criteria for choosing content.

If your wireframe doesn't already specify the format for displaying the content, you may need to be specific about what information gets displayed. For small lists of recommended products on an e-commerce site, this might be nothing more than a thumbnail image, the name of the product, and the price. On the itinerary site, we might specify the associated image, the name of the itinerary, the short description, average user rating, and total number of reviews.

Your wireframe may contain more specific content areas, variables that specify different individual pieces of information. For example the account link at the top of the page that says "Hi, Dan!" might be specified in your wireframe as "Hi, [Firstname]!" While the content rule may seem self-evident, use an annotation to specify additional information like:

- **Source:** Where is this information drawn from? Is there a particular database or particular field in the user database?
- **Format**: Any special rules about formatting the information? (For example, always render this with a capital letter first, regardless of what's in the database.)

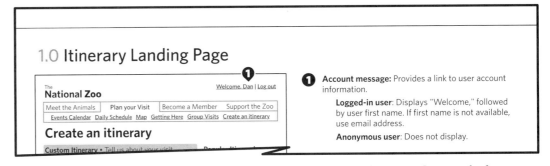

Figure 7.24: Content rules for a specific variable help developers know exactly where to draw the information from.

- **Default**: What does this look like if there is no information? (For example, maybe this whole statement changes to "Need to update your account info?")

States

If an area of the page appears differently in different circumstances, this is called a "state." A state is a scenario affecting the display of the page or the component. Like content rules, states are based on a set of criteria, but these vary based on the specifics of the application. Unlike content rules, a page or component has a discrete set of states, and they're usually named based on the circumstance or summarizing the effect on the design. A form, for example, may have three states—blank, prefilled, or error.

From a documentation perspective, you may need to create a wireframe for each state, especially if the differences between them are dramatic. At the component level, putting all its different states on one page in the document helps people compare the variations and understand the circumstances that drive them.

When documenting states for pages, it can be challenging to spell out the differences between them all on one page. In this case, include an overview page dedicated to highlighting the circumstances of each state, and then dig into the details of each screen on subsequent pages.

Connecting Wireframes to Other Deliverables

Wireframes are powerful because they can describe the user experience in great detail. But reviewing wireframes (especially when you aren't their author) can be challenging because they often appear out of order or out of context. Readers don't get a great sense of the flow, of the more subtle interactions, or how the wireframe might deal with different situations.

The Flowcharts chapter discussed wireflows, one technique for integrating wireframes with that diagram. Here are some other ideas on building a bridge between wireframes and other diagrams.

Providing context for pages

To understand a wireframe means understanding where it fits into the overall user experience. Site maps and flowcharts can help provide context for the wireframe, showing how it relates to other pages or templates in the site.

Some tips:

- **Zoom in on the appropriate portion**, especially if the flow or site map is too big to be recognizable when shrunk. When talking about a flow, I may even remove everything except what comes immediately before and what comes after.

- **Strip most or all formatting** from the structure. You may have used various colors and line weights to differentiate nodes on the site map, but those will just be distracting at a small scale. Use only the barest minimum to ensure the structure is still recognizable.
- **Highlight the relevant page** in the structure. Use a dark color to mark which page you're talking about, even if you've focused on just a handful of pages in the structure.

Providing context for components

The context for a component is a page; components fit into pages like pages fit into structures. Show where components fit into the site by incorporating a small thumbnail of the relevant page and highlighting the component. In most cases, you can use a small version of the actual wireframe, as in Figure 7.26.

If components may be used across different templates, you can use a small version of a generic page layout. The generic page layout shows the structure of the page in terms of regions, highlighting the appropriate region where the component might fit.

Prototyping and Usability Testing with Wireframes

Though the thrust of this chapter is using wireframes as diagrams to describe priority and functionality, wireframes can serve as the basis for something more interactive. Rather than describing the behaviors and flows, you can demonstrate them by stitching together wireframes. Describing how is beyond the scope of this book, but Todd Zaki Warfel's *Prototyping: A Practitioner's Guide* (Rosenfeld Media, 2009) provides a great overview of different approaches to creating interactive prototypes. Meanwhile, I'll leave you with some thoughts:

Figure 7.25: Flowcharts appearing alongside wireframes can help people understand how the screen fits into the overall experience.

- **Establish scenarios**: Wireframes for documentation require a different treatment of scenarios than testing does. With documentation, you can simply acknowledge changes of state, but with a prototype you need to show them. Outline the scenarios you want to demonstrate at the outset, so you can anticipate the range of assets you'll need to create.

- **Select prototyping approach**: Just because you create wireframes in a diagramming application like Visio or OmniGraffle doesn't mean they can't be turned into interactive prototypes. There are a number of ways to generate semifunctional demonstrations using PDFs, Flash, or slide-based applications like PowerPoint or Keynote. Each format comes with pros and cons, but understanding the capabilities of the selected tool will also help drive asset creation.

- **Incorporate out-of-scope pages**: Some pages may not be in-scope for the design effort, but may be necessary for demonstrating the new concept. The site's home page or the log-in page, for example, may be dependencies in the user experience, but may not be part of the design effort. Establish a means for incorporating these pages in a way that doesn't add unanticipated burden to the design team.

On-the-Fly Wireframes

Proficiency with your wireframing tool-of-choice can lead to some new and interesting techniques in designing screens. Combine that proficiency with an increased focus on collaborative design, and you might find yourself wireframing during the course of a meeting. Reacting to and incorporating design ideas on-the-fly can be a powerful technique for making design decisions efficiently and involving the entire project team. Rather than take notes on a design and then translate those notes into a new iteration, you're creating the next version right then and there.

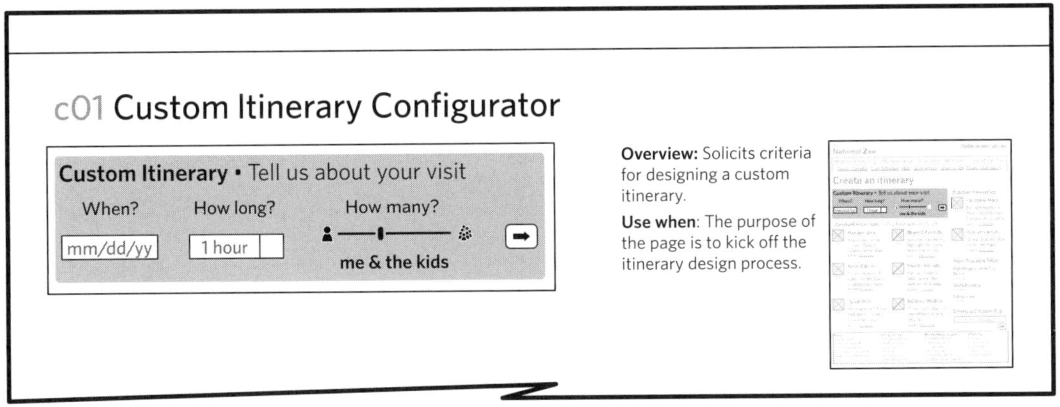

Figure 7.26: Providing context for a unique component, a thumbnail-size page wireframe shows where the component fits into the screen layout.

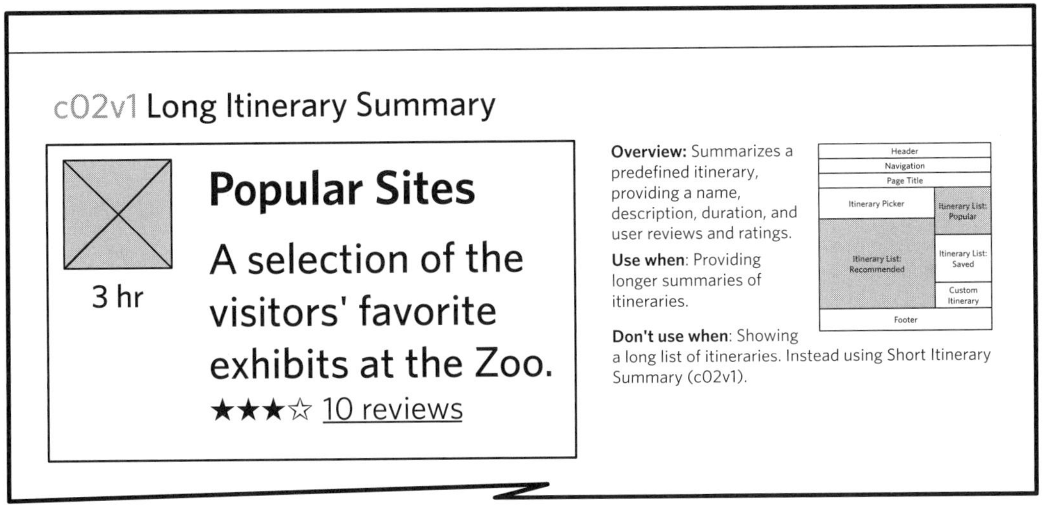

Figure 7.27: Providing context for a reusable component, a simplified thumbnail of the screen highlights which regions of the page are valid placements for the component.

The main challenge with this approach is sacrificing your role as a designer for the production efforts. Don't lose the thread of the design conversation, and don't neglect your own contribution to the design conversation in favor of incorporating feedback from the assembled team.

Personally, I've seen this done successfully by only one person, my business partner Nathan Curtis.

DESIGN IN BLACK AND WHITE

The power of wireframes, in a nutshell, is the universal acceptance that we can sketch what goes on the screen with rectangles and lines. The ability to zero-in on the content and priorities of an information display is essential on every design project. When design teams ask the question, "What do users see on this screen," they really want to know, "What do I see here?" Is a wireframe a tool for the ego? Maybe, maybe not. But a wireframe certainly is a dose of reassurance, a stake in the ground regarding What Goes Here.

Wireframes persist as a documentation tool because they are flexible. As diagrams describing content, behavior, and priority, they give us a lot of room to play with the exact presentation. Styles of wireframes emerge to suit the designer and design team. As the team becomes more cohesive, or the design system (the visual standards for the web site) becomes more mature, the wireframes can be more informal, simplifying the communication process. On the other hand, complex products, elaborate production processes, and other influences can keep wireframes highly formal. Neither extreme is better: that a diagram can occupy such a broad space *is* the value.

Modern production tools can make wireframes easy to produce, and there are many different approaches: vector artwork (Adobe Illustrator or Adobe InDesign), vector diagrams (Microsoft Visio or OmniGroup's OmniGraffle), or embedded with a prototyping program (like Axure).

Simple, portable formats offer a range of reuse. We've used wireframes as the starting point for Flash-based prototypes or clickable PDFs. The simplicity of the format allows designers to explore using other media, like HTML, to create wireframes. Combining wireframes, a historically flat diagram, with greater interactivity gives designers more opportunities to communicate complex behaviors. It provides tools to allow designers to test their concepts.

Wireframes are born out of the simplest way to represent a screen displaying interactive content: a bunch of rectangles. Stand up at a whiteboard or sit down with your sketchbook to diagram a screen and you will draw rectangles. The screen can take up a wall or fit into the palm of your hand, but they're all rectangles, and their content may be similarly represented. Whether or not the display of information continues to exist in such devices, there's a good chance that rectangles persist as the dominant form because of their simplicity.

Trends, however, suggest that screens will persist:

- Technological innovation is working to fit more information (higher resolution) on screens we can take with us. High-definition video, a novelty only 10 years ago, has become more pervasive.
- The screens themselves are becoming input devices as well as display devices. Any sophisticated phone you buy these days will be likely to have a touch screen.
- Innovation is going the other way, too, allowing us to put projectors in our pockets, so we can take over a wall with an information display anywhere we go.

When asked to design for any one of these devices, you'll draw a rectangle.

What changes is the layer of information on top of these rectangles: their behaviors, state changes, and responses to our interactions. As new interactive gestures become available—whether people tap, click, wave, or talk to the display—the content itself remains trapped in rectangles.

But let's say you can transcend the screen. Let's say technological improvements allow for cheaper ubiquitous computing—computers are embedded everywhere. How do you describe a user interface when the information is conveyed with sound alone? When consumer products have complex interactions that don't involve screens (like the refrigerator that can place your grocery order), how do you explain the interaction model? When the conveyance of information transcends screen-based devices or visual stimuli, it will be interesting to see whether or not designers develop a different method for representing information.

Wireframes are representations of screens, but ultimately they are about the kind of information presented and their relative priorities, as well as the range of behaviors available to users. Wireframes took on the form of our primary means for interacting with information (screens) and will evolve to accommodate other media. What we know of as a wireframe today may not look the same tomorrow, but its essence will persist. Ultimately, this tool (like any other design tool) is for illuminating the dark recesses of complexity, no matter what form it takes.

EXERCISES

1. Reverse-engineer a wireframe by using a page from a favorite site and boxing out the content areas. This exercise works best with a large content site, but creating wireframes for other kinds of sites often yields interesting insights about the structure. Keep the practice wireframe very low fidelity, focusing on just carving out the important areas of the page and giving them meaningful labels. Add a layer of information by distinguishing different types of content areas: navigation, content, forms, and so on. Also distinguish between static and dynamic content areas, and reusable components. Eliminate any key identifying information from the site (its name, for example) and show your wireframe to a partner. Have them ask you all sorts of questions about the functionality, and see if they can guess the site it came from.

2. Take your low-fidelity wireframe and create two higher-fidelity versions: one with lots of abstraction and one with no abstraction. That is, the first should have very little real content, using mostly variable names and other kinds of placeholders to demonstrate its flexibility and range. The second should be as concrete as possible, using real content from the original page. The fidelity should remain well short of a fully rendered page, but it should be something beyond simple rectangles.

3. Practice annotating by taking a screenshot of a favorite site and pretending it is a wireframe. Embed it in a document, add some markers and notes. Create multiple versions of your annotations: one to describe behaviors and another to describe content rules. Share the annotated screen with a colleague or your study group and see if they understand all the behaviors, interactions, and business rules.

Part

2

Design Deliverables

Chapter 8

Deliverable Basics

di'·liv·ər·əbəl (n.)

A document submitted during the course of a web design project to facililtate communication, capture decisions, and stimulate conversation.

The first edition of this book treated the artifacts described in the preceding chapters as separate deliverables—distinct documents produced in the course of a design project. Something's changed since I wrote the first edition in 2005. While I don't think design process and methodology have evolved significantly, I have a greater sensitivity to how deliverables and the design process work together to move a project along.

I should credit my partner at EightShapes, Nathan Curtis, with formalizing this awareness. Through his work on creating modular deliverables, he successfully distinguishes the story we're telling (the deliverable) from the characters in the story (the artifacts).

Site maps, flowcharts, wireframes, and the rest may be little stories in and of themselves, but they are part of a larger whole. A deliverable, as a stand-alone document that tells a complete story, must convey the "larger whole," the entire project to which each diagram contributes.

This distinction between artifact and deliverable yields a different approach to creating documents, too. On paper, most design methodologies call for producing a distinct document or two at the end of each phase. Research ends with a research report and personas. Discovery ends with a user experience strategy. Information architecture ends with a deck of wireframes.

About the Specific Deliverables

The four remaining chapters in this section elaborate on deliverables to use in specific situations. Usability plans and reports are the setup and payoff of usability testing. Competitive analysis and design briefs come at the beginning of the project to set context.

Noticeably absent from that list is functional specifications. The chapter you're reading now, however, can serve as your

One document: A big deliverable, but good continuity

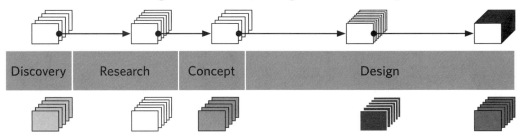

Multiple documents: Less continuity, but more discrete focus

Figure 8.1: Deliverables relative to the project timeline, can be one or multiple documents.

guide for functional specifications. This is the document that captures all the details behind a web site design: how the screens behave, where the content comes from, and the behind-the-scenes rules that drive the user experience. I wrote this chapter with those challenges in mind.

This chapter is inspired by functional specifications because I've been doing things a little differently. Instead of composing multiple separate deliverables, I produce one document over the course of a project—call it the Design Specification. This Design Specification grows and evolves with the project, its contents expanding as design work proceeds, or contracting as other activities in the project wane and become less important.

Why one document?

- **Maintenance**: It's easy to maintain a single document. With one deliverable, managing dependencies is simpler because you're not having to create a mechanism for referencing other documents. Instead of pointing to a personas document (and who knows what happened to that document anyway), the single deliverable already includes the personas.

My firm, EightShapes, released a collection of templates for Adobe InDesign, called EightShapes Unify. These templates are primarily for composing deliverables and incorporating artifacts into those deliverables. Having EightShapes Unify at our disposal makes document production significantly easier, accommodating much of the administrivia and automating as much as possible.

Using a set of templates, whether it be EightShapes Unify, some other collection, or making your own, helps the process of creating the deliverables substantially.

You can learn more at http://unify.eightshapes.com.

Approach	In which you...	Benefits	Challenges
Multiple deliverables	Create a separate document for each activity in the project schedule. Iterate on a document only within the space of the activity.	Clear delineations of activities.	Enforcing consistency between the documents. Ensuring all the deliverables are telling the same story. Ensuring continuity between the activities, such that they're all contributing to the same vision.
One deliverable to rule them all	Create a single document whose contents will evolve over the course of the project.	Only one document to track and maintain. All information is in one place.	Different activities have different owners, each of whom may want to produce their own deliverables. Different activities may happen in parallel, making it difficult to manage the composition of their outputs. The size of the document may become unwieldy.

Table 8.1: Comparing deliverable strategies, using one document throughout the life of a project versus creating several different deliverables.

- **Context**: Instead of having to set context with each new deliverable, the document preserves the "historical record" of the project.
- **Focus**: You can adjust the contents of the document to preserve focus on what's important. This is true for the project as a whole, too. Many methodologies became mired in the outputs and not the results. Documents are a by-product of creativity, not the desired outcome.
- **Continuity**: It can be easy to lose the thread of a project when it's structured around multiple documents. As the project evolves, the singular document does so in parallel, tracing the series of design decisions.

Of course, creating a single document presumes:

- **Flexibility in format**: You can let the document grow and change over time.
- **One team**: Yours is the only team responsible for the content of the document or the outputs of the design process.
- **One file owner**: You can name one person in charge of pulling everything together.
- **One track**: Your team is operating on a single stream of work, not dividing up the scope of work.

In choosing the right approach (one document vs. several), consider the benefits and challenges, in Table 8.1.

Creating Multiple Separate Documents

In some cases, multiple documents will be unavoidable or preferable, because of the following:

- **Corporate culture**: Some organizations have particular ideas about how design documentation should look. In large or bureaucratic companies, format might be dictated on high and the project team has little say in how to communicate design. In most cases, however, the organization is indifferent to the exact format of the deliverable, so I can easily let it grow and change over time. Corporate culture dictates the need for distinct reports and design documents for each activity.
- **Multiple contributors**: My clients sometimes use multiple vendors on a project, and each vendor is assigned a different activity. If my firm is doing information architecture and interaction design, another vendor may be focused on graphic design, and others may be engaged to

do testing and research. The client may handle implementation internally. This array of people and teams can make it challenging to use a single document from beginning to end for the entire project. For my portion of the project, however, that is how we will operate. Project logistics, such as separate funding sources for different aspects of the project, can make it difficult to proceed gracefully from one activity to the next.

- **Production logistics**: For better or for worse, current technologies operate under the assumption that there is one person who is the final "owner" of the file. Many applications try to simplify the process of integrating content from contributors, but ultimately don't make it easy for people to be working on different parts of the same document. If Nathan and I are each working on a different part of a deliverable, we'll break it up but designate one of us to be the "final owner," the person responsible for integrating all the content.
- **Multiple tracks**: Large projects will sometimes support multiple tracks of design, each track pursuing a different piece of the pie. Like one team and one owner previously, one track is not essential—there are ways to use a single document on a multitrack project—but it is easier.

These and other circumstances have nuances that will demand different approaches to documentation. In this situation consider taking steps to preserve continuity, such as:

- Establishing documentation standards and universal conventions at the beginning of the project
- Insisting that everyone working on documentation create good and consistent summary pages. These pages will be the easiest way to incorporate key information from one document into another.

WHAT MAKES A GOOD DELIVERABLE

The things that make for a powerful diagram—legibility, relevance, actionability—are the same things that make for a good deliverable. Like diagrams, simplicity in deliverables is paramount.

Good Deliverables Tell Stories

A good deliverable tells a story, and telling a good story is hard. (Seriously, turn on your television in prime time any night of the week and you're more likely to hit bad storytelling than good.) So, let's take a good look at what this means in the context of a design project.

Theme

Good stories have a theme, an essence, a "what this story's about." It is, in short, a concept that ties ideas together and gives them meaning. Theme has been, well, a major theme in the earlier chapters in this book because it's a useful mechanism for keeping a diagram, artifact, or conversation focused. Themes provide direction for design, a basis for making design decisions. Can design projects proceed successfully without a theme? Potentially, but experience shows that having a single unifying idea can keep design activities focused.

The design project may have an overall theme, but it's useful to devise such a focus for the deliverable itself. This is more than just the purpose of the deliverable (to communicate the latest design ideas or to solicit feedback or to facilitate decision-making). A theme for the deliverable constitutes the primary takeaway, the one thing that readers get from reading the document. Some examples:

- **The swim against the tide**: "This project is fraught with external challenges. Here's what we've been able to accomplish within the established constraints, but here's why they're not optimal."

- **The fresh eyes**: "This design challenge is very complex, and would benefit from a new perspective. Here's a new way of thinking about this problem and what insights it yielded."
- **The refactored challenge**: "This approach to the design challenge doesn't accommodate all the requirements, but it does address user needs as described in user research."

Stating them this explicitly as a planning exercise is good. Stating them this bluntly in the document may challenge team dynamics.

Beginning, middle, and end

A deliverable that tells a story acknowledges what came before. This reference is more than just a mechanism to remind the project team what they just did. References to prior work lend credibility to the current work, normalize the underlying assumptions shared by the project team, and, ultimately, drive the design.

One way to position the most recent work is in contrast to what immediately came before: Version 2 improves upon version 1 in this way. A version history, as such, not only helps people follow the trail of the design process but know what to focus on. With the increasing complexity of projects (in terms of requirements, technical capabilities, quantity of stakeholders, and depth of reach into the organization), a "previously on our show" message reminds people what's important.

Recent work may also lead into the next set of design activities: A site map sets up wireframing, personas provide context for up flowcharting. The "end" of a deliverable is not just the design punch line, but also how it sets up the next steps.

Conflict, contrast, and comparison

When denied a viewing of the latest commercial flick due to the potential fear factor, my son often asks us, "Why are there scary parts in movies?" At an early age, he learned about drama—it's what makes stories interesting. In the hopelessly nonfiction, unanimated, explosion-free world of design documentation, we can still use conflict to make an impression on project participants. (And I'm not talking about 3D PowerPoint animations.)

In this case, conflict comes from contrast and comparison. The project plan provides one way to draw comparisons: time. We can compare between the state of the design today and the one previously; between the current design activities and the ones to come. But there are other kinds of contrast a deliverable can use as the basis for a story:

- **Different approaches**: In short, the deliverable presents two different ways to solve a design problem. It lines up the options side-by-side to highlight the tension between them and make it easy to pick one over the other.
- **Conflicting priorities**: Even the simplest design problems come with inherent conflicts. With all the different people working on the project, all the different objectives, all the insights from user research, the design team is bound to encounter requirements that conflict. Conflicting requirements call for two different design approaches, or one solution that successfully mediates between the two. There are multiple ways of addressing such conflicts, but regardless of which direction you choose, the document can tee up your approach by illuminating the distinction.
- **Ambiguity in requirements**: Another kind of conflict is between reality (what you have) and the ideal (what you'd like to have). Positioning the starting point against the ideal can help stakeholders understand the gaps in knowledge. Perhaps you're trying to fill these gaps through research or brainstorming, or perhaps the gaps

in knowledge help explain the state of your design direction or the approach you took to get there.

Tension draws people in. The more you can use these conflicts inherent in the design process as a framework for the document, the more you will engage the project team to participate.

Characters

Stories have characters, the seemingly autonomous actors who, with the right amount of depth and empathy make readers care about them and interested in the story. The stories I'm most attracted to are those whose characters I care about long after the show or movie or book is over. It isn't the plot lines that linger in my imagination: It's the definition of the characters—who they are and the decisions they made.

It can be easy to default to thinking of personas (or even project team members) as the characters in your story, but this approach does a disservice to the deliverable.

Can you treat design artifacts as characters? At the simplest level, I've seen good art directors name their design concepts. Some of the best names are abstract, evoking the concept without necessarily being an accurate, objective description. (Think "Blizzard" for a design concept in cool colors rather than "Gray and Teal with Rounded Corners.")

As the artifacts emerge, think of them as distinct personalities, each relating to the theme (the overall design concept) in a different way. Independently, they can't describe the theme fully: They need each other to explore the theme and overarching concept fully. As their author, you need to ensure that they are believably part of the same universe, making use of the same visual language, resting on the same assumptions, and working toward the same objectives.

Storytelling in design documentation

Therefore, after reading a deliverable, someone who hasn't been along for the ride should be able to describe:

- What the current state of the project is.
- How the current design decisions relate to previous activities and how they set up the next set of activities.
- What the overall theme of the design project is.
- What the most important design decisions are, and how they relate to the overall theme.
- What the major issues facing the design project are.

Make sure you incorporate content in your deliverable that accomplishes these objectives.

Good Deliverables Encourage Conversation

All designers hope to prepare deliverables that are compelling enough, thoughtful enough, and well-written enough to encourage enthusiastic conversation. Frequently, project parameters (timelines and budget), constraints (requirements), and challenges prevent design teams from achieving this on their documentation. This is as it should be, as the focus for the design team should be on developing the design.

I'm sure there are great design deliverables that stand on their own, products of great minds (and greater budgets and timelines) that yield productive brainstorming sessions. Don't expect every document on every project to achieve that level of engagement. You'll drive yourself crazy. Frankly, my assumption these days is that the best conversation must be explicitly encouraged, not simply hoped for.

Why care so much about conversation? The purpose of a deliverable is to advance the project. Like the scene in a movie that shows the ne'er-do-well kids finding a treasure map stuck inside an old library book, the purpose of a

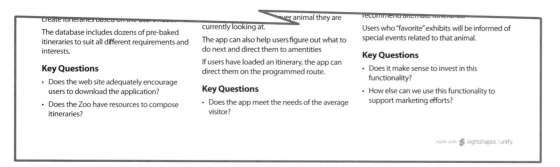

Table of Contents

made with eightshapes | unify

Figure 8.2: A table of contents makes a nice meeting agenda. In this case, I've highlighted different sections of the deliverable and assigned them to different times in the meeting.

create itineraries based on the user's needs.

The database includes dozens of pre-baked itineraries to suit all different requirements and interests.

Key Questions

• Does the web site adequately encourage users to download the application?

• Does the Zoo have resources to compose itineraries?

...ver animal they are currently looking at.

The app can also help users figure out what to do next and direct them to amentities

If users have loaded an itinerary, the app can direct them on the programmed route.

Key Questions

• Does the app meet the needs of the average visitor?

recommend alternate itineraries.

Users who "favorite" exhibits will be informed of special events related to that animal.

Key Questions

• Does it make sense to invest in this functionality?

• How else can we use this functionality to support marketing efforts?

made with eightshapes | unify

Figure 8.3: Questions embedded in the deliverable make it easy to kick off the conversation.

deliverable is only to move the plot. If it's not getting you closer to launching a product, why make it? The next sections offer some techniques to make sure you have something to talk about.

Table of contents

The value of a table of contents? It makes a great meeting agenda. Nathan introduced me to this technique. Within the first 5 minutes of a meeting, he lingers on the table of contents as a means for establishing the discussion for the next 25 to 55 minutes.

Explicit questions

Lace your deliverable with questions. Also known as the "brute force" approach, by putting questions in your deliverable you:

• Remind yourself of remaining issues to be discussed
• Inspire conversation by feeding participants one half of the dialog

You can put questions:

• **Adjacent to the design artifacts** about which you have specific questions
• At the **beginning of the document**, as a way to set the agenda for the meeting ("we need to answer these questions")
• At the **end of the document**, as a way to kick off conversation after reviewing the latest iteration of the design

For ideas on the different kinds of questions you might embed in a document, look through the "Presenting…" sections of each of the preceding chapters. The meeting agenda section deals with soliciting feedback and offers different questions related to each artifact. Generally speaking these questions fall into these categories:

- **Clarifying the design problem**: Any activity after framing the design problem inevitably sheds more light on the design problem. This is one of the frustrating (or perhaps intoxicating) truths about creative endeavors: the more you try to solve a problem, the more you understand it. By the same token, the more you try to define a problem, the harder it will be to solve. Philosophical conundrums aside, your efforts may yield additional questions about the design problem itself.
- **Identifying gaps**: By "gaps" I'm usually referring to scope: what's missing in what you've designed so far. Does the design adequately address all the different scenarios? Does it accommodate all the requirements? Does it leave out any crucial information?
- **Validating the approach**: Your questions may try to get at whether your approach is right. This is a superset of the previous questions. Are you solving the right problem? Are you missing anything that renders the design concept "incorrect" in any way?

Decisions

Depending on where you are in the design process, some deliverables may represent crossroads—an opportunity for stakeholders to push the project on one direction or another. Perhaps you're presenting two design concepts and the project team is responsible for selecting one. Perhaps there are three different aspects of the project and you need the project owner to select one aspect as your focus moving forward.

When positioning decisions, make sure the deliverable:

- **Clearly identifies the options**: You can go east or west. That's how explicit the deliverable should be. No doubt your project has nuances that makes such a clear divide challenging, but if you can position it that way at the outset, it will be easier for your stakeholders to weigh in.

- **Describes the implications for each option**: Choosing one option over the other will have a ripple effect downstream. Preceding chapters have a discussion of implications in the "Presenting…" sections, and the book's introduction has a framework for describing different kinds of impacts design decisions might have. Use these as a reference for identifying the different impacts of each decision.
- **Provides a recommendation**: Indicate which option you prefer, and provide a rationale. No doubt some readers will disagree here, but experience shows that my clients (internal and external alike) value my opinion. Recommendations especially make an impact if they have strong justifications behind them.

Good Deliverables Are Actionable

Actionability, another concept I owe to Nathan, is the document's ability to carry project participants into the next set of activities. Actionable documents are more specific than those with a set of "next steps" at the end. Instead, they position each insight, conclusion, or decision in terms of how it informs the next activity. Strictly speaking, nothing should be in the document that doesn't explicitly inspire the next set of decisions.

- Deliverables describing research results should provide explicit direction about what the design should or should not do.
- Deliverables establishing a structure for the web site should clearly inventory the range of templates to be designed.
- Deliverables providing functional specifications should provide developers enough information to take the concept to coding.

This is the main reason why artifacts can't stand on their own. A diagram depicting a site structure, for example, isn't usually explicit in what such a structure means to the project activities. Therefore, to integrate actionability:

- **Use imperative tone**: That is, conjugate your verbs as commands, much like the first phrase of each of these bullets does. It may come across as rude, but ultimately your design artifact isn't trying to make friends by using a casual, breezy tone. The document's purpose is to move the project along.
- **Preface the document with key takeaways**: Research documents are ripe opportunities for a one-page preface summarizing everything learned in the user study or usability test. In fact, most documents can benefit from a one-page summary explicitly stating what the team needs to keep in mind as they move forward with the project.
- **Frame each page in the document with a purpose or conclusion**: Each page in the document is another opportunity to provide direction to the next step in the design process. Research documents are ideal for this: present your findings, but conclude the page with a main takeaway. Set this conclusion apart visually, even providing an icon to highlight the severity, importance, or type of direction it is. But not every page in the document can have a clear call-to-action. Those pages should instead be framed with a purpose: explaining why this page is here, how it contributes to the overall theme and/or purpose of the document. These aren't conclusions, but instead a summary or gist. If readers read no other annotations on this page, what do they need to know about it?

Documents with purpose

To make deliverables actionable, you must start with a purpose, to know what you're driving toward. In fact, everything that makes deliverables good (storytelling, conversation, actionability) drives toward this one quality: You must have a reason for making the document.

Even if you create one document that evolves over the course of a project, each draft of that document may have a different purpose, but it has a purpose nonetheless. If you

are working on a document and have no idea why, stop and ask yourself:

- How will this move the project forward?
- What do I need from the project team in order to do my next set of tasks?
- Is the document positioned to get me that information?
- What information in this document will people later in the process use?

A purpose is different from a theme:

Purposes	Themes
Describe the role of the document in the design process	Describe the overall message of the document, which should serve the purpose
Explicitly reference project activities	Don't really care about project activities
Drive the positioning of the content in an actionable way	Prioritize the content in terms of what best illustrates the key messages

Table 8.2: Differences between purposes and themes.

Your document needs both of these.

ANATOMY OF A DELIVERABLE

Now that you have an idea of what makes for great documentation, let's make a couple of assumptions about deliverables:

1. **The Container Assumption**: They are a container for artifacts, but they have additional information beyond the artifact itself.
2. **The Format Assumption**: Deliverables are multipage documents on standard-sized pages.

Deliverables can, of course, break both assumptions. You could deliver a single-page poster containing just a site map. (The value of such a deliverable may be questionable, but you can do it.) You could deliver a series of clickable wireframes (format = electronic).

Once you start breaking the assumptions, you're talking about a different breed of deliverables—no less valuable or meaningful, but definitely beyond the scope of this book.

While these assumptions may be restrictive, they do not enforce a particular level of formality, detail, or any other qualities about the content itself. The takeaway is this: These assumptions identify a framework for telling good stories in the context of web design. Let's now look at applying that framework in the best possible way.

Title Page and Other Identifying Elements

The first sheet in a deliverable is the title page. The title page should include:

- The name of the client
- The name of the project
- The name of the deliverable
- The names of the authors
- Contact information for the authors
- Date of delivery
- Versioning information

For a good discussion of why putting authors on the document is important, see Tufte.

The first six items are pretty self-explanatory, but versioning a document is fraught with controversy. (Though that may be overstating it.) Versioning can be frustratingly (and unnecessarily) complicated. If yours is a team that likes a complicated versioning system, be sure to collaborate with them at the beginning of the project to establish standards. The most common approach is distinguishing between major changes in the document and minor changes. A version 4.3 means this is the fourth major version of the document and the third iteration of that version. If your team can successfully differentiate between major and minor changes, this may be the approach for you.

ASIDE

To version or not to version

Version numbers are curious. Ostensibly, they help readers validate that they're looking at the most up-to-date copy of the document. This, of course, is kind of silly if you don't have the author in front of you because how are you supposed to know if version 13.2 is, in fact, the latest version?

I think teams like them because they demonstrate progress. A version number like 13.2 sounds impressive: "We've been working on this a LOT. We have been thinking about your problem a LOT. Your problem is important to us."

Modern project management technologies make it relatively easy to store one and only one version of a document, while preserving a history of those versions. Cloud-based technologies are especially robust in this area.

Can version numbers go away? I think version numbers are here to stay (see the later section "Version history"). They are a convenient shorthand, and until we have a quicker means for demonstrating progress, we need them.

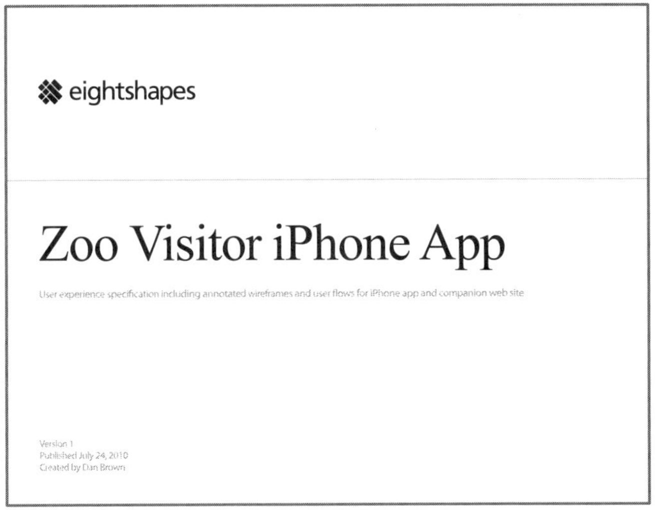
eightshapes
Zoo Visitor iPhone App
User experience specification including annotated wireframes and user flows for iPhone app and companion web site
Version 1
Published July 24, 2010
Created by Dan Brown

Figure 8.4: A deliverable's cover page with all the essential information.

My team generally uses a single integer for each version. Team members may append other numbers for internal reviews, but the document sheds those when delivered to the client. It's just as meaningful to say "version 6" as it is to say "version 1.5."

SHEET A page in a deliverable. Distinguishes it from pages on the web.

Figure 8.5: Document metadata
appears on every page in the document.
The metadata elements should match
those appearing on the home page. Of
course, individual pages should also
include page numbers.

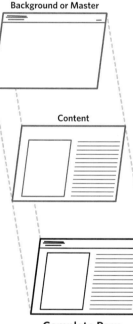

Background or Master

Content

Complete Page

Figure 8.6: Backgrounds or masters
are special pages in a file that can be
applied to other pages. Elements on a
background appear on every page to
which they are applied.

One approach to consider is "expiration date." This idea
emerged at a workshop I was teaching. In addition to a
version number, the document includes a date when the
author knows the information to be obsolete. For projects
with even a high-level plan, this should be pretty straightforward: The schedule indicates when the next iteration is
due or when the next set of activities starts. A document in
its final iteration expires at the end of the project. (It can be
tempting to put "Expires: Never" on the final version, but
this could lead to problems if the document needs updating later. Instead, better to encourage contacting the document's author to determine if there's a newer version than
to assume the document is actually up-to-date.)

Document metadata

The elements listed above for the title page are the document metadata. They should be incorporated on every sheet
in the document. The one other piece of information to
include is the page number.

A couple of tips for document metadata:

- **Use backgrounds/masters**: Most good diagramming
  and page layout applications let you establish a "background" that can be applied to certain pages. The background consists of elements that will appear on every
  page to which it is applied.
- **Use document variables**: The other useful feature for
  this endeavor is document variables, which may be
  inserted on both regular sheets and backgrounds. Typical
  variables are [page number] or [total pages] or [today's
  date]. They are usually accessed from one of the menus

in the application. Insert these babies into the document
metadata area of your background, and it practically
builds itself.

- **Create a visual hierarchy**: Document metadata is a little
  story in and of itself. There are meaningful distinctions
  between the pieces of information. Create a title box for
  the deliverable that implies these distinctions. A little
  typographic treatment goes a long way.

Front Matter

To set context, the document should include two sections
at the very beginning—a version history and a table of
contents. Is this overhead really necessary? Let me make the
case and you decide for yourself.

These context-setting elements provide some structure as
you tell a story. You can use the table of contents to set the
agenda for in-person discussions (as described earlier)
and help people looking at the document for the first (or
hundredth) time get a lay of the land. The version history
helps people focus on what's changed since their last viewing and provides accountability, demonstrating that you've
heard feedback.

Version history

I put the version history before the table of contents. In
reviewing the document in person, this is a natural progression. We go from "Here's what's changed" to "Here
are the areas of the document we'll focus on for this
conversation."

Version histories generally include:

- The version number
- The date of the version
- The author of the new version
- An account of the changes

The first three elements on this list are pretty straightforward. (Though I should mention that you should spell out names in full in the author portion. Initials can be ambiguous. There are two guys on my team with the initials JM. 'Nuff said.)

Where the variation occurs is in the account of changes to the document. These can range from the very cursory to the painstakingly detailed. As much as I would like this to be a function of the author's personality, it really depends on who uses the document. Experience shows that developers require the detail to ensure they don't build something they shouldn't.

Cursory description of document changes	Detailed description of document changes
Page 6: Stakeholder feedback incorporated throughout	Page 6: Updated links to include ellipses.
	Provided wireframes for all three states of the "log-in" button: logged in, recognized, anonymous.
	Incorporated messaging for error scenario when user is recognized and they attempt to login with a different user name.
	Changed annotation for submit button to indicate that the business team receives an email notification.

Table 8.3: Version history accounts of document changes can range from the very basic to the very detailed.

Note that both approaches do indicate the page number for the changes.

Table of contents

If you're lucky, the application you use to prepare deliverables will create a table of contents for you. (I'm especially lucky because EightShapes Unify has a built-in table of contents format already associated with styles from the document. You should download it!)

ASIDE
Versioning at the Page Level

I've tried a few other approaches to incorporating version history, driven by my inherent laziness:

- **Reflecting edits and conversations**: Using the strikethrough style (~~like this~~) and different color text, I illustrate the edits made on each page relative to the previous version.
- **Micro histories**: Instead of (or in addition to) one big version history at the beginning of the document, I put a small version history on each page. The small version history is detailed, but it only includes changes from the previous version. Using this approach, the micro history has to be explicit about which was the previous version. For example, if page 6 gets edited in version 5 but not in version 6, it will still include the micro history from version 5. So just be clear about this.
- **Version annotations**: In short, a collection of icons and "stamps" that indicate where the sheet stands in its version history. If the purpose of a version history is to call attention to things that have changed, it can be boiled down into a simple mark that says, "Look here! This is new!" These require careful monitoring though, so they are updated appropriately between versions. Some possible stamps for your arsenal: Approved, Awaiting Approval, Updated Since Version [XX], Feedback Needed.

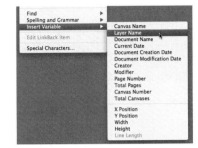

Figure 8.7: Document variables in OmniGraffle include X, Y, and Z. These let you do everything from automatic page numbering to incorporating the name of each sheet into the document metadata.

Table of contents features all use the same basic principle, but have been designed somewhat differently from application to application. They depend on your having defined "heading" styles for your deliverable. The template my team uses, in EightShapes Unify, includes Chapters, Pages, and Sub-Pages, along with several variations. The table of contents feature in Adobe InDesign will create a three-level table of contents based on these styles, so long as you used them throughout the document.

Obviously, the table of contents should reflect the structure of the document, and we'll talk more about that shortly. Suffice it to say that the table of contents is a good diagnostic tool: If it shows a long list of pages without much structure, you should find ways to break up the document. Structure helps preserve the storytelling aspect (three acts anyone?) and provides a useful mechanism for setting the agenda of discussions.

Summary

See this scar on my lower abdomen? I'll tell you what this scar is from. Picture your intrepid information architect on a two-week sprint to prepare a deliverable, a wireframes deck rife with detailed annotations. They were 10-hour days, trying to hit a deadline so the engineering team could ramp up their development efforts. Your gallant information architect had but one gate to hurdle, an in-depth review with a key business stakeholder. The day of the meeting arrives, two hours set aside to walk through the document and solicit feedback.

For better or worse, the stakeholder hadn't been present throughout the design process, and your handsome information architect was worried. Worried that they hadn't accounted for every scenario with the business rules on the configuration page. Worried that he could have done a better job designing the acknowledgement screen. Worried that his hair was kind of sticking up in the back.

The stakeholder arrives five minutes late. Your humble information architect demurely fires up the projector to walk through the deliverable, offering a freshly printed version. He directs the stakeholder to flip to the table of contents. After a brief glance, the stakeholder says, "I'm double booked. I've got to get to my other meeting. What do you need from me?"

I tell you this now to save you from scars. If you can't compact a two-hour conversation into five minutes, you're in the wrong line of work.

The first content page of your document should:

- Describe the *highlights* of the document, including any major design decisions or directions.
- Summarize any *findings, observations, or conclusions* that came out of any analysis work.
- List out the *main questions* you have for your stakeholders.

You should prepare this page whether your document is 14, 44, or 144 pages.

This will be the hardest page of the document to compose, because every opportunity to summarize, boil down, consolidate, or compact will seem like the murder of a perfectly good idea. Situations like this one happen, as unlikely as an information architect being handsome might seem. You might be in a conversation that veers way off course, or actually get to sit down for two hours with an important stakeholder who has never seen the project before. The "5-minute rule" for deliverables is more than just giving you a way to have important conversations in the space of 300 seconds. It's a way for you to ensure the integrity of your story and to be sure you can tell important parts.

The summary page needs to be *informative* (give me the essential information) and *actionable* (answering the question, now what?). If you're reducing the type size or increasing the margins to squeeze more in, you're missing the point.

Introduction and Context

An introduction is kind of a summary, but different. Introductions are not so much "what do you need to know in 5 minutes" but more "here's what I'm about to tell you."

Introductions	Summaries
Establish a framework giving the lay of the land to make it easier to process the details as they come	Capture all the essentials from the document
Focus just on the content to come	Incorporate questions, insights, recommendations, and required decisions, as well as highlights, from the content
Anticipate setting up following detail pages	Are self-contained and portable, making them easy to cut-and-paste into other documents

Table 8.4: Differences between and introduction and a summary.

There are two ways to introduce a document: describing the contents of the chapters or describing the position of the document relative to the project plan.

Chapter-based introduction

If your document is divided into chapters, the introduction can summarize what happens in each chapter. In this approach, the introduction provides a lay of the land of the document, a more detailed table of contents.

This approach is useful if the document is presenting a lot of new material, outputs from activities that haven't involved other people. The introduction doesn't emphasize the activities as much as the conclusions from that work.

Project-based introduction

Fast-moving projects with highly involved stakeholders might benefit more from a project-based introduction. In this case, the introduction sets context by describing where the team is relative to the project plan, so that the team doesn't lose the thread of the project. The key messages are "here's where we are and here's where we're going."

The appropriate picture for this kind of introduction is an abbreviated project schedule. The schedule clearly indicates

Summary

Enriching the experience of the Zoo means providing pertinent information at the moment visitors request it. Curious about the sloth bear's eating habits? Wondering why the lemurs sunbathe? Standing at an exhibit and firing up the app is all visitors need to do to learn more.

Before the Visit

Web-based application to plan trips to the Zoo.

The primary feature of this application is to create itineraries based on the user's needs.

The database includes dozens of pre-baked itineraries to suit all different requirements and interests.

Key Questions

• Does the web site adequately encourage users to download the application?

• Does the Zoo have resources to compose itineraries?

At the Zoo

Geographically-aware iPhone app that informs visitors about their current location in the Zoo.

The primary feature is to give users more information about whatever animal they are currently looking at.

The app can also help users figure out what to do next and direct them to amenities

If users have loaded an itinerary, the app can direct them on the programmed route.

Key Questions

• Does the app meet the needs of the average visitor?

After the Trip

Visitors checking in at exhibits and events earn "badges".

Badges earned on this visit
• Panda spotted
• Baby sighting

Follow-up interactions allow them to "cash-in" badges for offers and prizes.

The system remains aware of prior trips and can recommend alternate itineraries.

Users who "favorite" exhibits will be informed of special events related to that animal.

Key Questions

• Does it make sense to invest in this functionality?

• How else can we use this functionality to support marketing efforts?

made with eightshapes | unify

Figure 8.8: A document's summary page must provide essential information and explicit direction.

where you are, relative to activities before and after. The emphasis with this approach is less on the content of the output, per se, and more on how the outputs feed the next set of activities (see Figure 8.9).

If the project team is familiar with the details of the project schedule, you can use a Gantt chart itself to set the context of the document. Figure 8.10 shows a page from the document with the project schedule, where the project team is, an agenda for the discussion, and the necessary next steps.

Figure 8.9: Project-based introductions position the deliverable relative to the project plan.

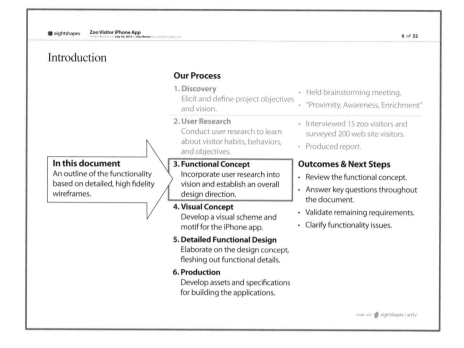

Figure 8.10: Using a project schedule to introduce a document sets the context relative to the specific activities and deliverables. It gives you an opportunity to provide status on the progress of the project.

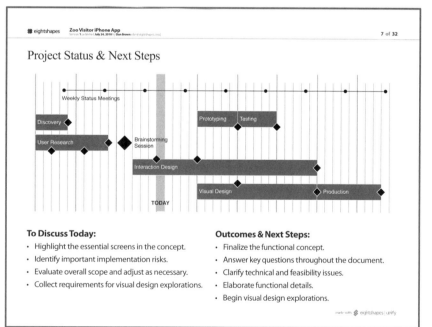

Chapters

Everything we just talked about for the document as a whole you can do for a chapter. A chapter is a document within a document and should be positioned, summarized, and introduced in much the same way just described. The real questions are, what kinds of chapters do you need, and what goes into each chapter?

Structuring your chapters

The bulk of document planning goes into the structure. How should you cut up the content? These decisions, no doubt, must be rooted in the content itself. An outline for a functional specification will not parallel the outline for a research report. In short, there is no one right way to structure the document.

Some tips on preparing the structure:

- **Spend more time on this than you think you need to**: Give yourself a 15-minute block of time to think through how you want to structure the chapters. If you have a default approach, take a moment to consider the pros and cons of alternate approaches to see if you can find a more effective structure for telling the story.
- **Support the theme and purpose**: If the theme is, for example, "We face more difficult challenges than anticipated," consider structuring a document around those challenges.
- **Draw a picture, not just an outline**: Our document planning sessions involve drawing thumbnails of sheets from the document on a whiteboard. By drawing thumbnails, we can take our structure discussion further, thinking through how we're going to present information on each page. You could also use stickies to make it easier to move stuff around.
- **Collaborate with content contributors to determine the structure**: Ideally, you don't have to do this in a vacuum. If other people on the team are contributing to the document, even a little, ask them to join you for 15 minutes of brainstorming the structure.
- **Show the picture to the people who will use the document**: As much as I abhor the phrase "content consumer," it does pretty clearly define the people who care about the document the most: those who will have to use it as part of their work. "Here," you say in a short conversation with them, "This is what I'm putting together. Can you think of anything else you need? Does the structure of the document make sense?"
- **Carve out space for future content**: Don't conceal parts of the outline that don't yet have flesh. Let them all hang out in their skeletal glory. If you know something's coming, prepare a space for it in the document. (More on this shortly.)

Letting the structure emerge

A lingering challenge: How to reconcile a document structure with the unpredictable nature of projects? Is it possible to use a single document (as I've recommended earlier) with a predetermined structure when design projects are inherently uncertain?

- **The vision**: Establish a document structure with placeholders for content you know will come. The document is born during a project's discovery phase, but you know you'll eventually have site maps and wireframes and usability testing reports. Your ideal approach is to establish an empty chapter for each of these things and fill in the content as it emerges.
- **The reality**: Projects are completely unpredictable. You don't know what's going to happen. I'm not even talking about the project derailing; I'm talking about uncertainty on a smaller scale. Requirements get "de-scoped" or you miss a minor deadline or a new requirement emerges. All of these things make it difficult to follow a structure you put in place weeks or months ago.

- **The practice**: A table of contents that changes is OK. Establishing a structure at the beginning lets you set expectations with the project team to help them understand the kinds of information that will emerge over the course of the project. Changes to that structure are useful topics of conversation. Highlighting why you had to change the document is meaningful to the project team because it captures important shifts between expected outcomes and actual outcomes.

Chapter cover sheets

Like the introduction for the document as a whole, chapter introductions should provide a lay of the land: What will readers see in the next few pages and what are the main themes addressed?

Earlier, I distinguished between summaries and introductions—two different sheets that serve related but clearly separate purposes. The cover sheet for a chapter more closely aligns with an introduction than it does with a summary, but could still include some clear actions or unsettled questions.

While chapter introductions may require only a bullet list, content in some chapters may lend itself to something more elaborate, as in Figure 8.11, which uses two sheets. The chapter's cover sheet hits the main messages, and the first sheet describes the content of the chapter.

Next Steps

Design documents don't have a conclusion, at least not in the way your high school English teacher expected. But these deliverables should still have clean demarcation at the end.

Remember, in composing a document, your job is more like a journalist than a joke-teller. A good design document gets the conclusion out of the way at the beginning, then uses the rest of the document to support it.

Instead your document should end with "next steps," an account of where to go from here. Your document also started this way, positioning the content as a stepping-stone to lead the project to a subsequent set of activities.

Figure 8.11: Introducing a chapter on the chapter's title page by spelling out the major elements of the chapter in a bulleted list. The first sheet in the chapter provides an overview of the chapter's content.

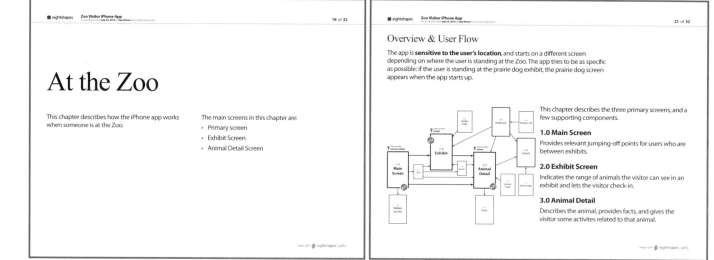

Conclude the document in the same way, answering the question, "Now what?"

Next steps are really between you and your project manager, but here are some ideas:

- **Validation activities**: People need to ensure that the approach, direction, and conclusions described in the document are correct.
- **Elaboration activities**: People need to take what was established in the document and flesh out details.
- **Directional decisions**: People need to choose from two or more options presented in the document.

Remember, the best next steps are:

- **Accountable**: There is a specific person to whom the steps are assigned.
- **Measurable and constrained**: There is a clear definition of success and the responsible party understands the deadline.
- **Specific**: The task is clear about what needs to be produced. (Not "additional screens" but "five additional annotated wireframes").

Next steps and evolving documents

If you're using a single document throughout the process (rather than creating a new document for each activity) the next steps described at the end of the document will change with each new iteration. Next steps change from one milestone to the next, and so they should in the document.

The nice thing about this approach is that you can annotate the next steps from the previous milestone to account for their disposition. Figure 8.9 incorporates both upcoming next steps and those from previous activities.

The Final Product

Incorporating all these pieces, Figure 8.12 shows what your structure might look like.

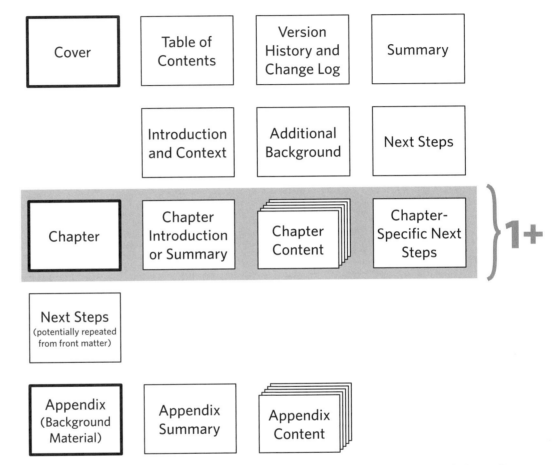

Figure 8.12: The structure of a document. Each row represents a chapter, and the rectangle with the heavier lines shows chapter cover pages. The gray box shows a repeated structure for one or more chapters in your document.

LAYING OUT PAGES

Composing a document is more than just assembling the right structure of pages. It implies creating page layouts that communicate appropriate "plot points" in the story.

My team uses the concept of a document "recipe" to describe both the *structure of the document* and the specific types of *layouts used for each sheet.* We refer to a layout as a "page pattern," founded on the relatively simple idea that most design deliverables consist of the same page layouts over and over again.

The templates included with EightShapes Unify reflect dozens of page patterns for almost any imaginable situation. We add to this library all the time as we devise new ways to communicate complicated ideas. Here are some of the general types:

Pages That Explain

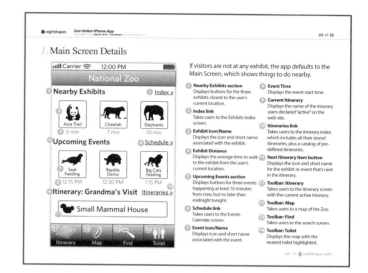

Figure 8.13: Use annotations to elaborate on a design artifact.

Explanation pages elaborate on the details of a design artifact, using annotations to point out important elements and narrate some detail about it. Annotations consist of a numbered marker on the artifact and a similarly numbered marker next to a description. Typically, these appear with wireframes or screens, but they could be used for more abstract artifacts, too.

This layout is our go-to approach for functional specifications. While it would be nice for our design diagrams to stand on their own, annotations describe details that may not be depicted easily. The format can support a high-level description (aka "light annotation") that provides an overview of the screen's behaviors. It can also support a more detailed level of annotations for digging into the complexities of a page.

To help tell the story, annotations may be grouped based on their function or the target area of the design they describe.

Pages That Evaluate

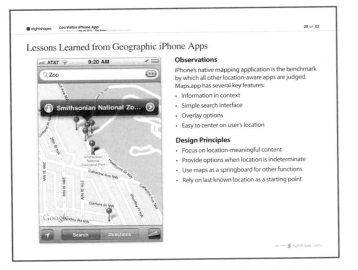

Figure 8.14: Capture critiques as annotations, but also conclude with a strong, actionable takeaway.

Similar to pages that explain, pages that evaluate provide a critique of a design artifact, usually a screen. You can format the annotations like those in explanation pages, but there may be additional pieces of information to include, like a measure of severity or priority.

These are useful in competitive analyses (see also the upcoming section "Pages That Compare") or expert reviews, in which you provide some feedback on an existing design based on industry standards and your experience as a designer.

An evaluation should conclude with a key takeaway, providing an insight based on the evaluation.

Pages That Introduce

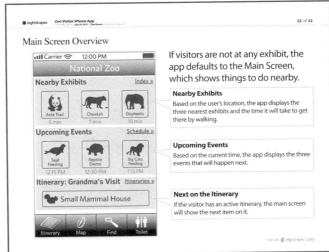

Figure 8.15: Use distinct regions of the page to provide a short overview of each thing you're introducing. Tie these things together with a unifying message at the top. Make sure the layout reflects the relationship between the things: distinct approaches, linear progression, and so on.

Unlike explanations or evaluations, which elaborate on details, introductions should provide a lay of the land, zooming out to show a wider range of content. An introduction points out highlights, major landmarks. Introductions connect the detailed content to larger themes or messages.

I'll use a page format like this one for just about any set of concepts that together form a whole but have enough detail to warrant at least one page on their own. Imagine using this page for a rogues' gallery of personas or storyboarding the four most important pages in a flow.

Pages That Compare

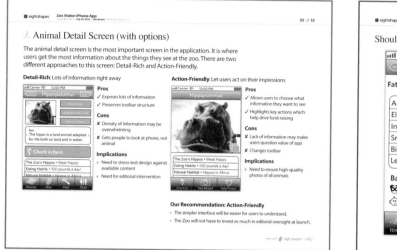

Figure 8.16: **Place artifacts side by side** to highlight their differences.

The design process may yield multiple directions. Background research may identify competitors with new approaches. At the very least, it may be relevant to compare the as-is state of the web site with the to-be, to ensure you've addressed all the needs. Annotations remain important in these comparisons because they describe the comparison.

These pages are ideal for competitive analyses, which may show more than one way of solving the same design problem. I have also used this layout for usability tests to compare observations made of two different users.

Comparison pages require a strong conclusion: What's the point of comparing if you don't gain an insight from it? Whereas explanation pages may set the tone of the design concept by highlighting an overall theme or purpose, comparisons need to highlight a takeaway, answering the question, "So what?"

Pages That Require a Decision

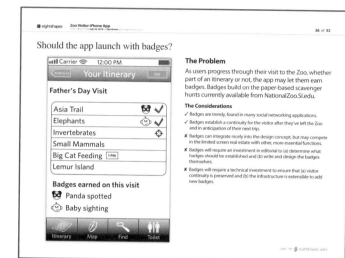

Figure 8.17: **Describe the problem and then spell out the options** for pages meant to drive a decision.

Whereas comparison pages hope to highlight differences in order to gain a particular insight, decision pages pose a question and provide sufficient information to drive toward an answer. A comparison will only focus on differences or similarities, but a decision page will also provide criteria for making a decision.

You may be reluctant to use decision pages. It may feel like your design work should not be subject to a one-page mechanism for deciding upon direction, or that you can't boil down decision-making criteria to a simple list. That said, the purpose of the deliverable is to move the conversation forward. It should be less a voting ballot and more a means for spelling out the options and the relevant topics of conversation in the context of the decision.

PRESENTING DELIVERABLES

In each of the previous chapters, I've described an approach for presenting individual artifacts. This presumes that the focus of your conversation is a particular aspect of the document.

What if you need to walk through a whole document? The structure established in Diagram Basics (Chapter 2) is appropriate for walking through a whole deliverable. It follows a flow that would follow the structure of the document, if you used the one described earlier. Table 8.5 applies the presentation framework to deliverables.

A WORD OF WARNING

Self-Indulgent Deliverables

To me, the situation was as clear as day. Each template could accommodate up to three different content types. A template consisted of regions. Each region was a pattern (tabs, list, filters, etc.), but the specifics of the region varied depending on the content type. A single template could address up to nine different scenarios! Oh the joy of abstract thinking!

So, to everyone else, not so clear.

Still, I persisted with the model, creating a diagram to explain these multiple levels of abstraction. I showed it to the primary stakeholder on the project, expecting an enthusiastic expression of awe. But the expression was more like, "Huh?" His exact words were, "I don't know what to do with this." Ouch.

Ultimately, the deliverable was by me, about me, and for me—utterly self-indulgent. A simple peer review would have helped prevent this.

Presenting Deliverables vs. Presenting Artifacts

So, are you presenting a deliverable or presenting an artifact? The book covers both, but which is the "correct" approach? You may be faced with either situation, sometimes both on the same project. If the choice isn't clear based on the circumstance, use the guidelines in Table 8.6.

In this part of the meeting...	You should discuss...
Establish context	Where the document fits into the project and what parts of the document you will be talking about in this meeting.
Describe visual conventions	If you've used any special annotations to structure the document (such as a badge for pages requiring sign-off), you can mention those here. Also, if you use a page pattern to structure individual pages, use this time to show people how the pages are structured.
Highlight decisions	Use this portion of the meeting to walk through the major design decisions described in the relevant portions of the document.
Offer rationale	No change: This is your chance to provide reasoning behind the design decisions.
Point out details	If there are pages you need to skip due to time constraints, consider pointing them out with a quick flip-through.
Communicate implications	In addition to the implications of the design decisions in the document, you should talk about the implications of the document in the context of the project. When do you need reviews complete? What happens if the project team introduces major changes?
Solicit feedback	If you've embedded questions in the document, point those out.
Provide framework for review	Return to the table of contents and show people which sections require their attention.

Table 8.5: Presenting a deliverable follows the same basic framework used throughout the book to structure discussions about design.

Discuss an artifact when...	Discuss a deliverable when...
Meeting participants have been involved with day-to-day activities on the project, and larger context is not immediately necessary.	Conversations with project stakeholders happen infrequently, and a deliverable will provide context even for specific design decisions.
You need a peer review on a first draft of a new diagram to gauge its effectiveness.	Perhaps conversations do happen frequently, but the scale of the project is of a size where you can't focus on iterating one artifact: You need to address different aspects of the project in different meetings.
You're seeking feedback on very specific design decisions reflected in the artifact.	The design decisions extend beyond a single diagram.
The artifact sets the tone for an upcoming deliverable meeting.	You need to provide some detailed context on a specific diagram by walking through a few pages of background to validate that all participants are aligned.

Table 8.6: Presenting artifacts or deliverables and artifacts, some situations to consider.

THE DELIVERABLE LIFECYCLE

Deliverables are conceived and born. They mature and eventually go where all good deliverables go, to that great archive hard drive in the sky. (Cloud storage solutions make that metaphor almost literal.) Maybe it's easy for you to think of your documentation as inanimate, but I just can't. A cradle-to-grave metaphor persists throughout this section. Bear with me.

The lifecycle of a deliverable—where it is in its maturity—depends on three factors:

* **Ratio of content to placeholders**: Initial documents contain more placeholders for content than they do actual content. As you replace placeholders with content, the document matures until there are no placeholders left. This is one way to measure the document's stage in the lifecycle.
* **Relationship to project plan**: Your ability to add content to a document is directly dependent on the project's activities. You can't incorporate findings from a usability study until you've conducted the study. Deviations from the project plan don't need to stunt the growth of the deliverable if the plan is adapting to new circumstances while bringing the team ever closer to the project's objectives.
* **Serving the project objectives**: And that brings us to the last criteria by which we can judge a document's maturity. Is it doing what it set out to do? Does a design specification sufficiently capture the functional details of the product? A usability results report, for example, that doesn't provide sufficient marching orders to the design team based on the test hasn't likely reached full maturity.

The stages of the lifecycle described in the following sections are a loose framework based on these criteria. They provide a sense of where you might be and things you can do to help mature the document.

The description of the document lifecycle implies a particular situation or organizational culture. Depending on your situation, it might strike you as antiquated or obsolete, especially in the later stages of the lifecycle.

One observation I made in writing these descriptions is that in modern software engineering methodologies, the deliverable lifecycle is abbreviated. I'd explain this by saying that deliverables in such methods have a very specific, targeted purpose. They play the same role (communication, alignment, etc.), but they have a significantly shorter half-life. Conflicts that might arise in the very late stages of a more "old-school" process do not arise in modern development practices. In these methodologies, questions about whether to keep a document up-to-date become irrelevant because the document is more disposable.

Conception: Document Development

In the very beginning stages of a document, things are pretty messy, not unlike other forms of conception. This process works best in front of a whiteboard with the people who will be collaborating with you on the document. During the conception of the document, you're identifying the overall structure (Table of Contents) and (if this is how you operate) the page layouts you'll use in each section. The whiteboard you end up with might look like the one in Figure 8.18.

This is the shortest phase, perhaps lasting only a few hours as you work with your project team to sketch out the basics of the document and then translate that outline to your page layout application. At this stage, the document is pretty rudimentary, unlikely to have much, if any, content.

I'll tell you right now, I have no idea how to react when someone tells me the sex of their baby. Congratulations are due in either case, so "That's awesome" seems somewhat disingenuous, but whatever. On the flip side, if a team member shows me a nascent deliverable, I can provide all kinds of feedback. Here are the things I look for in evaluating a team member's initial document:

- Is the document purpose clearly articulated?
- Does the structure support the purpose?
- Is there a clear place for next steps, and are they specified early in the document as well as at the end?
- Will the structure of the chapters make a natural progression?
- Are the layouts suitable for the purpose?
- Are there opportunities to consolidate pages?
- Is there a need to separate out pages?
- Does each new chapter or idea have a good introductory page or two?

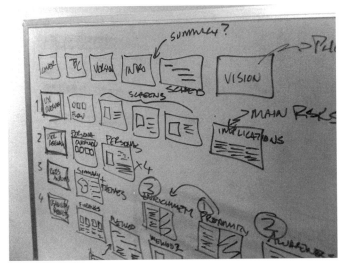

Figure 8.18: Conceiving a new document is less intimate but just as messy as other types of conception. In the results of this brainstorming session, the team worked together to establish the structure of the document. While this sketch may look like a mess, the participants have a good idea of what the structure of the document needs to be and what each page of the document should look like.

Birth: The First Presentation

When you show the document for the first time, it should have more content than the initial scaffold developed in the conception phase. There may not be enough content for the document to stand on its own, but the main messages and ideas have been incorporated.

When you're looking at the initial version of a new document, a few things should jump out:

- **Potential**: Even though the document can go in lots of different directions (and you'll be proud regardless of which direction it goes in, unless it becomes an actor), it has placeholders for content to come. These placeholders will in part evoke an enormous amount of work required to fill them, but should also communicate opportunity. You're building something new here, and you know what you need to do—what information to provide—to make it successful.
- **Alignment with plan**: Those placeholders represent opportunity, but they should also align to upcoming activities. Looking at a nascent document, still limited in its content, I should still be able to picture the project plan. A document alone should let me know where the project is going.
- **Illuminated challenges, constraints, and parameters**: As the story starts to shape up on paper, you'll uncover potential obstacles that lie between you and your objectives. The mere act of telling the story, even in rudimentary form, shines a brighter light on the project. This light brings greater insight into the things that constrain the project and present challenges, but also helps you refine the ideas within the story.

You might detour in your very first presentation of a document to address these three things. Putting something down on paper, even if it's the physical manifestation of your anticipated design process, always yields insights you hadn't considered previously. Incorporate some of these thoughts into the first, second, or third parts of the basic meeting framework (see the previous section "Presenting Deliverables").

Puberty: Still Some Maturing to Do

A document is considered pubescent if chunks of content remain missing. Enough of the story is in place to allow for sufficient momentum on the project, to propel you from one set of activities to the next. The document captures insights and conclusions from your initial set of activities, such that the project team can react, validate, clarify, or decide as necessary to move you along to the next set.

Documents can spend a long time in this stage: Placeholders you anticipated filling in eventually remain untouched. You might quietly eliminate them. (Documents, unlike humans, don't ever regret the road not traveled.) If you don't feel right making the executive decision to do so, you can highlight these portions of the document in the Solicit Feedback section of your meeting. In evaluating these sections, you (and potentially others) should ask the following questions:

- Are they connected to future activities?
- Do other parts of the document now address the same need?
- Can they be consolidated or refactored to reflect future activities better?
- Can key points from them be integrated into existing sections?

Maturity: All Content Present

A fully mature document is one in which all the placeholders have been replaced by actual content. This isn't to say that there isn't room for updates or even additions. A

document is mature when it matches the initial vision of what it's meant to do.

The preparation of each iteration of the document has been the by-product of the team's activities. A mature document might still grow and change depending on those activities, but it's unlikely there's much left in the project plan that can contribute to the document.

Retiring portions of the document

One of the risks with creating a single document in the course of a project is that the utility of content may recede over the course of a project.

Imagine your document structure starts with a chapter summarizing the results of user research. You might have a dozen pages, describing the type of research and providing insights into the observations and subsequent analysis. As you move into detailed design activities, keeping this information in the document (a) weighs it down with unnecessary pages (and megabytes) and (b) distracts from the new content.

In short, as the project progresses, outputs from prior activities may be less relevant. This is where introduction pages are especially useful. Your introduction page should include a reasonable summary of the key takeaways from all your project activities. By reducing the content from that section to just that introductory page, you can preserve the spirit and value of the activity without bogging down the document with obsolete details.

End-of-Life: Shelving the Document

The death of design documents is quiet and unassuming. In short, people on the team just stop opening them. The project activities require your attention elsewhere. The demand for their content diminishes as deadlines related to the deliverable pass and the team moves onto other things.

But, how does that old quote go? "Reports of my death have been greatly exaggerated." This is especially true for deliverables.

Documents you perceive to be casketed might be, in reality, still making the rounds. Just because the design process has concluded and there's nothing more you can do on a design document doesn't mean that its life is over. On the contrary, other parts of the team (engineering, quality control, and maybe even customer service or training) refer to them constantly. The mettle of a deliverable's utility is put to the truest test as people use design documentation not just as a tool for implementation, but for all the activities that come with it and after it as well.

Here's what might happen long after you turn in the "final version" of the document:

- **Clarification**: The caller ID isn't someone you recognize or maybe you get an email and the "from" field contains a vaguely familiar name. Like someone you might have met a long time ago at a company function. Your tech lead mentions this name sometimes. Oh, right, that's the QA guy. He's using your document. Actually using it. Like in his job. Of course, he's asking you about some pretty obvious scenarios you left out.
- **Update**: Same guy. He's now translating your designs into test scenarios. There's a pretty egregious error on page 6, something with the wireframe annotations not reflecting the correct values in a drop-down. He's asking that you update the document to correct the error. As you hem and haw, he reminds you that a QA team of five people is using this as the document of record to test the system in the development environment.
- **Kicking off the next project**: The quality assurance team found a handful of bugs, nothing to prevent the first version from launching, but things that need to get integrated into the next release. Also, feedback from the business unit's customers has been rolling in, and they

have a wish list a mile long. The product manager gives you a call, "I've been reviewing the design document and making notes about things we need to upgrade for the next release."

Maybe these scenarios read as a little "old school." Most modern engineering methodologies short-circuit the old-fashioned, endless timelines of software development.

Maintenance: Keeping It Healthy

The topic of document maintenance comes up a lot at workshops I teach on design deliverables. The question isn't so much about keeping a document up-to-date during the design process: Every team has its own way of sharing files and scheduling updates. (Yours, too, right?) Most people are asking about after the death of the document.

If a design document serves as the document of record for what the product is supposed to be, you might be on the hook for keeping it up-to-date in these circumstances:

- **Changes in design during implementation**: The very act of implementing something changes the design. Nothing created looks as it does on paper.
- **Insufficient documentation during implementation**: Later in the process (as in the QA activities described earlier), people working on the project may identify places where the documentation does not provide enough or the right kinds of information.
- **Updates in production**: Small bug fixes and minor upgrades can cause a discrepancy between what's in production and what's documented.

Are you on the hook for keeping the document up-to-date? The best advice is this: Don't ask this question in the same moment someone is demanding updates to the document. Instead, integrate this topic into your kick-off meetings. You might ask questions like:

*Nathan Curtis,
Principal and Founder,
EightShapes, LLC*

ASK THE EXPERT

DB: How much document planning and management is too much planning and management?

NC: *Planning documents with many artifacts can be challenging when you can include so much: maps, flows, page designs, component variations, the works! Predictably and efficiently evolving documents is hard, too. Those early concepts feel light, breezy, vital, even fun as you create and iterate. But over time, the document can balloon into a morass of unorganized mush. That's not fun. That's fat, unwieldy, and hard to change.*

Therefore, don't be hard and fast about evolving that "one deliverable." Instead, here are some ideas to break rules about the (presumably single) deliverable to fit what a process and team need at a given time:

Welcome a One-and-Done

Don't feel compelled to plan a long, detailed document with an extensive lifecycle if circumstances don't call for it. For example, suppose your project scope and design ideas are very unstable. Don't try to predict unknown page inventories and exact details not needed for six weeks. You aren't writing a book. You are designing an experience, so forsake such temptations. Sometimes, the right answer is to throw in pictures, sprinkle a few informative callouts, publish, get feedback, and then... throw the document away. And that's OK.

Anticipate Pivotal Moments

Communication objectives change over time, like shifting from high-level concepts to ironing out devilish details or from selling to stakeholders to delivering to engineers. The posture of a document—or even pages within it—can shift quickly from introducing, comparing, and deciding to a hefty amount of detailed explaining. These changing objectives call for changing communication techniques including page layouts and annotations. So take time to zoom out from your familiar page layouts, ask yourself "Is this page meeting it's objective?" and don't be afraid to replace a layout (like haphazard callouts bursting at the seams) with something more effective (like a scalable, formal list of specs—especially when you know you'll be authoring so many more just like 'em).

Iterate Before You Integrate

Larger design projects call for dividing work into smaller chunks that are worked on independently, even across multiple designers. In such situations, smaller and independent documents can sometimes provide freedom and focus. For example, while my team worked together on a large-scale design progress, I focused on a stand-alone yet high-profile component: the video carousel. My first deliverable compared alternatives that didn't work, but a second version proffered new ideas that hit the mark, and subsequent versions layered in annotations consistent with other deliverables and familiar to project participants. Once complete, this isolated deliverable was transformed into a chapter of the team's much larger design document, which hadn't been burdened with maintenance or disrupted out of its predictable publishing cycle.

- My deadline is May 30, but the product won't launch until August. Who will make use of the documents between now and then?
- Who is responsible for fielding questions from these people after May 30?
- What is the expectation for keeping this document up-to-date during implementation? If the project team identifies any problems with the document, can these be addressed through an addendum or do we need to create a new version of the document?
- After the product launches in August, who will be responsible for accounting for discrepancies between what's in production and what's documented?
- After the product launches in August, what will become of the document? Will it be used as the basis for subsequent releases for the product?

THE FUTURE OF DELIVERABLES

The beginning of this chapter states explicit assumptions about the definition of a deliverable. In light of newer trends in design methodologies, these assumptions start to seem antiquated. But, as of this writing, I'm still working on documents delivered as PDFs and laid out on standard-sized pages. Sometimes we even print them out.

The word "deliverable" implies only that you create something to be delivered to someone else. Format and style are not inherent properties in what we call our work product, and no doubt there's room to evolve. Design teams that remain mired in old habits will struggle to keep up. Even simple adaptations of existing deliverable frameworks may not be enough because ultimately documentation is a function of four things:

- **The product**: The documentation should do a good job of describing the actual thing you're designing.
- **The people**: The design team, the development team, and all the other people who have to collaborate to make a product real must buy into the approach for capturing

the plans for the web site. Blueprints remain useful to architects and contractors alike because the common language works for both groups.

- **Organizational context**: Deliverables are part of a larger ecosystem defined not just by the project team, but by the corporate environment. Degrees of formality, integrity, accountability, and history all come from the organization and establish a tone for the deliverables themselves.
- **Methodological trends**: The way we structure design activities will impact the by-products of those activities. Longer timelines, broader scopes, and multidisciplinary contributions yield one type of document, while quicker burns with narrow objectives yield another.

"Deliverable," however, does imply certain limitations. This label, as well as "documentation," suggest both a one-way-ness and finality. Deliverables are something we send along. In practice, we discuss them, collaborate on them, and let them morph with the project's progress, but you wouldn't get this from the name.

Maybe we should start calling them "shareables."

Our **obligation** as designers is not to the deliverable, but to the product. We are **accountable** only to the product's user. But the path to get there is filled with dozens of other people who may have similar objectives with differing agendas. Deliverables are tools to help us navigate that landscape. Our **responsibility** is to communicate design ideas and capture the details of a design concept in the most frictionless way possible.

EXERCISES

1. Reflect on a recent project, picking a deliverable from the project and plotting on the graph from Figure 8.1. How long did you spend conceiving the deliverable? How many iterations did it go through? What happened to the document? Is it still around?

2. Imagine you were creating one document for a recent project (instead of, perhaps, many). Write a table of contents for the single deliverable, accounting for both initial and future project activities. Make the table of contents as detailed as possible, defining what goes into each chapter. As an exercise, avoid structuring the chapters based on the project plan. Imagine you were structuring the chapters around different aspects of the user experience. Try to use real people as the target audience for the document, but if you can't, imagine the document's readers. Consider their role and personality as you structure the document.

3. For each entry in the table of contents from exercise 2, assign a page pattern from the "Laying Out Pages" section. There are six patterns to choose from. Consider what you are saying for each entry in the table of contents and identify the most appropriate page layout. Create thumbnails representing each page layout and put together a diagram showing the structure of the document. Walk colleagues or your study group through the diagram and solicit feedback on the structure of the document. Was there content they were expecting to see? Does the story make sense? Do they think the structure will be effective in communicating with the imagined target audience?

Chapter 9

Design Briefs

də'·zīne brēf (n.)

A document describing the design problem and establishing a foundation of objectives, principles, and requirements.

A design brief is a document prepared at the beginning of the project to summarize its objectives and parameters from the design perspective. To varying degrees, it:

- Articulates the objectives of the project
- Positions the project in a larger context
- States the design problem
- Establishes other parameters, like timing
- Summarizes any inputs, like technical, content, or user requirements
- Defines the direction or approach the designers will take

The problem with design briefs is that they sometimes don't make an appearance much beyond the initial activities of the project. That is, they are a useful tool for defining the design problem and perhaps establishing direction, but design teams don't tend to refer to them once they commence "serious" design activities.

With this chapter I hope to rescue design briefs from the virtual dustbin. A good design brief can serve as a reference point throughout the project to ensure alignment with goals and direction, and that designers remain focused on the right problem.

WHAT MAKES A GOOD DESIGN BRIEF

There's no fountain of youth for design briefs, but to boil the challenge down into a single idea, design briefs suffer from ambition. Designers think they need to make their design briefs monumental, sweeping, and meaningful with a capital M. While moral and aesthetic weight can make design briefs inspiring, they don't make for long-lived documents. Why? Documentation, as part of a design project, is not about winning the Pulitzer prize.

It's about practicality.

Clearly State the Problem

If you do nothing else in a design brief, make sure you state the problem. Looking at design as a matter of problems and solutions oversimplifies the endeavor, but certainly ensures that everyone on the team is working toward the same objectives.

For the most part, you should be able to boil down the design problem into a single statement (or diagram!), but the process of solving that problem will require a more extensive set of statements to frame it up truly. That is, while you can summarize the design objectives in a single sentence, the design brief includes further information (like requirements, constraints, and objectives) to establish a more complete picture.

Examples of single-statement problems:

- The new web-based application for customer service representatives needs to incorporate the functionality of two legacy applications, known as Update and Dispatch.
- The new marketing site needs to provide users with detailed feature information about our mobile product, and allow them to see the range of mobile platforms on which it's available.
- The current client-server application is ugly, difficult to learn, and out-of-date. The new one needs to take advantage of modern web technologies and design trends.

Each statement gives you a pretty clear idea on what the design team needs to work toward. The remainder of the design brief elaborates on the problem. This process, of achieving a deep understanding of the design problem, is crucial to our work as designers.

In one project from a couple years ago, I completely misunderstood the scope of the project; we were designing two pages, not the two dozen I thought we were. This led us to a very difficult conversation about a month in where we had to clarify expectations. Fortunately, we were supposed to do less than we planned, so this issue was less about "But you're only paying us to do this much" and more about "Wait, you want us to focus on what now?"

You know, a site map would have really helped.

Pictures, like the diagrams from the first half of this book, can be useful tools in clarifying the problem:

- **Site maps**: As-is structures that have problems with navigation or poorly classified content.
- **Flowcharts**: Current business processes or user flows that make it difficult for users to complete their tasks.
- **Concept models**: Underlying structures that leave out particular pieces of content.
- **Personas**: User needs that go unaddressed, especially mental models that show gaps in content or features that directly address specific user needs.

A design brief is filled with all kinds of statements, assertions, principles, and guidelines. Use pictures wherever possible to hammer the point home.

Statements Supported by Examples

In articulating the problem and outlining the prospective solution, design briefs make statements about the project to help designers keep their efforts on track.

Design briefs may include statements like:

- **Objective**: Create increased awareness of our newest product families.
- **Guideline**: Always display products with photos that show them being used by actual people.
- **Requirement**: Our user research shows that people want to compare products.

All useful principles. You can further enhance their utility by supporting them with examples, which makes for a more powerful design brief. Give readers, in other words, something to hang their hat on.

Picking examples can be difficult. They need to walk a fine line between providing a good illustration of the principle and being accessible to project stakeholders. Need to show how a large site establishes a content strategy? News sites like CNN.com or WashingtonPost.com might provide great examples, but the stakeholders behind a high-tech marketing site may not be able to relate, even though the challenges overlap. Here are some ideas on how to pick examples.

Where examples come from

A design brief should not be a competitive analysis. It might draw on the results of a competitive analysis, but its mission is broader. So, while the competition provides a rich source of examples, the design brief needs to walk a fine line between illustrating principles and setting direction for the design team.

Competitive sites need not provide the only source of examples. It's a good idea to use other examples with which your team and stakeholders will be familiar:

- **Other sites**: There are the canonical web sites (Amazon.com, for example, or CNN.com) that provide a common experience to draw from. (Even people for whom the web is not all-encompassing have bought something on Amazon.com.) They also tend to be trendsetters in terms of design, so new patterns usually emerge there first. At the same time, their success and usually conservative approach to design generally means that design patterns on those sites are best practices.
- **Other kinds of products**: Like canonical sites, there are interactive products (phones, digital video recorders, music players, and so on) that everyone is familiar with. They provide a useful reference for interface concepts (like menu systems) and also demonstrate how a product can fit into a larger scenario.

- **Other experiences**: I like drawing comparisons to other experiences, like borrowing a book from the library, researching strollers, or planning a home renovation. Simple photographs can evoke these experiences and help people make the connection to this project. No doubt you'll have someone in your meeting who got into an argument with the librarian just the other day over a late fee, so position these experiences as useful frameworks to consider all aspects of the design.
- **Examples are powerful**: They can entrench a statement from the design brief (whether objective, requirement, or guideline) deeply into the corporate culture. Having your examples come up time and again during design conversations can be gratifying, especially when one colleague uses it with another. Make sure in setting up the examples you extract the general principles, such that an example doesn't become, "We want to be just like Amazon!"

Using examples

There are two approaches for illustrating statements in a design brief, and each is the converse of the other:

- One statement per page, with associated examples: Each principle (or objective or requirement) gets a single page, and the bulk of the page is for describing the principle and providing one or more examples. This approach is ideal when you are working with a limited set of assertions.
- One statement per page, with associated principles: If a single example can illustrate more than one assertion, you can have each page dedicated to a theme. The example supports the theme, and the page lists all the principles (or objectives, and so on) associated with the theme. The challenge here is to avoid creating a competitive analysis. The principles, guidelines, and requirements don't describe the example; the example must support them.

Figure 9.1: Using examples to support design principles. Principles can each have a dedicated page or can share an example.

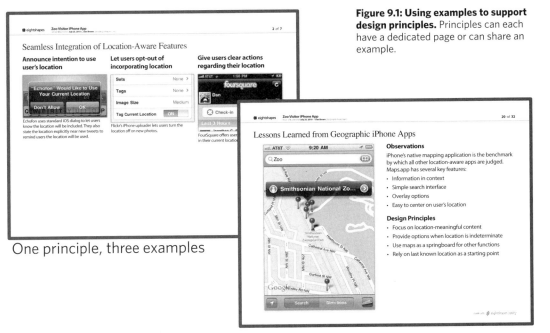

One principle, three examples

One example, many principles

Traceability

The content in a design brief consists of objectives, best practices, requirements, constraints, project parameters, design concepts, design vision, and other assertions that guide designers. In some cases, these statements represent very high-level design decisions that set direction for the project. In most cases, these principles capture the constraints—things outside the control of the designer exerting pressure on the design process, establishing boundaries for the creative effort, and providing criteria by which to judge the result.

Design, in one view, is a series of increasingly specific decisions. Early decisions are "What tasks should we support," and as the design progresses the team decides what screens are necessary and then how to prioritize the layout of the screen, and then what color the buttons should be. Such decisions have an implied hierarchy: I can't make one set of decisions without having made previous decisions.

A good design brief, in a word, captures that hierarchy.

A hierarchy of assertions

Is there one, immutable, objective Hierarchy of Design Statements? A ladder representing each kind of constraint and requirement, every level of abstraction for design decisions? Beats the heck out of me. But they generally follow the pattern described in Table 9.1.

It is possible to overthink this. You don't need a complex hierarchy accommodating every possible design principle that emerges. But you do need to be able to provide a rationale for design decisions. Designers who expect "Because I said so" to be a legitimate justification for a design will have to wait a long, long time for that to be true.

Instead, having an airtight decision-making process means demonstrating that you've considered different approaches, landed on the one that solves the problem best, and justified the approach by referring to prior decisions.

Reflecting the hierarchy

The brute force approach to referencing earlier material is to number items as granularly as possible and then embed those identifiers as appropriate in the document:

- On a flowchart, reference requirements identifiers to show which parts of the problem are being solved.
- On a wireframe, reference standards identifiers to show which components from the library are being used.
- In requirements, reference objectives identifiers to justify the inclusion of specific features and functions.

Such references are useful only in so far as they demonstrate thoroughness and attention to detail, and some project teams may need this rigor.

On the other hand, while putting together these references can be painstaking, the real problem is that they are abstract. In the context of a wireframe or screen design, citing requirement IDs provides no real context. (Except

Objectives	→	Requirements	→	Design Decisions
What the project will accomplish. How the business will change with the implementation of this product or web site.		More specific need on what the product should be able to do. It focuses on system behaviors. Presumably, every requirement should support a project objective, though some requirements will be derived from constraints.		The team will make a series of design decisions for each requirement. The mapping won't be one to one. Some design decisions address multiple requirements, and some requirements will require multiple design decisions. Design decisions also have a hierarchy, but this is more about levels of abstraction. Some design decisions are very broad (like deciding upon a set of templates) and others are more detailed (like the layout of a particular field on a template.)

Table 9.1: The hierarchy of statements suggests that every design decision should trace back to a project objective. In reality, some requirements come from external factors or constraints, yielding some design decisions that appear arbitrary or counterintuitive, but necessary for the success of a project.

maybe for the person who wrote and encoded the requirements document.)

One way to overcome the abstraction is to be explicit, listing references in full adjacent to design decisions. Of course, a complete list of requirements on a wireframe is impractical. (The requirements may change, there may have been some intervening interpretation of the requirements, and frankly, there may not be enough room on the page of your deliverable.) Instead, I will use sentences or phrases that summarize a set of requirements or objectives.

Figure 9.2: Simplified objectives statements allows me to reference them throughout the design process. A statement can evoke prior conversations about objectives and principles, whereas an abstract identifier separates the design from the rationale.

The exception: design standards. My firm has worked with many design teams that have started building internal standards libraries. In such repositories, a systematic codification of standards can become embedded in the language of design. Teams will become comfortable referring to design components by code, especially if the rationale behind the encoding is meaningful.

Articulated Boundaries

A good design brief draws a line around the project to clarify what the design team should and should not work on. Boundaries are crucial because creative endeavors can easily explore design problems ad infinitum. Boundaries are what let design teams get pragmatic. Two typical ways to express boundaries are in terms of time and features.

One reason why I rely on these approaches is that they can be expressed as pictures.

Schedule

Perhaps the simplest way to stop a project is simply to name a date when everything has to be done. A well-managed design team should be able to triangulate "what's possible" from "objectives" and "deadlines." The design brief should clearly state any predetermined deadlines.

Features

Another way to establish a focus for a project is to identify which pieces of the experience the team will address. A prioritized feature list is a good start, but a more detailed view into features may be easier:

- **By screen or template**: One typical way for us to establish the scope of a project is to say that we're focusing on one set of screens (sometimes even just one screen). Though translating a feature into a distinct quantity of screens is difficult, it can provide enough of a level of effort estimate for the purposes of a design brief.
- **By user scenario**: A more abstract way to establish scope is to describe what set of user behaviors we need to design for. Also difficult to define, but perhaps a more realistic quantification of user experience, scenarios allow us to talk in terms of what we expect users to accomplish. A scenario's complexity (dependencies, inputs, outputs, and consequences) will provide a basis for establishing a level of effort.

Additional constraints

There may be other factors that impact what the team focuses on, how much they can get done, and their timeline. These could include any other logistical constraints, like which team members are (or are not) available to work on the project. Key decision makers out of town during crucial parts of the project will force the team to frame up their deadlines to accommodate.

The corporate culture may come with additional constraints: content vetted by the legal department or other reviewers, specific engineering lifecycles that drive the deadlines, or technological frameworks that impose particular requirements.

The Plan

A good design brief describes how the project team intends to accomplish the objectives within the boundaries. This is the team's opportunity to take everything they know about doing design and apply it to the specific design problem.

The more specific the plan, the better, but a design brief may not be the right place to capture every last milestone. High-level plans—sketching the primary activities, deliverables, responsibilities, and hand-offs—are usually sufficient for a brief, so long as they lead to more specific plans. These are the things a plan needs to communicate, relevant to a timeline:

- **Activities**: What tasks the team will be performing.
- **Deliverables**: What the outputs of those tasks will be.
- **People**: Who is responsible for performing the tasks.

Remember, a plan is meaningless without objectives. The main message in a plan is how it drives toward objectives.

Ever-evolving

While design briefs should be the foundation upon which all design is built, doing design means having an increasingly intimate understanding of the challenge. It means refining and elaborating the vision and principles to provide more specific guidance and design direction.

There are two things that make a design brief easy to update:

- The document has to be *structured to allow change*: Beautifully produced design briefs set a good tone for the project, but unless there has been a conscious effort to design for change, they are difficult to update.
- The document has to be *useful*: That is, people need a reason for keeping it up to date. People forget a design brief that isn't useful.

If the purpose of the design brief is to reflect the design vision, it should never go out-of-date. And if you agree that this is the primary purpose, you should design the document with this kind of flexibility in mind: What if the principles change? What if you add more principles? Have you left room to elaborate on the vision? Have you established criteria to qualify new objectives? Can you add information to requirements as your understanding of the scope evolves? A good design brief is structured to permit these kinds of changes.

Set the Tone of the Project

A good design brief establishes the tone of the project. This is not something that happens explicitly: The document's executive summary doesn't include a line indicating that the project's tone will be light with occasional bouts of seriousness.

Instead, the degree of formality, structure, and polish of the design brief sets expectations on how the project team will communicate. It would be difficult to go from a finely tuned design brief to reams of disorganized and unannotated sketches.

A design brief can also be a vehicle for introducing the range of project management tools to be used. Project management tools are used to:

- Track "doneness" of different parts of the project
- Plan the activities for achieving objectives
- Refine the scope as the design problem becomes clearer
- Manage risks as they arise
- Document feedback on the design artifacts
- Capture to-do items for various team members
- Assign funding and commitments to different activities

Whatever tools you use to address each of these, the design brief offers an opportunity to provide a gentle introduction. The brief can show an excerpt or sample from the tool. If enough information is available, the tool shown should include baseline information.

Considerations for showing tools

As you present these artifacts, consider adding a layer of information adjacent to the project management tool itself:

- What it's for
- Who is responsible for maintaining it
- Who should use it

Example: Showing a progress matrix

For example, some teams use a matrix to track completeness for different aspects of the project. There are lots of ways to frame a project. One way is by deliverable, but more of my projects have multiple design streams as we pursue different aspects of the design. These are sometimes staggered on purpose at the outset, or later become staggered as feedback rolls in at different paces. In the example in Figure 9.3, we've structured the Zoo iPhone app project from Wireframes (Chapter 7) around three main workstreams: the app itself, the supporting web site, and the content creation.

Each stream of the design is based on a different piece of the product. The team may have a good idea of how they want to break up a project, but that framework may change

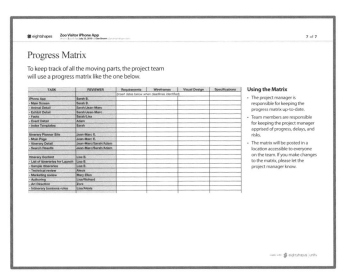

Figure 9.3: A progress matrix can be seeded with sample information based on the initial concept of the project. In this case the matrix is embedded in a page to provide additional information.

during the course of the project. The design may yield a different approach, feasibility assessments may render certain parts of the project out-of-scope, or stakeholders may reprioritize the features.

Moderate Level of Effort

Think about how much effort you want to spend on a design brief. Some considerations:

- **Purpose**: Every design brief should capture the design problem and objectives and set direction for the design. The document can serve either as a centralized bible used throughout the project or merely as a way to get the ball rolling on the design process. If the latter, plan for less effort on the design brief.
- **Overall budget**: If you need to dedicate a chunk of your budget to the design brief, you don't want to eat up too much, sacrificing later design activities. At the same time, design briefs can establish direction for later activities, making them more efficient and focused.

- **Inputs**: Design briefs may be positioned as a quick exercise at the beginning of a project to align expectations. They may also serve, however, as the summary of a series of requirements, research, and discovery activities.
- **Perceived value**: I always try to incorporate some initial design concepts in my design briefs, lest my customer think they're paying me to simply regurgitate the inputs. If your design brief won't offer much more than capturing the objectives and requirements, your level of effort should err on the lower side.

A reasonable starting point for level of effort is 20 percent of the overall design budget. If you have 400 hours to put together a design, spending 80 on composing a design brief generally works. (Eighty hours is one person full-time for two weeks. Most people can get a lot done in that amount of time if they have no other commitments.) Much more than this, and you start to encroach on the design endeavor. Much less than 10 percent and you just don't have the time to wrap your head around the design problem in a way that lets you state it clearly.

Of course, this rule of thumb is just a starting point. Design briefs can be much simpler, or they can require substantial inputs (for example, user research).

Communicate Priority

One of the overall messages of a design brief is that different principles have different priorities. There are various methods for identifying these priorities, but regardless of which you use, the outcome is the same: Some principles have a stronger influence on the design process than others.

Rather than communicate weight explicitly, by assigning some pseudo-quantitative value (numbers or "moon phases" for example), I organize my document around the prioritization. The most important ideas should come first in the document. They should be repeated often. They should appear at the top of lists.

In the next section, Anatomy of a Design Brief, I'll explore the different kinds of information appearing in this document. Priority is a key message throughout this section, because you may generate dozens of design principles for each type (objectives, guidelines, constraints, requirements, and so on).

Arbitrary lists of principles do not help the design team.

While it may feel like a step in the right direction, numeric weights also aren't very helpful. The design team will be looking to the brief as a constant source of inspiration and direction. The most important messages need to jump out at them, not be buried among others, a sole bullet or icon the only indicator that this concept is more important than another.

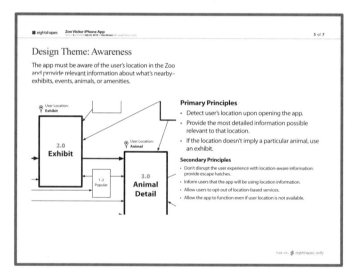

Figure 9.4: Communicating prioritization means using the layout and structure of the document to imply relative importance. In this example, which highlights one of the themes of the design concept, more important principles from the theme appear at the top of the page and are rendered in a larger type size.

Tips for Presenting Design Briefs

If you are the designer preparing the design brief, this may be the first document you share with the project team. If you haven't worked with the team before, this meeting can feel very important. The project team will be seeing work for the first time. They'll have the opportunity to provide feedback in real time. They will start to see how the process works. They will get a sense of how well you understand the design problem. They may have high expectations about the initial concepts. And, they may not really know what a design brief is, so they may not be prepared for what you show them.

In short, there's a lot riding on this conversation, and a lot that can go wrong. (I'll be honest, these are my least favorite presentations.)

Socialize concepts beforehand

One thing I do to help moderate the risks is talk to my key stakeholders about the content of the brief well before the meeting. This is an opportunity to gauge the concepts, set their expectations about the brief, and solicit feedback about the content.

In such a conversation, you can focus on the high-level pieces of the concept—the vision statement, the design objectives, the primary design principles, the characterization of the scope. Talking to the main project stakeholder about these things, you're interested in his or her estimation of the project team's reaction. You may need to ask pointed questions, like:

- Does any of this conflict with the general understanding of the project?
- Is it too soon to talk about these ideas?
- Our vision focuses on the concepts of Proximity, Awareness, and Enrichment. What's your first impression of those concepts?

- We'll be presenting a project plan that's a few weeks longer than anticipated. What do you think we can do to help justify that?
- We're not presenting any specific design ideas, but we do want to make sure we have the design problem right. Do you think the team will get that?

Another approach I take in this conversation is to share the table of contents. With this, my stakeholder will have a more solid understanding of the range of topics covered in the design brief. He or she can then react to what information might be missing, what might be premature, and which content is going to garner the most focus from the project team.

Depending on your relationship with the project stakeholder, you might share an early draft of the document.

Regardless of whether you get to have this conversation, you can also send around an agenda for the meeting, drawn from the brief's table of contents. Solicit input on the agenda from the meeting participants to ensure that it addresses all the things they expected to discuss.

Avoid "Ta-da!"

Be careful treating the design brief conversation as an unveiling of a Big Idea—whether that be some initial conceptual designs, some sketches to make sure you have the problem right, or a central vision statement. The sad truth is that no one is ever as excited about your ideas as you are. (And I mean no one, and I have a Jewish mother.) Other members of the project team consider the concept from other perspectives, which may render the concept as, well, disappointing.

Many people come to this meeting with their own idea of what the product should look like. Rarely will you find a project team ready, willing, and able to take ideas that you spoon-feed to them. (Frankly, I'm more suspicious

Russ Unger,
Director of User Experience,
Happy Cog

DB: *What makes for a good design brief?*

RU: *Design Briefs are a lot like job descriptions—they can vary depending on who writes them, their experience, and their perspective on the most important aspects.*

That said, a good design brief should have some key components to it. I like to include:

- *Project summary/overview*
- *Target audiences*
- *Design/interaction goals*
- *Business objectives and design strategy*
- *Supporting research and data*
- *Related personas snapshot*

The project summary/overview assures your client that you know exactly what you're working on. In most cases, this is something that it is already agreed upon, but possibly not articulated clearly in a document.

Target Audiences are essential—clients will tell you that "everyone is a target," but designing for everyone is nearly as fun as designing for yourself. That is, it isn't. If you can't identify your primary, secondary, and tertiary audiences, you need to have some in-depth discussions with your client.

Design/interaction goals can help guide you when it comes to prioritizing content, and may give you some insight into a content strategy (and hopefully you've got one of those, too!). In addition, the goals can provide you with ways to approach your design solution.

Business objectives and design strategy is the one piece that I wish every single brief could have, right on the cover, in bold text and maybe even a <blink> tag around it. In his book Creating the Perfect Design Brief, Peter L. Phillips says, "This is your 'contract'. If done well, it is your best opportunity to obtain agreement to experiment and pursue a variety of creative concepts. It will also become a key ingredient in preparing your final presentation of a design solution for approval, and acceptance." I couldn't agree more—work with your client so they can create the business objectives and then provide a clear design strategy for each.

It's nice to have supporting research and data, but at the same time, this could be an entire document of its own if you're not careful. A summary or overview of the research and data with direction to an external document can provide your team with primary findings and the ability to take a deep dive if necessary.

Finally, if available, a related personas snapshot is a great way to provide additional insight into the target audiences and supporting research and data. A thumbnail photo with key demographic information and a personal quote (with reference to fully detailed personas, of course) can go a long way toward supporting your design brief.

One last thing: The word "brief" is often, in my opinion, misconstrued to mean that there should be a finite number of pages to the document. In general, a design brief should include all the content it takes to get the information across clearly and concisely.

when other team members do not push back on the design ideas.) What you show will inevitably conflict with what they have in their heads. Sometimes it's a completely different concept, and sometimes their own conception of the web site is more detailed. (From their perspective: "Wow, so much effort to lay out the basics? Where are the details?")

So, instead of "ta-da!":

- Treat the concept as a starting point, a foundation from which the rest of the design will be built.
- Build a strong connection between the design concept and the design problem. In other words, don't position the design concept or vision as a stand-alone, but as a first step in hashing out the design problem. Show the relationship between different elements of the design problem and how the vision would treat those problems.
- Use the design concept to validate the objectives of the project, and clarify your understanding of what you need to accomplish.

Don't skimp on logistics

So, if doing an unveiling is a recipe for disaster, how should you focus the conversation? Beyond the tips in the previous section, the conversation around a design brief should address the How. As stated in the Designing Processes sidebar earlier, your role as a designer is as much about describing the approach for meeting the project objectives.

Spend as much time (if not more) describing the scope, activities, deliverables, and points of overlap with other members of the project team. Describe how your design philosophy (presumably the catalyst for hiring you) is realized in the approach.

If you spend the most time on the page of the document that describes the process, consider that the sign of a successful meeting.

ANATOMY OF A DESIGN BRIEF

The content of a design brief is the set of principles driving the design project.

Organizing Design Briefs

Here's a good table of contents for a design brief:

Chapter	Pages
Front Matter	Cover
	Table of contents
	Executive summary
The Vision	The design themes
	How the world will be a better place
	The context: What's happening today
The Challenge	Scope
	Requirements
	Constraints
Design Principles	One page per principle
Our Plan	Project plan
	Activity descriptions
	Deliverable descriptions

Table 9.2: The design brief should establish the overall vision and themes at the beginning of the document, then elaborate on additional principles and constraints.

This structure for the design brief follows the general philosophy of documentation laid out throughout the book: It starts with the punch line and digs into details in later chapters.

It may be tempting to start with The Challenge, which describes the design problem, and you are welcome to do so. Here are some considerations:

Starting with the Vision	Starting with the Challenge
If the client stakeholders are confident that you, the design team, understand the challenge, starting with the vision is more powerful.	If you, the design team, want to show that you that you understand the challenge, regurgitating it to the client stakeholders is useful.
Clients don't need you to regurgitate the challenge immediately, and they expect to see some progress on the design front. A solid vision feels like more progress than restating the challenge, especially if it's been the subject of kick-off meetings and stakeholder interviews.	You should start with the challenge if you're positioning it in a new way, some approach that the client hasn't considered.
	Another reason to start with the challenge is if you've determined you can't address the whole thing, and you're setting up that your approach will focus only on part of it.

Table 9.3: The vision or the challenge is the "Once upon a time..." to your whole story. Which you start with depends on the current state of the project, the activities so far, and your relationship with the clients.

Design Objectives, Themes, and Principles

One set of principles establishes the design direction. They provide different perspectives on the vision for the project.

In general, the design direction guides designers by providing inspiration and suggestions. At one level, they're rules that say "always use active verbs for buttons," and at another they point in the general vicinity of a concept, like "this product needs to help co-workers share information about specific projects."

As described in What Makes a Good Design Brief earlier, articulating the design direction benefits from moving beyond a simple bullet list. Examples are powerful; they illustrate elements of the design direction and provide context. Some other considerations:

- **Classification**: Categorizing the principles under different themes (like "navigation") will help you establish an overall direction for specific areas of the project. Such groupings help designers know which principles to focus on for particular design problems.
- **Prioritization**: As the project progresses, you may identify a large quantity of principles. Prioritizing them from the outset, giving some principles more weight, will help maintain focus during the design process.
- **Language**: Principles should be rendered in the imperative voice (verbs that are commands). Use simple statements, and make them as concrete and as specific as possible. "Be friendly" is pretty vague. "Lean toward understated and warm color palettes and geometric patterns" is less vague.
- **Sketches**: Illustrate principles with concept sketches. My documents frequently contain scanned pen-and-paper drawings.

Vision statements

One way to summarize the overall direction is to establish a vision statement, which defines the central theme that drives subsequent design decisions. This singular sentence or phrase can provide focus for the design effort, making an appearance throughout the process to qualify ideas and new requirements.

Here are some vision statements we've used:

- As powerful as you need it to be.
- Building bridges between areas of the organization.
- Let experts escape administrivia and be experts again.

(They may seem meaningless to you, here, now, because you're not familiar with the specific project. A vision is rooted deeply in the context of a project. Don't feel like your vision statement has to move the Earth. It just needs to be meaningful to the people involved in the project.)

Frequently, we use a visual metaphor to reinforce the vision statement. A simple statement superimposed on a large photograph is a powerful way to establish the vision.

Design Context and Scope

A second set of principles draws boundaries, clarifying project parameters. Instead of pointing designers in the right direction, boundaries let them know where they should avoid treading. These parameters are more specific to the particular design project, and have less to do with logistics (like deadlines) and more to do with areas of focus. Some considerations for defining boundaries:

- **Specificity**: If you're searching for a way to articulate a boundary in a more concrete way, start with quantity. Whether you're talking about number of screens, number of interface components, or number of iterations, establishing an order of magnitude can help the project team get at least a rough sense of how big the project is.
- **Source**: Some of these boundaries are more arbitrary than others. Why are we only focusing on press releases for launch? Why can't we touch the header? Documenting where these scope notes come from can facilitate traceability.
- **Weight**: Like any other design principle, those that provide context and scope should be weighted.

Figure 9.5: A vision statement paired with a photograph can produce a powerful foundation for the design process. Making the photo full-bleed adds further power to the image (in this case an innocent preschooler confronted by a male peacock during mating season).

Illustrations also help to communicate scope. Use a site map, flowchart, or concept model to draw the part of the site that you'll focus on for this particular project.

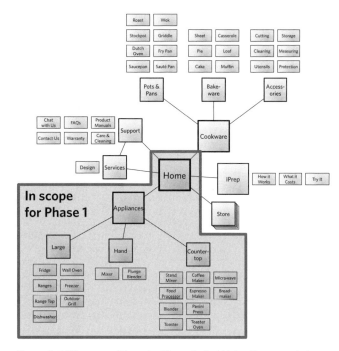

Figure 9.6: Site map with project boundaries. Using the example from Site Maps (Chapter 5), we can communicate which parts of the new site structure the team will focus on in the first design phase.

Design Concept

It's easy to picture the design process as spanning two key tasks—understanding the problem and solving the problem. This book makes heavy use of that dichotomy to help clarify the roles of different diagrams and documents. The design process is obviously much more complex, and frankly, not much more needs to be said about it.

ASIDE
Wait, What?

Incorporate a design concept into the design brief? Shouldn't we make sure we have the problem right? Don't we need to validate the requirements? We don't have a full understanding of the constraints!

Yes, but we're experimenting with a new philosophy at my firm. It's called, "Shut up and design." Before we dig into the details of presenting a design concept, some further rationale for incorporating one:

- **Use it to validate your understanding:** Don't try to solve the problem in the first go. Put an idea down on paper and see what works and what doesn't. That gives you a point of comparison to drive your discussion.
- **Keep your effort minimal:** Your aim isn't to solve the problem on the first go. (Didn't I just say that?) Spend a couple of hours kicking around some ideas. Exposing the project team to this thought process can help you iron out the other aspects of the design brief.
- **Engage the project team early:** All our attempts to avoid putting an idea down on paper are excuses to keep the rest of the project team away from design. The project team just wants to see design work. Let them get their hands dirty as soon as possible.

A design brief, in reflecting this complexity, doesn't need to stop at "stating the problem." Powerful design briefs provide an initial glimpse into the design direction; nothing illustrates a design direction better than the design itself. Not sure you agree? Check out the Wait, What? sidebar.

The design concept should help readers understand:

- The *experience*, but avoid providing too much detail: This is more a practical consideration. If you had the time and money to flesh out the details, you wouldn't be working on the design brief. (Conversely, if you have the time and money, you don't want to blow it all on the design brief.)

- The *design challenge*: Sometimes a design concept is a good way to illustrate the constraints and issues faced. Design problems become clearer as the design team solves them—why wait until later to uncover particularly sticky issues?
- The *scope*: A concept can show where you expect the project to begin and end. A drawing showing a new approach to the structure of the site gives a pretty clear indication of what you will and will not be working on.

Exposing design concepts early in the project comes with some risks. The benefits—clarifying the vision, establishing a direction, providing concrete illustrations to elicit reaction—far outweigh those risks. There are some things you can do to keep design concepts from getting out of hand:

- **Focus on one screen**: Regardless of the size of the application, use only one screen to illustrate the concept. Use an important screen (log-in just won't capture the direction in the same way), one that captures the essence of the application or the scope of the project.
- **Keep it sketchy**: If you can't create a hand-drawn concept, use line styles in your illustration application to render the concept "sketchy." Delivering a perfectly polished design concept is not appropriate for the brief. It may be tempting to position the brief as "locked up," but you know as well as I do that your understanding of the design problem will change. A "sketchy" style implicitly communicates a lack of finality.
- **Avoid committing to a particular direction**: I always position design concepts as throwaway—useful for framing the problem and setting us on the right direction, but requiring substantially more elaboration.

Structural concept

Instead of showing screens in your design brief, you can incorporate preliminary structural sketches—flows, storyboards, comics, site maps, and concept models. While these are useful diagrams for communicating an as-is state, and pointing out problem areas that might be the focus of the project, they can also show how to realize the design vision through structure. Before-and-after flows showing how a new approach to the design better addresses the design problem and establishes an overall direction.

As described earlier, you can use such a model to communicate a plan—which parts of the site or application you plan to deal with first. More generally, such a model can represent a stake in the ground, your first set of design decisions.

Summary of Requirements

Requirements, typically (historically?), are expressed with "The system shall…" statements. I've worked on projects that generate reams of paper etched with statements like these, like some errant software engineer being punished by writing inane phrases over and over again on a blackboard. "Shall" statements express the design problem, describing every behavior, business rule, and objective.

While such artifacts are not as common in more recent memory (and yet the psychological trauma remains), the spirit lingers in some corporate cultures. Stream-of-consciousness documents that are meant to capture the design problem have their place (who am I to shift the corporate culture of a Fortune 500 company?), but they don't serve your purpose as a designer very well.

But let's not throw the baby out with the bathwater. Requirements define the design problem and let project teams have important conversations about planning, scope, constraints, and feasibility. Requirements don't have to come from esoteric engineering methodologies. You might also find requirements through:

- User research
- Business needs and objectives
- Operational issues
- Corporate design standards
- Technology

Summarizing all of this information, especially if you have it at the outset, is useful because it further refines the direction for the design team. Some ideas on boiling it down:

- **Extract themes**: Far be it from me to encourage you to leave out details. Within the scope of a design brief, however, themes are sufficient. For the mobile zoo application described in Wireframes (Chapter 7), for example, the mobile app makes heavy use of geolocation. A detailed technical requirements document might elaborate on every variation. For the purpose of the design brief, stating that the application, well, makes heavy use of geolocation, is likely sufficient.
- **Use imperatives**: "The system shall…" is so passive. Designers like concrete direction: "Show users that the application is aware of their location." "Use location data to prioritize content."
- **Express from user's perspective**: Whether or not the requirements derive from user research, you can express them from the audience's perspective. You can phrase the design problem in terms of what users want to accomplish and what they expect to see.

Generally, I can avoid messing with requirements too much if I can express the design problem in a picture. If I can successfully articulate the design concept (as described in the previous section), I may not need to summarize the requirements at all; the picture is sufficient for generating conversation about what the system can and cannot do.

Summary of Constraints

The line between a requirement and a constraint is thin. Ultimately, both establish a boundary, but constraints are outside the control of anyone on the project team. "The content management system cannot incorporate any new templates within the timeframe for this project." Constraints are mostly technical, but could also be operational, "The content development team has limited resources and cannot author any new content for this project." They could be logistical, "We need something online by the end of the quarter in advance of our large marketing event."

Capturing constraints in the design brief is a lot like capturing requirements. Extracting themes and using imperative voice help. (Constraints do not define the design problem, only draw boundaries around it. They are, therefore, very much *not* from the user's perspective.) Here are a couple other things that can help:

Categorization and organization

It's hard to escape the straight list of constraints. Illustrations and photographs won't necessarily help you here. This is a case where biting the bullet and starting with a flat list of these things is worthwhile information. If you can build a picture around it, so much the better.

In the meantime, you should capture at least two things about each constraint: where it comes from and what it impacts.

The source of the constraint usually falls in one of these categories:

- **Technical**: You're building a product inside a technical platform (maybe even multiple layers of a technical platform), and the design must conform to any restrictions imposed by the platform. For example, the content management system may be picky about the kinds of content types or templates you use.

- **Operational**: The organization is on the hook to maintain and feed the design long after the project team creates the design. Operational constraints describe the organization's ability to maintain the design. For example, an organization may have only one person dedicated to editing site content, which would make it difficult to sustain a site that expects lots of new content every day.
- **Logistical**: Some constraints have to do with the project execution, and usually relate to deadlines or people assigned to the project.

If the constraint isn't obvious in the implication, you should spell out the area of impact. For example, with a technical constraint in a content management system, you should state explicitly that the project entails creating one new template for the content management system. This will make the constraint clear to anyone reading it in the context of the project.

Standard fields

Constraints usually follow a pattern. That is, there are some common ways to establish boundaries around a project. Your design brief template can include a page summarizing these standard fields, described in Table 9.4.

Constraint	Indicates...
Deadline	When the final design must be turned in.
Intermediate Milestones	Any major events happening between now and the deadline that may impact the delivery.
Approvals	Who must review and approve the design before it moves forward. On many of my projects this is an internal standards-enforcer.
Contributors	Who must participate in the design process. On my projects, these are people who lead downstream teams.
Prior Work	References to earlier activities that will drive the requirements on this project.

Table 9.4: Standard fields for defining constraints. Remember, these are determined outside the project team. If you have ultimate control over a deadline, it's not really a constraint, is it?

Late-breaking constraints

Unfortunately, many constraints don't emerge until well into the design process. Working through the design of the user experience and assessing feasibility of design concepts reveals constraints.

Letting these constraints fall through the cracks can be disastrous. Individually small, constraints have a big impact on the design. The team should maintain a separate tool (a spreadsheet, for starters) that tracks constraints, a checklist constantly updated so the designers have a reference tool at their fingertips. Whether you incorporate late-breaking constraints in the design brief depends on how entrenched that document is with the team. It also depends on how easy the document is to update, and whether the team would benefit from a separate tool.

Use a table in the design brief to capture constraints identified at the outset, supporting the table with supplemental illustrations as necessary.

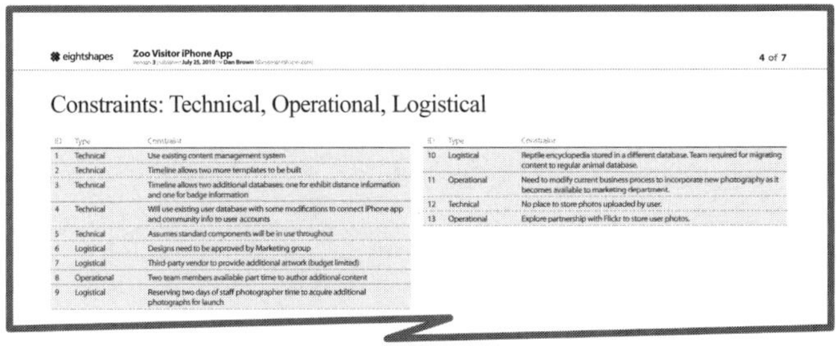
eightshapes Zoo Visitor iPhone App 4 of 7

July 25, 2010 Dan Brown

Constraints: Technical, Operational, Logistical

ID	Type	Constraint
1	Technical	Use existing content management system
2	Technical	Timeline allows two more templates to be built
3	Technical	Timeline allows two additional databases: one for exhibit distance information and one for badge information
4	Technical	Will use existing user database with some modifications to connect iPhone app and community info to user accounts
5	Technical	Assumes standard components will be in use throughout
6	Logistical	Designs need to be approved by Marketing group
7	Logistical	Third-party vendor to provide additional artwork (budget limited)
8	Operational	Two team members available part time to author additional content
9	Logistical	Reserving two days of staff photographer time to acquire additional photographs for launch
10	Logistical	Reptile encyclopedia stored in a different database. Team required for migrating content to regular animal database.
11	Operational	Need to modify current business process to incorporate new photography as it becomes available to marketing department.
12	Technical	No place to store photos uploaded by user.
13	Operational	Explore partnership with Flickr to store user photos.

Figure 9.7: A table of constraints in the design brief is easy to update and easy to expand with late-breaking information.

Project Schedule

Besides defining *what* the project will accomplish, a design brief also should assert *how* the team intends to get there. As described in the Plan section earlier in this chapter, the essential pieces of information in a project plan are the activities and the outputs. Nothing describes activities and outputs over time better than a Gantt chart.

Gantt charts are diagram outcasts. Appropriated (some might say bastardized) by Microsoft Project, these visual project schedules had their elegance and simplicity drained from them. Bars on a timeline, however, can be beautiful once again, and are great for telling stories.

Great Gantt charts depend on simplicity and focus. And, like any design endeavor, those things start with understanding the target audience.

Needs of the target audience

It can be tempting to incorporate every last detail of the project plan into a Gantt chart, but this approach undermines the overall story. Too many crisscrossing lines, illegible labels, and timelines that spread across multiple pages

render these diagrams inaccessible, and make it easy to lose the thread of the story.

A project plan's focus in the context of a design brief should be those things that project stakeholders care about:

- When do I need to get involved?
- What kind of commitment does my team need to make?
- What am I getting at the end of the day? Am I getting my money's worth?
- How soon will I have the most tangible design work in my hands?
- Are there additional costs on the project?

To that end, great Gantt charts have:

- **Meaningful timelines**: Use the width of the page to represent the length of the entire project. (Perhaps you can define this either by what part of the project is funded, or by a deadline established externally.) This may prevent you from revealing the details of individual phases or activities. Create separate Gantt charts for each of those. Practically speaking, you'll generally only have enough information to create a high-level project schedule across the whole timeline and then a detailed schedule for whatever phase you're embarking on right now. Your design brief will then have two charts: overall plan and activities right now.
- **Right level of detail**: On top of the timeline, you need to specify activities and deliverables. Sometimes, you need to specify dependencies between these things. Things get tricky here in determining how much detail to include. Generally speaking, I include activities that have discrete beginnings and endings. If I have the room, I'll break down an activity into smaller tasks, but I usually just list these in the annotations that accompany the schedule. Every activity should have a deliverable, and I'll incorporate intermediate deliverables throughout the activity if people outside the design team expect to see them or it will have a major impact on the project.

- **External inputs**: Sometimes people outside my area of influence (usually other stakeholders or subject matter experts on the client side) are responsible for providing an input to the project.
- **Participation commitments**: My project plans always show the cadence of regular status meetings, to let stakeholders know what their commitments are.
- **Relevant external factors**: Team member vacations, for example. There's a pang of resentment or guilt whenever these things get stated explicitly on the project plan, but the presence or absence of someone on the team can have an enormous impact on delivery.

THE ONE-SLIDE CHALLENGE

The design brief describes a project's objectives, the vision for the design, and how the team will get there. It establishes boundaries to help keep the design endeavor focused and documents some of the principles the team will use to drive the design process.

For a document called "brief," this is a lot of information.

Can you summarize everything in a single slide or single page? Shrinking down your text and artwork doesn't count.

I've heard a simple idea from several different sources, including Dan Roam, who wrote the book *The Back of the Napkin*. This idea is this: The person who can clearly state a problem or challenge is the person best positioned to solve it.

A design brief captures essential information, and good ones get pretty detailed, and they should not sacrifice that information for brevity. On the other hand, the design brief should include a page that boils it all down, that provides the team with **objectives**, **vision**, **direction**, **constraints**, and **approach**, in the space of a single page. From that page, I should understand how the design team will be spending the next few months.

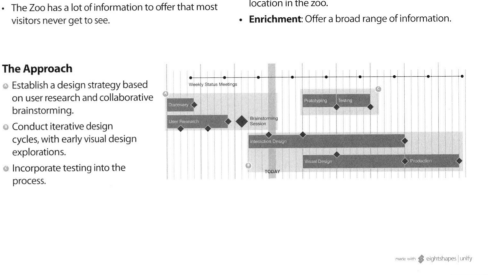

Figure 9.8: Focusing on the project schedule, the one-pager displays the Gantt chart with overlays to describe the overall approach.

Of all the pages in the design brief, this is where you should spend the most time. (Perhaps second only to those pages that put a stake in the ground for the design direction.) A one-page summary of the project will prove most useful to the team, something they can hang next to their computer. It will help them remember that, as they're pushing pixels around the screen or digging into recordings of usability tests or adding painstaking annotations to wireframes, they are making an important contribution to a larger effort.

Figures 9.8, 9.9, and 9.10 provide some ideas on what that page might look like.

Challenge Focus

New technologies make kitchen appliances especially powerful cooking tools. Downloadable recipes and guided cooking let the average consumer step-up his or her skills. The web site needs to communicate these new capabilities and make appliances and accessories easy to find.

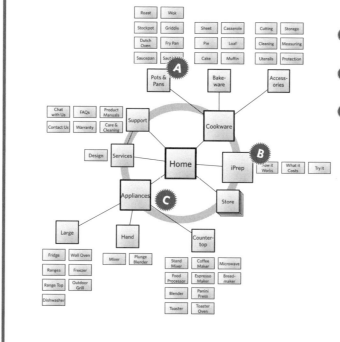

The Challenge

A Complex product hierarchy makes it difficult for users to find related products.

B Information about new technology buried and separate from actual products.

C Value of new technology lost on users who are focused on browsing the catalog.

Our Approach

1. Conduct user research to observe users with new technology and identify strategies for online marketing.

2. Develop prototype sites with two different approaches to incorporating new technology information into catalog.

3. Use prototype as starting point for web site redesign.

made with ❋ eightshapes | unify

Vision Focus

The online comic experience has come a long way even in the last year. But the model remains trapped in brick-and-mortar thinking.

Objectives

- **Engage more users** in the online comic book experience by creating more accessible virtual retail venues.

- **Reduce the dependency** of knowing the backstory of major comic book characters.

- **Create venues** for more age groups to let both kids and adults enjoy their favorite characters.

Vision

Readers love stories. What can online comics do to make the stories more accessible to more people?

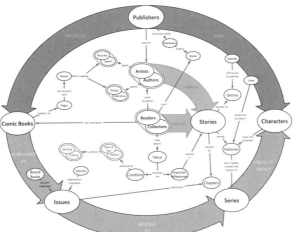

made with ❖ eightshapes|unify

Approach

1. Establish relationships with major publishers to make content available through this venue.

2. Design an online venue that leverages the extensive comic book character information on Wikipedia to structure the browse experience.

3. Pilot the experience with new readers.

Figure 9.10: Stating the vision for the project can show the project team how you're bridging the gap between the objectives and the approach. In this case, the concept model is not explained directly. When using diagrams that are more abstract, be sure they've already been socialized. This page would not be effective if the project team were seeing the diagram for the first time.

Chapter 10

Competitive Reviews

kəm'·pət·ət·iv ri'·vyoō (n.)

A document comparing one or more web sites to a set of criteria or design principles to illustrate or validate those principles. Often used as an input into the design process.

A competitive review is a document that analyzes other web sites, extracting lessons learned to inform subsequent design activities. There are lots of reasons to perform a competitive review:

- Find out how other people solved the same design problems.
- Validate desired features and priorities against a similar site.
- Explore approaches to solving similar problems.

"Competitive" may be a misnomer. Sometimes you can look at sites outside the circle of competition to inspire new approaches for solving the same problems. Sometimes we call these comparative reviews.

One caution: A competitive analysis shouldn't be the sole source of design inspiration. Don't do something just because someone else is doing it.

WHAT MAKES A GOOD COMPETITIVE REVIEW

Like any deliverable, a competitive review must be actionable; the lessons learned from looking at other sites must be immediately applicable to the design endeavor.

Focus

In the entire process of creating a competitive analysis, preparing the document is the easy part. You'll have some tough decisions to make about the document—for example, whether to present a simple table or something more elaborate—but ultimately, this is not what makes the process challenging. Once you've established the criteria and the range of competitors, gathering the data is also fairly straightforward, albeit time-consuming. Drawing a box around your analysis, however, and establishing boundaries to define what's relevant to your project, is the more difficult task.

This will be a lot easier if you identify your purpose before you begin your analysis. A purpose statement can drive not only the types of information you collect about each competitor, but also how you present the data. That purpose may be as simple as "We're struggling with widget X in our site and we want to see how it is done on 20 prominent web sites." Or, it may be as complex as "We're building a system to support user group Y and we want to find out how this group has been supported elsewhere." If you've decided to do a competitive analysis, spend some time with the team brainstorming about what you want to get out of it. Articulate a purpose statement and compare notes with the rest of the team to make sure they have the same understanding of the purpose. In the end, you'll define an agenda for the research and set expectations about how the information will be useful on the project.

Regardless of how you organize your competitive analysis, with size comes a potential lack of focus. As you expand the reach of your analysis, either by adding more criteria or more competitors, you don't want to lose sight of why you're doing the analysis. Including a statement of purpose in the document itself is a great reminder, and also helps the document's audience understand the context for the analysis.

Strong Competitive Framework

The competitive framework is the structure you use to tell the story, and what drives the moral of that story. A competitive framework is the technique for extracting conclusions—a set of criteria for judging sites deemed relevant—but it also gives you a way to tell the story.

Prior to looking at sites for comparison, make note of what conclusions would be most useful to the design team. Do they need:

- Direction on how to design a carousel?
- Inspiration on structuring a complex product catalog?

- Thoughts on labeling navigation items?
- Ideas for structuring page layouts for landing pages?
- Models for reconciling multiple levels of navigation?
- Sample flows for purchasing services?

The document should capture these questions: the inquiry that drives the study.

With these objectives in mind, you can derive criteria for evaluating the competition, for doing a more nuanced review. Criteria identify specific aspects of the design to explore. Consider these criteria for the objective, "How should we design a carousel that displays how-to videos?":

- Size of video relative to entire component
- Mechanism for displaying range of videos available
- Mechanism for displaying overall topic of videos available

The design team might not care about other parts of the carousel, like whether users can navigate between videos linearly, or how big the video thumbnails are.

Criteria may not be necessary. You may just want to see how different sites accomplish the stated objective. Criteria, however, form a checklist that can help make your research more efficient and more focused. You don't need them strictly to evaluate design ideas.

Ultimately, whether you rank the competition is up to you and your objectives. Stating that one approach is "best" may not be useful to the design team because it boxes them in: If it doesn't look like site X, it's just not good enough. On the other hand, ranking against individual criteria can give you a sense of which competitors provide appropriate inspiration for different aspects of the design. Your intent isn't to create a Frankenstein's monster carousel (just the thought of that…), but instead look at a range of inspiration and see how different sites accomplish the same thing.

Meaningful Comparisons

A competitive review against Apple or Amazon may yield some great lessons learned, but if these sites don't overlap with your project, those lessons may not be very useful. Emulating big-name sites can only get you so far, especially if you're not a computer manufacturer or a huge online retailer.

Balance conclusions from those sites with conclusions from sites more directly related to your work. Such an approach at the very least allows you to benchmark sites and see how they've used techniques from Amazon and Apple.

Tips for Presenting Competitive Reviews

Walking through a competitive review should always start with the lessons learned. How you elaborate on those lessons can take one of two forms. A competitor-driven story focuses each chapter on a different site, ideal for a small number of competitors. A moral-driven story dissects each conclusion and may draw from a range of competitors.

Option 1: Competitor-driven story

It may seem counterintuitive, but since the competitors will form the basic structure of the meeting, you should actually start with an account of the criteria. Provide an overview of the competitive framework at the top of the meeting to set the stage and then dig into each competitor more specifically. Describe how each competitor measured up in each aspect.

This approach works well for laying the landscape and for addressing broader issues, like how each site serves the needs of its target audience. By taking the stakeholders on a tour of the competition, you give them a sense of what they're up against. This walking-tour approach helps answer broad strategic questions, such as which features are available on the site, what appears most prominently on the home page, and how the site prioritizes content, but not specific design issues, such as comparing the treatment of "add to cart" buttons.

Though a competitor-driven approach is best for discussing larger strategic issues, it can also work well for specific design problems. If you're looking at just one aspect of the design, your meeting can show how the particular design problem was solved for each competitor. When discussing a specific design problem, your meeting can end with the conclusions, drawing together lessons learned from all the competitors.

Option 2: Moral-driven story

Instead of structuring your presentation in terms of the competitors and walking through all the issues for each competitor separately, this approach takes the opposite tack: For each issue, you talk about how each competitor stacks up against the others. To set the stage, provide a short overview of the competitors. You don't need to get into comparing them at this point, but instead describe why they were included in the study.

The presentation then focuses on your conclusions. For each conclusion, you'll first need to describe the criteria you looked at to arrive at the conclusion—in other words, what you analyzed on each site.

For example, you might conclude that the highest level navigation categories on a pet-related web site are usually pet type, but that this isn't the only system of categorization used on the site. To support this conclusion, you looked at three different criteria: the navigation categories on the home page, the metadata attached to products in the catalog and other content, and the structure of intermediate "gallery" pages (galleries are lists of products or content that appear on the user's path between the home page and

the product or content page). Finally, within each of these criteria, you make observations about each of the competitors. This structure is useful for both high-level strategy analyses and specific design problems; the content of the conclusions may be different, but the logic behind them is essentially the same. In this approach, the criteria do not disappear, but they become a bridge between your conclusions and your observations.

Besides the structure of the meeting, however, you should also set the tone of the competitive review.

Maintain perspective

The worst way for a meeting to get off topic is to get too caught up in the competition. Although you've invited people to the meeting to discuss your site's competitors, it can be easy to lose perspective on the purpose of the competitive analysis. Symptoms of this problem include getting stuck on one particular design element in a meeting about strategy, or spending too much time talking about one competitor over others. Even though your competitive analysis is meant to address one particular design problem, you might find conversation straying from that design problem into other areas of the site, or your participants might start talking about more strategic issues.

If the conversation is productive, you may not see this as a risk at all. However, if you have a specific agenda and certain goals for the meeting, these kinds of digressions may not be productive regardless of how interesting they are. To get back on track, jump in and remind the participants of the purpose of the meeting. One way to help stop this problem before it happens is to write the purpose of the meeting on a whiteboard or flipchart at the very beginning. If someone attempts to stray too far, you can always point to the meeting purpose and look very stern. You won't be popular, but you'll be respected for running a good meeting.

Know the rationale behind your methods

As you present the results of your competitive analysis, you may run into troublesome meeting participants who question your methodology. They may raise questions about your selection of competitors or criteria, or your technique for capturing data.

Say you're building this pet web site, for example, and your analysis looked at a handful of sites. That might not stop one of your participants from saying, "I do all my online shopping at JeffersPet.com. Why isn't that in your competitive analysis?" If you've done your homework, you can respond with, "Given the time constraints on the competitive analysis, we had to keep the number of sites down to four. We included DrsFosterSmith.com among our reviewed sites to represent the non-retail-store competitors, and think we've got a pretty good set of lessons learned. If, after our presentation, you think there are some aspects represented in JeffersPet.com that we missed, you can tell us about some lessons learned from there."

Open your mind to varying interpretations

Meeting participants will have their own opinions about what works and what doesn't work about different competitive sites. They may have their favorite sites and deem that approach the only one to follow. While discussion of the specifics of a site might be worthwhile, your role is to keep the conversation ultimately focused on the conclusions. Try not to sound like a jerk when you ask, but ultimately your focus is, "So what?" Since "Design our carousel to look like Amazon's" is not an acceptable conclusion, you need to help meeting participants extract lessons learned not already covered by your competitive analysis.

Communicate your willingness to look at other competitors or consider other criteria, but emphasize that the purpose will be to provide direction to the design team.

To facilitate this conversation, ask them to start with the existing conclusions and identify what's missing. "What is it about Amazon's carousel that you like that's not reflected here?"

If any of their conclusions conflict with ones you've already established, and you're not willing to throw away either one, perhaps this indicates that you need to seek design direction elsewhere. Sometimes multiple perspectives on a competitive analysis point to the method's inability to provide a solid direction.

ANATOMY OF A COMPETITIVE REVIEW

The essential elements of a competitive analysis are the purpose statement, conclusions, and evidence.

Organizing Competitive Reviews

Here's a good table of contents for a competitive review:

Chapter	Pages
Front matter	Cover
	Table of contents
	Summary: Objectives, study questions, and criteria
	Summary: All the lessons learned
Conclusions	One sheet per conclusion, with supporting evidence
Criteria and Competition	For each study question or objective, list of criteria considered
	How you chose the competitors
	Profiles of competitors

Table 10.1: The competitive review should start with the lessons learned and then provide a detailed look at each conclusion. If necessary to spell out further detail, you can include a chapter of "raw data," the competitive framework and profiles of the most important competitors.

By structuring the meat of the document around the conclusions, you can keep the endeavor focused and give designers one destination when dealing with a specific design problem.

The downside to this approach is that it can seem to take the sites out of context, providing only a narrow view of them.

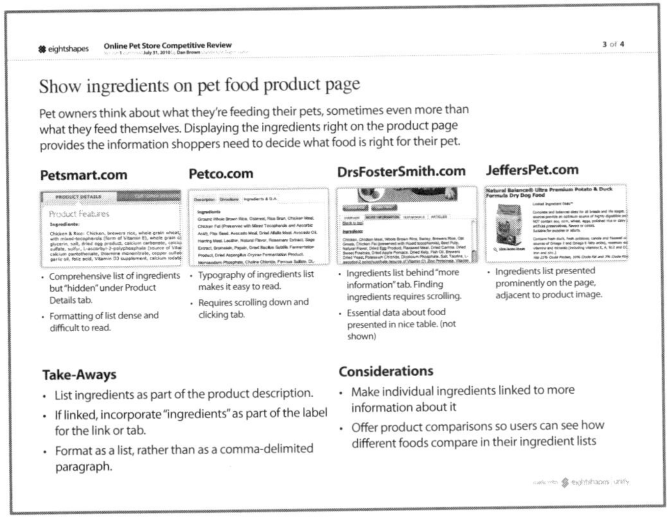

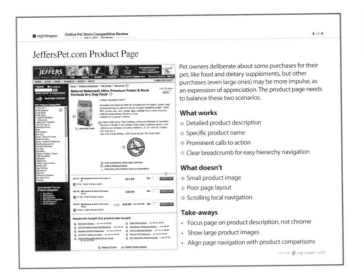

3 of 4

Figure 10.1: A conclusion summarized in a competitive analysis clearly states the lesson learned, offers some details about it, and provides evidence in the form of screenshots.

Another approach

Another way to organize the document is by competitor. Each sheet deals with a different site, and draws conclusions from that site. In this case, the competitive analysis reads as a sort of rogues' gallery of sites, each one having a separate profile. Within each profile, the site is described with various criteria. This approach offers a holistic view of the user experience for each site, but it is more difficult to compare between sites.

Figure 10.2: A competitor profile can speak more holistically about the site, but lessons learned become spread throughout the document.

Conclusions and Takeaways

Like any story part of the design process, you start at the end. What did you learn from looking at all these web sites? Did you get your questions answered? What should designers think about as they embark on this design project?

By putting your conclusions into words, you are establishing a partial direction for the design team, who will take their cues for the design from these assertions. The description of the competitive framework is meant only to support and illustrate the takeaways.

When embarking on building a pet-related site, for example, the design team may seek out best practices from the competition. A cursory study of the landscape allows them to conclude that most pet-related sites use pet type (dog, cat, and so on) as the main navigation. A more in-depth study, however, leads to more detailed data—how sites specializing in one kind of pet categorize their content, how frequently sites use the same categories, the order of the categories (cats first or dogs first), how sites

Show ingredients on pet food product page

Pet owners think about what they're feeding their pets, sometim[...] than what they feed themselves. Displaying the ingredients right on the prod[...] provides the information shoppers need to decide what food is right for their p[...]

Conclusion

Evidence

Design Direction

Petsmart.com

- Comprehensive list of ingredients but "hidden" under Product Details tab.
- Formatting of list dense and difficult to read.

Petco.com

- Typography of ingredients list makes it easy to read.
- Requires scrolling down and clicking tab.

DrsFosterSmith.com

- Ingredients list behind "more information" tab. Finding ingredients requires scrolling.
- Essential data about food presented in nice table. (not shown)

Jeff[...]

- Ing pro adj[...]

Take-Aways

- List ingredients as part of the product description.
- If linked, incorporate "ingredients" as part of the label for the link or tab.
- Format as a list, rather than as a comma-[...] paragraph.

Considerations

- Make individual ingredients lin[...] information about it
- Offer product comparisons so [...] foods compare in the

Figure 10.3: Conclusion pages must prominently show the takeaway and explain how the illustrations support it.

deal with uncommon pets (turtles). With data like this, the conclusions—and therefore design direction—can be better informed.

Assuming you've organized your document as in Table 10.1, you'll have a separate page dedicated to each conclusion, illustrating that conclusion with screenshots of pages or components from various sites. Some considerations as you lay out those pages:

- Make the conclusion very prominent.
- Provide a more detailed description of the conclusion.
- Show just enough of the site to illustrate the conclusion, providing short descriptions explaining the connection.
- Consider incorporating an "anti-example," a site that illustrates the wrong way to implement the conclusion.

Summarizing the Conclusions

While designers will find detailed treatments of each conclusion and assertion useful, the document needs a summary at the beginning, a cheat sheet to boil down the lessons learned. The summary should capture the principles established through the competitive analysis and a snapshot of the competitive framework.

Note in Figure 10.4 that summarizing the competitive framework means identifying the range of sites examined and the criteria by which they were evaluated. The deeper and broader the analysis, the more you'll need to abstract the framework. Looking at a broad range of sites along many criteria means barely scratching the surface of that depth on the summary page.

Characterize the range of sites visited by naming them explicitly; it's even better if you can show a screenshot of the site itself. If you looked at many, many sites, be sure to quantify the range and identify the kinds of sites you looked at. For example:

- We looked at 20 different sites, all Fortune 500 companies.

- We looked at 35 different "Web 2.0" sites, all with a social or community aspect.
- We looked at two groups of a dozen sites each: product marketing sites and service marketing sites.

The criteria may be too numerous or too nebulous to spell out. Instead, characterize them through subject matter:

- We looked at how each site handled navigation and classification of content.
- We looked at how the sites adapted the experience in response to user preferences that were gleaned implicitly from the patterns of clicks.
- We looked at a range of user experience issues, from finding information to account management.

Incorporate comprehensive lists of both criteria and subjects (sites) into an appendix and reference them on the summary page.

Summarizing the Landscape

Even the simplest competitive analysis displays two critical dimensions: the competitive web sites and the criteria. Together these comprise the competitive framework. The purpose of the competitive framework is to present the data in a way that makes it easy to compare the various sites across the different criteria.

One simple way to display a comprehensive view of the competitive framework is to use a table; the competitors run along the top of the table and the criteria along the side. Tables 10.2 and 10.3 show two examples of this kind of competitive framework.

A different kind of competitive framework is the two-by-two, plotting competitors on a simple grid depicting only two criteria as in Figure 10.5.

Notice that with a two-by-two, the number of criteria is shrunken down to two, so they tend to be broader. This type of graphic is useful for identifying holes in a

eightshapes | **Online Pet Store Competitive Review**
version 1 published July 31, 2010 by Dan Brown (dan@eightshapes.com)

2 of 4

Ecommerce Sites for Pet Owners

What we did

Conducted **competitive review** of other prominent pet supply web sites.

Our objective

Establish **common practices** for selling common pet supplies on the web.

We compared 5 sites

DrsFosterSmith.com 1800PetMeds.com JeffersPet.com Petco.com Petsmart.com

Across 20 criteria, including:

- Navigation structures
- Product displays
- Gallery pages
- Product classification
- Merchandising
- Home page features
- Calls to action
- Account management

What worked

✓ Navigation categories based on pet type.

✓ Navigation categories with common supplies (like food and toys).

✓ Recommendations based on previous purchases.

✓ Home pages that highlighted new products, specials and the range of the catalog.

✓ Prominent calls to action taking users to the next step in the shopping process.

What didn't work

✗ **Dense product pages:** Squeezing all the information onto a single page with tabbed panels hides information that may help users make a purchase.

✗ **One-size-fits-all product page:** Users require different kinds of information about different product pages.

✗ **Long lists of category links:** User research shows that some products are clearly more important than others, and navigation should reflect that.

made with eightshapes | unify

Figure 10.4: Summarizing the conclusions at the beginning of the document gives the project team a rundown of all the lessons learned from the competitive analysis.

	PetSmart.com	Petco.com
Home Page Features	Special offers	Special offers
Search	Prominently displayed in header above navigation, text field with scope drop-down	Prominently displayed in upper left below navigation, text field only
Navigation Categories	Animal type only	Pre-coordinated terms combining pet type and product type (e.g.: Fish Food)
Contact Information	None	Toll-free number displayed in header
Ecommerce	Standard shopping cart model	Standard shopping cart model

Table 10.2: Simple competitive reviews establish criteria and evaluate competitors relative to them. While useful inputs, this information doesn't provide designers with clear direction on what's working and what's not.

Does the home page...	PetSmart.com	Petco.com
introduce a range of products, illustrating the breadth of the store?	no	no
make the search function easy to find?	yes	yes
display off-line contact information?	no	yes
Does the navigation...	**PetSmart.com**	**Petco.com**
meet user expectations by including pet type?	yes	yes
provide access to ecommerce functions?	yes	yes
change seasonally?	no	no
incorporate links to sales, specials, or other product categories?	yes	yes

Table 10.3: Positioning the criteria as questions allows readers to compare and contrast the two sites quickly, and hints at the desired approach.

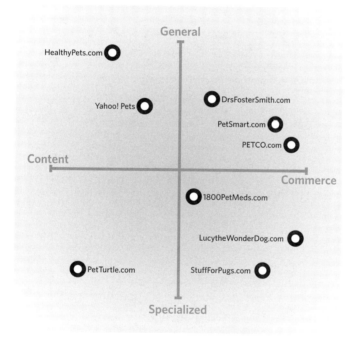

Figure 10.5: A comparative two-by-two establishes a simple framework for comparing a handful of web sites. Such an approach offers worthwhile insight if the criteria provide concrete action for the design team.

landscape. Competitors clustered around certain areas of the two-by-two can indicate that there are opportunities for your site to fill those holes.

There's one other kind of competitive framework that appears in comparisons of different user experiences: the small multiples. This term belongs to visualization guru Edward Tufte. In his *Visual Display of Quantitative Information*, Tufte writes: "Small multiples resemble the frames of a movie: a series of graphics, showing the same combination of variables, indexed by changes in another variable." Small multiples, in other words, allow the viewer to easily compare similar sets of information. In the case of interface design for the web, this approach is most effective for comparing page layouts, as in Figure 10.6.

Types of comparisons

While most of my competitive analyses present subjective data, you can attempt to quantify the comparisons you make. The data can be as simple as yes-no values, indicating whether a site meets a particular criterion, or it can be descriptive, going into some detail for each criterion:

- **Yes-No Values**: You've seen these kinds of competitive analyses on infomercials where the product in question is lined up with "other leading brands." For each feature, the product gets a checkmark while its competitors get an X, to show you how versatile the product is. When it comes to web sites, the straight yes-or-no comparison is most effective for considering features, in other words, whether a set of web sites has a specific feature or not. In such a comparison, however, the subtle differences between the competitors may be lost.

- **Scores**: Some competitive analyses score the competitors in different criteria. You'll see this approach in restaurant reviews where every place is scored on the quality of its food, the ambiance, the service, and the expense. For web sites, scores help give a little more substance to the comparison, though it may be difficult to generate the data.

- **Descriptions**: Used more frequently than yes-no data or scores, descriptions specify how the competitors meet each criterion. Descriptions allow you to be more explicit about how the competitors stack up against each other, without resorting to potentially skewed numbers.

Methodology

Spelling out your process can help address any possible methodological inadequacies, especially for stakeholders who take these things seriously. What's most worthwhile is rationalizing the selection of competitors and criteria.

The range of competitive web sites out there will vary, of course, depending on the site you're building. The number may seem finite because your site is in a niche category and all the competitors are known players. The number may seem infinite because the web is vast and there are lots of sites competing for attention. You'll have to narrow it down some way, and whatever way you choose makes for worthwhile content for your document.

At the same time, there are infinite criteria by which to compare sites. They can be as broad as the main navigation categories, or as narrow as the label on a button in a particular area of the site. You've made conscious decisions to include certain criteria—maybe they are a standard set used by your client or your company, maybe they were defined ahead of time by the stakeholders, or maybe you devised a special list just for this project. Whatever your methodology behind determining the criteria, this is excellent fodder for your competitive analysis.

ACKNOWLEDGING THE COMPETITION

A competitive survey, no matter how rich the information gleaned from it, will always play second fiddle in the design process. After all, just because your competition

Figure 10.6: Small multiples of thumbnail layouts allow you to compare the structure of different pages across different sites. What might not be apparent from the grayscale is that different areas of the page have been highlighted with different color transparencies. Each color represents a different feature. This approach allows you to see how different sites treat different features, like navigation, sample products, product browsing, etc.

does something doesn't mean you should. The competition is a good place to get ideas and to establish a baseline, a cost of entry. But the value of that information in making design decisions is limited at best.

Innovation moves fast online. Regardless of how the design process evolves, information about how other sites address the problems you face will always be valuable, because it keeps you abreast of the latest trends in technological change. With innovation comes a change in landscape. At the most basic level, your audience has to make a choice, and it's our job as designers to make that choice easy, even when we don't understand all the factors that go into the decision.

When the commercial Internet emerged, retail stores faced a new kind of competition. Suddenly, competitors were lurking around every corner. This is still the case. What drives your understanding of the competition, therefore, should be a keen understanding of your audience. On the Internet, the competition is more than simply every other site trying to do the same thing you're doing. The competition is nearly any site that can attract and hold a user's attention. By knowing how your audience spends its time and how it makes decisions, you can anticipate how other sites or technologies are getting their attention, thereby expanding your survey of the competition.

Chapter 11

Usability Plans

yoō·zə·ˈbil·ət·ē plan (n.)

A document describing the objectives and approach for conducting a usability test.

The usability test plan describes the goals, method, and approach for a usability test. The test plan includes several different components, from profiles of participants to an outline of a discussion with users. The test plan described here incorporates test objectives, test logistics, user profiles, and the script.

Usability testing is an essential part of the web design diet. In a nutshell, it's a technique for soliciting feedback on the design of a web site. Usability testing is usually conducted on one participant at a time and attempts to have participants use the site in as close to a real-world setting as possible. Design teams have different approaches to usability testing at their disposal but two crucial milestones remain consistent—the plan describing what you will do during the test, and an account of what came out of the test. This chapter describes the test plan—the document you prepare in advance of testing—and the next chapter describes the report.

There are several aspects of a usability test that need planning, and some people give each its own document. Other usability researchers create a single test plan, addressing all aspects of the test in a single document. This chapter will treat usability test plans as single documents but will indicate where you might split the document if you need to have several deliverables.

WHAT MAKES A GOOD USABILITY PLAN?

The basic elements of a usability test answer three questions: What do we want out of this test, how will we conduct the test, and what will we ask users during the test? With those questions answered, you've got the barest information necessary to make a test happen.

Establishes Objectives

Objectives for a usability plan answer the question, "What will we get out of this test?" For usability testing, objectives establish boundaries and constraints, allowing us to focus on important areas to inform the design process. Imagine we're designing a health encyclopedia for a medical insurance company. The objectives for such a test might look like this:

- Determine which version of the disease description page helps users retain the most information about a particular disease.
- Determine which version of the disease description page is the most actionable, giving users a clear idea of what they can do next.
- Determine if the new navigation structure makes it easier for users to locate a particular disease.

Centers on Scenarios

Test scenarios run from the general to the specific. For example, in some cases your scenarios may be as straightforward as "present screen to user and ask for impressions." In other cases, you may want to ask the participant to imagine himself in a specific situation and use the web site to address the situation: "You have just come down with the flu and you want to see if any of your symptoms put you at high risk."

Your plan should list, in one place, all the scenarios you'll test. If necessary, you can elaborate on the scenarios on separate pages. Ultimately, you need to create a tool for the moderator to help him or her facilitate the test.

> *TIP*
> ## How to Write Good Scenarios
>
> Determining exactly what scenarios to test is beyond the scope of this book, but not beyond the scope of *The Handbook of Usability Testing*, by Jeffrey Rubin and Dana Chisnell.

Directs Moderator

The two main audiences for usability test plans are the project stakeholders and the test facilitator—the person doing most of the orchestration during the test. There may be other players in the test—people taking notes, people managing the facility, people working the recording equipment—or there may be one person who does it all. The facilitator may be someone on your team (i.e., you) or it may be a contractor or freelancer you've hired for this purpose. In either case, make the script as specific as possible.

During the test the moderator will be thinking about so many things at the same time—what the participant is doing right then, whether the recording devices are working, what will happen when the user clicks a button or link—so the script needs to guide the moderator, and be a source of comfort and focus whenever he or she looks down at it.

Formatting your document like a script helps the moderator distinguish between "stage directions" and things that he or she needs to say to the participant. Other kinds of useful information are specific questions to ask participants as part of a scenario, what kinds of "gotchas" participants might run into, and where to go next.

Acknowledges Limitations of Test Materials

In the ideal world, every usability test will be run against a fully operational prototype. (Perhaps by the time you're reading this, that will be true. Things move very quickly around here.) More often than not, we find ourselves soliciting feedback on sketches, hacked-together PDFs, HTML screens devoid of real content, or just one comp.

COMP Short for "composite," a flat screen design, not yet transformed into HTML.

Can you still get reasonable usability results out of these kinds of tests? As a designer, my philosophy is this: Some feedback is better than no feedback. As a guy on the hook for writing a test plan, I'm concerned with crafting a script that acknowledges where our test materials fall short. The plan should describe the materials used in the test and highlight potential obstacles in specific scenarios. Make sure the script doesn't ask moderators or participants to do things that the prototype, sketches, or comps can't do.

Tips for Discussing Usability Plans

A test plan isn't a hard story to tell, especially if the project team has bought into the idea of usability testing. While other documents in this book lend themselves to different meeting structures, the only decision you'll need to make for a usability test plan is how much time to spend on each section.

If you have only one meeting to review a test plan, make sure you cover each part—don't leave anything out—but you don't need to go into great detail on the logistics and methodology. If your stakeholders aren't big "detail people," you can also just hit the high points of the script, describing what scenarios you're testing and how those correspond to the different functions or areas of the web site.

Scope creep: Losing sight of objectives

When presented with the opportunity to talk to actual end users, some stakeholders and team members are like kids in a candy store. They may start suggesting questions and tasks—reasonable though they might be—that are outside the scope of the test. Some stakeholders may use the post-test questionnaire, for example, to solicit feedback about other areas of their business. When this happens, the stakeholders need a reminder about the purpose of the test.

The flip side of this coin is that the suggested questions and modifications may fall within the scope of your script, but the script has become so long that there's no way to get through it all in the time allotted. This is a good indication that your objectives are not specific enough—they're not serving as an effective filter to keep the test focused.

Usability newbies

Inevitably, you'll be presenting your test plan to a roomful of stakeholders, one or two of whom aren't familiar with usability testing. They may start questioning the purpose of the exercise, or worse, your methodology. If your discussion is derailed by these kinds of questions, you should whip out your usability testing elevator pitch—the three-sentence description that at once gives an overview of usability while shutting down this line of questioning. Don't have a usability elevator pitch? This is your reminder to come up with one, or just use this one, free of charge:

> **Usability testing is a means for us to gather feedback on the design of the system in the context of specific real-world tasks. By asking users to use the system (or a reasonable facsimile) we can observe opportunities to improve the design, catching them at this stage of the design process rather than later when changes would be more costly. Usability testing has been built into the project plan since day one. We need to get through the plan because we have users scheduled to come in next week, but if you want to talk further about usability testing, we can discuss it after the meeting.**

Feel free to modify this to suit your needs.

ANATOMY OF A PLAN

The content of the usability plan has to answer at least two questions: What are you doing, and why are you doing it?

Icing on the cake in a usability plan includes describing the methodology and the recruiting process. Providing a detailed script comprises the ice cream on the side. (Either I'm craving refined sugar or usability testing makes me think of birthday cake.)

Organizing Plans

Here's a good table of contents for a usability plan:

Chapter	Pages
Front matter	Cover
	Table of contents
	Executive summary
Methodology and Logistics	Methodology overview
	Logistics and timeline
	Recruiting
The Scenarios (may repeat this chapter if the scenarios vary by user group)	One or more pages, each describing a single scenario for use during the usability test
Next Steps	The test summary
	The test report

Table 11.1: The usability plan should provide a one-page summary of the whole test so the project team has an at-a-glance understanding of what it is all about. The scenarios chapter may be repeated if the test covers multiple user groups, and each group has a substantially different set of scenarios.

Summarizing the Plan

Describing the usability activities on a single page helps stakeholders and other team members understand the kinds of information you will get out of the test. It sets their expectations about what the test is and what it is not.

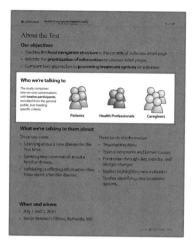

Figure 11.2: Summarizing participants with a picture, relating them to personas.

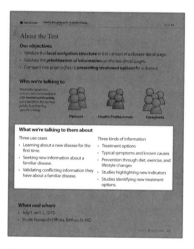

Figure 11.3: Listing scenarios describes the content of the test. In some cases, you might have to generalize or consolidate scenarios.

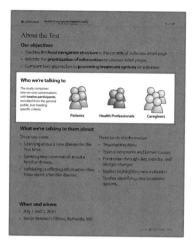

Figure 11.1: Summarizing the study on a single page answers the central questions about any usability test.

Who are you talking to?

The summary should describe the participants in the study. A simple sentence suffices for the summary page:

> We will talk to nine people: three caregivers, three patients, and three doctors.

You can use personas, if you have them, describing the range of recruits according to which profile or behavioral dimensions they conform to.

Providing a rationale for your focus may require too much space on a summary page. If recruiting, or the makeup of your participant pool is a hot topic, consider giving it a page unto itself.

What are you asking them?

Frankly, if you can't put a list of scenarios, generalized across user groups, on your summary page, your test might be too long. A list of scenarios best conveys the content of the test.

What are you looking for?

By basing test objectives on user motivations, you get objectives that look more like these examples for a fictitious health encyclopedia:

- To determine whether people who come to the site with a specific illness in mind are satisfied with how they located relevant information.
- To determine whether people who are doing research on behalf of another person can easily refer someone else to the information they find.
- To understand how people who have just been diagnosed with an illness want to revisit their research.

These objectives may be used together—nothing says your test must have only one objective. Once you've written up a couple, you can do a quick litmus test. If you state the objective in the form of a question, is it an answerable question? To take the first (bad) example, the test designers could ask themselves, "Is this site easy to use?" which would not be an easy question to answer. On the other hand, you could probably easily answer the question, "Are people who have a specific illness in mind satisfied with how they found relevant information?"

Scenarios

Scenarios make up the bread and butter of a usability plan. They describe what imaginary situations participants face, setting up a task or a challenge for them to address using the version of the site you put in front of them. (I dunno, stating it like that makes it seem kinda mean.)

From the plan's perspective, a bare-bones scenario consists of:

- **Setup**: The part you read to the participant so they understand the situation.
- **Expected results**: The description of how to deal with the situation correctly.
- **What's next**: The transition to where users go next.

ASIDE
Moderating Usability Tests

You never know what someone is going to say during the course of a usability test. My experience shows that strong scenarios with clear objectives for users to achieve keep the test moving and focused, but that the conversation varies from participant to participant. That said, having a list of questions to serve as a guide for the conversation helps remind the moderator (who may be getting old and easily forgets things he's supposed to ask from one hour to the next) about key topics.

When describing a scenario in a test plan, typography is more important than pictures. (Showing screens of what participants should be doing can be helpful, but the plan has a more important function.) With typography, you can distinguish the three parts listed earlier.

Putting scenarios on separate pages can help the moderator pace the test and provide a simple bookkeeping system for tracking each scenario.

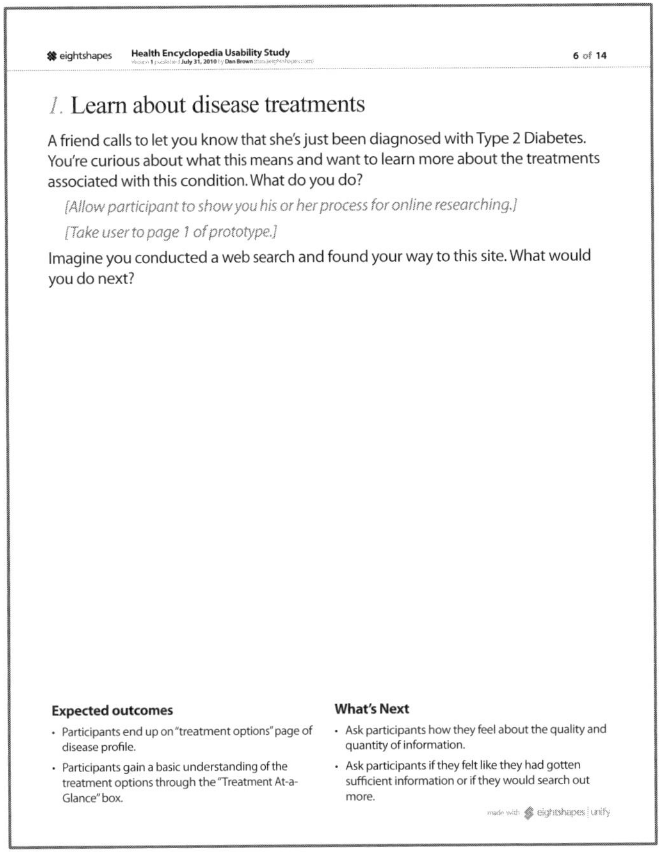

1. Learn about disease treatments

A friend calls to let you know that she's just been diagnosed with Type 2 Diabetes. You're curious about what this means and want to learn more about the treatments associated with this condition. What do you do?

[Allow participant to show you his or her process for online researching.]

[Take user to page 1 of prototype.]

Imagine you conducted a web search and found your way to this site. What would you do next?

Expected outcomes

- Participants end up on "treatment options" page of disease profile.
- Participants gain a basic understanding of the treatment options through the "Treatment At-a-Glance" box.

What's Next

- Ask participants how they feel about the quality and quantity of information.
- Ask participants if they felt like they had gotten sufficient information or if they would search out more.

made with   eightshapes | unify

Figure 11.4: The usability scenario description page may have a lot of white space, but giving one page to each scenario helps the moderator pace the test.

Questions

You can incorporate specific, targeted questions about the scenario into the scenario description. With explicit questions, the plan starts to look even more like a script, giving the moderator very specific things to say at specific times during the session. Somewhere in between "strict questions" and "no questions" is "questions as conversation guide." I like having them in front of me.

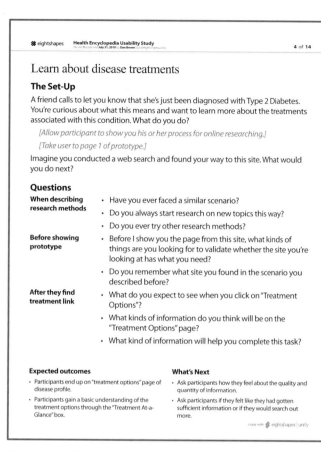

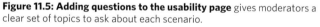

Figure 11.5: Adding questions to the usability page gives moderators a clear set of topics to ask about each scenario.

Scenario variations

The structure of the test might require varying the scenarios. (There can be any number of reasons to do this, but the most common is that the scenario changes for different types of users.) The structure of your plan should reflect the nature of those variations.

If only one or two scenarios vary, you can create a separate page for each variation and place it immediately following the main scenario.

If the majority of scenarios vary, you should give them their own chapter. This is clean if each chapter reflects a particular user group, for example. If user groups share some scenarios, you may want to repeat them in each chapter to make it easy to follow along the flow of the test. If you can get the common scenarios out of the way at the beginning or end of a test, you can dedicate a chapter to them before or after user-specific chapters.

I'd be hard-pressed to think of a reason to describe scenarios in an order other than the one you will use during the course of the test. Reviewing a test plan, the project team needs to understand how the test sessions themselves will run.

Pre-test and Post-test Questions

Some usability testing methodologies suggest that you ask users questions before and after the actual test. At the beginning of the test, before showing participants any screens or prototypes, you can establish their expectations with respect to the web site and their general level of experience. You can clarify their motivations for using your site and flesh out your profile of them.

The format for these questions will vary depending on your methodology. Some usability testers ask the questions of the user in person, recording their answers by hand. Others give participants a questionnaire that they can answer separately. (This approach allows the facilitator to spend more time focusing on the usability scenarios.) If you decide to let participants answer the questions on their own, you may want to separate these questions into a different document because it will be something you hand to them. In that case, you may need to format it differently, and—if the participant is to answer the questions without intervention from the facilitator—you'll certainly want to be explicit about directions.

Pre-test questions can help you get a handle on the user's expectations and experience before seeing the site for the first time. Questions after the test can gauge overall impressions and allow general pain points and suggestions to surface. Formatting for pre-test and post-test questions can include open-ended questions and questions with pre-defined responses.

Examples of open-ended questions:

- We're developing a new system to support your sales process. What are the most challenging tasks in the sales process for you?
- The web site we're building is called FluffyPuppies.com. What do you think you'd find on this web site?
- What system do you currently use to manage your family videos?

Examples of questions with predefined responses:

- On a scale of 1 to 7, where 1 is strongly disagree and 7 is strongly agree, how would you rate this statement: I found the web site easy to use.
- What level of Internet user are you? Beginner, intermediate, advanced?
- How long have you been involved with the sales process?

Regardless of how you deliver the questions to the participants, you should write the questions exactly as you intend to ask them. This can help ensure that you ask the question the same way every time.

Test Logistics and Recruiting

Good plans incorporate logistics and scheduling. Whether you need to state these explicitly in the document is up to you. Summarizing the when-where-and-how of the test on a single page might comfort stakeholders to know that you've taken care of all those things, even if they don't see all the little details. You can also use this section to remind the project team of the timeline. Generally they want to know when they will see results.

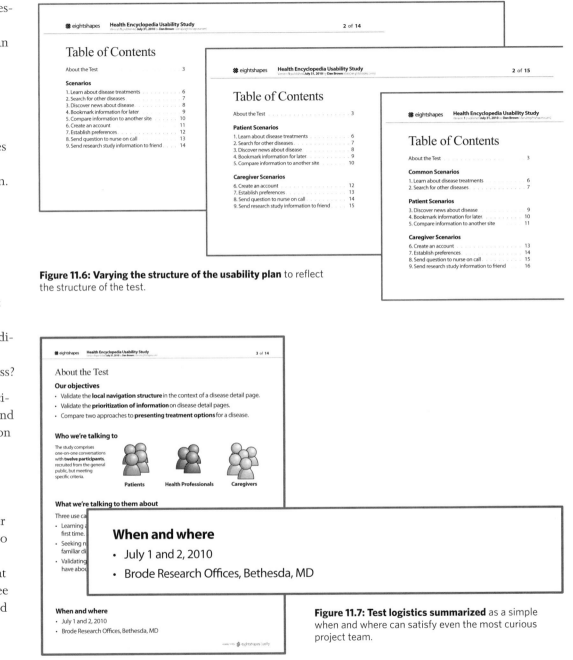

Figure 11.6: Varying the structure of the usability plan to reflect the structure of the test.

Figure 11.7: Test logistics summarized as a simple when and where can satisfy even the most curious project team.

Detailed Recruiting Information and Screener

Although the logistics information from earlier elements should reference the kinds of people you'd like to recruit, you can always provide more detail. The more complex the test, the more detail you'll want to give because you may be testing different user groups. Defining profiles for each group allows you to design an appropriate test for each group. If you've done user personas (described in the previous chapter) you can draw straight from those. Here's a user profile for a parenting web site:

> The Day Job Parent needs to work outside the home. He sees his kids in the morning, maybe drops them off at the bus stop, and then sees them again in the evening, when he comes home from work. The Day Job Parent may steal a glance at this web site during a lunch break, seeking advice on specific child-rearing problems. He may spend a bit more time on the site in the evening after the kids are in bed. In the Day Job Parent's house, both spouses work. They are both familiar with Internet technologies, and have shopped and researched health issues online.

High-level descriptions of users are one thing, but actually finding people who meet those criteria is another. If you don't have immediate access to people from the target audience, you need to put together a screener. A screener is a set of questions to ask potential participants to see if they fit your needs for the usability test.

You can embed the screener right in the plan, to show the project team what tools you will use to recruit participants. If you don't have a screener at the time you share the plan, insert a summary describing the kinds of criteria you'll use. Such a starting point gives the project team something to react to, and the recruiting agency a sense of what you're looking for.

Some screener questions are pretty straightforward, asking about experience with using the Internet or shopping online. Some will be more specific to your particular application. For example, for the fictitious online health encyclopedia, your screener might seek out people who have recently been to the doctor, or who visited a health site in the last three months. Such questions will help narrow the pool of applicants to those who best match your target user group.

Usually, recruiting from the general public is done by a recruiting agency. They have a large list of people to draw from. If you're using an outside agency, you'll need to provide as much detail in the screener as possible. Indicate when a particular answer to a question should eliminate a potential participant. Indicate quotas for particular answers. You may want, for example, half your participants to have visited a health site in the last three months, and half to never have visited a health site.

THE BEST-LAID PLANS

Gauging the usability of our design work is a method and process undergoing change. Whereas lab-based testing (recruiting participants, bringing them to a lab, watching them use the product) has been entrenched for years, it is being supplemented with other forms of testing. Technologies allow designers to watch people use web sites in real-time, gathering data as it happens. We can recruit people from across the globe, ask them to participate in an unmoderated usability study, and aggregate data across multiple sessions—all from the comfort of our desk.

These capabilities have raised some worthwhile and difficult questions in the design community. How much should design decisions be informed by data? Must we respond to every usability problem surfaced? How much feedback is too much feedback? For years we sought to be closer to the target audience, to be able to watch them in real-time and solicit input. Now that such a technique is a reality, we wonder if we should be careful about what we wish for.

To me, these controversies point to more careful planning, an increasing need to establish the parameters for studying users relative to the product. A document answering some basic questions provides, in a sense, a contract. Everyone on the project should have a shared understanding of what kind of information will come out of a usability study and how that information will be used.

A good usability plan does more than just incorporate some clever scriptwriting and scenario-building. It establishes a role for the usability test in the design process. It moderates the voice of the user, couching it in a context that helps the project team interpret the results. It positions that input among the countless others the design team needs to accommodate.

In assembling a usability plan, it can become easy to get lost in planning logistics, writing scenarios, composing interview questions. There is a lot to think about. In light of all of it, keeping things focused on the ultimate objectives is hard. And I'm not talking about the objectives for the test (though that's pretty hard, too). The ultimate objective is informing the design process. A good usability plan must imply, if not articulate explicitly, how the design team will incorporate the results; and how they will integrate it into the landscape of the project, treating it not as a stand-alone activity, but as a constant source of feedback and inspiration.

Chapter 12

Usability Reports

yoō·zə·ˈbil·ət·ē ri'·pôrt (n.)

A document prepared after a usability test, capturing the findings and observations and, potentially, recommendations.

After conducting a usability test, the design team will have a pile of data. This information provides useful direction for design activities, but the team's ability to respond to the results hinges on how the results are presented.

Usability results are usually presented as a report. In our industry we are resigned to expect a fat report coming out of usability testing. Experience shows that design teams don't need big reports, which generally include information not essential to the design effort.

This chapter positions usability results as a design tool, minimizing the extraneous stuff and focusing on how designers can use them as a valuable input into their process.

Different design teams have different conceptions of usability testing outputs. Some teams ask their usability person to perform tests and report on what the users thought. Others want to see design recommendations based on the observations. This chapter assumes that there's a clear delineation between the observations made during a usability test and the interpretation and analysis of those results, regardless of who's responsible.

WHAT MAKES A GOOD USABILITY REPORT

To be useful to the project team, a usability report must overcome three challenges:

- **Actionability**: Data coming out of a usability test can be so rich as to be difficult to boil down into digestible direction for designers. Reporting observations loses much of the flavor and context of an actual person reacting to the actual design. In an effort to avoid losing that information, you may be tempted to embellish results with the context or explanation. These distractions make it difficult for designers to know exactly what to respond to.

- **Authority**: What makes actionability especially challenging is that usability observations should reflect a rationale: They need to come with some authority. If you're summarizing lots of observations to provide the essential direction, it may appear as if you're simply critiquing the design without any basis.

- **Accessibility**: Finally, another danger of usability reports is that they try to justify themselves too much. Depending on the methods used, usability testing can be extremely complex. To explain the complexity of the tests, you might develop a report that buries the observations in elaborate analysis. At the same time, if you generalize too much, the reader may have a skewed view of the results.

The following sections describe attributes of good usability reports, ones that address these challenges and provide value to the project team.

Focus and Relevance

Usability testing can go in lots of different directions. Here are some typical objectives in conducting usability studies:

- Diagnosing problems with a design
- Establishing priorities for a design project
- Learning more about users and their behaviors
- Validating design concepts
- Validating and prioritizing requirements

A good usability report keeps content focused on one of these purposes. All the observations and insights captured in the document should support this singular focus. Stating this purpose at the beginning of the document helps set context.

If your study covered more than one of the themes above, that's OK, just be sure to clearly distinguish them in the report. For example, you might have made the following observations during a study:

- Users can't find the submit button during the checkout process.
- Two users (of eight) asked for the ability to ship to multiple addresses.

Though both of these are about the checkout process, the second represents a significantly larger endeavor from a design and implementation perspective. The first observation is a smaller fix, but more severe and immediate. The observations may be equally high priority but should occupy separate places in the document.

Prioritized Results and More

A good usability report distinguishes priorities, such that the design team knows which issues they need to pursue immediately. The usability report must be an input into a plan. The plan's timeframe is irrelevant for the purposes of a theoretical discussion; designers just need to know which issues to address now and which they can save for later.

In the next section, we'll talk about severity. While severity is an important and useful measure to drive priority, a prioritized document involves more than that. In preparing a usability report, you must not only prioritize observations but also how the document is presented.

To keep the document *actionable*, the results directly tied to specific design tasks must be prioritized over supporting information. Methodology, user profiles, and rationale for the approach are all relevant background, but they don't lead into concrete tasks for the design team. Exploring the psychological implications of the observations may yield valuable insights about the target audience, but doesn't give the design team a specific set of objectives for the next week.

Prioritizing observations over this context also keeps the document *accessible*. Contextual content like methodological theory may be ethically necessary, to provide a rationale for the kinds of results captured, but can muddy the content. Documents with too much theory can feel like scientific papers instead of design tools. The trick to a good usability report is balancing the needs of the design team with methodological integrity.

Tips for Presenting Usability Reports

The presentation outline described in Diagram Basics (Chapter 2) works perfectly for presenting usability reports. The structure allows you to communicate the main messages (step 3), elaborate on specific findings (step 5), and offer recommendations (step 6, implications). So, no need to depart from that framework, but here are a few things to consider as you prepare for presenting usability results.

Establish a purpose

Ideally, usability testing should lead to ongoing conversations within the team. The results should pervade every design discussion. If this isn't the team's culture, however, or if you need to kick off these discussions, determine what you want to get out of your meeting about usability testing. There are two flavors:

- **Establish a plan of attack**: In this meeting, your intent is to answer the question, "What should we focus on?" This meeting can be structured to describe the findings from the study. Alternatively, if the team is familiar with the tenor of the test, you can do a prioritization activity to determine which problems deserve attention first.
- **Brainstorm design directions**: If the design team is familiar with the range of problems raised during usability testing, your meeting might instead focus on solving those problems. The value of this discussion will vary depending on your team's ability to brainstorm design concepts. The role of the usability test report in this kind of conversation is to keep the team focused on the core problems.

Report findings ASAP

One of the greatest challenges with usability reports is that if the project team doesn't actively participate in the test, they don't get to see the observations in real time. A report helps bridge that gap (though if everyone was there to observe, the need for a report diminishes). A report can take some time to compose, and the relevance of the results diminishes over time.

In my practice, I've tried to reduce turnaround time on a report to a matter of days. Having a selection of templates helps with the formatting of usability reports. Eliminating any deep analysis means the report just needs to report what happened, and I can limit the amount of time we spend poring over results.

We also try to hold a meeting the day after the testing is complete. In this conversation we provide our initial high-level impressions and describe the most severe findings.

Be objective and honest

Usability testing, as practiced by most people, is an inexact science, and the results leave room for interpretation. During your presentation of the observations, be careful to distinguish between what happened and your interpretation of what happened. For example, users of a web application might consistently miss a submit button. You don't know why they missed it—perhaps it is too small, or the contrast isn't right, or perhaps it doesn't look clickable enough—but you might have asked users why they missed the button.

In reporting this observation, you can say that people consistently missed the button and then offer several explanations why. Unfortunately, the nature of usability testing is that you may never find an exact explanation, but the team may need to agree on one in order to develop a solution.

ASK THE EXPERT

DB: *What's the best format for communicating results from usability tests?*

DC: *The best format for your team and stakeholders can vary by where the team is in the life of the design, the culture of the team and the larger organization, and the purpose of the test. Typically, the assumption is that there will be a report of some kind. It is not unusual for the researcher to put together a highlights video, splicing together video clips from the session to illustrate issues. Often there is a presentation.*

Teams that create the best user experiences don't report results in those traditional ways. Written reports take a lot of time and often the content depends solely on the perceptions of (and data gathered by) the researcher. Instead, great UX teams find that the best format for communicating results is conversation.

Usability testing (and other user research) is most effective when everyone who touches a design observes sessions. When that happens, results are the shared stories, told orally by teammates to other teammates, of the experiences users had during the sessions. If the team observes users using the design in an exploratory, formative usability test, they're usually so excited that there is little need for a written report or a presentation because every person on the team was a witness.

If you're in a documentation-loving organization, though, there are a few ways to collaborate within a team on analyzing the observations and end up with a "report." A progression I've developed that seems to work well has two steps. First, keep a rolling issues list during the test. Second, prioritize individuals' observations within the group to identify the three to five most important issues by conducting a KJ activity.

Rolling issues lists are simple. During the break after each usability test session, the team identifies observations and issues and writes them on a whiteboard. Next to each observation, they note the number for the participant who had the issue. These observations might be issues or good things that happened. The key to recording them is that they're important to the design, and that they are only what was heard or what was seen—not design solutions.

*Dana Chisnell,
Independent Researcher,
UsabilityWorks*

Prepare for questions about design

The Recommendations discussion in the Anatomy of a Usability Report section that follows gives some suggestions for how to incorporate recommendations into your process and your document. Suffice it to say, regardless of what strategy you choose, the question of "What should we do?" will come up as you describe the problems with the site design.

Your strategy will dictate exactly how you respond, but here are some considerations for walking through the presentation:

- **Set expectations**: Even before you start testing, determine whether you'll make recommendations as part of your usability test report, and the extent of those recommendations. Communicate this approach at the outset, helping the project team understand the exact nature of the outputs of the usability testing.
- **Remind**: At every opportunity throughout testing, remind project participants about the scope of the test and the report.
- **Incorporate**: If you choose to incorporate recommendations into your report, consider how they will factor into the discussion. Your higher priority might be to convince the project team about a broader range of problems, and getting distracted with specific recommendations may not help move the project along. By contrast, there may be a few things the project team can do to address some of the major concerns. Each of these situations implies a different way to organize.

Don't get defensive about methodology

That the industry is still exploring different usability techniques (remote vs. in-person, moderated vs. unmoderated, prototype vs. live, paper vs. on-screen, small sample vs. large sample) shows only that there are a variety of tools for evaluating a design. Even the role of such studies is subject to controversy in the design community. To people not typically involved with these activities, this variety smacks of lack of rigor. The logic is sound: If you can't tell me how many participants is the right number, why should I trust that this work will give us meaningful results?

Deliverables aren't a silver bullet to addressing methodological concerns. Producing a nice report won't alleviate underlying doubts. The content of that report is crucial, but your work starts long before the study even begins. The following advice assumes you've laid groundwork early in the project, helping the team understand the technique you've decided to use and working with them to refine the approach:

- **Summarize methodology and rationale**: Your deliverable should summarize the methodology used and, if possible, include some rationale for the methodology. This justification is, hopefully, a summary of conversations you had with the project team at the outset. It should only, therefore, be a reminder of what and why your approach was selected.
- **Acknowledge methodological limitations**: You may be conducting testing even though lingering doubts remain with the project team. Be transparent, acknowledging that no technique is bulletproof. Enumerate the pros and cons of the technique you're using and be careful not to speculate on results outside what's permitted by the technique.
- **Capture departures from the plan**: Sometimes, a study benefits from some improvisation during the test. If you had to make changes to your approach on the fly (and again, the professionals' opinions on this vary wildly) be sure to document those modifications. On-the-fly adaptations shouldn't affect the quality of your results, especially if your plan or technique anticipated that such changes might happen.

ANATOMY OF A USABILITY REPORT

The primary purpose of usability results is to summarize observations made during a test and any other data gathered. Usability testing almost always happens in the context of a web site—actual screens, wireframes, or some kind of prototype. These artifacts provide a framework for documenting the results, too, as in Figure 12.1.

This is the basic building block of a usability report, but it can't survive on its own. Some ideas follow on how to build a document around this atom.

Organizing a Usability Report

Here's a good table of contents for a usability report (Table 12.1).

Two other ways to organize the observations' chapters:

Organizing by scenario and task

The example goes screen-by-screen, showing results for each screen involved in a particular scenario. The author could instead dedicate each page in the report to a task within the scenario. For example, here's one scenario for a usability test on an e-commerce site:

> It's holiday time. You've loaded your cart with goodies for the family, and you want to send them directly to the recipients. You have stuff to send to yourself, and stuff you want to send to two other addresses.

This might involve several tasks:

- Designate items to send elsewhere.
- Choose a destination address.
- Add a new destination address.
- Configure gift wrap options.
- Select shipping options.

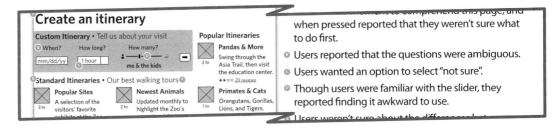

Figure 12.1: A simple usability result, using the screen (in this case a high fidelity wireframe) tested to provide context for the observations.

Chapter	Pages
Front matter	Cover
	Table of contents
	Executive summary
	Key takeaways/highest priorities
Scenario 1	Screen 1 observations
	Screen 2 observations
Scenario 2	Screen 3 observations
	Screen 4 observations
	Screen 5 observations
Scenario 3	Screen 6 observations
Scenario 4	Screen 7 observations
	Screen 8 observations
	Screen 9 observations
Other observations	Screen excerpts 1
	Screen excerpts 2
	Discussion
Participants	Persona summary
	Participant profiles
Background	Methodology
	Recruiting
Appendix	Comprehensive table of all observations, sorted by severity

Table 12.1: A usability report structure should summarize the key takeaways at the beginning of the document and then organize the observations around the scenarios of the test.

All these may happen on one single screen or across several different screens, depending on the design. The usability report can dedicate a page to each of these tasks. This helps put the observation in context and avoids cluttering observations on a single screen, especially if those observations relate to different kinds of tasks.

Organizing by theme

In analyzing the observations, you might identify certain emergent themes. Here are some themes that came out of a recent usability study:

- Users don't know what to do next.
- Users didn't understand jargon.
- Users didn't understand visual conventions.
- Users missed important content.

You might have dozens of observations that support each of these themes. Categorizing observations in this way can help provide an overview of the results, the bottom line summary of the test. On the other hand, it can be difficult to act on these themes if they all come from different scenarios and reflect different severity levels.

Observations and Severity

An observation is a single discrete behavior exhibited by a participant during a scenario of a usability test. User moves mouse around the screen looking for the submit button. User misses additional information because he or she didn't scroll. User indicates he or she has no idea what the shipping charges will be. All of these are observations.

When reporting observations, there are a couple things to think about:

- **Consolidation**: If we reported every specific observation, usability reports would be difficult to read. In practice, reports take liberty with the definition of an observation, frequently consolidating them when more than one user

(a) exhibited the same behavior or (b) exhibited such similar behaviors in the same scenario as to yield the same result.

- **Design context**: The example observations in the first paragraph are all pretty straightforward, but even so could do with a visual context. Attaching an observation to a specific design element helps readers clearly interpret the observation.

There are a few ways to format observations, much in the same way as there are a few ways to annotate wireframes (Figure 12.2).

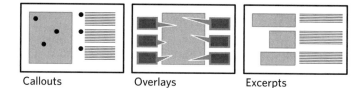

Callouts   Overlays   Excerpts

Figure 12.2: Capturing observations.

Some considerations for each approach:

- **Callouts**: The most effective approach for showing lots of observations on one screen is to annotate the screen. Though this separates the data (the observation) from the target (the design element) it doesn't obscure too much of the context.
- **Overlays**: With a short and sweet observation, overlays create the most direct connection between it and the design element. On the other hand, overlays can obscure the screen and therefore the context. Too many observations on a single screen, of course, and the overlays will obscure the screen completely.
- **Excerpts**: Removing the design element from the screen gets readers to focus on the specific area and places the observation(s) directly adjacent to it. This is ideal if one area of the screen comprised most of the observations. On the other hand, outside of the entire screen, an excerpt loses some context, and it may be difficult for readers to understand where it fits in.

Summarizing observations in a table

Frankly, your usability report may be ideally represented by a simple but well-designed list of observations. A good spreadsheet can capture the essential elements and drive next steps much more efficiently. A good project team generally needs nothing more than a spreadsheet of to-dos sorted by severity to jump into action.

Tables don't require a specific level of abstraction. That is, you can incorporate all kinds of observations in a table, especially in a sortable spreadsheet. You can make sweeping statements about the labeling throughout the experience, or you can identify the label on a particular button.

If you can't have a stand-alone table, you can still include one as an appendix in your report. The table should include at least all the key pieces of information discussed in this chapter:

- The observation
- The severity of the observation
- Design context

A note about design context: While pictures speak louder than words, screen grabs embedded in a spreadsheet look kind of tacky. Therefore, for tables to be successful, teams need a consistent way of referring to aspects of the design. The first few columns of the table should clearly locate the observation (Table 12.2).

Severity

An important data point you should attach to every observation is severity. Books on usability testing methodology can provide a better description of how to measure and assign severity. Suffice it to say that I generally use a scale related to whether users were able to complete a task (Table 12.3). Position severity adjacent to the observation.

ID	Category	User flow	Screen	Interface element
1	Navigation	Browse	ALL	Menu: section navigation
2	Transaction	Checkout	Shopping cart	Button: confirm cart contents
3	Transaction	Checkout	Shopping cart	Button: update quantities

Table 12.2: Summarizing usability results in a table must include an elegant way of addressing or locating the observations. This example shows the first five columns of the table, short of the observation itself, just to locate the observation.

Severity	Means
1	Users were able to complete the task without a problem.
2	Users were able to complete the task, but had to check their work or paused before doing so.
3	Users demonstrated or expressed frustration with the interface, but were able to complete the task.
4	Users were unable to complete the task without intervention.
5	Users were unable to complete the task, even with prompting from the moderator.

Table 12.3: Measuring severity in usability observations usually comes down to users' ability to complete a task. Severity might also incorporate the number of users who faced the problem. Your severity scale will vary depending on the technique you used in your study.

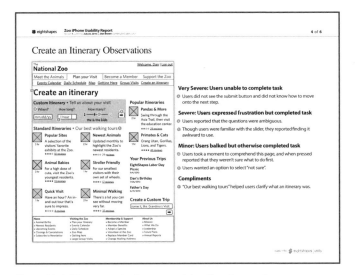

Figure 12.3: Use icons to show severity.

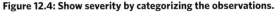

Figure 12.4: Show severity by categorizing the observations.

Further embellishments

Here are a couple other ways you can embellish reporting observations. Remember that the observation itself and severity are most important. Use these embellishments to provide further context or clarity. If they obscure the results, leave them out.

- **Category**: As indicated in the Organizing a Usability Report section, results are typically categorized by the scenario to which they belong. Other categories describe what part of the site or what kind of task is involved: navigation, browsing, search, checkout. You can attach a simple label on the observation to show category. Icons or other visual devices may distract from the purpose.

- **Sensitizing quote**: No doubt more powerful than another layer of categorization, direct quotes from participants can further clarify the observation and lend some credence to it. Consolidating observations opens the risk of misinterpretation: Readers may wonder how much license you took in summarizing what you saw. Quotes support observations by eliminating the interpretation.

Summary and Analysis

Perhaps the most important page in the usability report is the summary. Usability reports can seem overwhelming—packed with lots of data and rife with brutally candid feedback. A good summary page not only helps people focus on the most important findings, but it also sets the tone of the report.

Summaries should surface the main takeaways from the study, indicating the site's primary strengths and weaknesses, and giving the project team a sense of priority. The summary may have explicit next steps, but they also may be implied based on the characterization of the findings. Clearly articulated findings with unambiguous priorities may be all the next steps you need (Figure 12.5).

Successful summaries visually describe the mechanics of the test. Avatars representing user groups along with a numbered list of relevant scenarios may be all you need to describe how the test worked.

Analysis

Any time you attempt to interpret your observations to surface a pattern, theme, or motivation, you are analyzing the results. Analysis provides a unified explanation of the findings.

Incorporating such discussion into the document depends on the content. Table 12.4 identifies the different forms analysis can take, and offers ideas on how to include it in the structure of the document.

Figure 12.5: Summarizing usability results entails escalating key findings and providing a snapshot of what you did.

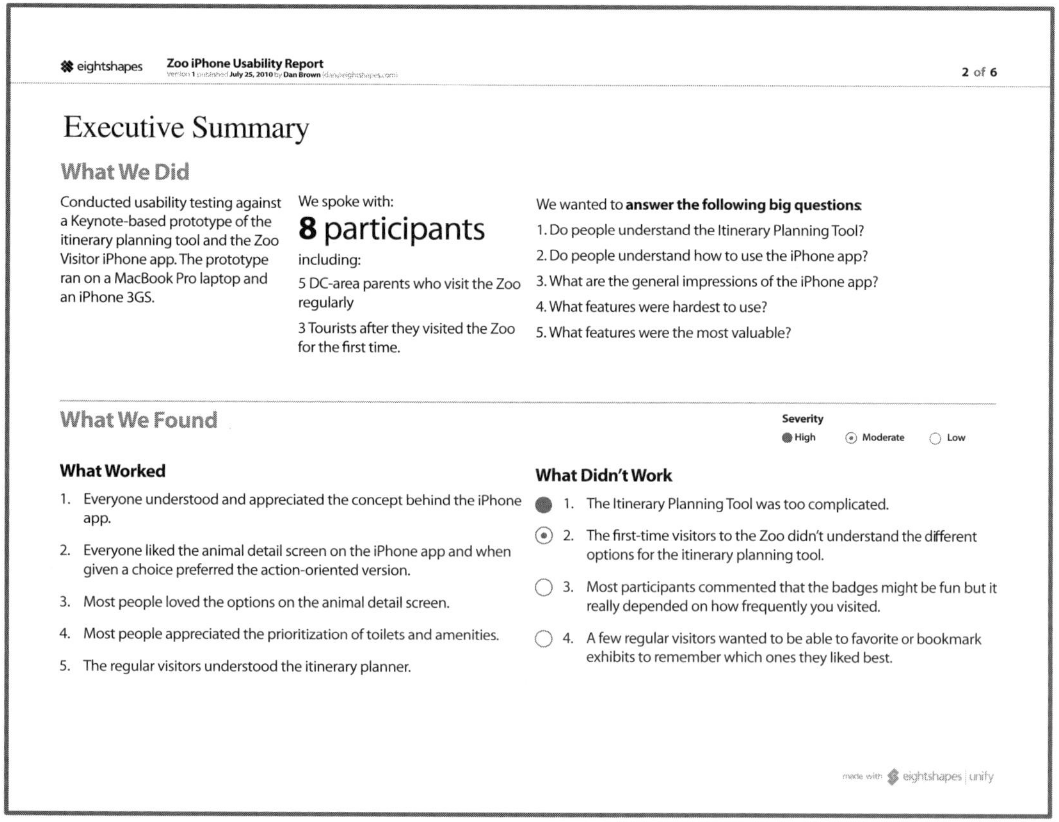

eightshapes   Zoo iPhone Usability Report
Version 1 published July 25, 2010 by Dan Brown dan@eightshapes.com
2 of 6

Executive Summary

What We Did

Conducted usability testing against a Keynote-based prototype of the itinerary planning tool and the Zoo Visitor iPhone app. The prototype ran on a MacBook Pro laptop and an iPhone 3GS.

We spoke with:

8 participants

including:

5 DC-area parents who visit the Zoo regularly

3 Tourists after they visited the Zoo for the first time.

We wanted to **answer the following big questions:**

1. Do people understand the Itinerary Planning Tool?
2. Do people understand how to use the iPhone app?
3. What are the general impressions of the iPhone app?
4. What features were hardest to use?
5. What features were the most valuable?

What We Found

Severity
● High   ◉ Moderate   ○ Low

What Worked

1. Everyone understood and appreciated the concept behind the iPhone app.
2. Everyone liked the animal detail screen on the iPhone app and when given a choice preferred the action-oriented version.
3. Most people loved the options on the animal detail screen.
4. Most people appreciated the prioritization of toilets and amenities.
5. The regular visitors understood the itinerary planner.

What Didn't Work

● 1. The Itinerary Planning Tool was too complicated.

◉ 2. The first-time visitors to the Zoo didn't understand the different options for the itinerary planning tool.

○ 3. Most participants commented that the badges might be fun but it really depended on how frequently you visited.

○ 4. A few regular visitors wanted to be able to favorite or bookmark exhibits to remember which ones they liked best.

made with eightshapes | unify

Recommendations

Beyond analysis, another way to interpret results is to offer some recommendations. To state the obvious, you can suggest how to improve the site based on the data you gathered through the study.

You could narrate a recommendation:

> Instead of a set of blue buttons for the controls, consider using a single button for the main action and links for secondary actions.

But this is a book about using pictures to help with the design process, so the natural conclusion is creating a mock-up of the suggested approach. There are, of course, several ways to do this. Figure 12.6 shows one approach.

In layering in recommendations, don't lose sight of the purpose of the document. It can be easy to get carried away with recommendations, but if they obscure the findings, you should leave them out altogether or include a chapter at the end of the document.

Saving recommendations for the end

Note that the table of contents in Table 12.1 doesn't include a chapter on recommendations. Basic reports probably don't need them; that's the role of the design team (see the upcoming Aside). With just a handful of recommendations, the approach just described will likely work just fine. When you're on the hook to provide a series of recommendations across the whole experience, trying to stuff them on the same pages as the findings can be challenging.

There are several ways to organize the recommendations chapter, and your choice depends on the kinds of recommendations, elaborated in Table 12.5.

If your analysis...	In which you...	You can...
Categorizes findings and observations	Create a limited set of categories to group the findings together based on the target of the observation or to show patterns of behavior across the experience	Organize the document around these themes. Explain the theme at the beginning of each chapter or at the top of each page.
Explains participant behaviors by identifying possible motivations or cognitive issues with the interface	Elaborate on a finding by offering insight into why users exhibited a particular behavior	Add a concluding page at the end of each chapter to sum up the chapter in these terms.
Summarizes the usability results by extracting key themes	Capture the main messages of the findings through a series of bullets	Include these in the executive summary.

Table 12.4: Forms that analysis can take.

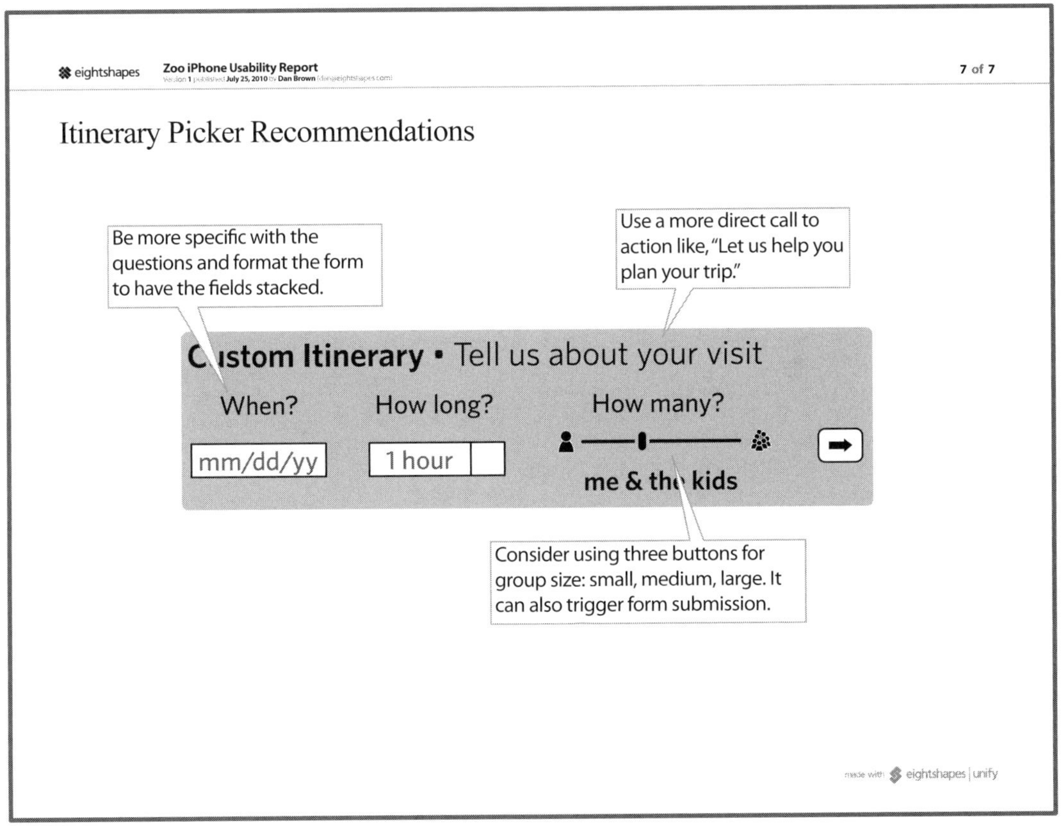

Figure 12.6: Incorporating recommendations into a usability report using overlays.

If recommendations focus on...	You can organize them by...	But be careful...
Interface elements (e.g., Change this button.)	Dedicating a set of pages to each screen tested, such that interface elements all appearing on the same screen are clustered together.	Some interface elements may be common across all screens. Interface elements removed from their screens lose context.
Screen layouts (e.g., Reorganize this screen.)	Putting them in the context of scenarios or tasks users.	Some screens may have a high density of recommendations: The project team may lose the spirit of your recommendations.
Structure of the experience (e.g., Change the order of this flow.)	Putting them in the context of scenarios or tasks users.	You may not be able to focus on particularly egregious usability problems at the interface level.
Overall themes (e.g., Reduce the range of options throughout the user experience.)	Increasing granularity; the more specific the theme, the later it comes in the document.	Such recommendations may not be actionable if they're too broad.
Additional design activities (e.g., Conduct additional testing on the product catalog.)	Impact and cost. Provide a range of options for the project team so they understand where they'll get the most bang for their buck.	Recommend activities you're prepared to do; key stakeholders may pull the trigger on your recommendations right then and there.

Table 12.5: Different recommendations call for different organization schemes in the document.

One last note on recommendations: In my experience, the most effective recommendations are expressed as themes ("revisit labeling") with supporting examples ("abbreviated field label 'Med Vert' caused confusion"). Give each theme its own page in the recommendations section and then show before and after pictures for two or three different prime examples.

Supporting Content

You might be surprised to find methodology under "supporting content." Presumably, usability reports need to describe what you did, right? Ultimately, the reason to deprioritize the methodology and other mechanics of the study is that they don't directly help the design effort. Actionability of results does not depend on knowing the method. The document is inaccessible if readers struggle to separate the wheat from the chaff.

Methodology

Summarizing the methodology of a usability test study requires these six points of data:

- The technique (for example, a moderated remote study)
- The number of participants
- The types of users represented by the participants (referencing personas, for example)
- The materials used in the study (a web site or prototype)
- Scope of the study (which part of the experience)
- A quantification of the study scale (number of scenarios)

When elaborating on the study's methodology, you could also capture the high points of the study's script. At the very least, you can list the scenarios or tasks users were asked to perform.

To boil down the methodology further, for including in the executive summary, I've also chosen three or four (at most!) of the points in the previous list. This makes for a very compact display appropriate for an early page of the document.

Incorporating such a summary may not be necessary if your project team is generally aware that the study is happening and the technique you're using. Stakeholders that aren't heavily involved or are unfamiliar with usability testing may benefit from the summary, especially as the document gets passed around.

Participant profiles and recruiting

Team members who weren't involved in the study are most likely to ask, "Who did you talk to?" They're more interested in who than they are in what. The motivations for asking are generally methodological:

- You didn't talk to enough people
- You didn't talk to the right people
- You missed people of a particular type

My reports sometimes include a separate page describing the participants to address these concerns at the outset. At the very least, such a page gives us something to speak to when we discuss these concerns.

The table-based approach to describing users lists out each participant and some key attributes. This is a good way of showing that you incorporated an appropriate variety of users.

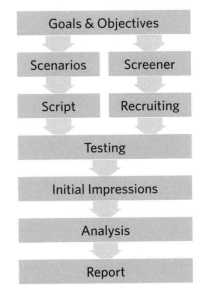

Figure 12.7: Summarizing the methodology in a very compact display makes a useful element on the first page of the report.

> ### ASIDE
> ## The Actionability of Recommendations
>
> Call me a purist, but I prefer usability reports that don't make specific interface recommendations. Piecemeal recommendations don't take the whole experience into account. And users experience the design holistically. In other words, solving each individual problem may, in turn, create problems with the overall interface. It's a forest and trees problem.
>
> A good designer will consider all the problems raised during a usability study, prioritizing and refactoring the design as appropriate to address the needs.
>
> On the other hand, recommendations can take other forms; they don't have to be concrete changes to the design, but instead can be more strategic without losing their actionability. For example:
>
> - Users struggled with some of the jargon in the interface. Consider running a card sort to zero in on more appropriate labels.
> - Though not rated as particularly severe, the color of the buttons was disconcerting to some users, since it does not align with the aesthetic. Consider revisiting the design of the buttons to match the overall visual design.
>
> Ultimately, the point is actionability. While a recommendation is actionable (structured right, a recommendation tells me exactly what I need to do), it is not necessarily efficient. It makes more sense to engage with the design team to talk through the problems raised and make changes to the design on the fly. Eliminate the middle step.

Our Participants

ID	First Name (Sex)	Last Visit	Frequency	Favorite Exhibit/Animal	Mobile Phone	Family	Role
1	PJ (F)	May 2010	Monthly	Elephants	iPhone	2 kids (4, 1)	Parent
2	Ana (F)	N/A	N/A	Pandas	iPhone	3 kids (5, 4, 2)	Tourist
3	David (M)	June 2010	Monthly or more	Invertebrates	iPhone	2 kids (3, 1)	Parent
4	Nathan (M)	June 2010	Monthly or more	Small Mammals	Android	3 kids (9, 7, 5)	Parent
5	José (M)	April 2010	Every few months	Kids Farm	Nokia	3 kids (12, 11, 5)	Parent
6	Dimple (F)	N/A	N/A	Pandas	iPhone	N/A	Tourist
7	Jennifer (F)	2001?	N/A	Elephants	Android	1 kid (7)	Tourist
8	Jason (M)	Sept 2009	Twice a year	Reptile House	Blackberry	1 kid (2)	Parent

eightshapes **Zoo iPhone Usability Report** 5 of 7
Version 1 published July 25, 2010 by Dan Brown dan@eightshapes.com

Figure 12.8: A table summarizing participants can highlight the criteria you used to recruit them, addressing concerns about talking to the "right" people.

ASK THE EXPERT

DB: Is there a good alternative to writing a usability results report?

DC: *If team members aren't involved in user research, it's difficult for them to keep users in mind as they design. If team members have not observed users themselves, no document will make the experience of the users real. By delivering reports and presentations, we risk objectifying the flesh-and-blood folks who helped us learn enough to make informed decisions about the design direction. People turn into data; they become abstractions.*

User researchers often complain that team members don't read their reports. They're too busy; the report is too large; they don't know how to apply what the report says; the users aren't real to them, so the results aren't meaningful. This leads me to conclude that writing a report is a poor way to convey test results to any team. The solution: Don't waste your time writing reports. Get the team to come to sessions instead. Let them tell the stories of their experiences observing the users' experiences to one another.

If you already have user segments or personas from work earlier in the project, you can use a cartoon-based approach. The cartoon-based approach shows groups of participants based on the preexisting segments. You can accompany these groups with bullet lists describing the key attributes you sought in recruiting participants from this group.

GETTING INSIDE THEIR HEADS

The conclusion of the last chapter implied that usability testing will live forever, in some form. Far be it from me to change my mind in the space of a chapter, but it's important to consider what form it will take.

Done correctly, usability testing is a great way to see whether a web site works, but it has some serious methodological concerns to overcome. Placing users in an artificial environment—outside the very place they'll use the site, sitting next to someone they'll never see again, responding to questions no one has ever asked them before—means that usability testing in its current form is a design technique trying to be a science.

Many user experience professionals these days advocate getting out of the lab, that is, shedding the artificial environment and going to where people actually do use the web. This sounds daunting. If we have a hard enough time finding the time to schedule a couple days of testing and getting a good selection of users to come to the lab, won't it be more difficult to visit their homes and offices? The answer is most likely "yes," but the bigger concern isn't logistical; it is, again, methodological. This kind of testing is not appropriate for every situation.

In fact, the evolution of the web and the web design process points to more immediate access to usability results. More and more web-based services launch so-called "beta" versions of their sites—mostly finished, but far from final.

Figure 12.9: Avatars representing participants can build on earlier segmentation analysis. Use avatars that directly relate to that previous work, incorporating the same iconography or color scheme.

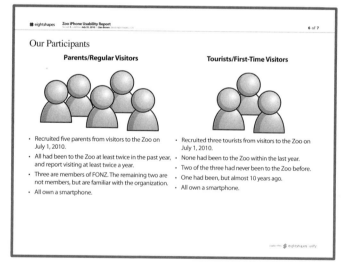

Some sites live in what the industry used to call "perpetual beta." Like the house up the street whose owners are constantly renovating, these sites are being tweaked daily. Basic assumptions about how the web is built and used shift constantly. (For example, since the first edition of this book, perpetual beta has fallen out of favor. Now, some designers just assume that the "final" version of a site is one that's constantly evolving. Still other teams can't escape the idea that a launched web site must be complete in every way.)

Early adopters of this methodological shift are probably not doing usability testing the way you and I are doing it. They're probably planning the initial site carefully, putting it out there, soliciting feedback, and issuing new "releases" every quarter, every month, every week in response. And now we get back to the point of this chapter: understanding how people use a web site. When you do a usability test, sitting with actual users, you get a rich array of data. The people who are building perpetual beta sites don't have access to that same depth of information. The next stage of usability testing needs to be a convergence of these two ideas: rich data with near-real-time response.

Like any deliverable, usability reports will need to adapt to pace the evolution of technique and method. Yet the essential content—observations, design context, and severity—will remain the same. It's these elements that trigger a response from the design team and help define what that response should be.

EXAMPLE
Justifying the Who

My colleague Chris Detzi did some in-depth user research for a government client. Early in the project, they identified about 10 different user groups. These groups were convenient ways of thinking about people (for example, the press or Congress), but they didn't speak to motivations, tasks, or behaviors.

Chris did some analysis to identify these aspects of each group and find common attributes across groups. Through this analysis, he identified two groups that represented the majority of attributes across groups, and those that were most important to the business. When conducting usability studies, Chris was able to recruit from these two groups, already having established that they represent the majority of user needs. The client needed no further convincing.

EXERCISE

Developing a good usability report depends on having good content. I would not recommend outlining an abstract usability report: You won't know if it makes sense or not. One good source for "usability" data is product reviews. What's great about product reviews is that they usually don't have recommendations: Reviewers aren't on the hook for making the product better, just telling you what's wrong with it.

Next time you're in the market for something (a baby stroller, for example, or a digital camera or a home theater projector or an espresso maker), find a few different product reviews online and translate the review into a collection of observations. You can start with a spreadsheet, entering each relevant quote from the review into a separate row in the table.

Analyze the "observations" to determine if they can be categorized, and if they're at a particular level of abstraction. (For an espresso maker, a review may focus on the range of features, or it may describe the usability of a particular feature. It will, hopefully, also address the quality of the coffee.) Assign severity levels to the observations. Decide on whether you want to incorporate recommendations.

The number of observations won't rival the scale of observations you'd get in a usability exercise. (Only one user and limited by the constraints imposed by the original publishing medium.) If you need more fodder, use three or four reviews, acknowledging they may come from different products. (You're just trying to generate some fake content.) Compose a report from the product review(s), including product images as if you were including screenshots.

If you have a study group, present the report to them. Make sure they wear their "project team" hats, each playing a different role on the team—designers, stakeholders, engineers. Offer to buy the product for the team member who plays their role the best. (Just kidding.)

RECOMMENDED BOOKSHELF ADDITIONS

Far from comprehensive, this selection of books does represent essential reading for people documenting user experience.

Classics

These books have been on my shelf for a long time. I keep coming back to them. They were both instrumental in my thinking about design.

Kristof, Ray and Amy Satran. *Interactivity by Design*. Mountain View: Adobe Press, 1995.

Raskin, Jef. *The Humane Interface*. Reading, MA: Addison-Wesley, 2000.

Web User Experience

Curtis, Nathan. *Modular Web Design*. Berkeley: New Riders, 2009.

Halvorson, Kristina. *Content Strategy for the Web*. Berkeley: New Riders, 2010.

Kalbach, James. *Designing Web Navigation*. Cambridge: O'Reilly, 2007.

Morville, Peter and Louis Rosenfeld. *Information Architecture for the World Wide Web* (3rd Edition). Cambridge: O'Reilly, 2006.

Saffer, Dan. *Designing for Interaction*. Berkeley: New Riders, 2007.

Tidwell, Jenifer. *Designing Interfaces*. Cambridge: O'Reilly, 2006.

Wodtke, Christina and Austin Govella. *Information Architecture: Blueprints for the Web* (2nd Edition). Berkeley: New Riders, 2009.

Wroblewski, Luke. *Web Form Design*. Brooklyn: Rosenfeld Media, 2009.

Project Planning

Unger, Russ and Carolyn Chandler. *A Project Guide to UX Design*. Berkeley: New Riders, 2009.

Design

Lidwell, William and Kritina Holden and Jill Butler. *Universal Principles of Design*. Beverly, MA: Rockport Publishers, 2003.

Comics

Abel, Jessica and Matt Madden. *Drawing Words & Writing Pictures*. New York: First Second, 2008.

McCloud, Scott. *Making Comics*. New York: Harper Paperbacks, 2006.

Presentations

Duarte, Nancy. *slide:ology*. Cambridge: O'Reilly Media, 2008.

Reynolds, Garr. *Presentation Zen*. Berkeley: New Riders, 2008.

Prototyping

Zaki Warfel, Todd. *Prototyping*. Brooklyn: Rosenfeld Media, 2009.

Users, Personas, Usability Testing

Beyer, Hugh and Karen Holtzblatt. *Contextual Design*. San Francisco: Morgan Kaufmann Publishers, 1998.

Krug, Steve. *Don't Make Me Think*. Berkeley: New Riders, 2005.

Mulder, Steve and Ziv Yarr. *The User Is Always Right*. Berkeley: New Riders, 2006.

Pruitt, John and Tamara Adlin. *The Persona Lifecycle*. New York: Morgan Kaufmann, 2006.

Rubin, Jeffrey and Dana Chisnell. *Handbook of Usability Testing*. Indianapolis: Wiley Publishing, 2008.

Young, Indi. *Mental Models*. Brooklyn: Rosenfeld Media, 2008.

Making Diagrams

Buxton, Bill. *Sketching User Experiences*. Boston: Morgan Kaufmann, 2007.

Roam, Dan. *The Back of the Napkin*. New York, Penguin, 2008.

Tufte, Edward R. *Envisioning Information*. Cheshire, CT: Graphics Press, 1998.

ABOUT THE AUTHOR

Dan Brown is founder and principal at EightShapes, LLC, a user experience consulting firm based in Washington, DC, that has engaged with clients in telecommunications, media, education, health, high-tech, and other sectors. Dan has been practicing information architecture and user experience design since 1995.

Prior to founding EightShapes, Dan consulted with organizations ranging from the U.S. Postal Service, the World Bank, and the Federal Communications Commission to US Airways, FirstUSA, and Fannie Mae. From 2002 to 2004, Dan was a federal employee, leading the content management program for the Transportation Security Administration. His portfolio includes work on public-facing web sites, intranets, and extranets, and addresses most aspects of the user experience, from information architecture and content strategy to interaction and interface design.

Drawing on his expertise in communicating complex ideas and abstractions through high-quality visual documentation, Dan wrote a book on user experience deliverables—*Communicating Design* (New Riders, 2006). Amazon reviews call it "authoritative," "practical, personal, comprehensive," and "a cool nerdbook." He has written more than a dozen articles for *Boxes and Arrows*, an online journal dedicated to information architecture, on topics ranging from Power-Point to the information architecture of home audio devices.

Dan has conducted seminars and workshops for most major user experience conferences, including the IA Summit, Interaction, An Event Apart, Nielsen-Norman Group, and Jared Spool's Web App Summit. Most recently, Dan taught a workshop on using diagrams to plan web sites at the School of Visual Arts for the Interaction Design Program.

Having earned a bachelor's degree in Philosophy from Wesleyan University well before the web was mainstream, Dan attempts to reference Plato as often as possible in his design work.

You can follow Dan on Twitter (@brownorama).

Follow @uxdeliverables for information about updates to *Communicating Design*.

CONTRIBUTOR BIOS

Tamara Adlin is the founder and president of adlin, inc., a customer experience consulting company located in Seattle. Tamara is the co-author of *The Persona Lifecycle: Keeping People in Mind Throughout Product Design* (with John Pruitt, Microsoft), which has been highly recommended by Jakob Nielsen, Don Norman, and Alan Cooper.

Stephen P. Anderson is a speaker and consultant based out of Dallas. He spends unhealthy amounts of time thinking about design, psychology, and leading intrapreneurial teams—topics he frequently speaks about at national and international events.

Dana Chisnell has helped thousands of people learn how to make better design decisions by giving them the skills they need to gain knowledge about users. She's the co-author, with Jeff Rubin, of *Handbook of Usability Testing*, Second Edition (Wiley), and writes a blog about user research and usability testing techniques at www.usabilitytestinghowto. blogspot.com.

Nathan Curtis has been practicing design since 1996, with interests that include information architecture, interaction design, usability research, front-end development, and an obsession he shares with his partner—documenting and communicating design ideas.

Liz Danzico is chair and co-founder of the MFA in Interaction Design Program at the School of Visual Arts. She is an independent consultant, columnist for *interactions* magazine, on the boards of Rosenfeld Media and Design Ignites Change, and writes at Bobulate.com.

Christopher Fahey is a founding partner and user experience director at Behavior Design, an award-winning interaction design consultancy. He also writes and speaks about user experience, and teaches at the School of Visual Arts' MFA in Interaction Design Program.

James Melzer is a user experience designer for EightShapes in Washington, DC, specializing in design documentation, information architecture, and interaction design. He has been a researcher, a developer, a librarian, and a project manager, but his first love has always been design.

Steve Mulder is VP, Experience Strategy, at Isobar, where he transforms customer insights and business and brand strategies into engaging online experiences that drive results. He is the author of *The User Is Always Right: A Practical Guide to Creating and Using Personas for the Web* and a regular speaker at web conferences on topics such as digital strategy, social media, customer research, information architecture, interaction design, and usability.

Donna Spencer a freelance information architect, interaction designer, and writer for her company, Maadmob. That's a fancy way of saying she plans how to present the things you see on your computer screen, so that they're easy to understand, engaging, and compelling.

Russ Unger is a User Experience Director for Happy Cog, a web design firm in New York City, Philadelphia, and San Francisco. He is co-author of the book *A Project Guide to UX Design* from Peachpit Press (Voices That Matter) and is co-authoring a book on guerilla research methods with Todd Zaki Warfel due out in 2011.

COLOPHON

The text was written on a MacBook Air running OS X and Pages '09.

The majority of diagrams were created using OmniGraffle Pro (v5.2.3) on a MacBook Pro with a 30" Cinema Display.

Most of the deliverable layouts were created using Adobe InDesign CS4 and EightShapes Unify, a set of deliverable templates. (Learn more at http://unify.eightshapes.com)

Inspirational music provided by Pandora:

- Django Reinhardt Radio: www.pandora.com/?sc=sh39302326603468870
- Johann Sebastian Bach Radio: www.pandora.com/?sc=sh25531845408706630

Index

I

inclusive flow, 145
industry standards, 25
information
    actionable, 49–50, 211–212, 275, 285
    version, 213, 214–215
    See also layers of information
insight, 3
institutional personas, 37, 39
interactive elements, 176–177
internal design teams, 10
introductions, 216–218, 223
isometric layout, 110–111

K

Kahn, Paul, 111

L

labeling
    flow charts, 130
    personas, 43
    site maps, 118
    wireframes, 174, 175
large-format printers, 161
late-breaking constraints, 249
layers of information, 15–16
    in concept models, 71–77
    in flowcharts, 128–141
    in personas, 38–43
    in site maps, 99–106
    in wireframes, 170–179
layouts
    for deliverables, 222–224
    for site maps, 101–102, 110–111
    for wireframes, 173–174
leadership, 9
Lenk, Krzysztof, 111
lifecycle of deliverables, 226–230
lines on flowcharts, 130–131

links
    in concept models, 72–73, 82
    in site maps, 100–101, 105
    in wireframes, 196
logistical constraints, 249

M

maintenance, document, 229–230
Mapping Web Sites (Kahn and Lenk), 111
master pages, 214
meetings
    buy-in, 53
    challenges in, 29–31
    establishing objectives for, 23
    pausing for questions, 26
    pre-meeting, 32
    virtual, 32
    See also presentations
Melzer, James, 110
mental models, 48–49
Mental Models: Aligning Design Strategy with Human Behavior (Young), 49
Merholz, Peter, 53
metadata, 67, 90
metaphors, 76
modular approach, 185
Modular Web Design (Curtis), 122, 180
moral-driven story, 257
motivations of users
    flowcharts and, 140
    personas and, 40
Mulder, Steve, 60

N

names, persona, 39
navigation models. *See* site maps
navigation strategy, 107
next-steps statement, 220–221
nodes
    in concept models, 66, 72–73, 82
    in site maps, 99–100, 103, 104, 105–106
Novak, Joseph D., 68

O

objectives
    meeting, 23
    persona, 40
    project, 24
    usability study, 265, 275
one-page summary, 251–253
on-the-fly wireframes, 199–200
open-ended questions, 271
operational implementation, 25, 27
    design briefs and, 249
    flowcharts and, 153
organizational politics, 118–119
organizational standards, 25
org-chart-like site maps, 101, 102
orthogonal lines, 131
overlays, 280

P

pages on site maps, 99–100
    groups of pages, 99, 103–104
    page details/distinctions, 102–103
pain points, 41
Particular-General-Particular (PGP) approach, 26
paths on flowcharts, 130–131, 137
people, personas as, 56–57
perpetual beta, 286–287
personal background info, 42–43
personas, 34–62
    applying, 59–61
    audience for, 35, 45
    challenges of, 37–38
    clarifying, 51–52
    comparisons between, 47–48
    context for, 35, 54
    creation of, 43–50
    definition of, 34
    demographic info in, 43
    describing to clients, 56–58
    design documents and, 60
    design process and, 60–61

WATCH READ CREATE

Unlimited online access to all Peachpit, Adobe Press, Apple Training and New Riders videos and books, as well as content from other leading publishers including: O'Reilly Media, Focal Press, Sams, Que, Total Training, John Wiley & Sons, Course Technology PTR, Class on Demand, VTC and more.

No time commitment or contract required! Sign up for one month or a year. All for $19.99 a month

SIGN UP TODAY

creative edge